For Love of Reading

For Love of Reading

A Parent's Guide to Encouraging
Young Readers from Infancy
Through Age Five

Masha Kabakow Rudman, Ed.D.,

Anna Markus Pearce, Ed.D.,

and the Editors of Consumer
Reports Books

Consumers Union
Mount Vernon, New York

Published by Consumers Union of United States, Inc., Mount Vernon, New York 10553.

Library of Congress Cataloging-in-Publication Data
Rudman, Masha Kabakow.
For love of reading.
Includes bibliographies.
1. Children—Books and reading.   2. Family—Books
and reading.   3. Reading—Parent participation.
4. Reading (Preschool)   5. Language arts (Preschool)
I. Pearce, Anna Markus.   II. Title.
Z1037.A1R85   1988   028.5′343   87-36409
ISBN Hardcover: 0-89043-208-2
ISBN Paperbound: 0-89043-209-0

"By Myself," from *Honey, I Love, and Other Love Poems* by Eloise Greenfield. (Thomas Y. Crowell). Text copyright © 1978 by Eloise Greenfield. Reprinted by permission of Harper & Row, Publishers, Inc.

Design by The Sarabande Press
First printing, April 1988
Manufactured in the United States of America

To my dear sisters and friends who nurture me.

MKR

To Masha with thanks, respect, and love.

AMP

Contents

CONTENTS

Acknowledgments

In a book of this sort it is impossible to complete all of the research, the hunting for books and titles, the organizing and compiling of information, and the myriad details that need to be attended to without the help of many people.

We give special thanks to: Cindy Asebrook, Michael Bernstein, JanetLee Beswick, Syd Cherney-Clark, The Children's Book Council, Pat Drake, Joy and Howard Gerson, Eric Heller, Norma Kent, Teresa Lomotan, Valeria Lovelace of the Children's Television Workshop, Dee McWilliams, Ella Pearce, Sondra Radosh and her staff, Sue Rayner, Marie Sorensen, and Irene Taafaki. We thank our supportive and patient husbands, Sy and Tony.

For Love of
Reading

INTRODUCTION

The Road to Reading

Researchers agree that the single most important factor in a child's academic success is the model that parents set. If parents regularly read newspapers, magazines, and books, children will learn that reading is a valued activity. When parents watch television actively, that is, when they talk about what they are viewing rather than sitting silently in front of the set, they demonstrate that television can be a mentally stimulating resource rather than a soporific.

Parents' and caretakers' responsive behavior is another element known to be essential to children's attitudes toward learning. Do they talk to their children and listen when their children speak? Are they attentive to their child's developmental level? Do they provide an environment that is neither boring nor overwhelming?

Parents can actively engage in their children's informal education. If they read aloud to each other and to their children, starting from when the children are infants, their children will see that reading is a pleasurable and important activity. As a family, do they play games, go on trips, go shopping, and watch movies, plays, or television together? Researchers agree that these factors influence a child's attitudes, behaviors, and abilities.

Since the ability to read is key, it is important to begin early to motivate and prepare children to become competent and enthusiastic readers. Literacy is one of our most basic survival tools. We need reading to help us when we drive, shop, cook, assemble a piece of equipment, apply for a job, plan a trip, select a movie or television show, find the telephone number or address of a doctor or plumber, and, in general, pursue our everyday activities.

Beyond the basic level, people read newspapers, commentaries, periodicals, nonfiction, advertisements, dictionaries, and other reference works, manuals, and correspondence to keep up with the world and to inform themselves about subjects of possible interest, from antiques to space travel, from computer technology to auto repair, from history to current events. Reading and writing include more than print; we read pictures, expressions on people's faces, signs, maps, and the weather.

Reading can entertain us and others. Whatever our tastes in relaxation, there are magazines, novels, comic strips, mysteries, comedies, and other light fare available to us in many forms and styles.

Through reading and writing we can also explore, expand, clarify, confirm, and communicate our own thoughts, ideas, and feelings as well as discover those of others. Every one of us is a writer: we write in diaries or journals, notes and reminders, lists, instructions, checks, and letters. Some people use the act of writing to see on paper what it is they are thinking. Many people use the processes of reading and writing to clarify how they think and feel, and to communicate their emotions and thoughts.

Good poetry, drama, and literature enrich our lives. Through the artistry of authors we are enlarged and deepened in a way that everyday interactions cannot accomplish. We share the wisdom of centuries. We taste the flavors of all cultures. Reading is useful as an escape to imaginary worlds as well as a way to find our own world explained. It can be used to find out about other people and cultures, and to explore different ways of viewing and dealing with the world.

To be a good reader a person needs a number of tools: visual discrimination; the ability to see and hear differences and similarities; the ability to question; the ability to recognize and understand feelings; the ability to infer what is not specifically stated; the ability to recognize and understand individual words as well as concepts; the ability to use and understand figures of speech; the ability to compare, contrast, and classify; the ability to remember; and the ability to predict what words, ideas, or phrases will come next. Although these tools are vital, it is important to know that they will not suffice unless the reader has a solid base of experience and language pertaining to the written text. We understand, describe, and read best those things we know something about, and, ideally, have encountered as part of our life experience.

Since the quality of the reading depends largely on how much language a person understands, children's talking and listening are vital factors in their preparation as readers and writers. Parents are enormously important as active builders of their children's experiential and linguistic foundations. This occurs when they talk, listen, and read to the children, and provide them with experiences that make language enjoyable.

This book is designed to help parents and caretakers of children from birth to kindergarten assist in the development of a love of reading. The developmental stages through which children move during these crucial years are discussed and resources appropriate to each stage are suggested. The book encourages an informal, unpressured approach that allows learning to be natural, enjoyable, and an ongoing part of everyday life. It is, above all, an invitation to parents to take advantage of their own and their children's abilities in a pleasurable and productive way. Select from the suggestions and information what you want, and make them your own. You serve your children best when you use your own values, judgment, style, and pace.

Each chapter approaches the subject in a slightly different way. Taken together, they form a comprehensive view of the road to reading and to a love of books. The chapters provide information of a theoretical as well as practical nature. Specific books are discussed to exemplify the points being discussed, and sometimes a book might be discussed several times to illustrate different points the chapters make.

Immediately following the nine chapters and five appendices is a section called "The Bookshelf," which is an extensive annotated bibliography. It not only includes the books mentioned in the chapters, but also hundreds of additional titles that you will find appropriate for use with your child. The titles were selected from dozens of lists produced by educational and library organizations, and from texts and journals that regularly review and recommend children's literature. As specialists in education and children's literature, we have included only those books to whose quality we can personally attest. It is impossible to list all of the fine books available, but our hope is that you will use these as a beginning, and apply the criteria we have outlined to your search for other books and materials.

Chapter 1, "Classics Old and New," follows this introductory chapter and discusses books that have continued, long after they were published, to reach the minds and hearts of readers. The chapter presents criteria that establish these books as classics for infants through age five. Many genres are included so that a wide variety of excellent books can be made available to your children. Although every title in "The Bookshelf" has merit, the books in this chapter serve as the standard against which other books you find may be judged.

Chapter 2, "The Magic of Story," offers advice on how to select materials that lend themselves to reading aloud, and those stories dramatic and memorable enough for storytelling. In this chapter you can find information on how to tell stories, and how to make your reading aloud an experience that will attract your children and hold them entranced, making them eager to come back for more. For children too young to read for themselves it is essential that you learn to present the books in as attractive and engaging a manner as possible.

Chapter 3, "The Reading Infant," encourages parents to respond to the child's need for appropriate sensory stimulation and social interaction from the moment of birth. It documents how infants "read" their environment and how they communicate with their caretakers. It provides parents with information on books, materials, and activities that meet the needs of babies from birth to one year of age as well as beginning a foundation for a positive attitude toward reading. The chapter discusses books that provide labels for familiar objects and simple actions, thus helping to build a receptive vocabulary for babies in the second half of their first year.

"Stocking the Storehouse: Food for Thought," the fourth chapter, looks at the stages of children's cognitive growth as they move beyond infancy. It discusses books that are resources to children between the ages of eighteen months to five years. Labeling and exploring the concepts of number, shape, color, opposites, spacial

4

relations, as well as mastery of the alphabet and the gathering of information, are presented and reinforced through the books listed in this chapter.

Children from age two to five want to apply their growing store of knowledge. Chapter 5, "Whistle While You Work," shows how children can join their caretakers in the daily activities of running a household. These activities can enliven routines and provide the content for further learning. Many books related to these activities are described.

Chapter 6, "The Beginning Book Bag: Books That Touch the Heart," focuses on the child's emotional growth in the period from birth through five years of age. It takes a close look at developmental issues and books that deal with the earliest needs for a sense of belonging, security, and protection; the quest for competence and independence; the stages of temper tantrums and fears; the ability to form relationships outside the family; and the burgeoning sense of autonomy and self-acceptance. Children feel confirmed and understood when their parents and caretakers share books with them that respond to the emotional challenges facing them.

Chapter 7, "Mirrors and Windows," acknowledges children's needs to see themselves reflected in books as well as to use books as windows to the larger world. It discusses books, mostly for the three- to five-year-old, but includes some books for toddlers, which take into consideration both the cognitive elements of providing information with the awareness of the emotional aspects of such sensitive areas as divorce, special needs, and death. It also includes books that respectfully present information about non-majority cultures. In all four areas the aim is to enable the children who are directly experiencing the issue in the book to have their worth confirmed and to permit other children to acquire sufficient perspective so as to develop empathy. When a story or poem containing this sort of material entertains rather than preaches, it is literature rather than tract, and the information is much more likely to remain with the young reader and become part of his or her values system.

Children develop and practice many of their social skills with their siblings. The sibling relationship, as evidenced in many books, assists children in seeing not only their own perspective, but also that of their siblings and parents. Chapter 8, "The Enduring Bond: Exploring Sibling Relationships," is devoted solely to this single issue, because of its near-universality, and because there are so many books that deal with it from many aspects, both positive and negative.

Books are not the only resource for encouraging children to think, read, and write. Handled wisely, television can provide hours of entertainment, enlightenment, and stimulation for children from age two and a half to age five. Chapter 9, "Taming the One-Eyed Monster," while not ignoring the possible negative effects of indiscriminate and passive viewing, provides parents and caretakers with a scheme for using television to its fullest positive extent. Current research is reviewed, and books that can be used in conjunction with TV are listed.

This is not a book on how to teach your child to read at an early age. It *is* a book that affirms the value of literature to entertain, inform, convey a sense of beauty, and model enduring values. Loving and responsive parents, aware of their children's changing needs in the earliest years, should consistently share with their children books that are satisfying and of high quality. If parents do so, their children will continue to turn to books for love of reading.

1

Classics
Old and New

Books offer many rewards to readers: knowledge, pleasure, heightened awareness of self and others, deeper appreciation of the world and its visual and cultural treasures, the opportunity for armchair travel, a nurturing of the imagination, an aid to the development of a moral sense, and, for many, a greater understanding of what it means to be human. Extraordinary books last beyond the period of their authors' lives. When they continue to delight and reach the minds and hearts of readers for generations, these books are called "classics."

Each year the publishing world of children's literature presents awards to those books deemed to be of the highest quality. You will discover the two top awards that recognize excellence (the John Newbery award for writing and the Randolph Caldecott award for illustrations) have been granted to some of the selections described in this chapter.

The dictionary defines a classic as "of the highest quality or rank; having recognized and permanent value; of enduring interest and appeal." This chapter describes books that have withstood the test of time and are acknowledged to be classics, as well as books which, because of their grace and beauty, compelling insight, depth and originality, are sure to become classics of the future.

Above all, this chapter discusses books that exemplify appropriateness for a young audience and excellence in illustration, language, characterization, and plot. In addition, these books often explore and convey matters of enduring truth while at the same time responding to universal human needs.

Some books contain stories, songs, and verse that have been handed down orally from generation to generation. When selecting books of this sort parents and caretakers would do well to examine the text to see how respectful the adaptor has been of the original material. Sometimes modern versions cut the originals so drastically that their flavor is lost. Adults also should decide whether or not they want music included with the songs or verses. Sometimes the music is so familiar that it is unnecessary to include it in the text. If the music is included, parents may want to check to see that the melody is the one they prefer. A single lullaby or folk song often has several different melodies accompanying it, and parents may be disappointed to discover that the book they have selected contains an unfamiliar melody. Whatever the edition, it should provide a blend of authenticity, visual beauty, and listening enjoyment.

Birth to Five Months

For the youngest population, newborns to five months, there are some beautiful songbooks and nursery rhyme editions that have remained favorites. *The Fireside Book of Children's Songs* contains an excellent assortment of traditional lullabies and other songs for children. *The Fireside Book of Folk Songs* (illustrated by Alice and Martin Provensen) is also a fine staple.

One book, *Nursery Songs*, published by the Metropolitan Museum of Art in 1980, arranged by Joseph Moorat and illustrated by Paul Woodroffe, includes such favorites as "Three Blind Mice," "Yankee Doodle," and "Ding Dong Dell," and some lesser known old songs such as "The Frog and the Crow" and "Good King Arthur." The book provides music and visual entertainment at the same time that it presents the entire texts of the songs.

F. Warne and Company has produced a series of Caldecott Collections containing the original nineteenth-century text and illustrations by Randolph Caldecott of such traditional nursery rhymes as "The House That Jack Built," "A Frog He Would A-Wooing Go" (*A First Caldecott Collection*), "Sing a Song for Sixpence," and "The Three Jovial Huntsmen" (*A Second Caldecott Collection*). The illustrations are tinted pen-and-ink drawings, a mixture of realism and cartoon. The flavor is decidedly Victorian-English. The format of these tiny volumes, containing a minimum amount of text with many illustrations, makes this series one that parents will enjoy reading to infants, and one that will probably continue to provide entertainment for the children as they grow older, when they can appreciate the pictures as well as the music, rhythms, and rhymes.

Arnold Lobel, whose *Frog and Toad* books are among the best loved and popular contemporary classics, has selected and illustrated a veritable treasure chest of rhymes and images to delight both parents and children in *The Random House Book of Mother Goose*. More than three hundred rhymes are included in this collection, along with colorful illustrations throughout, some covering the entire page, some bordering the edges, and some marching in an orderly fashion in rows. Although published in 1986, the book can already be considered a classic because of the care taken in insuring a diverse and comprehensive selection of rhymes and because of the flavorful and humorous illustrations.

Some nursery rhymes have merited their own separate volumes. Paul Galdone's *Little Bo-Peep* accurately reflects the dress of an eighteenth-century shepherdess. Again, the text is provided in its entirety. We follow Bo-Peep to where she finds and refastens the tails on her sheep. Color and line attract the reader's attention to the large, bold, and humorous illustrations. Galdone is a prolific illustrator of many children's books. Some of his other classic nursery rhyme books are *Old Mother Hubbard and Her Dog* and *The Old Woman and Her Pig*.

Tomie dePaola is an award-winning illustrator of many children's books. His illustrations of *Mary Had a Little Lamb* are based on his research and photographs of the town of Newport, New Hampshire, the birthplace of Sarah Josepha Hale, the reputed author of the original rhyme. Although most scholars agree that Mrs. Hale is the author, the controversy about the authorship of the rhyme continues, perhaps because Mary Sawyer Tyler claimed that the verse was written by a man who visited her school on the day that her pet lamb had followed her to school.

A classic rendition of songs and stories suitable for singing and/ or telling to infants under five months of age is *Walk Together Children,* a collection of Black American spirituals selected and illustrated by Ashley Bryan. The two dozen songs, with music, are illuminated by Bryan's bold, stylized woodcut illustrations. The songs are respectfully and authentically rendered.

Not only Mother Goose rhymes and familiar songs are appropriate for infants. Adults can read aloud anything of their choice for their own and their babies' pleasure. If adults want to read poems with content suitable for babies, there are a number of volumes that provide time-tested verses. *Poems to Read to the Very Young* is a profusely illustrated collection by such authors as A. A. Milne, Elizabeth Coatsworth, Walter de la Mare, Aileen Fisher, Margaret Wise Brown, and Vachel Lindsay. The illustrator is Eloise Wilkin, and the editor is Josette Frank. This selection is aimed at children under five and includes a varied assortment of poems encompassing a range of young children's experiences.

The collection *Illustrated Poems for Children* contains poetry by such greats as T. S. Eliot, Emily Dickinson, Walt Whitman, James Joyce, and William Shakespeare. As the children grow older they will appreciate the poetry more, but as infants they will surely enjoy their parents' pleasure in the reading aloud of these timeless poems.

A recommended collection of rhymes for very young children, *Readaloud Rhymes for the Very Young*, is a recent edition illustrated by Marc Brown, containing verse selected by Jack Prelutsky, who is a popular poet in his own right. As Jim Trelease points out in his introduction to this volume: "the first sound a child hears is actually a poem—the rhythmic, rhyming beat-beat-beat sound of a mother's heart. This early and fundamental relationship sets the stage for a natural and lifelong love of rhythm and rhyme." All 200 of the poems in this collection rhyme as well as contain a rollicking, regular rhythm. The softly colored illustrations complement the verses.

A Child's Garden of Verses by Robert Louis Stevenson has been a part of many adults' childhood heritage for a long time. The volume published by Rand McNally looks like a Victorian showcase because of its delicate and flavorful illustrations by Tasha Tudor. By introducing these poems to infants, parents and children can continue to enjoy their familiarity as the children grow.

Before infants can sit up and grasp objects, they do not pay much attention to either the text or the pictures of a book. Adults read the stories and poems and sing the songs and rhymes to infants without necessarily sharing the actual book with the child.

It is the sound of the adult's voice and, perhaps, the rhythm that is attractive to this age group.

A great change occurs when babies are sitting up and attending to their immediate environment. The book itself becomes attractive. The pictures and structure of the book add to the experience of the story, song, or rhyme. The same books that caretaking adults have used for infants may still be appropriate for the toddler. Or it may take a year or two longer before the children appreciate the texts their parents have been reading to them. But do not discard the earliest books you have used for your baby; at some point your child will be ready to take them into his or her own hands and enjoy turning the pages and rediscovering the songs and verses you sang and read when he or she was "just a baby."

Five Months to One Year

At five months to one year, the sitting-up, grasping, sensory-aware child is ready to play with books as toys as well as to take pleasure from books' appearance and content. At this time, books that invite children's active participation become popular. Many such books exist, but very few merit the designation of "classic," probably because these books are toys rather than books. *Pat the Bunny* by Dorothy Kunhardt was one of the first of such books and has remained a perennial favorite for almost fifty years. In it the infant is invited to feel different textures such as soft bunny fur or the scratchy stubble of daddy's beard; smell the flowers; look into a mirror; try on a ring and read a miniature book. The language is not condescending. A predictable pattern is created that permits an older child to chime in with the reading. Although the book is appropriate for children at six months, it is versatile enough to remain attractive to toddlers through age two. Older children may also remember it fondly as one of their very first books.

A similar book that has attained the status of a modern classic is *Where's Spot?* by Eric Hill. Babies enjoy searching through the flaps and hiding places in their quest for Spot. They may need some help at first in managing the mechanics of this "peek-a-boo" book but even after their initial surprise at what they find has worn off, their delight in manipulating the pages will probably not abate.

Board books made of sturdy, chewable laminated cardboard contain such classic material as familiar lullabies and nursery rhymes. *The Pudgy Rock-A-Bye Book* illustrated by Kathy Wilburn is one of these and Alice Schlesinger has illustrated a *Baby's Mother Goose* in this board-book format. Although the text is abbreviated, toddlers will recognize the songs and verses that they heard when they were babies. Now they may turn the pages themselves and play with the books while at the same time identifying the pages as the source of their current and previous pleasure. While these board books themselves are not the original format, their depiction of classic material helps in the process of attracting children to reading and books.

One board book, *Meet Peter Rabbit*, is intended to introduce babies to a classic, and uses the original illustrations from Beatrix Potter's *Tales of Peter Rabbit*. The words can be omitted, as they bear no resemblance to the genuine text, but the pictures may capture the attention of babies, and telling the story to accompany the pictures can convey the flavor of the original.

Helen Oxenbury is an author/illustrator whose books invariably appeal to young children. In *Animals,* her perspective on what animals and children each can do provides the reader with an opportunity to savor the humor as well as learn to search for similarities.

Since children usually do not even notice print until they are about eighteen months old, for very young children the picture is the most engrossing attraction of a book. Talented artists will compel attention and invite repeated examination through their design of the page, their use of colors, lines, shapes, and different media such as woodcuts, water color, and collage to create a visual context and tone for the story and add to the emotional impact of the words.

One Year to Eighteen Months

By the time children are a year old they can identify books and distinguish among them. They know that the turning of a page will bring new images to their attention, and they love the adventure of turning the page for themselves. They begin to anticipate what will come next, to remember sequence, and to understand that pictures stand for real objects. They appreciate the naming of objects and characters, and they will find their favorite books and bring them to you to read.

One such book is likely to be a board book called *Baby's Things*. It is simply a book of brightly colored photographs, most of them as large as life, of things such as an apple, a brush and comb, sneakers, yarn, keys, and other ordinary items. The placement of the objects (one to a page), the varied textures, the vibrance of the color, and the three-dimensional quality of the photography combine to make this book aesthetically and conceptually compelling. Of the many similar naming books available, this one stands out.

One book that builds on the naming process, and incorporates it into a classic loved by countless children, is *Good Night Moon* by Margaret Wise Brown. The setting is a familiar environment for both young middle-class urban and suburban readers, but because of its universal features it does not exclude those children who live in different parts of the nation and the world. The room is furnished with traditional bed, lamp, rocking chair, braided rug, and fireplace. But the unconventional use of color (the walls are bright green; the floor is red) transforms the setting into one that goes beyond reality.

The child in this book conducts a bedtime naming ritual that secures the identity and safety of each familiar object in the child's environment, a brush, a comb, a telephone; and then reaches out to the universe: stars, air, "noises everywhere." The reader is drawn into the book and is encouraged to examine each object and each picture carefully. The moon rises in the sky; the light in the room changes; the kittens give up their game and curl up in the chair. A tiny mouse can be discovered somewhere on each of the pages. Children often make a game of finding this mouse.

The illustrations alternate between black-and-white and color, and in each subsequent picture, move from bright and light to a gradual absence of light. The child takes leave of the daytime world with assurance that he is secure. The figure of the old lady in the rocking chair conveys a sense of the adult guardian who cares about the child and who will not leave until the child is ready to be alone. The author and illustrator show a profound understanding of how difficult it is for many young children to let go of the securities of the daytime world and go to sleep at night. The book helps to calm children as they make this transition. The rhythmic and repetitious, well-selected but deceptively simple, language

13

creates a tone and atmosphere that fit well with the pictures.

Children request *Good Night Moon* over and over again. It seems as though the ritual of reading the book becomes a safeguard for the child's passage into the unknown and sometimes frightening world of sleep. Margaret Wise Brown is a trustworthy author. Her books can be counted on because she has her finger on the pulse of children's feelings.

Another of her books, *The Runaway Bunny,* was written in 1942 and has become an enduring classic. It is described in detail in chapter 6, because of its appropriateness in connection with children's emotional development. The illustrations by Clement Hurd use full-color double-page spreads in the sections that picture the mother's promises. Black-and-white sketches record the reality-based interactions between the baby bunny and his mother. The technique is analogous to the film "The Wizard of Oz" where color was used for the fantasy and Kansas was all in black-and-white. Although the book is developmentally appropriate for the one- to-two-year-old whose sense of autonomy and separation from his mother is emerging, the book can remain a favorite for years afterward.

Another classic that can be introduced to children at this young age is *The Snowy Day,* a Caldecott Medal winner by Ezra Jack Keats. At about fifteen months, children become more aware of themselves and their external environments and they are increasingly eager to use their senses to explore the world. At eighteen months they begin to organize thoughts into symbols and form mental images. *The Snowy Day* incorporates all of these competencies with a sense of joy and independence as young Peter plays in the snow. His feet make patterns; he hears the crunching sounds as he walks along. He builds a snowman, creates snow angels, and slides down a hill. Even though Peter is older than the young reader may be, the book will endure for several years, retaining its interest while the children grow into its action as well as appreciate its appeal. As with most of Keats's books, the protagonist is a young black child. The illustrations appear two-dimensional because they are made with blocks of colorful paper cut into simple shapes. The jaunty angle of the tail of young Peter's snow hat serves as a symbol of his spirit and energy.

The appeal to the senses—patterns and color—combined with the sparse but appropriate text all add to the total impression of authenticity. The book confirms the one- to-two-year-old's "love affair with the world" (to use Mahler's terminology) and it does it with freshness.

Another modern classic that accomplishes this feat is Ruth Krauss's *A Hole Is to Dig,* with illustrations by Maurice Sendak. Subtitled *A First Book of Definitions,* it presents objects and activities through the eyes and attitudes of a very young child. "Hands are to make things; a package is to look inside; a book is to look at." "Mud is to jump in and slide in and yell doodleedoodlee-doo." The joyousness of a child's life at this stage is reflected in the text and accompanying energetic and childlike illustrations. The book will retain its appeal through the age when children begin nursery school, but it can be introduced before a child is two.

Eighteen Months to Two Years

At about eighteen months to two years of age children start to know that books tell a story. This is when they begin to understand that looking at a book is called "reading."

Most of the "simple" stories that have been handed down to us through the oral tradition contain messages. *Goldilocks and the Three Bears* deals with disobedience and a lack of respect for other people's possessions. In the version by Paul Galdone the type size for the baby bear's words is tiny, and the type is correspondingly larger for the mama and papa bears.

Folktales are all in the public domain. Do not assume that because you heard a certain version of a story while you were growing up that all printed versions will be the same. The Galdone version of *Goldilocks* ends with, "No one knows what happened to Goldilocks after that. As for the Three Bears, they never saw her again." For parents and children who would prefer to be kinder to Goldilocks, Janet Stevens's version ends with a more comforting, "Goldilocks ran and ran. 'I'm never going to wander alone in the forest again,' she said when she got home. And that suited the three bears just fine!" Read any texts carefully before sharing them with your children. Select the wording and illustrations that satisfy you most, and that you know are most appropriate for your child.

There are also timeless stories that were invented by authors, rather than handed down orally from a preliterate tradition. The series of *Curious George* books by H. A. Rey has been enjoyed by children for more than forty-five years. The inquisitive little monkey often behaves in a foolhardy, somewhat thoughtless fashion, but he always manages to escape permanent harm and to be returned to safety and security at the story's end. George represents the inquisitive and clever, but sometimes errant, child. The man in the yellow hat symbolizes the protective and caring adult.

The representation of the child exploring the world, but still requiring the safety and affection of the adult, appears in the books written by Beatrix Potter as long ago as 1902. These stories are best told using their original language. Some of the vocabulary may seem old-fashioned or too sophisticated for the not quite two-year-old, but it is so flavorful that children deserve the pleasure of being introduced to it. You may need to explain some of the terms or add your own interpretations, but it may be well worth the effort. In *The Tale of Peter Rabbit*, her best-known work, the theme, characters, and plot are simple enough for this age level. It contains the age-old moral that children should obey their mothers, but even when they don't, their mothers will care for them.

Another simple tale, published in 1933, describing a similar lesson, is that of *The Story About Ping* by Marjorie Flack and Kurt Wiese. In trying to avoid a reprimand for being late, Ping, a little duckling whose home is a riverboat on the Yangtze River, stays away all night. Like Peter Rabbit, he narrowly escapes being served for dinner, and, like Peter, he goes home to accept both his punishment and the security of family life.

Two to Three Years

When children attain the age of two, language development accelerates. They begin to put two or three words together into sentences, they become enamored of new words and the power that speech gives them, and they are able to follow more complex stories and to understand those that contain humor and exaggeration. They often repeat catchy phrases or refrains as they begin to match their own emotions with those of the characters in a story.

In some classics, animals reflect young children's emotions. *Little Bear* by Else Holmelund Minarik with pictures by Maurice Sendak is a gentle book that six-year-olds may be able to read for themselves, but that two-year-olds enjoy listening to. The loving mother bear responds consistently and positively to the little bear. She makes clear not only that there are limits on his behavior but also that she will love and nurture him always. In the other books in the series, the father and grandparents similarly embody their human counterparts, but still magically retain the essence of bear. The pictures, in combination with the text, demonstrate respect for individual dignity. The dialogue is simple and straightforward; the pictures are more subtle and complex. The facial expressions and body language augment the message in the text. Children will ask for these stories again and again.

In contrast to the quiet and gentle understatement of *Little Bear* is the exaggerated, fantastic story of *Millions of Cats,* by Wanda Ga'g. First published in 1928, it is still in print and enjoyed by youngsters. The hand-lettered, illustrated story portrays a world as it might be seen through the eyes of a child. An old couple are lonely; they want a cat, and the old man goes out to search for one. He comes upon a hill containing an enormous number of cats. The refrain, "Cats here, cats there. Cats and kittens everywhere. Hundreds of cats. Thousands of cats. Millions and billions and trillions of cats" captivates young listeners. In their attempt to decide which cat to keep, the old couple inadvertently instigates a huge war. The violence of the cats' quarrel is portrayed as a cartoon, and toddlers will know, because of the refrain and the tone, that this is a make-believe story. They may also understand that one lesson presented here is to avoid physical conflict. One little scraggly kitten, because it did not participate in the war, emerges as the sole survivor. The old couple tenderly feed and care for the kitten, and in the end it grows into a beautiful and healthy cat. The story is of the love and care that the old couple lavish on the kitten. Together with the recurring refrain, the black-and-white pen-and-ink drawings roll across the pages and arrive at a satisfying conclusion depicting the contented couple with their playful cat.

Children at this age begin to enjoy nonsense, exaggeration, and playing with language. They love books such as *May I Bring a Friend?* by Beatrice Schenk de Regniers, illustrated by Beni Montresor. The little protagonist in the story tests the hospitality and congeniality of the king and queen by bringing an assortment of "friends" to dinner. All of the occupants of a zoo eventually dine with the royal couple, who maintain their amiable demeanor throughout. This book is indeed a royal romp that children and their parents can be heard quoting from time to time: "My dear, my dear,/Any friend of our friend/Is welcome here./"

When children get to be about two and a half, they become interested in how things work, and what is going on around them. One book that will sustain their interest at this time, and that is sure to be popular many years from now, is Eric Carle's *The Very Hungry Caterpillar*. The illustrations of crayon added to layers of colored tissue would alone make the book a worthwhile experience. The story is of the life cycle of a voracious caterpillar who eats his way, one day at a time, through an enormous amount of food.

The book's pages reflect the caterpillar's journey culminating in his metamorphosis into a gorgeous butterfly. Each day of the week has its own specially sized page. The food is pictured, complete with the hole the caterpillar has eaten. Children like to poke their fingers through the holes that indicate the caterpillar's journey. Each page gets larger as the quantity of food grows. The caterpillar grows as well. The book is a clever counting book as well as one that names the days of the week. Although the variety of food the caterpillar eats (ice cream cone, pickle, swiss cheese, salami, lollipop, cherry pie, sausage, cupcake, and watermelon) is very attractive to a small child, it is undoubtedly beyond the realm of a real caterpillar. The point is made that a caterpillar eats enormous quantities of food before building its cocoon. Not many informational books are this lavish in color and concept. Carle makes the whole complex structure succeed in conveying a coherent set of information while at the same time entertaining and enriching the reader.

Lois Lenski's *The Little Farm* was first published in 1944. Despite the many books that have since been produced on this theme, this book and its companions (*The Little Family, The Little Auto, The Little Airplane, The Little Sailboat,* and *Cowboy Small*) have remained in print and popular. *The Little Farm* pictures a toylike farmer (aptly named Farmer Small), accomplishing his chores on a cheerful and picturesque farm. There are no complexities in this bucolic life, but the details of real farm existence are there: the early rising; the feeding of the animals and milking of the cows; the ploughing, harrowing, cutting, and hauling of hay;

the sale of his produce, and more, are depicted. Children enjoy noticing the humorous touches in the illustrations, such as the piglet climbing onto its mother's back at the feeding trough and the bird's-eye view of the entire farm. The author accompanies the pictured information with prose that is simple and direct. The ending page has the same good-bye ritual that marks all of Lois Lenski's books about the Small family: "And that's all—about [Farmer] Small."

A modern classic for this age group reflects the interest children have in animals, and in using their senses actively to understand the world around them. *Just Me* by Marie Hall Ets follows a little boy in his attempts to mimic the movements of the animals on his farm. The child recognizes his limitations. He can't fly like a bird. But he *can* hop like a rabbit, climb like a squirrel, and imitate many other animals' modes of locomotion. The best thing of all, though, is that he can run just like himself, to join his father on a boating expedition. The black-and-white textured illustrations aptly portray the movement and feelings of the child. The combination of independence and competence coupled with the need for contact and companionship makes this little classic just right for the two-year-old age level.

The little boy in *Just Me* lives in a rural area. So does the little boy who sparks the unfolding of *The Park Book* by Charlotte Zolotow. He asks his mother, "What is the park like?" And his mother proceeds to describe it with personalized and sensitive detail. H. A. Rey's illustrations faithfully reflect the spirit of the description. The reader sees, hears, and experiences the park from early morning into the night. The illustrations capture the characters and the setting at a moment in time. Although this is not a story with a plot and a continuing cast of characters, we come to know certain important details about the inhabitants of the pages. We identify some of the people by what they had for breakfast, what hour they go to bed, and what their family is composed of. We wonder about the shoeshine man who seems not to be doing any business at all, but who observes all of the goings and comings in the park.

The portrait of the park (the illustrations make it apparent that this is Washington Square Park in New York City) is an accurate one. The activity, changing pace, detail, and multiplicity of perception is conveyed in an unhurried, concise but rich text-and-picture partnership. The book is a classic for good reason: its quality and appeal are timeless. Children from age two upward will find great satisfaction in looking at and hearing this book time after time, and each encounter with the book will give them something new to think about.

Another real park, the Boston Public Garden, is the setting for the 1942 Caldecott Medal winner, *Make Way for Ducklings*, by Robert McCloskey. The story outline is deceptively simple: a mother mallard needs to find a safe home for her ducklings, and the home that she does find is in the Boston Public Garden. But the characterization, theme, flavor, and details that the author lovingly inserts into the story make it a classic.

Although the text by itself would be enough to make this book a treasure, it is the illustrations that raise the book to a level beyond most others. Each double-page spread presents us with a dramatic episode, while at the same time attracting our attention to a myriad of details, each one contributing to our understanding and enjoyment of the story. The attractions of the park are lovingly rendered; we see the various visitors to the park enjoying their individual activities. The swan boats are loaded with an assortment of people, each of whom we might recognize if we met them on the street.

The police officer, Michael, stands out as the mallards' best friend. He not only feeds peanuts to the mallard parents while they're building their nest, he also stops traffic for them so they may cross the Boston streets safely. The images of cars from the 1940s convey a duck's-eye view that is humorous and dramatic at the same time. The background views of the buildings in downtown Boston also add to the pleasure of reading this book. Older children like to trace the ducklings' route on a real map. Readers of any age get a truer picture of Boston from this book than from many nonfiction accounts. This is a book that satisfies many requirements for this age level: the wish to know, the appreciation of characters and plot, and a sense of humor. And it does so with consummate skill.

Children's fascination with mechanical objects is part of the basis for the lasting quality of such books as *Little Toot, The Little Engine That Could, Mike Mulligan and His Steam Shovel*, and *Katy and the Big Snow*.

Little Toot by Hardy Gramatky, published in 1939, is a story of maturation, an issue that two- to-three-year-olds are very much concerned with. Along with the little tugboat's fears come growing competencies. Gramatky's watercolor illustrations reflect well, and then move beyond his Disney training in animation. They are free, fresh, expressive, and memorable. The little tugboat's movements reflect his internal condition. He soars, sags, and steams ahead visually as well as textually.

In *The Little Engine That Could*, written in 1930 by Watty Piper, the famous rhythmic refrain: "I think I can, I think I can" touches a chord in everyone, young and old, who has struggled with a seemingly impossible task. A pop-up book with an abbreviated text has been retold by its original author. Though the pop-up is fun for youngsters to see, the original, complete story is worth the telling. The pop-up illustrations differ slightly from the original but they are similar in style and tone. Both versions are worth having. A surprising number of adults, when asked about the books they remember from their childhood, select this one.

Two famous female machine-characters, the steam shovel named Mary Anne in *Mike Mulligan and His Steam Shovel* and the snow plough Katy in *Katy and the Big Snow* are memorable primarily because of their pictures by the author-illustrator Virginia Lee Burton. The movement and swirls are reminiscent of the illustrations in Wanda Ga'g's *Millions of Cats,* but color is an important feature in Burton's work. In *Katy and the Big Snow,* the borders, the maplike quality of the pages, and the design of the space all combine to convey the story and its message of competence.

Three-Year-Olds

All of the books already mentioned as classics for younger toddlers and infants can be read to older children. By the age of three, children are ready to be introduced to somewhat more complicated stories and can appreciate the literary interaction with characters that these stories afford through their unfolding plots.

Plot is an important ingredient in the making of any story, but it must contain certain vital elements if the book is to be a classic. Although some predictability is important, a plot must contain enough tension or surprise so that the outcome is not obvious. The beginning must set the stage well enough to draw the reader into the rest of the story. It must pique the reader's curiosity, stimulating anticipation and speculation about what will happen next. The middle should provide enough details to carry the plot through its intricacies and sustain the reader's attention. The rise and fall of the action must lead to a final peak and resolution. Timing and detail are essential.

Some fairly complicated stories have appeared in books that have no words. *A Boy, A Dog and a Frog* by Mercer Mayer uses humor and some exaggeration to tell the story of a boy and his dog who try to catch a sassy frog. After a series of slapstick events, at the expense of the boy and his dog, the frog is dismayed to see that his two antagonists are giving up their quest and going home. The frog leaps after them and happily joins them in their bathtub. Children at this age derive pleasure from telling the story in their own words, predicting what will happen next, and labeling the frog's expressions.

Another classic book that amuses young children is *Caps for Sale* by Esphyr Slobodkina. The illustrations, which resemble colorful paper cutouts, enliven the text. The story of how the peddler manages to outwit the monkeys who have taken his stock of caps entertains children with its predictable humor.

The Three Billy Goats Gruff is a story that comes to us from Norway through the oral tradition. Several artists such as Paul Galdone and Marcia Brown have retold and illustrated this tale, but its greatness lies in the universality of its theme. Children acquire a sense of relative size as the story unfolds. They readily identify with Little Billy Goat Gruff. Both younger siblings are aware of their vulnerability and trust that their big brother will protect them. They also use their wits to prevent the wicked troll from eating them up.

In this story Big Billy Goat Gruff vanquishes the troll and saves the entire family. Three-year-olds often think about their relationships with their siblings, their relative size and power, and their ability to control their world. These themes may seem complicated, but a story like *The Three Billy Goats Gruff* simplifies and clarifies the issues. Adding to the pleasure and the value of this story are the billy goats' contrasting voices and the noises of their feet as they make their way across the bridge. Select for your child a version of this story whose ending suits you. Do you demand that the troll be killed? In some editions he repents and becomes a pleasant fellow; in some he simply disappears. Every folktale has multiple versions. You can judge best which ones will appeal to, rather than frighten or repel, your child.

The more complex folktales can be introduced now. *The Little Red Hen* and *Henny Penny*, both retold and illustrated by Paul Galdone, are examples of stories that involve several characters with whom the young child can identify, and whom they can keep track of in the story. Children at this age are beginning to extract concepts from their experience. They are beginning to understand with greater clarity what a moral is. They are pleased that the little red hen's housemates do not get to share in the eating of the food after they refused to assist in its preparation. They chuckle over as well as empathize with the predicament of the character who acted hastily on the basis of too little information.

Paul Galdone's version of *Henny Penny* ends with the fox and his family's eating up all of the foolish fowls who are running to tell the king that the sky is falling. A gentler ending to the tale is dramatically illustrated by Ed Young in *Foolish Rabbit's Big Mistake*, retold by Rafe Martin. The story, from the traditional Jataka tale, perhaps 2,500 years old, tells of a little rabbit who broadcasts the alarm that, "The earth is breaking up!" Eventually, because of this assertion, a mob of animals starts to run for their lives. At last they encounter the wise lion, who, unlike the fox in the story of Henny Penny, is not a predator but rather a sage king of the animals. The story ends with everyone the wiser.

The illustrations alone make this a book worth keeping. There is a visual surprise on every page. The paintings are notable not only for their intensity of color, but also for the impact of their enormous size and unusual perspective. In one double-page spread all we see, filling the page, are the giant front paws and claws of the lion. In another we see only the lion's eyes and snout, with a suggestion of his shaggy, hairy mane. The effect is intense and dramatic.

Outstanding writers use language to paint vivid images even in books for young children. Sometimes the words are secondary to the illustrations, but they must, nevertheless, be clear, original, respectful of the audience, and must pack into a brief space as much meaning as possible. The sentence structure as well as the vocabulary must create a mood. The words must be chosen so as to delight and engage the audience. Even in picture books each word is carefully selected for its sound, its implications, and its particular meaning. Names of characters, verbs, and nouns convey special attributes.

Madeline, a series of books by Ludwig Bemelmans, would be less memorable if the protagonist had a different name. Madeline is the smallest and spunkiest of all the twelve little girls in Miss Clavel's care. The story, told in rhyming lines, includes words such as "disaster," but, in general, manages to tell its story of Madeline's appendicitis surgery and hospitalization with simple words and charming humor. The setting is France, and the illustrations of Paris add immeasurably to the attraction of the book.

In addition to the plot, language, and illustrations, characterization is an important element to consider in judging whether or not a book merits entry into the ranks of the classics. Characters are usually memorable not only for their external characteristics, but also for their intrinsic qualities. *Winnie the Pooh* by A. A. Milne, with pictures by Ernest Shepard, concerns Christopher Robin, and Pooh, Piglet, Rabbit, Owl, Tigger, Kanga, Little Roo, and Eeyore. The little animals are not just toys, although the story was stimulated originally by the love of a young boy for his stuffed bear. The characters are recognizable and endearing because of their personalities and their idiosyncrasies. Their traits, both negative and positive, combine to make them sympathetic, understandable, amusing, and endearing.

We all know people who exhibit the same sort of inadvertent "bounciness" that makes Tigger a difficult guest. We can point to incidents in our own lives that echo Pooh's preoccupation with food. We empathize with Kanga's overprotectiveness and Roo's quest for independence. And we wryly recognize ourselves in Eeyore's gloominess. In each case language, picture, and plot all help to create the strength of characterization. Each character's foibles and strengths emerge as integral parts of their escapades. Ernest Shepard's tiny pen-and-ink sketches sprinkled throughout the text in unexpected places such as the middle of a sentence or paragraph transform the little stuffed animals into complex, believable characters whom we come to know in great detail.

At age three, children begin forming friendships with peers. In *I'm Terrific* by Marjorie Weinman Sharmat, illustrated by Kay Chorao, the softly textured line drawings in shades of gray and orange complement the story. Jason Everett Bear must confront his own behavior when none of his peers will play with him. His mother supports his ability to work through his problems. The language of the text accurately reflects the developmental level of the three- to four-year-old.

Friendship is the major theme in the *Frog and Toad* series written and illustrated by Arnold Lobel. Frog and Toad are recognizable to children because of their specific personalities. Their behavior is predictable and consistent, but always of interest because of their well-defined characterizations. Frog is usually the more mature, more giving helper, and Toad is usually the immature, somewhat neurotic member of the team. The differences in their approach to the world permits readers at different stages of development (even adults) to identify with the characters and situations.

Acceptance and gentle responsiveness are qualities that pervade all of the *Frog and Toad* books. These modern classics also provide models for kindness and sensitivity while at the same time presenting problem-solving situations. Each episode brings out the characters' weaknesses and strengths, conveying to the reader that no one need be perfect in order to earn the friendship and love of another person.

Lobel narrates the exploits in language simple enough for beginning readers to manage for themselves, and clear enough for precocious three-and-a-half-year-olds to appreciate. Despite the simplicity of the language, the plot is complex and interesting. This series of books and stories touches the hearts of adults as well as children with its wry but sympathetic look at relationships and the human condition embodied in the forms of two amphibians.

Four-Year-Olds

Children at this age are energetic and inquisitive. They continue to enjoy playing with language and want to know more and more about how everything, including the language, works. They have probably shown some interest in written words and the alphabet for a number of months now, but most experts recommend waiting until they are four to emphasize these books. If alphabet books of very high visual and conceptual quality are introduced, not as teaching tools but as entertaining items of interest and pleasure, then children's initiation into the mechanics of the written word will be a fruitful and unpressured one. Parents err when they impose the alphabet on children. Reading skill grows from interest and attraction, not from drills and a premature emphasis on learning the alphabet. Children are more likely to remember certain individual letters of the alphabet when they can associate the letter with objects and words that have special meaning to them.

Children at this age are ready to have books with several chapters read to them. They can retain what they have already heard, and can anticipate what is to come. They can use their imaginations and play with the notions of make-believe and reality. This is the age of the imaginary playmate, the age when they begin sorting out their relationships with peers and family. This is an age of exploration and wonder.

One book that consistently entertains four-year-olds who love new and amusing words is *A Peaceable Kingdom: The Shaker Abecedarius* by Alice and Martin Provensen. The rhyming text is taken from the Shaker Manifesto of 1882 and includes, in addition to the more conventional animals such as Alligator and Elephant, unusual creatures such as Ibex, Yellowhammer, and Xanthos. Each page depicts doll-like Shakers engaging in their daily occupations, and almost every page includes a short homily, carefully lettered in tiny italics. The text provides twenty-six individual rhyming lines, using a successive letter of the alphabet at the beginning of each line. The illustrators have faithfully retained the sense of Shaker life and design. Children can enjoy the whimsy and humor of the illustrations and words at the same time that they acquire new vocabulary and a sense of the alphabet.

Another alphabet book that comes to us from long ago is *A Apple Pie* by Kate Greenaway. First published in London in 1886, it is based on a rhyme that can be traced back to the 1600s. The huge apple pie in question miraculously reconstitutes itself throughout the pages, and the somewhat quaint and awkward text ("E eat it; F fought for it") labels the actions without a hint of judgmental disapproval. The illustrations of the unusually pretty children dressed in costumes of Greenaway's invention (so appealing that it is said that Victorian mothers began dressing their children in the style that Greenaway designed) generally depict the children as demure and proper, and looking much like little adults. It is probably the appeal of "days gone by" and the use of verbs as the symbol for the letter of the alphabet rather than the more commonly used nouns, that account for the continuing popularity of this book.

On Market Street by Anita Lobel, with words by Arnold Lobel, takes us on a tour of Market Street where a young child stops at each of the shops to see what there is to purchase. Anita Lobel's paintings, inspired by seventeenth-century French trade engravings, depict fanciful storekeepers constructed entirely from their wares: The apple-seller has apples for hair; her body is a basket of green apples; her arms branch out into apple-laden boughs. The book progresses through the proprietors of shops that sell books, clocks, doughnuts, eggs (some fried sunny-side up, some hard-boiled, some still in their shell, decorated and plain, and in creative containers), flowers, gloves, and so on through the alphabet. Each illustration invites many moments of exploration and attention. The book earned a Caldecott Honor Award in 1982.

Among the many books that the award-winning Mitsumasa Anno has created is *Anno's Alphabet*. Its subtitle, *An Adventure in Imagination*, is apt. Each double-page spread contains on one side a letter wrought of wood, and on the other, an object representing the letter. Each page has a black-and-white border filled with drawings of more items that begin with the pictured letter challenging the viewer to study it and discover the surprises hidden there. On each of the two pages dedicated to the letter, *R*, dense rose vines encircle the pages, and, not as obvious, is a rabbit hiding in the roses.

Some of Anno's work is reminiscent of the trompe l'oeil of Escher, a little sophisticated for young children, but attractive nevertheless. Adults, too, enjoy Anno's books. They, as well as the children, may need to consult the guide provided at the back of the book of the items found on each page.

Wait until age four to introduce *Anno's Counting Book*. It is complex and sophisticated. Each page of this book consistently reflects the author-illustrator's desire to convey the *sense* of numbers to his readers. The clock tells the appropriate time on each numbered page. We move through the months of the year as we progress from one to twelve through the seasons. The objects that we count are items that are real, and that we would count in real life. They are related to one another in a way that not only takes into account the abstract quality of numbers but also translates them into meaningful units. The objects are not simply clumped into the number depicted; the groups are set in different configurations so that children can understand that nine can be four and five, six and three, and so on. The ability of this book to attract and sustain the attention of very young children as well as adults is a strong part of what makes this book a modern classic.

All of Anno's books demand thought and the application of creativity. They give readers the opportunity to consider what is real and what is imagined. Anno uses a blend of the mundane and the fantastic that is at once sophisticated and attractive to the child in everyone.

Children at this age are inquisitive. They love fast action; they are impatient with long descriptions and overly involved dialogue. They can appreciate imaginative settings and situations; their own imaginations are in flower. On the other hand, they require security and the assurance of a stable world. Most folktales and fairy tales provide these characteristics. Fantasy can constitute a vehicle for escape into a strange and different world, but it must be noted that the best of fantasies affirms the aspirations and virtues of this world and helps people sort out their fears and hopes.

Some classic fairy tales may be introduced at this time, but take care not to overload a child with too much violence or retribution. Search for the versions that your child can tolerate. Avoid the saccharine or stereotypic stories that are so watered-down as to be without any drama or life. They may retell the classic stories, but they omit the basic elements that make the stories classic: the sense of credibility and internal truthfulness, the accuracy of the details, the avoidance of stereotypes or gratuitous violence, the respect for human dignity, the universality and depth of the themes, the logic of the plot, and the presentation of a clear values structure.

Each rendition of a fairy tale or folktale varies in its details, depending on its source, the point of view of the storyteller, the medium, and the audience. The classic Cinderella theme, for example, appears in every culture, with male as well as female protagonists, and in modern as well as traditional dress. There are more than eight hundred versions of the Cinderella story. All of them share the theme of the innocent, kind, and worthy young person who is persecuted by a selfish and unkind caretaker, but who emerges triumphant in the end.

The oldest of these stories is from China. The oral version is hundreds of years older than the first written Chinese Cinderella, which dates back to the seventh century! Ai-Ling Louie and Ed Young have collaborated on *Yeh-Shen: A Cinderella Story from China*, a recent retelling of this ancient tale. The illustrations are set in panels like those of a standing folding screen. They are painted in watercolors with pastels that give the appearance of textured fabric. The details of the story differ somewhat from the European versions; the Asian renditions all involve a magic fish and golden shoes, but in the end, as with the European versions, the wicked stepmother is punished, and Cinderella and the prince live happily ever after.

In fairy tales and folktales wickedness is usually punished; virtue is rewarded. The predictability of the fairy tales adds to their attraction. Children expect a "happy ending" after the hero (male or female) has braved harrowing adventures. The best books, by means of their unfolding plot and modeling of virtuous behavior, as well as their exemplification of deep and basic emotions, help children to construct their own values system. These books are not sermons, nor do they have as their major intent the teaching of a lesson. Rather, they present characters, with whom the reader can identify, engaged in a struggle against powerful forces.

The characters are universal. The situations, even at their most fantastic, contain the roots of reality. We all war with the monsters within us. Fairy tales reassure us that we can persevere and aim for great heights. They make us feel that our personal fantasies are acceptable and that we are not alone in our imaginings.

E. B. White's *Stuart Little* and *Charlotte's Web* exemplify the best of modern fantasy. *Stuart Little* is the story of a mouse that was born into a human family. It is a mark of the author's talent that we believe that this situation could occur. Stuart goes on many adventures, struggles with the jealousy of his older brother, and accepts, understands, and takes full advantage of his differences from the rest of his family, and, indeed, the world. Children relate to Stuart's small stature, kind and gentle nature, spirit of adventure, and to his strength. The story has humor, suspense, and pathos.

Charlotte's Web, too, contains all of these elements plus a profound philosophical view of life and death, as told to the reader by a wise and loving spider named Charlotte. Readers have no problem accepting the fact that a spider can spin words into her web. White's characters remain with us as individual personalities as well as prototypes. Wilbur, the insecure runt of the litter; Templeton, the street-wise, cynical rat; Charlotte, the ideal, generous friend are all as real as any character in a work of nonfiction or real life.

The *Frog and Toad* books by Arnold Lobel can be read and reread at this time as well. Each "chapter" is a self-contained story. Children will recognize the two friends' continuing characteristics: Toad is petulant, insecure, and moody; Frog is helpful, understanding, and competent. But they are each much more complex than this listing of attributes suggests. All of the stories contain original situations and deep interactions that provide food for much thought and reflection. While at age three children will enjoy the plot, now, at age four, they will begin to appreciate the open-endedness of the issues, and they will begin to examine and discuss the possible implications of each of the characters' behaviors.

In one story, "The Swim," in *Frog and Toad Are Friends*, Frog and Toad go swimming. Toad doesn't want Frog to see him in his funny bathing suit. Frog obligingly hides his eyes while Toad dons his bathing suit and gets into the water. After the two friends have been swimming for a while some animals appear at the riverbank. Toad pleads with Frog to make the animals go away; he doesn't want them to see him in his funny bathing suit. Frog's efforts prove fruitless, and when Toad finally emerges from the river, all of the animals, including Frog, laugh at how funny he looks.

The last scene shows Toad going home, with an expression on his face that could be interpreted as either angry, chagrined, obstinate, or a host of other somewhat negative reactions. Encourage your children to discuss the feelings of the characters as well as their motivations and behavior. They may talk about how they would have behaved had they been in that situation. They may want to discuss Toad's reasons for wearing the funny suit. And they may want to discuss possible options for Toad's future behavior. They will enjoy the fact that neither Frog nor Toad need be perfectly well behaved or wise in order to be loved and accepted.

Another set of books that is endearing and endlessly rewarding for children of this age level is the *Frances* series by Russell

Hoban. The first one, *Bedtime for Frances*, was illustrated by Garth Williams. Lillian Hoban illustrated the others. Frances is a badger, but she, in common with most of the memorable characters in classics, is really each one of us, and certainly, each child. She is a bright and feisty youngster who composes little songs that she sings to herself, revealing what she is thinking and feeling. Her responses to her baby sister in *A Baby Sister for Frances* and *A Birthday for Frances* reflect the older child struggling against her negative feelings and trying to do what is right. The struggle is a classic one, and it is poetically and sensitively detailed in these two books.

Frances could possibly be introduced at a younger age, but it is the four-year-olds who will fully understand and appreciate her little fantasies and inventions. They will make the best use of her songs and her solutions to the ethical problems that confront her.

Five-Year-Olds

By the time they are five, children's social world has expanded to include people outside the family. Many five-year-olds go to kindergarten and have attended day care and nursery schools. They have developed patterns of interaction with others and are emerging as thinkers and talkers. They are increasingly concerned with their autonomy. They are testing their own power and strength. They are ready for stories that help them try on different personalities. They enjoy seeing children who take risks and emerge with a sense of control over themselves and their environment.

One book that responds to children's imagination and sense of humor as well as their growing concern about how to deal with the adult world is *What Do You Say Dear?* by Sesyle Joslin with pictures by Maurice Sendak. Subtitled *A Book of Manners for All Occasions*, the book poses absurd situations that call for routine polite responses. For example, when having dinner with the queen, after having been served spaghetti for the appetizer, main dish, and salad, and upon being offered spaghetti for dessert, "What do you say, dear?" When we turn the page, the answer is, "May I please be excused?" Each of the preposterous situations is illustrated with young characters enjoying themselves thoroughly and demonstrating that they know that the whole situation is delicious nonsense.

Sendak's *Where the Wild Things Are*, a story no doubt familiar to millions of readers, tells that Max, who has "made mischief of one sort and another," is punished by being sent to his room without eating. He dreams a wonderful dream of sailing away to a far-off land where he becomes king of the wild things. Although he tames the wild things and they love him, he decides to leave them and return to his home, where there is a hot meal waiting for him.

In this modern classic, the design of the page is very important to the effect of the story. The pictures grow in size as Max gets further and further into his dream until at last the text disappears, and for six pages (three double-page spreads) the monsters and Max occupy our attention with the images of their orgy and its aftermath. The light changes from moonlight to morning and the moods of the characters change from ferocious and wild to tame and contented.

The details of the illustrations are as important as their size and placement. Each wild thing is an individual; there is no special mold for one. Their noses, chins, feet, skin texture, and color vary from creature to creature, yet they resemble Max, and could probably be part of his extended family. It is clear throughout the story that Max is wearing his wolf suit, and is not a wild thing through and through. Each picture provides the viewer with details to notice: the size, shape, and color of the moon; the position and varying solidity of the furniture in Max's room; the human feet of one of the wild things; and the changing expressions on Max's face. Every aspect of this book raises questions for the reader to consider, thus adding to the enduring fascination of the story.

The ending is a satisfying one to Max and to the readers of this book. Max returns home, in control of himself and his world. His dinner is waiting for him, and we know that his family loves him. His feelings and needs have been acknowledged, and he can continue with self-respect.

Ira Sleeps Over by Bernard Waber details the dilemma with which young Ira is faced when he is invited to sleep at a friend's house for the very first time. Ira's sister taunts him about his teddy bear, so Ira decides not to bring it with him. He finally knows that it is OK for him to have his bear when he discovers that his friend sleeps with a teddy bear too. Ira's sister is not a sympathetic character, but Ira's parents are supportive and understanding and

Ira ends with a feeling of control and assurance. The situation is a classic one. In one conversation between Ira and his sister, she warns Ira that his friend will laugh when he finds out about the "silly, baby name" of Ira's bear. (It is "Tah Tah.") Ira decides not to take his teddy bear.

Ira's vacillation is characteristic of children this age. The author understands the needs of modern society. Both the mother and father are nurturing. Ira's father is shown in the kitchen cooking a meal alongside Ira's mother. The two children share responsibility for chores in the household. The setting is specific, but the situation is universal. Librarians note that this is one of the most frequently circulating books in the library.

Another book that has proved to be very popular in the years since its publication is *The Terrible Thing That Happened at Our House* by Marge Blaine, with pictures by John C. Wallner. Here, too, the blend of humorous writing and illustrations with a situation that is familiar and important to youngsters is the cause of its lasting popularity. The story deals with a young girl's chagrin at the changed conditions in her house now that her mother has gone back to being a science teacher. The girl complains bitterly about now having to find her own underwear and socks, eating lunch in school, and missing out on stories and games because her parents are now too busy to read to her and play with her. Eventually, the family listens and now arranges time for everyone to be accommodated, while at the same time making it clear that the proper running of the house is everyone's responsibility, not just the parents'.

The illustrations are framed as though they were snapshots from a family album. They depict a far-from-perfect cast of characters. The first few pictures exemplify the child's version of an idyllic life. As we progress through the period immediately following the mother's return to salaried work, the settings and characters look messy and convey a sense of turmoil. The final picture shows the family as a unit, composed and smiling, waving happily to the viewer. The book not only portrays a realistic problem, it suggests a solution. And it is sympathetic to all of the people involved, not just the parents or just the children. Although this book does not have the artistry or depth of many classics, its humor and pragmatism make it a book that belongs with old favorites.

Age five is a time when many children voice their fear of death.

There are many books now that help children and parents deal with this issue. Some of them have become classics because of their sensitivity, adroitness in handling the problem, and beauty of language and image. *The Tenth Good Thing About Barney*, by Judith Viorst, with illustrations by Erik Blegvad, is one such classic. The delicate black-and-white line drawings acknowledge the delicacy of the situation. The author displays an awareness of the stages young children go through, both in their knowledge about death and their reaction to it. She affirms the importance of the mourning period, and she helps young readers understand that death is a part of the cycle of life. In dealing with the death of a pet she is preparing children to deal with death in general. The language is almost poetic in its simplicity and cadence. The author has an excellent ear for children's authentic language. She is respectful of all of her characters, and the story unfolds as story, not as a tract.

Similarly, in Charlotte Zolotow's *My Grandson Lew*, illustrated by William Pene duBois, the tone of the story is neither saccharine nor condescending. The message that memories of loved ones who have died can comfort the living, emerges along with the portrait of a remarkable, tender, vital grandfather. It is not uncommon for five-year-olds to have to cope with the death of a grandparent, and this book will remain a treasure and a comfort for them as well as for those children whose grandparents are still alive and well.

In Lucille Clifton's series of books about Everett Anderson, Ann Grifalconi's soft sketches enhance the text and convey the characters' emotions and relationships in a sympathetic and evocative way. All of the *Everett Anderson* stories are told in verse. In *Everett Anderson's Goodbye*, which details the child's reaction to his father's death, the little boy progresses through each of the stages of grief: denial, anger, bargaining, depression, and acceptance. At all times, his mother is supportive. It ends with the assurance "and whatever happens when people die, love doesn't stop, and neither will I."

Clifton's special ability to portray accurately the language and cadence of each of the characters illuminates her books. Further, she provides readers with a sense of pride and the opportunity to understand that diversity is an important factor in the unity of mankind.

Children at this age can begin to look at people who are different from themselves and appreciate those differences. They are interested in other people and how and where they live. They are expanding yet further their understanding of the way the world works. A book of prize-winning photographs for adults, *The Family of Man*, can be appreciated by children at this stage. Parents and children together can look through this international collection of photos and see people, very different from one another, engaging in similar activities and experiencing similar feelings. The book contains photos collected and arranged by Edward Steichen into an exhibit that was first displayed at the New York Museum of Modern Art in 1954. The prologue by Carl Sandberg states that this is "A camera testament, a drama of the grand canyon of humanity, an epic woven of fun, mystery and holiness — here is the Family of Man!"

The Caldecott Award–winning book, *Ashanti to Zulu*, by Margaret Musgrove, illustrated by Leo and Diane Dillon, introduces twenty-six African peoples to the young reader. It is notable in its attention to detail; its author and illustrators were meticulous in their research. For example, the borders of watercolor and black ink use a design based on the Kano knot, symbolizing endless searching. The combination of brief, interesting facts about each of the peoples depicted and the portraits of the people in their African settings makes this a valuable book.

Some books convey the same sense of beauty, dignity, and authenticity about places here in the United States. Robert McCloskey's *Time of Wonder*, another Caldecott Medal winner, combines large watercolor paintings with prose that is so sensory and specific that the reader enters with the child protagonists into the life on this tiny island in Penobscot Bay off the coast of Maine. McCloskey catalogs people (Mr. Billings, Harry Smith, Clyde Snowman, Ferd Clifford), places (Camden Hills, Islesboro, Western Island, Hog Island, Spectacle Island), and flora and fauna (fiddlehead ferns, bees, hummingbirds, seals, porpoises, owls, eider ducks, fishhawks). The text and pictures take us from morning to night and across a summer. The images and senses of the island build until they form a palpable experience for every reader to cherish.

Books can move readers across time as well as space. *Ox-Cart Man*, another Caldecott Medal winner, by Donald Hall, with pictures by Barbara Cooney, takes the reader into nineteenth-century New England. The book conveys an important sense of the feelings of farmers and their families in the 1800s, the work that each family member, including young children, performed, and their interdependence with the land and their animals. We accompany a family through the year and travel with the father on his journey to Portsmouth Market where he sells his goods and then returns to his home.

Although the text simply recounts the details of the father's journey, specifying each item that the farmer packs into his cart and then sells, there are occasional hints of emotion in the terse sentences. "Then he sold his ox, and kissed him good-bye on his nose." There is rarely an adjective; the sparse text carries the reader through the seasons. It is not until the last sentence, when we have moved into late spring "and geese squawked in the barnyard, dropping feathers as soft as clouds" that the words give us anything but a literal image. The prose indicates the cyclical nature of the family's life. We know that in fall the farmer will carry bundles of these feathers to the market again and that the family will continue planting and gathering and selling.

Barbara Cooney's art supplies the adjectives that the bare text omits. It conveys to the reader a respect for each person, animal, and scene. The rolling blue hills of the New England setting; the vibrant colors of autumn; the houses, painted in primitive early-American style; the faithful rendering of the Portsmouth Market; the gentle and amusing portrayal of the beloved ox; the placid whiteness of the wintry landscape; the new, fresh greens, and whites and pinks of spring; and the unmistakable authenticity of the family's clothing, implements, and furniture, combine to make this a classic to be appreciated and enjoyed over time. Every rereading will yield a new discovery on the part of the observant child or adult.

Barbara Cooney's work is unfailingly worthy. *Miss Rumphius*, a book she both wrote and illustrated, has the ring of truth to it; the main character is based on a real person. But this person is larger than life. She is a Johnny Appleseed, beautifying the Maine coast with hundreds and hundreds of lupines. She is also a model for children to follow: a feisty female who travels around the world, comes home to live in a house by the sea, and makes the world more beautiful.

Again, as in *Ox-Cart Man*, the illustrations add inestimably to the value of the book. The details of each of the settings, the color, especially the vibrant colors of the lupines, the pastels of the far-off lands, and the intense blues and whites of the ocean, combine with the textures of the grass, stones, and houses to provide a visual banquet.

We cannot emphasize enough that although we must allow for differences in taste, experience, background, and personality, the wonder of a great book is that it manages to satisfy certain universal human needs and emotions. It communicates a sense of morality without becoming didactic or sacrificing its literary or aesthetic quality. Great authors bear in mind psychological, societal, cultural, and historical factors. They often research their themes extensively so that their details are accurate.

Children's literature, like adult books, touches the heart with its depth of truth and beauty. Enduring literature satisfies needs that cross boundaries of culture, nationality, religion, race, gender, and status. The beauty of a classic is that it changes to fit new generations and new demands. All of the components of such a book must work together to hold the reader's attention. A classic usually deals with familiar and even comforting truths, and contains such depth that readers want to return again and again to find something that captures continued attention and provides continuing satisfaction within its pages.

Young readers are fortunate to have so many great writers and artists who are producing books of quality, books that will foster the love of reading. We recommend any of the works by artists such as Mitsumasa Anno, Dick Bruna, Ashley Bryan, Eric Carle, Barbara Cooney, Donald Crews, Tomie dePaola, Diane and Leo Dillon, Marie Hall Ets, Tom Feelings, Ann Grifalconi, Tana Hoban, Trina Schart Hyman, Leo Lionni, Thomas Locker, Helen Oxenbury, Patricia MacLachlan, Maurice Sendak, Peter Spier, Tasha Tudor, Jane Yolen, Ed Young, and Paul Zelinsky. Look for writers such as Ludwig Bemelmans, Margaret Wise Brown, Virginia Lee Burton, Lucille Clifton, Arnold Lobel, Beatrix Potter, William Steig, Judith Viorst, E. B. White, and Charlotte Zolotow. No one list can include all of the excellent artists and authors, but these people consistently produce work of the highest quality, and they are not likely to disappoint you.

2

The Magic of Story

A good storyteller is like a magician who creates images and illusions and presents the world in a special, entertaining way and distracts the audience from the mechanics of the act, so that time and space are transcended and the viewer or listener enters another realm. Good storytellers build their skills carefully and over time. They learn to gauge their listeners' abilities and interests. They constantly acquire greater and broader repertoires of material from which to weave their tales. They use all of their life experiences to good advantage, and they don't neglect what is under the surface. They read, and experience; they listen, extract what is important to them, reshape it, and share.

Everyone has many stories to tell. A story is a narrative. It must have a beginning, middle, and end, and it should have a point. It may or may not be true, but it should always make the listener suspend disbelief. Authors who write fiction or fantasy spend much time and energy considering and researching their settings, eras, and characters' behaviors and appearances so that their stories will ring true. They also take great pains to learn about the psychological characteristics and responses that fit their characters and the situations in which they are involved.

A storyteller in the home differs from a professional storyteller only in that no one need pay an admission fee and the audience is not composed of strangers. Certainly all parents and caretakers can experience the joy of engaging an enraptured child in the web of a story. "When I was little . . ." is sure to capture a child's attention, especially if it does not preface an admonition ("I *always* was good to my little brother" or "I walked five miles to school in the snow" or "I never disobeyed my mother"). Family stories about how Uncle Harold got a lump on his head when daddy wound him up in a swing and then let go; or how Grandma Jenny met and married Grandpa Tom; or how Carlos lost his way one day, and his dog, Prince, found him and guided him home are tales that can be enjoyed over and over again.

Little children, in recounting the events of their day, are also telling stories and their narrative should be accorded the same sort of respect that older storytellers expect. Our interested questions and comments can help young children to learn how to make their stories more complete and sequential.

Professional storytellers, sometimes called authors, also provide good models. Any story that we enjoy reading aloud is probably a good candidate for a story to tell. The more stories we read to our children, the more they will learn what makes a good story. They will unconsciously internalize the structure, language, and cadence of a good story. One element that children love to hear and will imitate is the use of a ritual beginning to a tale. "Once upon a time . . . ," "Once there was, and once there was not . . . ," "A story is a story; let it come let it go," "I remember . . . ," "When you were very little . . . ," "Gather 'round me, children, I'm about to tell a tale" are all invitations to enter into a world of magic, even when the content deals with the mundane.

Although this chapter deals extensively with reading aloud, its advantages, and how to do it, the importance of *telling* stories should not be diminished. There are many occasions when it is not possible to read from a book, and it is at these times especially that storytelling is appropriate. There may, in fact, be many instances when, even if a book is available and it is convenient to read it, you may prefer the direct contact of storytelling.

From time to time, make it a practice to retell some familiar stories, or sing verses and songs while you're engaging in ordinary tasks. Use such occasions as pushing the shopping cart, wheeling the baby carriage, doing the daily chores, bedtime, bath time, meal time, waiting in dentists' and doctors' offices, driving the car, traveling in a bus or plane, or when you are just out for a walk.

Professional storytellers and librarians tell us that the best storytelling is a mutual creation. Children create their own mental images from what they hear. Their imagination is stimulated, and their creativity flourishes. The repeated experience of listening to stories also helps children learn and remember the rhythms and shapes of stories.

The art of storytelling is an ancient one. Prehistoric civilizations used storytelling as a way of explaining the world, controlling their fears, and transmitting their history and culture. Today we still use it in the same way, even though we have many new scientific and technological advances. As in times long past, we now learn to tell stories from our parents, grandparents, aunts and uncles, siblings, friends, and teachers. We have means of transmitting our stories to millions of people at a time, but the feelings we get when we are in the close and intimate presence of a live storyteller cannot be replicated in any other setting.

The benefits of storytelling extend beyond the family and home. When children have been exposed to people who love both the written and the spoken word, those children become enriched in many ways. Research indicates that these children do very well in school. Their vocabulary is sharpened and increased; their listening and comprehension skills are improved; they receive valuable knowledge and insight; they become more and more attracted to books and literature, and they learn to identify with people who are different from themselves while at the same time coming to realize that people share a common bond of humanity. They also learn that they can share in pleasurable experiences with adults.

The best storyteller is one who is comfortable with the material and enjoys the process of transmitting it to a listener. It would be a mistake to tell a story that you don't enjoy. Your feelings come across, no matter how much you try to hide them. Storytellers neither overact nor engage too often in elaborate or grand gestures; the words and tone usually suffice. In this vein, although sometimes a hand puppet or a special costume can be fun, it is usually unnecessary to use props or aids in telling the story. A story that is worth telling stands on its own and carries its own messages.

Children know when we are teaching them a lesson rather than telling them a story. Many good stories have lessons in them, but they are inherent to the plot, and not tacked on in an attempt to be didactic. Certainly, there may be a discussion, and questions that the child may have should be respectfully responded to, but sometimes a child may want to retain the sense of magic by simply remaining silent for a while after the story is over. It is also a good idea from time to time for the storyteller to make eye contact, ask questions, and initiate discussions with the listener. Good stories deserve retelling, and it is often in the relistening that a child will be moved to comment or actively participate.

In selecting a story to tell, take into consideration the developmental level of the child. What are his or her interests? How complicated is the plot? How clear is the structure of the story? Younger children cannot tolerate as many intricacies of character and description as can older children. You will need to be careful to organize your story into a clear beginning, middle, and end. Remember that young children are just beginning to develop their organizational skills along with a sense of time and sequence. Make the characters believable to your audience. Their actions should be comprehensible and suited to the plot. Their qualities should be inherent in their behavior, or should be described in clear and specific language.

Take into consideration your own personality, voice, and style. If you are a quiet, reflective person you may be attracted to the retelling of stories by authors such as Charlotte Zolotow, Judith Viorst, and Margaret Wise Brown. If you have a strong or deep voice, you may particularly enjoy the telling of such tales as *The Three Billy Goats Gruff, The Three Little Pigs,* or *Goldilocks and the Three Bears.* But your voice need not limit you; the more stories you tell, the more versatile you will become.

A light, loving touch is often more effective than a heavy dose of drama. Humor, short anecdotes, and brief episodes can begin your storytelling ventures. You may want to keep retelling a few stories with which you are very familiar. You can extend your repertoire and build to longer adventure tales, complicated plots, or serials as you get more adept and your child gets more involved. Respect your own values in your story selection and storytelling. Certainly, invite your child to contribute his or her own stories. And be sure to value and enjoy them.

When you prepare to tell a story, first become very familiar with it. Even if it is a story that happened to you, think about the sequence that you will use. Decide which details you will include, and which you will omit. When you're creating the characters, first imagine them. Choose three or four outstanding characteristics of their personality, mannerisms, physical appearance, and voice. Identify the climax, and be sure to build up to it. Decide how you will begin it and how you will end it.

Reading Aloud

When you tell and retell literary stories, try to find these stories in print. Then, when you read these aloud, you help your child to recognize the connection between print and speech and you prepare the way for your child to be more comfortable with the written word. The acts of storytelling and reading aloud are loving and attentive ones; moreover they demonstrate the value of reading and the spoken word.

Most people like to be read to. No one is too young to enjoy it; no one is too old; it does not matter whether or not the listener knows how to read. Reading aloud can be informative, entertaining, soothing, inspiring, and challenging. It is not a substitute for reading to oneself; by its very nature it is a sharing and intimate occasion, a special event no matter how regularly it is performed.

Don't be discouraged if your child fidgets or seems unenthusiastic when you first read a book. Try it again at another time, or simply let it go. Your attitude should be relaxed. This is, after all, a mutually enjoyable experience.

One of the first rules for successful reading aloud is that you select something you know *you* are attracted to. You will be especially successful if you love a book and can communicate this strong positive feeling to your child. Negative feelings somehow become transmitted to your listeners and you will defeat your purpose. So it stands to reason that you should read aloud only those materials that you have already read and feel some familiarity with. After all, reading aloud is a performance. Even if you are reading to only one small child, you still must remember that you have an audience.

With small beginning books you will usually read the entire book. Later on, with longer and more complicated books you will have to decide how much of the book you want to read, where you

42

will begin, and where you will end. Don't worry about reading each word, or even about the accuracy of each word you read. It is perfectly permissible to leave out some passages if you feel that for the sake of the action or the interest of the child you would like to do so. The more comfortable and natural you are, the better the story will be conveyed.

Especially when you are reading to a very young child, pick a chair that the two of you will be comfortable sharing. Books are even more memorable when the child is enclosed in the loving circle of a parent's arms. Take your time. Don't feel that you have to turn a page immediately after completing the text on that page. Allow some time for the two of you to savor the pictures. Repeat some of the phrases from time to time. Don't be afraid to point to the words as you read them. This helps the child to make a connection between what your voice is saying and what is on the printed page. If what you are looking at is a picture book, and the text simply labels the pictures, or if there is a refrain that recurs, try to say the words in different ways each time. For example, if you are reading the story of *Goldilocks and the Three Bears,* you can repeat "But it was too———" in a slightly different way by first accenting "But," then accenting "it," then "too," and finally, the descriptor ("hot," "cold," "hard," "soft," "high," or "low"). After a book has become a repeated event in a child's life insert some questions every now and then to heighten the interest: "What will happen next?"; "Where are the bears?"; "What other words would fit here?"

Once you have graduated into books with plot and adventure, don't forget how powerful the use of silence is. Pauses of several seconds' duration help to create a sense of anticipation and excitement. "Just then" (count silently to five) "the bears came home."

Other techniques for emphasis or dramatic effect are the raising and lowering of your voice, the speeding or slowing down of your pace, and the deliberate taking on of different voices to indicate the different characters. Try a coarse, hoarse voice for the papa bear, your own voice (even if you are a man) for the mama bear, a tiny, squeaky voice for baby bear, and a sweet, light voice for Goldilocks. If this makes you feel uncomfortable, try it in slow stages, with a special voice for just one of the characters and your own voice for all of the others. Once your child knows the story he or she can join in with the voice of a character. After many readings and tellings you may enjoy making puppets and inventing plays that you can perform just with each other or for family members.

When you are selecting passages to read aloud it is sometimes a good idea to avoid sections with long descriptions. The most satisfying read-alouds are usually those that communicate some action, contain dialogue or interaction among characters, or at least convey some point. But at times even descriptions can be satisfying, especially if they are read at nap time or at the end of the day. (Don't be offended when your audience falls asleep in the middle of these.) At every reading, note your child's reactions. Watch for signals of developmental readiness and postpone what doesn't seem to be working well right now. Maintain enough eye contact so that you can react and respond to signs of interest, or lack of it.

Don't worry about selecting books that are too easy for your child to understand. If the book contains elements of interest to you, it's likely that your child won't be bored. Some of the simplest picture books are fascinating to older children and even to adults. But make sure that the book is not too emotionally or intellectually demanding for your child. And do try to select books that are not empty of meaning or overly sentimental. Children don't like to be talked down to. Most of the good children's books are simple, but respectful of their audience.

The qualities of a good children's book are the same qualities as a good adult book. The plot should be plausible, engrossing, and flowing; the characters should be believable, interesting, and three-dimensional; the theme should be appropriately handled with authenticity and accuracy; the language should be rich and the illustrations should satisfy the aesthetic tastes and needs of the reader. Humor should be humane; no character or group should be demeaned.

The best books satisfy the needs of both the reader and the listener. We all share in our basic human needs, and we often go to books to have them acknowledged and satisfied. The need to feel competent, emotionally and physically secure, to belong, to play, and to experience beauty are all qualities that the best of books portray and that we, through our reading aloud, can bring to the attention, experience, and hearts of our children.

Reading Aloud to Infants

Any time is a good one for reading aloud, especially when babies are still at the stage of needing a great deal of attention. The primary purpose of reading aloud to infants is not to force them into early reading. Rather, it is to help them develop an enthusiastic attitude toward books and reading. Children should approach books and the process of reading with a sense of confidence and happy anticipation. When pleasurable experiences with books have not been a part of a child's regular home routine, the books that are introduced at school may be associated with academic expectations of a threatening nature. They may be perceived as an imposition rather than an extension of the child's interests and needs. Research indicates that children who come from home environments where books, magazines, and newspapers are in evidence and where reading aloud is a common routine, are much more likely to succeed academically than children whose homes are barren of print and where reading aloud has not been the practice.

Dorothy Butler reports in *Cushla and Her Books* that every time of day and night was used as an occasion for reading aloud. Reading aloud was introduced to Cushla when she was only a few months old. And even though doctors told her parents that Cushla should be institutionalized because of her multiple physical and mental handicaps, Cushla's parents persisted and read aloud to her more than ten times a day. By the time she was nine months old Cushla was indicating which of the books were her favorites, and by the time she was five she was reading!

Reading aloud while you are feeding an infant helps the baby to associate books with fulfillment of needs. Even when the child is too young to understand words, he or she can sense the connection between nurturing and the reading of a book. Over time, the child will come to savor the rich array of tantalizing and gratifying pleasures that the experience of books and literature can offer. The reading aloud of books can help children develop a sense of humor, build their feelings of emotional security and the necessary sense of belonging, address their need to know, enhance their sense of playfulness, awaken their openness to new situations, and help to develop their appreciation of beauty of sound, images, and words.

In the beginning a parent can read aloud from an adult book; it is the sound of the voice, and its association of the voice with the book that matters. It would not hurt to include some books of poetry, or even some joke books so that you will have an opportunity to vary your voice and rhythmic patterns as you read.

Infants respond to the rhythms, melodies, and differing tones of voice beyond mere conversation. In this way they are prepared to acquire a repertoire of language abilities and appreciation. This is an excellent time to introduce the songs and sounds of different languages, especially those of your parents, relatives, and friends. Songs may come spontaneously to your lips, without your even being aware that you remembered them from your babyhood.

The adult's voice is probably the most important part of earliest reading aloud and storytelling. Nursery rhymes, books of poetry, and songbooks provide a source of pleasure and early preparation in distinguishing between a "story" voice and an ordinary conversational tone. One book of verse, *As I Was Going Up and Down and Other Nonsense Rhymes,* with humorous illustrations by Nicola Bayley, will not be intelligible to infants, but will probably amuse the adult reader and entice the baby both by the rhythm and the obvious enjoyment on the part of the adult. Books of this sort have the added advantage of encouraging the adult reader to continue reading, because of the entertainment they afford. Some of the rhymes are impudent, some are like riddles, others are unadorned nonsense. Don't read this one at dinnertime:

> A diner while dining at Crewe
> Found quite a large mouse in his stew
> Said the waiter, "Don't shout,
> And wave it about,
> Or the rest will be wanting one, too!"

You may want to add some of your own favorite riddle-type verses to this one:

> The man in the
> wilderness asked me
> How many strawberries
> grew in the sea.
> I answered him

46

as I thought good,
As many as red herrings
grew in the wood.

The same illustrator whose detailed pictures captivate adults and older children (they are probably too small and delicate for infants to appreciate) has also published a beginning book of a dozen lullabies that does not contain the music, but that serves as a helpful list and reminder of the most commonly sung nighttime songs, among them "Diddle Diddle, Dumpling," "Hush Little Baby," and "Sleep, Baby, Sleep."

One recently published book of lullabies is notable for its well-crafted musical arrangements by Adam Stemple, its interesting and informative background information by Jane Yolen, and its full-color illustrations by Charles Mikolaycak. The title of this book is *The Lullaby Songbook*. It contains a broad cross-cultural selection of songs such as "Lulloo Lullay," "Raisins and Almonds," "Cum By Yah," "Suo Gan," and others. Another lullaby book is Jamake Highwater's *Moonsong Lullaby*. Color photographs accompany the lines of the poem inspired by traditional Native American tales. Consult chapters 1 and 3 for other appropriate titles.

Although the main attractions of lullabies are the melody and the circumstances surrounding the "reading aloud" of the songs, the words become an important part of the experience as children's understanding grows. Even from the very beginning it is a good idea to substitute the child's name whenever possible since the child's own name is usually the very first word he or she understands and reads. Thus, "Sleep, Matthew, sleep," or "Down will come Jessica, cradle and all." Another option is to invent a personal song for your child, especially if you like the melody of a song, but not its words. A number of parents sing different words to the tune of "Rockabye Baby" because they find the idea of the falling cradle to be a frightening one. It is worthy of note, however, that the words to this song have lasted through the ages.

Many of our most popular children's verses originated as material intended for adults. The rhyme and rhythm appeal not only to the ear, but also cause the young child to respond physically. An important part of the reading aloud or singing of Mother Goose rhymes is the physical action that accompanies it. You bounce your baby on your knees, rock him in your arms, and make responsive motions that become part and parcel of the experience. You can also involve your baby in the clapping of hands, rolling and patting of imaginary cakes, and gesturing to accompany the verses. Not only is this enjoyable, but also educational, since developmentalists have found that there is a connection between motor ability and language competence.

One of the easiest starting places for telling and reading verse is Mother Goose. There is a rich variety of versions from which to choose, depending on your tastes and wishes. One recently published set contains more than half a dozen Mother Goose nursery rhyme collections illustrated by Allen Atkinson. *Mary Had a Little Lamb and Other Favorites* and *Simple Simon and Other Favorites* are two of the little (5¼-inch square) paperbacks that each include about twenty of the more familiar of the rhymes as well as some that are less well known, such as: "Bat, bat, Come under my hat, And I'll give you a slice of bacon; And when I bake I'll give you a cake, If I am not mistaken."

Some anthologies are more elaborate, more comprehensive, and published in larger format. Arnold Lobel's *The Random House Book of Mother Goose* contains over two hundred and fifty of the rhymes, with the artist's color illustrations sometimes occupying a whole 8½-by-11-inch page.

You may own some Mother Goose collections that you have saved from your childhood. Such well-known illustrators as Randolph Caldecott, Arthur Rackham, Kate Greenaway, Feodor Rojankowsky, Tasha Tudor, and Brian Wildsmith have lent their talents to flavorful editions of the rhymes.

A number of individual Mother Goose rhymes occupy whole books. Illustrator Paul Galdone has selected *Three Little Kittens* for such attention. Large illustrations accompany the verses. Parents and children may sing the poem, take on the voices of the mother and baby cats, and make the sounds of the mewling kittens. ("Meow, meow, and they began to cry.") Once children are able to follow and enjoy the plot of these simple stories, you can begin to enrich the reading aloud by accentuating the drama of the story, relishing the suspense of guessing what will come next, and noting and appreciating the individual qualities of the characters.

Other individually depicted Mother Goose rhymes include Jeanette Winter's version of *Come Out to Play,* a whimsical rendition that may retain the child's interest for years to come because of its complex and detailed illustrations. At first the attraction will be the rhyme and the music. (Unfortunately the melody is not included in this book, but it is a simple one to find and sing.) The playful and amicable children in the book clearly come from different heritages. A gnomelike fiddler with a star on the tip of his cap follows the children in a benign, protective fashion.

There is never an age when you should stop reading songs and poems to children. These materials are very effective when the infants are focusing on their parents' and caretakers' voices rather than on the written source of the words. The rhythm, rhyme, and melody overcome the lack of understanding. These books can continue to delight and influence the development of children after the babies have begun to show an interest in books as attractive and meaningful in and of themselves.

As soon as the infant begins to recognize people and objects in the environment he or she enjoys and responds to bright colors and illustrations. Publishers have taken into consideration the fact that parents are introducing children to books at a very early age, and they have designed books that are made of cloth or laminated heavy cardboard and called board books. Babies can hold the books and even put them into their mouths without doing damage to either the book or themselves. The reading aloud of these books is an interactive experience. They generally do not contain stories, but usually have one picture with its label on a page. The child continues to enjoy the sound of the adult's voice, the colors and shapes of the illustrations, and the sensation of nearness to a loving adult. But the magic here is that the object on the page is beginning to represent something in real life that the child can recognize. In the zest with which the child and adult are sharing the sound of the words and the identification of the pictures, the message is conveyed that pleasure comes from books, not only as toys, but also as read-alouds that are shared with adults. Many of these books are listed in "The Bookshelf" and are discussed in other chapters.

Once babies have developed some control of their gross and fine motor skills (at about twelve to fifteen months) they become adept at turning pages. They return again and again to books that have become familiar and loved. These books can be reread hundreds of times, and even six-month-old infants will respond to, recognize, and request certain favorites. Research on informal prereading development tells us that in the first year, although books are viewed as objects by children, and are often handled as though they were toys, babies can recognize brightly colored illustrations and can distinguish one book from another. They enjoy responding to pictures that represent familiar objects.

Reading Aloud to Toddlers

Toddlers will continue to enjoy all of the songs and verses you have read to them as infants. Only after they are sitting up and taking note of pictures do they really attend to the books themselves. Peter Spier's *London Bridge Is Falling Down!* stands the test of time. The intricacy of the illustrations invites older children to pore over the details long after the song is so familiar that it has been committed to memory. In this book Spier not only gives us the verses and music for singing, and illustrations of each era, but also he provides for the adult, or older reader, a history of London Bridge through the ages. Readers learn that the first London Bridge was constructed in 43 B.C. and that the bridge was destroyed and rebuilt many times.

Another well-known rhyme that appears as a book is *Old MacDonald Had a Farm*, adapted and illustrated by Abner Graboff. The music is included on the back cover so that it is accessible, and will stay in place on a piano ledge if necessary. Part of the read-aloud fun here is to make the sounds of each of the animals, and, perhaps, to engage in some creative additions of your own animals to the list that appears in the book. Rhymes such as this one are called cumulative because each verse adds a new element while retaining the previous sequence. Young children take pleasure in exercising their memories as they sing these songs. They also are building their ability to understand categories and sequence.

Not only Mother Goose rhymes and songs are accorded their own place in books. Traditional songs, folk songs, and poems also can be found. A book that appeals to a child's need for a sense of belonging, especially appropriate at Thanksgiving, is *Over the River and Through the Wood* by Lydia Maria Child. Its muted-color drawings by Brinton Turkle are reminiscent of nineteenth-century paintings and depict the pleasures of being reunited with grandparents for a special holiday celebration.

Go Tell Aunt Rhody, illustrated by Aliki, transforms what could be a nonsense song into an occasion for demonstrating genuine sadness over the death of a farm animal, followed by the practical tasks of fetching and plucking the goose to make the warm feather quilt. One of the reasons for selecting a read-aloud can be the additional dimension of invoking some empathy in the listener for one or more of the characters. A number of researchers, in particular Jerome Bruner, have noted that even young infants can exhibit empathic responses.

At a very early stage of listening and talking, children will repeat some of the refrains in stories, songs, and rhymes that they have heard read to them many times. They may, on occasion, commit whole stanzas or poems to memory. Counting songs, the alphabet song, Mother Goose rhymes, and snatches of characters' conversations ("Go dog, go") will often emerge spontaneously from toddlers' mouths.

Once children have reached the toddler stage parents can introduce wordless picture books and invite the child to join in not only on the labeling of the pictures, but also the telling of a story. Although Helen Oxenbury's book *Animals* has no real story line and no written words at all, each double-page spread depicting a child mimicking the action of an animal could, in and of itself, spark the creation of a little story. On a more advanced level, the wordless Anno books, for example, *Anno's Journey*, where a tiny figure on horseback wends his way across European landscapes, cities, and time, attracts adults and children alike with its imaginative pages filled with objects, actions, and stories at many levels of sophistication.

Kjell Ringi's book *The Winner* presents a complex concept in a startlingly simple way. As soon as children can recognize action they will be able to interpret what is happening when the two characters in this book engage in an ever-escalating competition that finally destroys them both. "Reading" a wordless book requires the skills of observation, sequencing, making connections, understanding story structure, and using a wide range of vocabulary. Children acquire these skills after they have had models provided for them. That is the role of the caretaker in presenting these wordless books to their young charges.

From the beginning, the routine of reading aloud can be established as part of a family's everyday schedule. Nap time can prompt a look at lullaby songbooks or tone-poem books such as *Dawn* by Uri Shulevitz in which a little boy and his grandfather share a special outing together. Bedtime is, of course, a logical occasion for the comforting and loving reading aloud of stories, rhymes, or songs, new or familiar. *Good Night Moon* by Margaret Wise Brown tells no exciting story, but simply details a young child's saying "good night" to all of the objects and people in her immediate environment. It is a book that children may want to hear and see over and over again, partly because many children have trouble settling down at the end of the day, and partly because the rhythmic repetition of the predictable refrain is soothing. They may also want to add their own objects and people to the list for saying "good night" to.

This sort of experience with early books helps children to recognize that they can contribute to the meaning in a book. The author alone can not complete a book; it is the act of reading and responding to the book that really constructs its meaning. And as the reader grows and changes, the meaning of the book will grow and change.

Children often recite pieces of books and tell their own stories based on those that they have heard. Be careful to respect this practice. It becomes children's early reading; it is not simple memorization; it reflects the child's making of personal meaning out of the world of literature. It is very important at this time, even though the child is showing more independence with books, to continue the regular practice of reading aloud and storytelling. Children can become reluctant to learn to read on their own if they think that this prowess will cut off the very pleasurable activity of being read to by others.

Reading Aloud to Older Toddlers

After age two, children are ready for well-designed, developmentally appropriate informational books that help them discover the wonder in the world outside their immediate environment. Through their innovative formats and simple, predictable text, books such as Eric Carle's *The Very Busy Spider* help children start to make connections between the natural world and themselves. As you turn each page, the spider spins an ever more complicated (and tactilely inviting) web. The adult reader, in presenting books of this sort, should take care to turn the pages very slowly, communicating a sense of growing excitement and anticipation of the little adventure of each turning of the page. The repeated sentences (for example, "She was very busy spinning her web") can be said in different tones, speeds, voice registers, and with emphasis on different words in order to maintain interest while providing a continuity from one set of pages to the next.

Excitement and anticipation, plus the security of the predictability of a repeated pattern can be found in *Where's Spot?* by Eric Hill. It is a storybook that toddlers will enjoy. They can search for the missing puppy, Spot, by looking under and behind flaps that appear on each page of the book. Among the flaps children can open are the doors of a wardrobe and a grandfather clock. They can lift the dust ruffle of a bed and the lid of a trunk; and finally they can join mother dog in finding Spot. Toddlers will have no trouble keeping up with the story line. The adult reader can use pauses and questions to dramatic advantage in a book of this sort and can direct the story's question directly at the listening child. The physical act of peering behind each of the flaps gives the youngster the opportunity to participate and react to the story.

Poetry can delight children in the same way that songs and stories do. When adults make the mistake of communicating the notion that poetry is sacrosanct, children are likely to reject it. If you choose poetry that you enjoy and poems that are written with the voice of a child in mind, and if you read it among other material, then children will react favorably to your enthusiasm and will not feel threatened by poetry's unique format. Such books as *Honey, I Love, and Other Love Poems* by Eloise Greenfield with drawings by the award-winning Leo and Diane Dillon, reflect a child's feelings in small, potent doses.

Poetry reading should not differ from the techniques of reading prose. Don't let the rhythm or rhyme distract you from the meaning. In this selection, for example, be sure to vary the speed of your voice as well as the tone. Read the first two lines slowly, in a dreamy fashion, the next line in a staccato, short voice, varying your emphasis. "I'm a squeaky noise" should be spoken in a high, squeaky voice, and the next two lines should be said in a deep and firm voice. The last three lines of this poem should contain pauses, with the ending arriving in a strong, resounding tone:

By Myself

When I'm by myself
And I close my eyes
I'm a twin
I'm a dimple in a chin
I'm a room full of toys
I'm a squeaky noise

I'm a gospel song
I'm a gong
I'm a leaf turning red
I'm a loaf of brown bread
I'm a whatever I want to be
An anything I care to be
And when I open my eyes
What I care to be
Is me

A cumulative rhyme is one that begins with simple statements and carries these and each succeeding addition on to an ending that contains all the previous lines. Cumulative rhymes, such as *The House That Jack Built*, imaginatively and amusingly portrayed by Janet Stevens, can be appreciated by the older toddler who is able to remember more complex sequences. Each new addition to the cumulative rhyme is separated from the rhyme itself so that older children may pick out the words and associate them with the objects. A book well worth owning is *Bringing the Rain to Kapiti Plain* by Verna Aardema with pictures by Beatriz Vidal. It is based on "The Nandi House That Jack Built" in Alfred Hollis's book *The Nandi: Their Language and Folklore*. The story-poem begins with a description of the land and the problems that ensued when the rains were late in coming. The cumulative verse starts with the "cloud all heavy with rain" that must release its moisture in order to relieve the drought-ridden African plain. It ends with a young boy's successful intervention that makes it rain.

This is another book that will entrance children from infancy through early school years because of a magical rhythm combined with the story and striking illustrations. Remember to let the meaning, rather than the rhyme or rhythm, govern your reading aloud. Some people find it helpful to ignore the end of the line and simply read the poem as if it were a story. Do what you feel more comfortable with when you read aloud. Older toddlers are capable of sitting still for some storybooks. They can anticipate, follow, and obtain great satisfaction from brief, fairly uncomplicated plots and characters with distinct traits. Children at this age are social beings; they appreciate interesting characters. At this stage children are also interested in stories about animals, and can identify with their predicaments and feelings. *The Box with Red Wheels* by Maud and Miska Petersham, first published in 1949, is a classic. The story tells of the farm animals' reaction to a mysterious "box with red wheels" that has appeared on the farm. A baby appears from inside the box, and calls to her mother. When the mother worriedly shoos the animals away, both the baby and the animals are forlorn. Seeing this, the mother opens the gate and permits the friendly and gentle animals to play with her baby, and all of the characters are content.

This book is satisfying on many levels. It has simplicity, a clear story line, enough predictability to make it comfortable, and enough surprise to sustain interest. The text gives young listeners ample opportunity to participate in making the animal sounds and in predicting what will happen next. The characters are sweet without being artificial.

Reading Aloud to Three-Year-Olds

By the time a child is three years old the language used in books can be as important and enticing as the pictures. They will express their opinions, ideas, and questions in an almost steady stream of response to your reading aloud or storytelling. "Why?" and "How?" questions proliferate. Children also want to know what is true and what is make-believe. They work hard to sort out for themselves the answers and keys to these questions and concepts. This is a good age for some folktales. The language, exaggeration, cultural differences, and simple plots correspond with the developmental level of these children.

The Three Billy Goats Gruff is a Norwegian folktale that appears in many versions. Most importantly, in telling or reading this story aloud, the adult reader must clearly differentiate among the three goats, or the story loses its power. Using different descriptive verbs for the sound of the goats walking across the bridge, and changing the loudness and tone of your voice to dramatize the size and character of each of the brothers Gruff is a requisite. (See chapter 1 for more information about books containing versions of this story.)

All of the *Frances* books by Russell and Lillian Hoban are storybooks the three-year-old can enjoy. The little badger and her adventures reflect many of the situations and feelings of children at this age. Children love them. Especially at this age books about siblings strike a chord in the child. There are a myriad of books appropriate at this time; it is important to select books that will particularly appeal to your youngster.

At three, children's tastes are developing, and they are growing in independence and competence, experimenting with how relationships work, developing friendships outside the home, often struggling to find their place in the family constellation, and increasing their ability to deal with frightening situations. They are also beginning to expand their sense of humor to include exaggeration, word play, and the ridiculous.

Try Sendak's *In the Night Kitchen* or Wanda Gag's *Millions of Cats* to respond to the child's need for a humorous management of potentially frightening situations. William Steig's *The Amazing Bone* and *Sylvester and the Magic Pebble* can be introduced at this time with great success. To respond to the child's identification with animals and their longing for friends, *Corduroy*, by Don Freeman, is a comforting favorite. Remember that children do not seem to outgrow these books. They will come back to them even when they are years older.

Short chapter books may be introduced at this time, and read one chapter at a time. At this point, and certainly by age four, children are capable of identifying with characters and their escapades and can remember where the adult left off. Be sure to involve your child in predicting what will happen next, and in summarizing what has already happened in previous episodes. You need not make this a quiz session, simply make it a comfortable review and guessing game.

Reading Aloud to Four-Year-Olds

Four-year-olds enjoy pretending and are getting better at distinguishing between fantasy and reality. *Stuart Little* by E. B. White can be a wonderful book to read, episode by episode, at this time. The mixture of fantasy and reality coupled with Stuart's daring and cleverness as well as his coping with his special characteristics and family situation speak directly to a child from this stage on.

Since some children at the age of four begin to think and ask about such cosmic issues as death, there are a number of helpful books, such as *The Dead Bird* by Margaret Wise Brown, that provide examples of healthy patterns for confronting and coping with death. Sometimes adults find it difficult to acknowledge that young children need to mourn. Books on this topic are discussed in chapter 7. They deal with the questions children at this age may ask. If you find yourself crying while you're reading these books aloud, this is a good opportunity to acknowledge to your child that you are moved by the story and that it's OK to cry. Don't shy away from reading aloud a book that contains serious emotional issues.

It is logical that with their awakening interest in the larger workings of the universe, children at this stage also are interested in how mechanical things work. Books about trucks and tunnels and people working are very popular now. Donald Crews does an outstanding job of depicting these topics for young children. When adults are reading these books aloud they can expect their children to ask more questions than the sparse text offers. The read-alouds here become conversations accompanied by looking at the pictures. Reading aloud a book such as *Going to the Doctor* by Fred Rogers not only informs the child about the work of a doctor, but also prepares the child for visits to a doctor's office and can help to calm whatever fears the child may have about such visits. The book respects children, presenting vocabulary often reserved for adults. When you read aloud, use the words "examination table," "otoscope," and "tongue depressor" when they appear and clarify the concepts when the book's explanation is not sufficient. The author, incidentally, shows respect for children's need to see fathers in nurturing roles, and female and black physicians.

Reading Aloud to Five-Year-Olds

The world of the five-year-old is flavored with expanding relation-ships, particularly with peers. After all, this is the year that most children enter kindergarten, necessitating the building of new social skills. A number of books reflect children's interest in the challenges of learning to be a good friend. You can look at "The Beginning Book Bag" and "The Bookshelf" for read-aloud books to use as bases for discussing how friends behave with friends.

Five-year-olds are struggling with their desire for indepen-dence and the recognition that they are, indeed, dependent. Books such as *The Story About Ping* by Marjorie Flack and Beatrix Potter's classic *The Tale of Peter Rabbit* are good for parents to read aloud. By doing so, they assure their children that even when children are disobedient they can count on the love and concern of their parents.

All of the classics are appropriate for reading aloud. Try *Miss Rumphius* by Barbara Cooney for a stretching of the child's sense of self in relation to the world as well as an aesthetic treat for everyone. Miss Rumphius is a character who is vulnerable yet strong, independent, and productive. The reader first meets her when she is a young girl, and accompanies her as she grows into an old woman. This story of "the lupine lady" is based on fact, and the author-illustrator's drawings help us to see the magic Miss Rumphius has accomplished in the real state of Maine. You should take your time when reading this book aloud. Dwell on each picture and invite your young listener to observe the details and the colors on each page. Very often, fairy tales and folktales will contain particularly high-quality illustrations.

Folktales that have somewhat more intricate plots and charac-ters can be introduced at this time. Many different editions exist with different sorts of illustrations. We recommend you try sev-eral folktales for variety so that children may develop their aes-thetic awareness at the same time that they are enjoying the story. You can start with an old favorite like *Stone Soup*, retold and illustrated by Marcia Brown. Continue with any of the beautiful renditions of *Rumpelstiltskin*. The Paul Zelinsky version pub-lished by E. P. Dutton won a Caldecott Honor award in 1986. Paul Galdone's *Rumpelstiltskin*, published in 1985, provides another set of images for this time-tested story. You and your child may want to hunt in the library for all the *Rumpelstiltskins* you can find. Read them, compare their text and illustrations and, perhaps, talk about the foolishness and greed of the miller and the king. We recommend you try to find folktales from many countries and cultures to read aloud to your children. Not only are the stories entertaining, but also the different versions provide an opportunity for children to understand how universal these stories are, and how valuable the differences are.

If you enjoy putting rhythm, various voices, and special effects into your reading aloud, be sure to get a copy of Ashley Bryan's *The Cat's Purr*. The author-illustrator is a talented storyteller and folk singer who often travels around the country entertaining children with his read-alouds, songs, and stories. This old folktale from the West Indies is designed to be read aloud. In it, Cat and Rat are friends until Rat betrays Cat by playing Cat's magic drum without his permission. And that is why from that day to this, cats and rats are enemies. Cat swallows the drum by mistake, and ever since then has carried his drum safely inside.

If you would like your children to hear professional storytellers and actors, there are many cassette recordings of stories. Some are sold in packets with the books, inviting children to "read" along with the narrator. The best of them feature actors who do not talk down to children. *Parents' Choice* regularly reviews the latest cassettes or check with your local children's library.

Some storytellers publish their own cassettes, and they are worth looking for. Susan Klein, a popular storyteller who frequently travels to Alaska to tell stories to Eskimo children, has produced a tape, "The Spirit of the River," talking about her experiences in Alaska. Sarah Pirtle, a peace activist as well as storyteller and singer, has made "Two Hands Hold the Earth," a cassette of songs about peace. Laura Simms, an internationally renowned teller of tales, has produced a number of tapes, as has Diane Wolkstein.

You might go to your local children's bookstore to see what they have available if your local library doesn't have what you're looking for. Some particularly fine cassettes are Meryl Streep's narration of *The Velveteen Rabbit* (Random House); Alice Playten's rendition of *The Story About Ping* (Scholastic); Arnold Lobel's reading of *Frog and Toad All Year* (Listening Library); a charming dramatization of *Bedtime for Frances* featuring Arnold Lobel, Alice Playten, and Gloria Virgile (Scholastic); *Aesop's Fables* read dramatically by Boris Karloff (Caedmon); and *A Kiss for Little Bear,* narrated by Ted Hoskins (Weston Woods). New ones are continuously being made.

In "The Bookshelf" at the end of the book we have listed hundreds of books, most of which are suitable for reading aloud to children from infancy on. The estimated ages of interest are flexible. You may find some two-year-olds will love books aimed at five-year-olds; most good books last from infancy into adulthood.

3

The Reading Infant

Current research is changing our understanding of the nature of infancy. Newborns are not, as had long been thought, blank or passive when they enter the world. Nor are they mere reactors to their own inner needs and states. Babies begin absorbing and responding to outside stimulation from the moment they are born. They respond much earlier and more clearly than we previously thought to touch and texture, odor, light, pattern, rhythm, and sound. As they grow older they "read" the messages coming to them through each of their senses with increasing accuracy. They actively seek out experiences they enjoy, responding in different ways to the same information, which suggests that individuals are born with different thresholds for specific kinds of stimulation.

Babies also start communicating from the moment they are born, with facial expressions, body movements, cries, and other sounds. They express themselves to their parents and caretakers in characteristic behavior patterns or styles that vary widely from child to child. Some children's movements and sounds are small and subtle, some are much larger and stronger, suggesting that they bring different temperaments into the world with them. Parents have to learn to understand the messages their children are sending.

Besides taking in information about the people and things around them, babies communicate their reactions. Parents read these reactions, these messages. They notice facial expressions and body movements and learn to distinguish different cries, coos, squeals, and words. Parents' temperaments, past experiences, knowledge, present hopes, expectations, and feelings all influence the ways in which they react to their children.

The more you know about your baby's temperament and way of communicating, the better. It can also be very helpful to have as full an understanding as possible of what children are actually capable of perceiving through each of their senses at different ages and stages. The more you understand about infant development, the more appropriately you can respond and the better you can provide an environment that will fascinate but not overwhelm, and bring pleasure rather than discomfort.

One to Four Months: The Sense of Touch

Many infants' first reflexive reactions are to sensations they receive through their skin. When stroked on the sole of the foot or the palm of the hand, newborns grasp the finger stroking them. Touching the cheeks of newborns will cause them to turn or "root" toward the stroking object. But most important to infants is the manner in which they are handled. One well-known author of books about child development states that touch is almost a language for infants. Skin contact and warmth, especially from the mother's body, are probably the most potent stimulation for infants in the first few months of life. Like a radar screen picking up vibrations, your baby absorbs your feelings about him from your handling.

In many cultures babies are held most of the time, often by a number of relatives and caretakers. They do not feel that they are spoiling the baby, only that they are providing the contact that all babies need. Whether or not babies are held most of the time, it is evident that most babies will stop crying when they are picked up, held, cuddled, rocked, talked to, and walked.

The ideal time to introduce your baby to some of the earliest forms of literature—lullabies, songs, and nursery rhymes—is while you are sitting very near to or holding your infant. Long before the words make any sense, children will enjoy the vibrations of the sounds and rhythmic movement that automatically flow through your body as you sing or chant. Some doctors have found that very young children prefer to be held near the parent's or caretaker's heart. Some babies require more intense hugging and rocking for stimulation, while others are contented with gentle movements. Find the songs that particularly fit you and your baby.

Some parents derive pleasure from recalling songs that were sung to them as infants, and passing these family heirlooms on to the next generation. If these came to you in a foreign language do not hesitate to sing them in the original form. They will hold your interest and provide your baby with an experience that is enriching. A list of songbooks can be found in "The Bookshelf," and some of the most enduring are discussed in chapter 1. If you have no repertoire of remembered melodies or are someone who feels uncomfortable singing, seek out some of the many records or tape recordings of lullabies and nursery rhymes for children. You may even find yourself singing along.

During the first eight weeks of life, your baby's hands are not yet coordinated enough for touching and feeling things. Their fists are clenched, and although they may curl them tightly around your finger or an object you give them, they cannot open and close their fingers to investigate shape, temperature, or texture. A tactile experience that infants enjoy is mouthing and sucking. In fact, infants' mouths are important early channels of perception.

The mouth is, of course, used for eating, an intense experience for the infant, a crucial, life-supporting one. Note how children react when you respond to their howls of hunger with breast or bottle. Watch for signs of satisfaction, such as sighs or shivers. You should observe early indications of your child's eating style because, occasionally, these early tendencies signal later learning styles. Drs. Spock and Rothenberg, coauthors of the 1985 edition of Dr. Spock's *Baby and Child Care,* have identified various patterns. Your child might be an "eager-beaver" who sucks vigorously until satisfied. Or your child may be a "procrastinator," one who sips, pauses, and sips again and who resists any prodding. Some babies are "resters." They drink steadily for a few minutes, then wait for a few minutes as though pausing politely between courses. Whatever the baby's style, this is an ideal time to begin developing the roles of careful, respectful observer and resourceful and responsive helper. It is reasonable to expect babies to learn about respect for individuality and independence as they are permitted to proceed in their own style. If their caretaker is available and can be counted on for responsive support or for help when it is called for, babies will also learn about satisfaction and about limits.

How you react to your children's style will not only influence how they feel about themselves but will also be the foundation of your ongoing relationship. You may avoid a detrimental power struggle if you understand that a baby's style is not evidence of goodness or badness, malice toward you or kindness, exemplary or deficient behavior. You will be preparing yourself to respond to your baby's behavior in a rational, understanding, accepting, and loving manner.

In the literally hundreds of hours a caretaker and baby spend together at feedings each can learn a great deal about the other's style, preferences, and limits. It is important to accept the fact that styles can sometimes be amended, but they must first be noted and respected. In later years you may be struck by the similarity between your child's learning and reading style and his or her early eating style. Whether or not this is the case, if you have learned to recognize and accommodate yourself to one style, the process of encouraging and facilitating the child's future learning modes will be much more effective and comfortable.

In the early months infants use their mouths to explore objects. When, at about eight to ten weeks, babies unclench their hands, you can place safe, interesting objects into their palms. At first they hardly realize the object is there, which is why many rattles have noisemakers inside. The sound is needed to attract the baby's attention. Once babies recognize that objects are there, they are very likely to bring them to their mouths to explore. They will gum, suck, taste, rub, squeeze, and feel the texture and temperature of things that you put into their hands.

One to Four Months:
The Sense of Hearing

It is almost certain that newborns have the ability to hear while they are still in the womb. From the moment they are born they react with displeasure, by starting or crying, when encountering a sudden loud noise. Sounds in the womb were muted by the amniotic fluid. Some obstetricians have been making an effort to keep the delivery room free from all loud noises, even the sounds of an encouraging birth coach. Newborns have been reported to react with "soothed pleasure" when they are provided with a recording of human heartbeats soon after they are born. They also respond favorably to rhythmic sounds from almost any source. Rhythmic music seems to please them, and some mothers report that babies seem undisturbed by the steady sounds of appliances such as a vacuum cleaner. Other caretakers report that their baby's reaction to mechanical sounds varies with the baby's mood at the time the sound is begun. Many mothers report that their infants are lulled to sleep when riding in the car. This, however, is probably due to the vibration as well as the steady purr of the engine.

Studies tell us that even very young infants react to the different lengths of sound and different pitches, as well as the volume of sounds they hear. Reports differ on whether babies can identify the direction from which the sound is coming. Stand in different parts of a room and make a sound. Notice whether or not your baby turns in the direction of the noise. The sound that babies seem to prefer, in response to which they quiet down and become most alert and attentive, is the sound of a human voice. Be sure to talk frequently and warmly to babies and watch for their reactions. If they have been noisy, do they quiet down and seem to be listening? If they have been quiet, do they seem to become more alert?

By two months of age many babies can recognize the voice of their primary caretaker even in a room full of other voices and noises. By three months your baby may talk back, gurgle, coo, or squeal when you talk to him. Very young children are also apt to turn away from an unfamiliar person who is talking to them. Their ability to differentiate among fairly subtle auditory clues is already apparent. This ability to make auditory discriminations stands children in good stead later on when they are asked to distinguish among the sounds of letters where the differences are very small.

From the moment of their birth, talk to babies, let them know of your presence from the sound of your voice. Whisper how wonderful they are or simply describe in a natural tone of voice whatever you are doing or seeing. Your baby is sure to attend to and feel reassured by the sound of your voice. At around eight weeks of age, babies will begin to "answer" you. They will begin to make sounds in response to being talked to. Babies of this age will, it is true, vocalize to themselves, but they have been found to vocalize more in another person's presence, suggesting that there is already some rudimentary sense of their trying to communicate with others. By the age of four or five months your children will watch your face carefully while you are talking and will love the social stimulation that comes from your talking to them. It seems to be the social interaction that is important to babies; they respond with delight when spoken to. Researchers have tried rewarding children with the sweet tinkle of a little bell, but it has been received with far less satisfaction than the sound of the human voice.

Once again, lullabies, nursery rhymes, poems, and songs of all sorts are appropriate. "Ding dong dell, pussy's in the well," "Old Mother Hubbard went to the cupboard," "Ride a cock horse to Banbury Cross," "Little Miss Muffet sat on a tuffet," "Jack and Jill went up the hill," and other Mother Goose rhymes will please your baby. Their quick rhythms and rhymes make them lively and fun. Lullabies, poems, and rhymes with slower, longer lines and the softer sibilants and vowel sounds suit them when they need calming down. You may find that your own reactions to different rhythms and texts influence the way you hold, rock, and interact with your baby because your mood is also affected.

Besides talking to your children, it is of equal importance that you take the time to pause and listen to the sounds they are producing. This is not only because your delight will encourage them to produce "real words," but also because your listening to everything they say lets them know that you value their communications, that you want to hear what they have to say. It is never too early to give your child this message.

One to Four Months:
The Sense of Vision

At birth, babies have fairly good vision for things within eight to ten inches from them. At two weeks they seem to be able to discriminate among some colors. Given a choice, by one month of age, if you place objects before their eyes at the appropriate distance, they not only pay attention, but also they appear to have preferences for complex patterns or shapes over simple ones.

Through research we have learned that babies do prefer the human face to all other visual stimuli. In the first week of life, infants look toward the eyes of the people holding them. And research now confirms that four-day-old babies can already distinguish the face of their mother from the face of a stranger. By six weeks infants have been described as "reaching out" with their eyes. In short, they are already seeking, "reading," and responding to visual and social clues. Their focus gets better as does their ability to track moving objects. Their range of vision grows from a few inches to a whole room.

Babies need lots of practice focusing accurately and they enjoy mobiles immensely. At three months or even a few weeks earlier, babies become fascinated with small irregularly shaped multicolored objects that move. Strings from which you hang tinfoil, colored paper, or fluttering ribbons can be strung overhead. Changed often, such decorations interest babies and help them sharpen their focusing and discrimination skills. Babies may also learn to anticipate what they will see when they open their eyes or turn their heads in particular ways. They enjoy watching the shape, color, and movement of objects strung within their sight.

At two and a half months babies begin unclenching their hands and by three months do a great deal of what one educator calls "palm reading," studying their moving hands with great concentration. By the third month children explore their mouths and faces with their hands, gathering early rudimentary information about themselves.

Fairly large, unbreakable mirrors can be introduced at this age to stimulate the visual experience of self. Although there is some dispute about babies' ability to make sense of pictures at this age, try showing your baby some pictures of other babies, either photographs of themselves, siblings, or babies pictured in magazines. Their reactions may tell you that they recognize what the picture is.

Babies will begin to reach and feel things with their hands. Now mobiles can be kept within reach, only if it has been ascertained that every object is firmly attached, unbreakable, nontoxic, and not sharp. Items hung from a ribbon can be stretched across the crib, clearly out of baby's reach. Everything from Ping-Pong balls in mesh bags, to rattles and pieces of textured material and cloth can be used. Try objects of differing shape, texture, length, width, color, and brightness and observe your baby's reactions. Hand-eye coordination develops slowly, and it is one of the essential ingredients in the reading and writing processes. The early practice the child gets in focusing, reaching, touching, and exploring of objects provides enjoyable stimulation and practice.

You are your baby's first book. Just as babies seek out your voice, so will they seek out the sight of your face and will try to read your expressions and your moods. Your touch, the way you hold them, your expressions, your words and songs, the way you vocalize, will all be read by your baby in the very first months of life.

Over time, children need to be able to note changes, subtle or otherwise, in their caretaker's body language, tone of voice, and facial expression, just as you need to be able to note theirs. As long as you are consistent in providing for their basic needs and help your baby develop a fundamental sense of trust and safety, the baby will slowly be able to gain a basis for mutual accommodation with other people. Furthermore, observation and understanding of people are important skills for the good reader and writer, skills that will be useful in understanding or creating clues of character development.

Four Months to One Year: The Sense of Hearing

Being talked to seems to make babies more eager to produce sounds. Although they watch you carefully and listen attentively when you are speaking, they are now at least as interested in making and hearing their own sounds. At first these sounds are the result of the babies' experiments with a combination of gurgles and saliva. Babies love to play with what sound and moisture can do. If you can restrain your urge to blot their faces and wait a little bit, you can observe what the child is learning. Some experts think that this playing with saliva is the baby's way of performing some sort of scientific experiment: "What will happen if I dribble and gurgle at the same time?" "Where is all this wetness coming from and where is it going?" "How fast can I make it go?" "What will mother do about this now?" Even if these thoughts are not being verbalized, the actions, repeated over and over again, help children understand and gain control of their own functions.

It is easier for most parents to react positively to the gurgling sounds than the moisture accompanying them. Focusing on the sounds is the more important part. Earlier, babies perfected the art of communicative crying. Now they are beginning to babble. Their sounds have progressed from the cries of hunger, discomfort, boredom, fear, exhaustion, and pain to an increasingly wider repertoire of babbles. It remains important for adults to listen and respond. Give your baby lots of feedback, first responding positively to all efforts to produce sounds and then showing particular pleasure in sounds that approximate words. Even when you are merely repeating your child's first meaningless babble, you may find yourself engaged in your first conversation!

Babies soon show evidence of their growing awareness of the social power of language. Not only will they put forth a stream of different pitched babbling sounds while with their caretaker, they will also become effective in "interrupting" your conversations with other children or adults by means of their vocalizations. Although these interruptions may occasionally be annoying, it is important to understand that the baby has made a profound discovery—language is not only self-entertainment, it is one of our most powerful tools.

Somewhere around the age of five months when this social function of language is beginning to be understood, babies also will be observed carefully watching other people's mouths and trying to imitate their sounds and inflections. While it is still good practice to keep echoing your child's vocalizations, especially those that seem approximations of real words, now is the time when babies will have matured to the point that they will be hungry for the words that name the things in their immediate environments. Label everything you use: blanket, crib, diaper, wastebasket, teddy bear, and so forth. Repeat the nouns a number of times. Remember that your child will not be ready to articulate these words, but is building a receptive vocabulary very quickly.

It is important not to prod your child into parroting the words you say or to act disappointed when your words are not repeated. A child's speaking vocabulary develops very slowly in the first year, if, indeed, any spoken words are produced at all. Babbling is normal and when a "real" word pops out of your child's mouth in the course of babbling, it is almost certainly an accident. For example, at six months your child may be saying vowels with a few consonants thrown in. At seven months a few syllables may emerge. This is the time when his utterances may coincidentally have meaning or resemble words with meaning. If at lunchtime your child happens to say "mik," react with excitement, pleasure, and repetition, but do not try to pull the word from your child. It is unlikely to be reproduced.

At eight months some recognizable intonations may appear in your child's babbles along with two-syllable sounds. Once again this is evidence of careful listening and beginning efforts to approximate adult speech. A child's first meaningful word is often "ma-ma" or "da-da." Show your enthusiasm and repeat the word, but do not insist that your baby say it again. At ten months few children have more than four words and many have none. When babies reach a year, they rarely can say more than eight words, though these are repeated frequently and in different tones of voice. Remember, above all, that in the last months of the first year they are building a vocabulary of understood words called a receptive vocabulary. Long before they can talk, their interest in the names of things will be acute. Speak clearly while looking at your baby. Watch their intent looks. They are using their ears and mind with great concentration.

Four Months to One Year: The Sense of Vision

By four months of age babies can focus on people and objects at many different distances. Between four to six months babies have coordinated their hands and eyes quite well and have developed accurate grasping ability. They still learn almost exclusively through direct exploration and want to use their hands and mouth constantly to touch, taste, and gum everything they see. At around six months babies are beginning to sit with better balance and require less help, which also frees them to look around and to manipulate objects.

At five or six months your child will probably show an interest in pictures and begin to connect the picture of an object with the object itself. When you combine these interests and burgeoning abilities with the child's new hunger for words that label familiar things in his environment, this all adds up to being an ideal time to introduce books and add a reading time to your daily routine.

Introducing Books

Although you have been singing, talking, and reading to your baby before this point, the age of four to six months is when many babies can grasp an object fairly easily, and this is an ideal time to give them books. Since at this age babies can sit propped up in your lap or against carefully arranged pillows, they will now enjoy grasping books, gumming them, feeling them, and trying to turn the pages. Many books are designed for the sensory-motor development of the child younger than fifteen or eighteen months who has not yet achieved reflective powers, the ability to manipulate concepts, or to generalize, but who has begun to gather data and who understands that language labels it.

These books usually augment the fundamental sensory experiences that young children require to learn and will require for many years to come. They give pictorial representations and labels for objects that have been touched, seen, heard, smelled, and tasted. They provide pictures and labels for actions with which the child is familiar. Cloth books with some stiffening liner, plastic books, or board books made of laminated cardboard can be handled by very young children with no fear of damage. Many books provide special opportunities for tactile exploration.

Cloth Books

Cloth books are chewable and free of staples, sharp edges, tearable pages, or inedible dyes. They are generally six or seven inches square. Frequently their edges are cut with pinking shears. John E. Johnson's *The Me Book* has four pages in which a boy describes himself. He has two feet, ten toes, two eyes, two ears, two arms, and he is so-o-o big. The child describes things that he can do by himself: eat, wash, play, jump, swing, jump, and hide.

Another cloth book is Amye Rosenberg's *1, 2, Buckle My Shoe*. This somewhat smaller cloth book is cut in the shape of a shoe and contains a new version of the old rhyme. On each page rhyming directions are given for manipulating the closure device sewn onto that page. For example, "3,4, Button Panda's button and go on to do more," is accompanied by a button and button hole. Except for one page which uses a very narrow ribbon, all of the other closures, a shoelace, zipper, and button, are large enough for a toddler to manage. Younger children can enjoy playing with the book, turning its pages, and hearing the rhymes.

More recently, publishers have reduced the size and floppiness of the pages of their cloth books. These are particularly useful because they are somewhat easier for the very young child to hold. The twelve pages of Marsha Cohen's *Baby's Favorite Things* have a layer of padding and are easier to hold and turn. Each page has a picture of a single object with which many babies are familiar: a duck, blocks, a bottle, a puppy, a ball, a rattle, a teddy bear, balloons, and a toy truck. The colors and pictures are clear, outlined in black, and with little shading or detail. The children shown with one or two of these objects are of different races, reflecting the growing conviction that early introduction to multi-racial consciousness is important.

Norman Gorbaty has illustrated *Baby Animals Say Hello,* a book identical in physical format to the one above, but that shows animals on each page and describes the sound each makes. The pictures in this book are more complex, but are still simple and clear.

Kitten's Animal Friends by Carolyn Bracken comes in the form of a gray cloth kitten who is ten inches tall. It is lightly stuffed and soft, though not stuffed enough to be really cuddly. Sewn to the kitten so it looks like it is held in the kitten's hands, is a very small cloth book that shows the kitten playing with other little animals. Also appealing is the five-inch book *Little Rabbit Takes a Walk* primarily because it comes with a five-inch stuffed rabbit perfectly sized for a baby's hand.

Books Designed to Be Touched and Manipulated

During the first year babies experience many different tactile sensations and learn to differentiate the feeling, and perhaps the meaning, of each. In the second half of the first year they begin to reach out, grasp, and seek objects of interest. Books that talk about and give labels for sensations of touch are useful here. Books that can be touched and played with, which allow the child to feel different textures, will become favorites.

The Touch Me Book by Pat and Eve Witte, illustrated by Harlow Rockwell, allows babies to feel a soft dog, a hard table, a dress of bumpy fabric worn by a doll, a soft squishy sponge, scratchy sand, smooth plastic, stretchy rubber, and sticky tape. Each page has a two- or three-inch section of the material that is set into or onto the page in a manner that minimizes the possibility of damage by small, uncoordinated hands.

There are also a number of books constructed entirely of plastic. Each page is constructed of two pieces of plastic between which springy lining has been placed. These books can be pulled fairly hard by uncoordinated hands and can even be taken into the bathtub. One particularly appropriate example is *Spot Goes Splash*. In this book Eric Hill's beloved yellow puppy, Spot, splashes under the faucet in the garden, at the beach, in puddles when it rains, and in the bath every night. While some people will feel that books should always be treated with respect, these books allow babies to treat them as toys that can be floated, gummed, or sunk.

It is not until later that children enjoy the tactile experience of books that can be manipulated with finer motor coordination. At around a year of age they can thoroughly enjoy *Pat the Bunny* as well as the many superb pop-up books that have small tabs to pull. These books are especially effective and can hold up for quite a while if you are there to help your child handle them with some care. Teach your child to pull the tabs as gently as possible. Explain that animals, even those in books, like to be patted softly, and that they do not like chocolate or sticky lollipops in their fur.

There are also many books with flaps to open or turn over. One book with stiffened pages, *My First Book*, by Colin and Jacqui Hawkins, appeals to children and adults alike. On the first page, labeled "my first day home," there is a picture of a large crib filling the page. When the cover of the crib is flipped open, a tiny sleeping infant is revealed. On the second page, when the blanket that covers the baby from the nose down is turned back, "my first smile" is revealed. Each page has a flap that your child can turn over to show a first: the day he first sat, when he cut his first tooth, and so on. On the back of each flap is a place for the adult or older child to write the date on which the infant achieved each first. You can use this book for many years if you reinforce the flaps with clear tape or contact paper. Children enjoy being allowed to turn the pages of stiff books by themselves.

Another very popular book with stiffened pages and flaps is the peek-a-boo story *Where's Spot?* Children love to look for the little puppy, under the bed, and all over the house, until Spot is finally found in a basket. Other peek-a-boo stories are listed in "The Bookshelf." The creator of *Curious George*, H. A. Rey, has contributed a clever book for very young children. *Where's My Baby?* contains folded-over pages that hide infants beneath their folds. Babies can learn the names of animals as they engage in the game of unfolding each page.

The Importance of Labeling

Most early books label things with which your baby is probably familiar. This is developmentally appropriate. Babies have a rudimentary sense that language is a desirable form of communication. They have the urge to represent things they see and do with words. Often a single word stands for a whole thought. For example, "milk" or "mik" may mean "I want to have some more milk." As they build their repertoire of behavior, they also build their vocabulary, their repertoire of words. The first books babies are likely to become directly involved with which are not primarily toys, as the cloth and "feelie" books, are those that provide them with pictures of objects they can recognize. At first they will enjoy having you name the things in the pictures. They will ask for these books by bringing them to you over and over. Soon they will be able to say the words themselves and will revel in their achievement. They will be "reading."

Books made of laminated cardboard are easy for young children to hold. They have pictures of much higher quality than can be reproduced on cloth. Some of them are beautiful and carefully designed to appeal to very young children and to meet their needs. Children respond to them with great enthusiasm.

Labeling Objects

Two outstanding board books for very young children are Platt and Munk's *Baby's Things* and *Baby's First Toys*. Each book has just one photographed object per 7-by-8 inch page. The objects are pleasing to the eye, simple, large, colorful, beautifully shaped, and placed on a carefully chosen contrasting background. Because these books are of such high aesthetic quality, they convey respect for children while building their appreciation of beauty. Children smile with recognition when they see these objects, and after a few exposures, enjoy "reading" these books on their own.

A simple book that labels objects and uses photographs is Sabrina Withall's now famous *The Baby's Book of Babies*, which presents children with black-and-white photo close-ups of different babies in a variety of positions and moods. The author discovered that babies get great pleasure from looking at photos of babies when her baby's first real, warm smile was directed to the baby of the diaper box rather than at her. The book has a space for your baby's picture at its beginning and end. If you enjoy using a camera, take pictures of your child from time to time, in different moods, at different activities, with different people, and in different locations. Mount three or four pictures on colored paper and sew them together with a strong needle and heavy thread to make a book for your child.

Two introductory books of interest are *The First Picture Book* and *The Fifth Picture Book*, from the large Ladybird educational series published in England. The authors of the books, Ethel and Harry Wingfield, introduce parents and caretakers to the idea that children enjoy recognizing and naming familiar objects. This leads to a foundation for a love of books and reading. On each page of their *First Picture Book* is a painting of an object, which fills most of the page: a red sandal, a teddy bear with a blue bow, a ball with a multicolor design. At the bottom of the page are a few questions that the parent, caretaker, or teacher might pose to encourage comment or conversation. The stimulation of communication, of sharing language, is one of the important functions of books that name or label.

Very young children enjoy recognizing the objects that you name for them. Somewhat more mature children will be able to name the objects themselves. The adult can use the questions in small type to stimulate children's comments about the items in the picture. The most important feature of this series is that it is designed to help caretakers aid in the learning process. Although the series is not laminated, shiny, or exciting, it is useful, tried, and true.

Gyo Fujikawa's *Let's Eat* is also a book that labels objects. This time the objects are all foods. The author gets children immediately involved by asking them which of "the delicious things to eat" they like best. Children in the story are shown enjoying common favorites such as hot dogs, chicken legs, ice cream, candy, spaghetti, apples, and pancakes. They are also asked whether they like rice and tortillas and whether they know how to eat with chopsticks. This provides the adult reader with an opportunity to talk about different cultures and their special foods. The book also has an array of children of different races. Caretakers should read through this book, and all books, before reading them to children. Decide how the food choices in this labeling book fit with your own convictions about nutrition. See if you feel that all the foods presented in the story are ones you would consider "delicious," as the author does.

Disagreement with the author by no means necessitates discarding the book. It does mean that you may want to consider omitting the word "delicious" from the opening lines. It is acceptable to edit a text in this way or to openly disagree with an author. Teaching children that you do not agree, and that they do not have to agree, with everything in print is an important lesson. You may want to acknowledge that while your child may love the flavor of some items, they are not as nutritious as other foods. Even a very simple early book such as this one may give you opportunities for a discussion or statement of values, which might be more difficult in a less neutral situation. It is easier to talk about the nutritional drawbacks of a lollipop while it's on the printed page than when your child sees a real one and wants it.

Labeling Animals

Although very young children seem to get most immediately involved with books depicting children, they also identify readily with animal characters. Phoebe Dunn presents children with clear color photographs in her book *Farm Animals*. On each double-page spread she presents and names one, or sometimes two, common farm animals. The size of the book is unusual; each page is tiny, 3½-by-3½ inches.

Some children find drawings of furry animals particularly appealing. For them, the book *Pudgy Pals*, illustrated by Kathy Wilburn, may be ideal. In this small board book ten little animals are pictured and named. Each has a descriptive adjective, often beginning with the same letter as the animal's name. There are a few background details pictured, a grassy ground, a few flowers or butterflies, but nothing to distract the child from the animal on the page. All the background colors are pastels.

There is also Gyo Fujikawa's 8-by-8-inch board book entitled *Babies of the Wild*, which opens with Mrs. Elephant and baby and continues with two-page spreads of very benign-looking wild animal mothers with their babies. Although some adults may find the text and illustrations somewhat artificial, little children identify readily with the mothers and their babies. If this or any other books are not to your liking, skip them. With all the wonderful books available, choose the ones you respond to positively. The message of love for books is more important than the content of any one story.

Michelle Cartlidge has used a teddy bear as the character in her board book, *Teddy's House*. In each picture the teddy bear is interacting with a familiar object: he walks through a blue door, he talks on a red telephone, crawls under a pink table, looks out a light-blue window, and so on. Since teddy is always the same color, it is clear that the object to be labeled is the colored one. Children seem to have no trouble accepting that a teddy bear can walk, talk, and live in a colorful, humanlike house because they identify so readily with the little teddy bear.

Feodor Rojankovsky's Great Big Animal Book has been enjoyed by children for over thirty-five years. It is a large book with bright, full-page illustrations providing the child with appealing and unthreatening close-up views of animal families. One family appears per page, allowing the child to gain much information without being overwhelmed. The particular characterization of each animal is clearly pictured: the cow's large limpid eyes; the sow's round rosey snout; the turkey's full, feathered form, complete with waddle, and so on. The compact text of about five words per page is also clear. The color, texture, design, and warmth of the illustrations invite young readers to return to them over and over.

An innovative book labeling the animals is Eric Carle's *Catch the Ball!* The seal, at the beginning of the book, has a long string attached to its nose. So does the kangaroo at the end of this board book. The string passes through the center of a small red ball that hangs from the string and slides on it. Each page, except those with the seal and kangaroo, has a hole cut in it through which a child can pass the ball. The ball can be passed from the seal to the elephant, and then on to the deer, the bear, the stork, the snake, the lion, the crocodile, and the giraffe. It is finally "caught" by the kangaroo who has a slot in its pouch into which the ball can fit. Eric Carle is famous for his bright-colored animals. It is fun for children to try to remember what animal is coming next, to pass the ball through the holes and see the animals miss the ball.

Once children have learned the names of domestic, farm, and wild animals, they may become fascinated with the names and descriptions of obscure animals, living and extinct. Four-year-olds often have an obsession with dinosaurs that can be satisfied with books such as Dot and Sy Barlowe's *Dinosaurs,* a pop-up and manipulative book in which the longest dinosaur, the diplodocus, spreads beyond the edges of the book, and the huge brachiosaurus, first seen as just a small head above the water, can be made to emerge to reveal his impressive full form. Many strange and little-known animals appear in Alice and Martin Provensen's *A Peaceable Kingdom: The Shaker Abecedarius.* Finding books that stretch and fascinate your children's imagination without overwhelming them is a worthy challenge.

Valerie Greeley's *Pets* is a small wordless board book. She has drawn delicate, detailed color pictures of five animals against a finely designed background. It is hard to decide which animal and its environment is most beautiful, the rabbit in a flowery corner, the spaniel beside the spring bulbs, the birds on a branch of leaves and berries, the fish in their green world, or the cats in the meadow.

Peekaboo Rabbit by Helen Piers is also a book with no words. In each of its simple, carefully designed photographs a small tan rabbit is sniffing, hiding behind, looking at, crawling under or through a familiar object. For example, he hides behind a rag doll, touches his nose to a mirror, lifts his front paws onto a wheelbarrow, and sticks his nose into a pair of overalls. For the very young child, parents can simply say the name of the main object in the picture. Or, as your child's understanding increases, you may choose to describe in very basic language what the bunny is doing with the object. At a later stage you can make your descriptions somewhat more complex, adding adjectives or even making up a simple story about the bunny. As children's ability to speak increases, they can go through the same incremental process.

The fact that this book has no printed words is probably an advantage. It compels adults and children to use the book in the manner appropriate to them. One final observation: the book is folded accordion style. This makes it more difficult for the youngest children to handle by themselves but has the added advantage that the book opens up to become a long, two-sided mural. A second book with the same format, *Peekaboo Kitten*, is equally appealing.

Labeling Places

Children want labels for places, too. One small board book that meets this need is Sally Kilroy's *Babies' Outings*. Each double-page spread shows a young child in a different outside environment. The pictures are bright, clear, and simple enough not to overwhelm the child with distracting detail. Since very few books depict those places to which we regularly take our children, such as bakeries, post offices, libraries, doctors' offices, and drugstores, take the initiative to label these places for your children when you are there.

Labeling Actions

In addition to building a basic vocabulary of the people, things, and places nearest to them, young children want words to describe actions. As soon as babies can sit in your lap they will begin to enjoy *What Do Babies Do?* The color photographs, selected by Debby Slier, show babies involved in ordinary, everyday activities. They sleep, drink, read, look in the mirror, laugh, cry, stand, clap hands, and go for a trip in the stroller. Your baby may imitate the baby in the pictures who is clapping and reading. In fact, imitation is one of the primary ways children learn, and babies from ten months or so on are no exception. Through imitation of adults, real children, or those in books, babies practice many new skills.

The companion volume to *What Do Babies Do?* is *What Do Toddlers Do?* Here Debby Slier has again selected clear illustrative photographs showing toddlers at different activities. The concentration of the climbing child and the child who is carefully balancing his blocks, the gleeful face of the swinging child and the child banging on pots, and the total involvement of the child petting the rabbit will be easy for your child to identify with. Another plus is that the book has children of different heritages engaged in nonstereotypic gender tasks.

Another book about actions, with pictures of very young children, is Phoebe Dunn's *I'm a Baby,* which acknowledges growth and increasing abilities. It begins with labeled pictures of infants eating, playing with their toes, and sucking their thumbs. Then it pictures older babies sitting up and playing, bathing, squeezing a ball, and trying to put on a sock. It ends with children who are even older, a child showing a first tooth, a child taking a first step alone, and, finally, a child blowing out the candle on a first birthday cake.

One book that is just right for children in the last half of their first year is Helen Oxenbury's *Dressing.* This is the cumulative story of a little boy getting dressed. Since this activity is central in the life of a diaper-clad youngster, children appreciate seeing it reflected in print. At each stage the little boy appears with a new piece of clothing: diaper, undershirt, sock, shoes (bright-red sandals on his pigeon-toed feet), shirt, overalls, and finally an orange-and-yellow-checkered hat. In each picture the child's pleasure and stage of dress increases.

A small board book called *Munchety Munch!* by Harriet Ziefert contains color photographs of children eating. They inform the reader that they can take a big bite, lick, sip, drink, crunch, and taste. As your children mature they will seek more specific words to enlarge their vocabularies. Use somewhat sophisticated vocabulary from time to time. If it is linked to specific, identified behaviors or objects or if you immediately provide a synonym, your child should be able to understand.

Bill Gillham's *The First Words Picture Book* is more complex than its title suggests. In this book, the left-hand page is, in each case, a clear, close-up color photograph of a labeled familiar object. The right-hand page shows children and sometimes adults interacting with that object. This format invites children to describe action.

While children's active, spoken vocabulary is growing slowly in the second year, their receptive vocabulary, built of words they understand, is growing rapidly. You can find out a great deal about children's receptive vocabulary by asking them to get specific items, or to perform certain actions. This will tell you what nouns and what verbs they understand.

It is important to note that even in the second twelve months of life most children's speaking vocabulary develops relatively slowly. It is typical for a thirteen-month-old to have a three- or four-word vocabulary of words other than "mama" and "dada." Keep in mind, though, many children have no words at all at this age. Three months later, at fifteen months, on the average, children have a speaking vocabulary of just four to six words. At eighteen months they have an average of about ten words, and at twenty-one months only about twenty words, although some children now construct two-word "sentences."

Young children can often be helped in their understanding of action words if they see animals performing the same actions as humans. In Tana Hoban's board book *Panda, Panda*, a large panda has been photographed eating, sitting, rolling, standing, drinking, walking, climbing, yawning, resting, and sleeping. The protagonist is exceptionally appealing, and is sure to hold a young child's interest.

Children also enjoy hearing simple songs and rhythmic verses, especially when they are about animals, children, or, of course, themselves. A number of authors and illustrators have interpreted some all-time favorites. Barbara Emberley adapted "One Wide River to Cross" and Ed Emberley has made it come alive visually with his woodcuts mounted on backgrounds that fade from one color to the next. If you sing this song to your youngster and point to the animals in the text, soon you may find your child pointing to the animal and trying to say its name. Another example of a song used as the text for a book is "Over in the Meadow" that has been illustrated by Ezra Jack Keats. Here a number of animals from the meadow appear in the lyrics and on the printed page. The action most typical of their species is described and parents can act out the action.

Traditional nonsense rhymes are also perennial favorites. Nicola Bayley in *As I Was Going Up—and Down—* has illustrated some particularly funny ones, for example "I eat my peas with honey, / I've done it all my life. / It makes the peas taste funny, / But it keeps them on the knife." Although the content of many of these rhymes may be too sophisticated for infants to understand, their rhythm and the pleasure they bring the adult will be communicated.

Another book in this series illustrated by Nicola Bayley is *Hush-a-Bye and Other Bedtime Rhymes*. It contains a number of lullabies, some humorous, some musical and sweet, some very well-known, others more obscure. Children enjoy being sung to at bedtime. They become familiar with the tunes and some of the lyrics, and as they get older will appreciate recognizing them in books. Other books presenting familiar songs are Peter Spier's *London Bridge Is Falling Down* (see description in chapter 2), *Old MacDonald Had a Farm* illustrated by Abner Graboff, and *Go Tell Aunt Rhody* illustrated by Aliki.

Labeling Sounds

A very simple book of animal sounds is John Burningham's *Cluck Baa*. In each sketchy drawing a very small child (he is the size of the rooster pictured in this book) is shown with an animal, shaping his mouth as one would to make the animal's sound. At the top of the page a sound is written, "cluck," "baa," and so forth. Children may enjoy hearing, and later trying to imitate, the sounds presented in this book. They may also enjoy imitating the postures of the child or the positions of the animals.

On the cover of *Beep! Beep! I'm A Jeep: A Toddler's Book of Let's Pretend*, a tiny picture shows a little boy sitting in a yellow cardboard box that has wheels drawn on it. A giant picture on the same page shows the child in a real jeep. The caption reads, "Beep! Beep! I'm a jeep." On the next page, the tiny insert at the top of the page shows the child in a cardboard train made of three cartons. Below is a picture of a long, sleek train and the caption "Choo! Choo! I'm a train." Each successive page demonstrates a make-believe vehicle and its real counterpart, as seen in the child's imagination. This book not only provides children with words for different vehicles, but also with a label for the distinctive sound of each.

Another creative book that engages children directly is Frank Asch's *I Can Roar*. This large book has laminated pages, each with a picture of an animal. In the place where the animal's head should be is a large cut-out circle where your child's face can go. At the bottom of the page the text reads, for example, "I can baa like a sheep." Children pretend to be the animal of their choice and make that animal's sound.

The famous illustrator/author Peter Spier has given us an encyclopedic book about animals and their sounds, *Gobble, Growl, Grunt*. Each page is crowded with his distinctive color pictures of a class of animals, for example, fowl, and the various sounds each animal makes. Spier is as good a listener as observer, and his book will challenge both adult and child readers to cultivate these skills. Peter Spier's other book labeling sounds, *Crash, Bang, Boom*, is also entertaining.

In contrast to the myriad of sounds in Peter Spier's books, Helen Oxenbury has managed to write a noisy book, *I Hear*, that never verbally labels the sound. The book contains pairs of pictures, one showing an object making a sound, the other showing a child reacting to the object. Opposite the picture of a watch, is a smiling child, snuggled in his grandfather's arms, with his ear pressed to his grandfather's wristwatch. Even with the absence of descriptive words, the reader can hear the ticking.

In 1939 Margaret Wise Brown wrote her first story about sounds, and it is still in print and popular today. *The Noisy Book* is the story of a small black puppy who gets a cinder in his eye and is bandaged so that he cannot see. The book describes the sounds he hears, first the big noises, then the little noises. The book asks a series of questions: Could Muffin hear it when the sun began to shine? Could he hear it when it began to snow? and so forth. Children identify with this hurt puppy and the challenges he faces. Let them pretend that they are Muffin, blindfold them, and produce different sounds that they know.

Margaret Wise Brown's *Country Noisy Book*, illustrated by Leonard Weisgard in large bright blocks of brown, green, blue, yellow, and white, again tells about the little dog Muffin. On his trip to the country with his family, his hearing is tested because he is placed in a box where his vision is restricted. He travels by boat and train and soon arrives in the country where he listens to the sounds of the animals. Finally he falls asleep and hears no more noises. It is worth mentioning that there is a third book in this series, *The Indoor Noisy Book*.

Almost fifty years later, Cynthia Rylant has written a book called *Night in the Country* that also evokes country noises. It is illustrated by Mary Szilagyi. The dark night is full of movement and sound: the clanking chain of the dog, a creaking screen door, the plump of an apple falling off the tree. This is an excellent book to use as a jumping-off point for naming, imitating, and becoming familiar with and less frightened by the sounds surrounding children in the night. Familiarity and identification often diminishes fear.

Labeling Tastes

In the first twelve months most babies have also experienced a variety of flavors and tastes. The range of foods they eat has increased dramatically. They have noticed the temperature, texture, and the shape of what they have been given. They have also used their mouths to explore many things other than food, "gumming" many objects. Although there are no books as yet that allow children to taste, there are some that provide children with reinforcement of the vocabulary used to describe tastes. One book by Kate Petty and Lisa Kopper, *What's That Taste?*, describes oranges as fresh, apples as crisp and juicy, ice cream as creamy and cold, as well as other tastes such as tangy, spicy, sour, sweet, sugary, salty, bitter, and minty.

Labeling Feelings

It is difficult to capture feelings in words, to label them, because they aren't things at all. Probably the most effective way to teach children the names of feelings is to identify them as they are happening. Tell your children that they look, or are acting, happy, cheery, worried, scared, angry, annoyed, sorry, surprised, tired, hungry, and so on. It may also be helpful for you to describe and label your own feelings. There are a number of books for young children that aim at helping children find words for their feelings.

In Peggy Kahn's *The Care Bears' Book of Feelings*, these colorful, popular, pastel characters are shown expressing different emotions. They are happy at a picnic, sorry about spilt milk, excited about getting a present, surprised by a jack-in-the-box, lonely when home sick in bed, friendly when visiting their sick friend, scared of the water, brave in the waves, and sleepy when floating on clouds under the moon.

Anne Sibley O'Brien has written a series of board books with realistically drawn children confronting "small but difficult issues that arise in daily life." Three examples of books in the series are *I Want That*, in which two children show a range of anger, hurt, regret, and pleasure in their struggle to share; *Don't Say No*, in which a child experiences sadness and frustration when her parents repeatedly, though justifiably, say "no"; and *I Don't Want to Go*, in which a child kicks and screams when his playground fun is interrupted to go home for lunch. Young readers may find it helpful to see other children expressing feelings they have felt themselves. These books provide good opportunity to label the emotions when those feelings are overpowering a fictional character rather than your own child.

In Hugh Lewin's picture book *Jafta*, illustrated in brown, black, and white drawings by Lisa Kopper, a small, expressive black boy's feelings are compared to the actions of African animals. When he is happy he purrs like a lion cub, skips like a spider, or laughs like a hyena. When he gets cross, he stamps like an elephant and grumbles like a warthog. The illustrations clearly depict the mood of both the boy and the animal through facial expression and body movement.

Most of the books about feelings are for children who are a good deal older than babies up to twelve months. Many will be discussed at length in chapter 6. They, and others, can also be found in "The Bookshelf" at the end of this book.

4

Stocking the Storehouse: Food for Thought

Eighteen Months to Two Years

In contrast to the way infants manage information, at about eighteen months of age, rather than just temporarily retaining experiences as they come in through the senses, children will now be observed reflecting and pausing. At this stage they are beginning to retain images and figure out things in their heads. Although they now, and for a long time to come, will still learn much better when they have a concrete object in front of them to refer to, they are making their first forays into the world of symbols. They are beginning to have mental images, ideas, fantasies, and other thoughts. While they had to work everything out with physical objects through trial and error before, they are now beginning the abstract process of "trial and error grouping" in the mind.

It is characteristic of children of this age that they have an increased interest in the world around them and are busy trying to make sense of how the world works. Children spend a great deal of time sorting, organizing, and trying to categorize objects and sensations. They also demand labels at this time as they build a basic vocabulary and learn the fundamentals of language.

As children strive to understand how the world around them works, they experiment for long periods of time with blocks, dolls, sand, water, soil, paper, glue, crayons, clay, paper, pots and pans, flour, spilled milk, the cat's food, dirty and clean laundry—any medium or object with which they are permitted to interact freely. In this "play," which has been described as children's work, they are exploring the laws of physics, chemistry, and mathematics. Children also investigate human relationships, trying to understand the principles of sharing, personal power, accommodation, authority, and friendship.

This chapter discusses books that encourage and reinforce children's intellectual growth. Books can confirm previous learning, stimulate new thinking, and cause old thoughts to be questioned and revised. They can also provide necessary bits of information for consolidation of an idea, concept, or category. Interpersonal and emotional issues will be discussed in chapter 6.

Children at this age are beginning to conceptualize basic mathematics. They look for the patterns of things and the relationships between them, which is the substance of mathematical thinking. They are beginning to work on the task of ordination (counting things in order) while at the same time struggling with the concept of numbers. Being able to count from one to ten is very different from the much more difficult and abstract concept of "eightness" that means that eight of any object, of any size, in any order is still "eight."

Once children start understanding how numbers work, they embark on an intuitive and sensory comparison of objects' size, weight, length, width, shape, and quantity. Later, given the proper simple instruments, they measure and weigh things more exactly, checking out whether their impressions and intuition were correct. Sometimes they will be startled to learn that their impressions were wrong, for example, that a large ball can be lighter than a small one because of the density of its content.

The development of these and all concepts takes a great deal of time, thought, and practice. Although toddlers can perform some abstract functions, it is still essential that they be constantly physically involved with materials and objects that can facilitate their thinking. They need to engage in experimentation with real objects. There is no need to search for elaborate materials; apples, stones, cars, people, spoons, books, buttons, and everything and anything will serve them well.

Books About Numbers

Although books can not and should not replace the fundamental and essential process of counting out real moveable objects, they can provide supplementary experiences. Books take into consideration all of the various aspects of mathematical understanding. They range from the simple presentation of objects to count, to a more complex notion of number theory. Children will be able to find in books all sorts of objects depicted in a remarkable range of artistic styles and media.

Tana Hoban's *Count and See* is a well-designed early counting book. Don't try to go through the whole book at one reading. In fact, one page at a time will provide ample material for a beginner. On the left-hand page of each double-page spread is a large white numeral on a pitch-black background. Beneath it the number's name is spelled out in simple block letters. On the same page are white dots corresponding to the number. Encourage your child to touch and count the dots.

On the right-hand page there is a black-and-white photograph of familiar objects in their usual setting: fire hydrants, children, buses, trash cans. Each of the photographs appeals to the child's aesthetic sense, a sense which should be cultivated, nourished, and not underestimated. Each is well-composed, clear, and interesting. The book presents the numbers one through fifteen. It then devotes a double page to each multiple of ten to fifty, showing objects in groups of ten. On the final page the number one hundred is depicted by a row of ten open peapods, each holding a line of ten peas. Because of its movement beyond numbers one through ten, this book can be used with children from two to eight.

In Robert Allen's *1 2 3: A First Counting Book*, the left-hand page labels the color picture at the right. For example, he shows and labels one kitten, two eggs, three dolls, and so forth. The pictures are labeled and have solid backgrounds and are, therefore, even simpler than Tana Hoban's. After Mr. Allen reaches the number ten, he provides pictures that are not labeled in which the child can count the number of objects. The book then provides pictures to show a bit of simple addition and to illustrate that when objects change in placement or in size this does not change how many there are. The sophistication of the latter part of the book means that it will be challenging and helpful for several years.

Eric Carle's *My Very First Book of Numbers* is designed for children who are ready to match two different groups of two, two different groups of three, and so forth. Each page is cut in half horizontally. On the top half of each page is a numeral and the corresponding number of distinct black squares. The bottom halves of the pages, which must be turned separately, display bright color pictures of several types of fruit. Each page has a different type of fruit and a different number shown. It is the child's job to find the bottom page that has the same number of objects (fruit) as the page with squares above. While the top halves are in numerical order, the bottom pages are not.

John Burningham's 1,2,3 combines the fun of a story with the opportunity to count the progression of children ascending and descending a tree. As the reader turns the pages, there are an increasing number of children playing. They are typical Burningham children, simply drawn, but full of facial expression, body movement, each uniquely clad. After ten pages have been turned, and ten children fill the tree, a tiger appears and runs to the trunk. On the last page the ten children have descended and the tiger is viewing them from the branches.

Eric Carle's *1,2,3 to the Zoo* is a large book. Each page contains one flatbed train car with huge, colorful circus animals standing on it. The number of animals progresses from one to ten. Each page contains only one species of animal. For the very young child, just naming the animals will be enough. For the somewhat older child, counting them will be appropriate. Some observant children will notice the small, cumulative picture of the train on the bottom margin of each page. Older children will understand these small pictures and perhaps try counting the total number of animals on the train at each stage and predicting what the next page will hold.

Another aesthetically pleasing book that works with the numbers one through ten is Sheila Samton's *The World From My Window*. Through a window the reader first sees one moon on the first page, two clouds on the second page, then the picture enlarges and the reader moves beyond the window frame to see three stark, black, conical hills on a background of red earth and blue sky. Out of the mountains spill four streams, and in one stream swim five bright pink and orange fish. The scene becomes filled with numerous objects, the vivid colors and cut-out shapes abound. It is no surprise to learn that this is the work of a muralist, designer of banners and wall hangings, whose creations have appeared in public buildings, institutions, and private collections across the country.

Mitsumasa Anno is the author/illustrator of *Anno's Counting Book*, a gift to children and adults alike. On the page labeled 0, there is nothing but a light blue river, white earth, and sky. When you turn the page one fox, one child, one adult, one snowman, one flag, one house, one bird, one bare tree, and one snow-covered tree are added. Each object is small, detailed, colorful, and carefully placed in the large space. By the time you reach page twelve, there are twelve of each of the objects and a busy scene that invites the reader to look more closely and, perhaps, make up a story as well as count. The picture also serves as an impetus for questions. Are there also twelve windows on each of the twelve buildings? No. Is it twelve o'clock on the church tower? Yes. Was it eleven o'clock on the previous page? Yes. The questions can go on and on. Both children and adults may find this book rewarding, reading after reading. An exceptionally large and diverse array of number and counting books exist on many different levels of complexity. Several are listed in the bibliography of this book.

If you are not sure of your child's developmental level, begin with a book like *1,2,3 to the Zoo*. Let your child enjoy the pictures and the story they tell first. Then casually pose some simple question about the single elephant. If your child knows how many there are, applaud and praise him. If not, count together with the child. Young children need to manipulate objects as well as simply see them. Remember that everyone thrives on success. It gives a person the confidence to meet challenges.

John Burningham's *Viking Number Play* series presents many different ways to approach the understanding of our number system. There are six small books in this series. The same format is used in each of the books. Each one opens up accordion-style to display five flaps on which there are pictures. Each flap lifts to show another picture. Children learn about addition, subtraction, sets, numbers as words, numbers as signs, and about groups. Some of the books could be excellent tools to supplement basic manipulative work. They are also useful as a reminder that there are many mathematical concepts and no single right way or right order in which to learn about them.

Books About Time

Time is a complex mathematical concept and children develop their understanding of it very slowly. They probably begin their rudimentary understanding recognizing the pattern of their own day. First they will connect the sound of their caretaker's footsteps with his appearance and the subsequent experience of being fed. One precedes the other. One happens "before" and the other "after." This understanding comes long before words do. But, in time, if you talk to children as you care for them, they will begin to understand "now" and "later," "then" and "now," "this morning" and "this afternoon." It is not until the school years that children begin to learn to tell time by hours and minutes, or learn the specific details of the calendar.

There are very few books that tackle these concepts, perhaps because it is difficult to communicate sequencing to a very young child. There are, however, a few books about the seasons for young children. They give concrete examples of what one can see and do at different times of the year. Harold Roth's small board books *Spring Days* and *Summer Days* picture and describe the activities toddlers engage in at these times of year. Heidi Goennel is an artist whose work has often appeared on the cover of *The New Yorker*. Her book *Seasons* presents all four seasons with an understanding of how children perceive them. She also gives examples of what children can do during each season. The unusual combination of bright and muted colors makes her pictures memorable.

Anne Sibley O'Brien has written a story about a child's sense of time, taking into consideration the immediacy of a child's feelings. *It's Hard to Wait* demonstrates how very difficult it is for a child to wait, to accept that something he wants cannot be had right away.

Children will identify with the little boy in the story who has to wait to play with his father because his father is doing the dishes. He then has to wait again because a telephone call takes precedence. He struggles to look at a book rather than cry, and he is finally rewarded by his father's appreciation of his patience.

The story of *Joshua's Day* by Sandra Lucas Surowiecki tells of one full day in Joshua's life. He rises at home, has breakfast with his mother, walks to day care with her, and says good-bye. He goes to day care where he engages in many activities and plays with many friends. At five o'clock his mother picks him up and they walk home. They eat dinner, get ready for bed; they talk and go to sleep. It can be instructive for children to see the pattern of the day in print, and, in this case, to learn that other children separate from their parents and are reunited with them at the end of each day. You may want to talk with your children about the pattern of their day and yours. Begin with descriptions of what you are doing and then ask your children to recall what you did immediately before. Tell what you will do next. Slowly, in gamelike fashion, you can lengthen the period you remember together or the list of activities.

Books About Shape

Children enjoy playing with simple sorting boxes, with blocks that fit only into the slot of the same shape. Children will be able to place these blocks in the proper spot well before they can label the shape of the object. Children can also practice recognizing the basic quality of, for example, roundness, which applies to all round objects—big ones, small ones, black ones, yellow ones, striped ones, transparent ones, two- and three-dimensional ones. It is best to begin by sorting objects of just two shapes. Put aside one object of a specific shape and ask the child to find all the other objects like it. In time label the shape of the object. You can make this a game. When they are ready, children love the challenge. Reinforce their understanding of shape with well-designed books, but do not expect the books to do the initial teaching. Children need the chance to learn by doing.

Some of the best books for children working on the concept of shape are those that necessitate children's active involvement with the text. Tana Hoban's *Round & Round & Round* presents a single shape. Each large color photograph contains one or more circles. For example, the photograph on the cover is of six pinwheels. Each pinwheel has an outer rim that is a circle, an inner hub that is circular and it is held to its stick with a very small round yellow pin. A round-cheeked child with two round blue barrettes appears at the left of the photograph. In this photograph alone there are twenty-one round shapes to be found. Younger children will probably be able to locate only the more obvious circles, while older children and adults will enjoy finding the hidden circles in many of the photographs.

Karen Gundersheimer's *Shapes to Show* is recommended for children between the ages of three and six. It appeals to children who enjoy animals and who can appreciate the story implied by each of the illustrations. On the left-hand page of each double-page spread, a black shape is drawn against a white background and is labeled in large, uppercase purple letters. On the right-hand page, two small mice are shown doing something with an object that has that same shape. On the page illustrating the octagon one little mouse is playing with toy cars while the other is holding up a red octagonal stop sign. Children may enjoy making up simple stories about the pictures as well as discovering the objects that are examples of the shape being presented.

Bill Gillham and Susan Hulme have used color photographs by Jan Siegieda in their book *Let's Look for Shapes*. Again, as the title implies, children are challenged to find shapes in the photographs. In this book, however, the initial presentation of the shape is seen as a real object from close-up: a round clock, square kitchen tiles, and the triangular sail of a boat. On the right-hand page, children are shown a more complex and abstract picture that contains the shape just presented, for example, a child with a Hula Hoop, a child eating a waffle, and a child eating a sandwich cut in half diagonally.

In Rosalinda Kightley's large book called *Shapes*, the left-hand page shows a large, very brightly colored shape. The right-hand page then presents an object made up of a number of different-sized examples of that shape. The child is asked to see how many circles have been used to make up the object. In the example of the circle, thirty-two different size circles make up the amusing pink bug on the right-hand page. As the book progresses and more shapes are introduced, the pictures on the right-hand page include all of the previous shapes as well as the new one. At the bottom of the right-hand page is a small line of the shapes that can be found in the picture.

In *All Shapes and Sizes*, Shirley Hughes uses a rhyming text and expressive colored drawings to show how people, familiar objects, and playthings come in different shapes and sizes. One sequence reads, "Hats can be many sizes. So can feet. Children of all ages are playing in the street." The first of the four lines is illustrated with a drawing of seven preschool children wearing an array of distinctive hats. The drawing for the second line shows a father who has taken off his shoes wiggling his toes as his barefooted daughter sits on his lap and a barefooted infant sits propped up against the chair. The last two lines are illustrated with a double-page spread of twelve youngsters enjoying themselves in different ways in the street. This book demonstrates that everything has a shape, and it subtly celebrates the differences among people.

Boxes! Boxes! by artist Leonard Everett Fisher presents eighty boxes, boldly colored, interestingly detailed, having many shapes and purposes. The boxes are seen close up, from unusual angles and perspectives. Each box is filled with unexpected contents (puppies, paints, flowers, a wooden soldier, chocolates) and is constructed of a different material. One value of this book is that it demonstrates how varied a single object, with a single label (box), can be.

Spence Makes Circles by Christa Chevalier is the story of a little boy who enjoys his new ability to draw circles rather than a didactic book to reinforce recently taught shapes. While experimenting with circles, color, scissors, and glue, Spence gets himself very sticky, but remains in his mother's good graces and confident in his ability to make circles by himself. The book is a good model of the way children like to use the skills they have learned. It is also a good model of a parent who values the child's growing knowledge although it comes at a price.

Eric Carle's *The Secret Birthday Message* is a large and complex book not only using many shapes but also including such concepts as through, below, behind, open, and biggest. Its format includes a rebus (picture reading) using shapes, and pages with different shapes cut out of them, through which the next page can be seen. All of this is embedded in a motivating story.

Books About Color

The concept of color is mastered much in the same way as the concept of shape. Children often enjoy sorting things by color. They can seek all the red things in the house. They may enjoy having a green day in which everything they wear is green, every book they read with you has a green cover, every car they count is green, and so forth. They will certainly enjoy the many beautiful books designed to help reinforce their learning about color.

It is difficult to find a book that deals with a single color. Dorothy Savage's Peephole series illustrated by Gillian Chapman is one such book. In *The Yellow Peephole Book*, for example, every page has a hole in the same place on the page. Since the last page is yellow, the color showing through the hole on all previous pages is always yellow. On the first page, the circle makes up the yoke of a fried egg. On the second page it is the sun over the ocean. On the third page it is a yellow balloon, and so forth. This book has two drawbacks, however. When the page is turned and the circle appears on the left side of the book, no yellow shows through. However, this side of the page can be covered by the adult reader's hand to avoid confusion. Or you can use a sheet of yellow paper to place under each left-hand page as you read the book. Because the text labels only the object that the circle represents, to reinforce the color concept when you read the text, add the adjective "yellow" in each instance. Then labeling the object takes its place alongside the primary task of identifying the color.

Tana Hoban's *Is It Red? Is it Yellow? Is It Blue? An Adventure in Color* contains photographs that reinforce and stretch a child's concept of color. The bottom of each page contains colored circles of about an inch in diameter. Each circle is a different color, a color that is matched by an object or part of an object in the photograph above. Some of the photographs contain only one or a very few colors, and the example of that color is quite large and obvious. In some of the pictures, one or more of the colors is exemplified in only a very small part of the picture. For example, in a photograph of a black child on a bicycle with training wheels, the circles beneath the photograph are red, green, and yellow. The child's socks and shirt are red, and the grass is green. These are easy to find. But the child also has a yellow hair fastener and a very narrow stripe of yellow on her vest and shorts. The book is without any text other than the title.

Karen Gundersheimer's *Colors to Know* presents a color word and shape in that color on the left-hand side of each double-page spread. A tiny child dressed in that color and with a large object of that color is found on the right-hand page. The format is unconfusing because the color is presented by itself. The same is true of John Burningham's *Colors*. On the left-hand page the word naming the color is written in simple black lowercase letters. Directly below it is a drawing of a bowler hat of that color. On the right-hand side of the page against a sketchy background of the given color, a figure completely clad in that color and white is shown with objects of just the color. The only contrast is the face of the character and its flesh-colored hands. For children who appreciate John Burningham's art, this book will have great appeal.

For children who love clowns and their antics, Sara Lynn's *Colors* may be a favorite. On the left-hand side of each page a huge square of the new color is found. On the right side of the page a clown is shown painting large objects in that color. As the pages are turned the objects being painted are always the new color, and the clown's costume accumulates all the colors presented up to that point. This allows beginners an opportunity to focus on only the new color, and it affords more sophisticated learners an opportunity to review the colors they have already mastered.

Brown Bear, Brown Bear, What Do You See? written by Bill Martin, Jr., and illustrated by Eric Carle invites children who already know their colors to put their knowledge to use in a highly imaginative fashion. The book models and encourages divergent thinking, while affording the comfort of a predictable pattern. The rhyming text introduces animals that are normal in color, as well as two that are not. (There is a blue horse and a purple cat.) The book initiates a game that can be played from then on. Parents can challenge their children (and vice versa) to imagine or to draw animals of exceptional color. They will be stimulated further by reading Mwenye Hadithi's *Greedy Zebra*, illustrated by Adrienne Kennaway, in which the animals and their backgrounds are depicted in bold, dramatic, and unusual colors and patterns.

Many other books can be used to help children learn their colors. Some of them are very well-designed and clear. But many of them are confusing and will need a great deal of input from an adult to make them useful. You may want to weed out those books that try to overload the child with too much information at once, those with colors that are not true to their label, those with illustrations you do not enjoy, and those that may convey stereotypic or demeaning messages. Don't restrict yourself to books that are specifically designed with the particular purpose of teaching children colors. Many books can be used to that end. Have the child tell you about the colors in the picture or simply add color words to the text as you go along to reinforce each color that captures your child's interest.

Comparisons

Once children have developed an understanding of some of these very basic concepts such as number, time, shape, and color, and have mastered enough language to describe them, they will begin making comparisons and seeking ways to describe the similarities and differences between things. Children at about two years of age will be found working for long periods of time with all sorts of containers. They love to have objects to put in and to dump out of them. As they are exploring the concept of "in" and "out" through play, they will welcome being given the words for the concept.

Once they have the words, many children will practice them over and over as they play. They also experiment with and refine these concepts, and will, for example, be found allowing objects to overflow the edges of the container as they explore first "full" and then, dumping everything out, "empty."

Given the chance, children of three, four, and five will spend hours at the sink or in the sandbox with different size containers. That children of this age love sand and water is no accident. These media provide opportunities for experimentation with such concepts as "wet" and "dry," "light" and "heavy," or "clean" and "dirty." Reinforcing such concepts can be done with storybooks like Gene Zion and Margaret Bloy Graham's *Harry the Dirty Dog*, a story of a pet who returns home and is, at first, unrecognized because he has gotten himself so very dirty. Often, an entertaining story will crystalize a child's understanding of a concept. Look for books that use concepts in the context of a story as well as those that isolate concepts and consciously teach them.

George Kern's colorful small board book *Circus Big and Small,* contains bright, cheerful drawings of circus animals and entertainers illustrating big and small, short and tall, plain and fancy, up and down, in and out, alone and together. The contrasts are clearly depicted. It would be a good idea to use this book in coordination with stuffed or plastic toy animals. Ask your child to find a play animal that is big and put it next to one that is small. Or simply ask the child to act out the opposites with you, sitting "alone" in a corner of the room and then "together" with you on the chair. Remember that children are just beginning to think and will develop a still deeper understanding if they learn concepts actively.

In Cristina Ong's board book *Back and Forth!,* five basic opposites are illustrated by pictures of children playing. Through their play they demonstrate up and down, small and big, in and out, and so forth. Encourage your children to imitate the behaviors of the children in the book. They may be ready to think of different behaviors that will illustrate the concept labeled. For example, one child might act out "up" and "down" by climbing up and down the staircase in your house, although it is much larger than the one in the picture. Or the child may stand up and sit down, climb up on the bed and down from it, or pick up an object and lift it up above his head and then set it down again. In fact, the more examples of a concept you and he can perform, the more thoroughly it is likely to be understood.

J. P. Miller's brightly colored board book *Big and Little* uses animals to illustrate opposites. A very large long-legged bird looks down at a small duck, a very fat green frog sits bloated on a lily pad while an elongated, thin frog stretches to catch a firefly. The pictures in this book are so striking that the concepts are likely to be remembered by the images presented here. As always, it is a good idea to think of more examples of each pair of opposites than the book does so that the child has enough examples to begin understanding what it is they have in common, what attributes make them a part of a class.

The search for attributes forms the basis for children's thinking in *What's the Difference?* Once again Bill Gillham and Susan Hulme have collaborated with photographer Jan Siegieda to illustrate concepts using photographs containing children. Young readers are asked to view the photos on each double-page spread, and to discover and then name the differences between them.

Often concepts are presented in the context of a good story. Look for books like Crockett Johnson's *The Blue Ribbon Puppies*. Since its publication almost thirty years ago children have enjoyed this story about two children who decide to award a blue ribbon to the best puppy. First they tie the ribbon on one pup. When the little girl says that he is too fat, the little boy says, "He is the best FAT puppy." Then they tie a ribbon on another puppy. The little girl declares that the puppy is too spotty, but the little boy looks at her and says, "He is the best Spotty puppy." The story continues until each of the seven pups has received its own blue ribbon and children have learned to distinguish them one from the other.

Rosalinda Kightley has used very simple, large, brightly colored pictures on intensely colored backgrounds to capture and hold children's attention. In *Opposites* twelve basic opposites are presented, each occupying a full double-page spread. On the second to last page, the pictures are all reduced greatly in size and shuffled. Children are challenged to find the opposites. The last page shows the pictures correctly paired. The pictures on the next to last page could be cut out, covered with clear plastic, and made into a pairing game.

Tana Hoban, filmmaker, television consultant, and prize-winning photographer, has created three books about opposites. The simplest, *Push/Pull Empty/Full* uses large black-and-white photographs to illustrate each of fourteen opposites. Particularly striking are the large pictures demonstrating "in/out" of the turtle with its head and feet retracted next to a turtle whose head and feet are showing, and the photograph of "thick"-legged elephants juxtaposed with "thin"-legged flamingos.

Tana Hoban's second book of opposites *Big Ones, Little Ones*, presents pictures of animals with their young. The relative size of the animals does not change as distance from them changes or as they change position with each other. One animal is always bigger while others remain smaller. This is not an easy concept for young children to understand and may not be clear to them for a number of years. Much experience with real objects will be needed for them to truly grasp the idea. Books such as this should be used in conjunction with concrete material until children are six or seven and their reasoning is logical rather than based on appearances.

In *Over, Under & Through,* Tana Hoban uses black-and-white photographs in an urban setting to present spacial concepts. After the first exemplary photograph, the pictures are all unlabeled, adding a certain challenge and mystery to the "reading" of the book. The author provides six photographs to illustrate each concept. Spacial concepts are difficult, but this book makes them more accessible to youngsters.

Robert Crowther's captivating *The Most Amazing Hide-and-Seek Opposites* book contains tabs to pull or flip open, as well as creatures and features that pop up automatically. Possibly the most unusual feature is the snake who makes a ratchety noise as he pops up at you but who is quiet when pictured earlier, wrapped around a branch.

Fast-Slow, High-Low: A Book of Opposites by Peter Spier is one of the more sophisticated of the opposites books. The upper right-hand corner of each double-page spread labels the pair being illustrated and gives a pictorial example of it. The rest of the large spread is covered with carefully drawn, often amusing, and frequently unexpected, examples of the concept. For example, on the page labeled "Big-Small," among the many other sketches is a whale balancing a goldfish bowl on his back. Each page is filled with pictures that pose as well as answer questions.

With many examples, Peter Spier's book reminds us that concepts are learned by extracting common attributes from many objects. This process is a long one, particularly in the case of difficult concepts. Many of the concepts discussed here are understood by children beginning around the age of two or three years, but continue developing and being tested, refined, and corrected through the preschool and elementary school years.

Review the concepts from time to time. Use an old book that has become a friend. Use a comprehensive book like *Richard Scarry's Best First Book Ever.* Its huge pages cover a variety of topics such as school, playground, supermarket, farms, the railroad station, and harbor as well as colors, parts of the body, months of the year, the alphabet, counting shapes and sizes.

Your child may explore and struggle with these concepts for many years. Do not be discouraged when your child makes errors. Just as your children need to practice other behaviors over and over in order to master them, and make successive approximations as they learn to sit up, grasp accurately, pronounce words, and so on, so too will they become increasingly accurate as they work toward mastering concepts.

Imagination

For some children at the age of two and a half and three, the imagination is beginning to develop. Not only are they working hard at the basic concepts already discussed, using materials that can be manipulated and books that confirm or challenge their hypotheses, they also use blocks and other materials inventively. They create their own special versions of farms, villages, harbors, ice cream stores, fortresses, towers, and dungeons. As before, they are using these materials to test their growing ideas about things. They are also developing another extremely important skill, the ability to differentiate between reality and make-believe. *Changes, Changes* by Pat Hutchins could be used to help children examine the real possibility of building the pictured block structures while watching the fantasy wooden characters in the book magically transform their block-edifices.

At about fifteen months there are, perhaps, glimmerings of the beginnings of this important ability to separate fantasy from reality. At this stage children are acting out either their own feelings, or they are mimicking someone else's observed behavior. Children imitate the roles and behaviors they have seen most often. They pretend to be mother, father, caretaker, teacher, doctor, storekeeper, or letter carrier. Some two-year-olds expand the sophistication and complexity of what they are remembering, and increase the number of themes they will play out. This is in relation to their increased memory and their growing number of life experiences, not yet because of real growth in their imaginative powers.

During the third year, and sometimes earlier, children start to use their imaginations to do more than simply imitate. Often imaginative play is a way of working on feelings of powerlessness or inadequacy. We see this when children become bossy with their stuffed animals or play at being superheroes. Sometimes children use their imaginative powers to conjure up images in their minds of frightening things that they have heard of or have been warned against but have never seen. Books like Sendak's *Where the Wild Things Are* and Mercer Mayer's *There's A Night-*

mare in My Closet are reassuring for children at this stage because they show children conjuring up frightening images and learning to control them. Three- and four-year-olds can use books of this sort to help conquer their fears of such things as wild animals, large earth-moving machines, thunderstorms, or water going down the drain.

Slowly, children who are using their imaginations begin to sort out and comprehend the difference between what is real and what is fantasy. It may be helpful to provide the label "pretend" for the child. For example, "Let's pretend that you are riding on a tall giraffe." When children are ready, they will start to use the word appropriately themselves, indicating that this difficult distinction is beginning to become clear. The ability to understand the difference between what is real and what is not opens up a huge new field of literary enjoyment.

In *What Can You Do?* written by Bill Gillham with photographs by Fiona Horne, the left-hand page shows an object: a tire, sofa pillows, bath bubbles, orange rinds, and other common things, and poses the question, "What can you do with . . .?" The right-hand page shows children making a beard out of the bubbles, monster teeth out of the orange peel, and a doll's bed out of a slipper. Children often use this book as a stimulus to their own imaginative powers.

Simple objects can be used in imaginative play. Parents would do well to provide their two- , three- , four- , and five-year-olds with props such as different types of hats, grown-up shoes and clothing, large boxes, blankets, and other items to make hideouts. Things to carry, like shopping bags and suitcases, keys, pots and pans, tools, and other articles suggesting different kinds of work are also useful. Wagons, boxes, and tricycles can be used to invent pretend adult-driven vehicles. Even after they reach the age of seven, eight, or nine, when they move into the stage that Piaget calls the "concrete operational thought" stage, children will benefit greatly from being encouraged in their creative, imaginative play.

Shigeo Watanabe's *Daddy, Play With Me,* illustrated by Yasuo Ohtomo, reflects how children may feel when a parent is willing to join or initiate fantasy play. In this story a little bear rides on his father's back and pretends that his daddy is a horse. He also takes pleasure in being lifted by his father and pretending that he is an airplane. Eventually, his father's exhaustion brings him down to earth. In Christa Chevalier's *Spence Isn't Spence Any More* both Spence and his mother pretend to be fantasy characters. In the end they both strip off their disguises and go back to being mother and son.

Children also engage in acting out familiar stories, ones they have asked to have reread many times. Some children may enjoy Marie Hall Ets's *Just Me*. It is the story of a little boy who tries to copy the behavior of the animals he meets. He walks like a cat and a rooster, he pretends to lie down and take a bath and nap like the pig, to hop like the rabbit, wiggle like the snake, and so forth. At the end of the book, the little boy sees his father, and runs to him "like nobody else at all. JUST ME."

Children often pretend they are Goldilocks or any of the three bears. This story is especially appropriate when children have been working on concepts of size. When they pretend that they are Little Baby Bear, Middle-Sized Mama Bear, and Great Big Papa Bear, they may use different voices as they act out the parts. They may also use such props as different-size chairs, bowls, and beds. Reading Paul Galdone's version of the story, or any other rendition of your choice, can spark the imaginative play.

Marjorie Flack's cumulative story *Ask Mr. Bear* is another old favorite that invites acting out. You and your child can take turns playing the part of the various animals the little boy meets. Your child may enjoy saying "Good morning" to each of the animals, asking each one "Can you give me something for my mother's birthday?" and telling the animal that mother already has what the animal has to offer.

In John Burningham's *Mr. Gumpy's Motor Car* children may prefer to be Mr. Gumpy, who invites the animals for a ride in his car that then gets stuck in the mud. Or they may choose to become one of the many animals that ride with him, push him out, and then go for a refreshing swim.

Children can create pretend scenes once they have acquired a certain ability with language. Both imaginative and language ability are stronger in children who have had a great many stories told or read to them. It is important that when children reach this stage, you not only relate many stories but that you also give your full attention to their storytelling. This is their first entry into the role of author and writer and should be encouraged and treated with respect. Once children have developed an awareness of the printed word, it is gratifying to them to have an adult write down a few sentences of their spoken words. Your child may be thrilled to see the story on paper and take pride when it is shown off to another adult or posted in her room with a border around it.

In fact, "the language-experience" approach to teaching reading is highly recommended and begins with children saying a little bit about the picture they have drawn. The adult writes exactly what the child has said directly below the picture and then reads it back to the child. Eventually children can read their own stories aloud. Some adults give their children small individual notebooks in which they write words the children can recognize from their own stories. The theory is that children will read first those words that are important to them. At their own pace children who are taught in this manner develop the complementary skills of both reading and writing. They understand the role of the author and come to appreciate the personal nature of authorship.

Alphabet Books

Once children take interest in writing and reading their own words, they are ready for a more focused investigation of the alphabet. Although children have been exposed to the names of the letters in songs, in signs, labels (their name on an item of clothing or on a birthday cake), and on programs such as "Sesame Street," most educators recommend waiting to instruct children in the alphabet until they are about four years old.

Alphabet books abound. Their variety ranges from books that are very simple to those that are extraordinarily complex. In the beginning, you may find the greatest success by teaching the first letter of your child's name. You might look for a book like Gyo Fujikawa's *A to Z Picture Book*. Each page contains numerous pictures of plants, animals, and objects exemplifying a single letter. You may be fortunate enough to find, or clever enough to make, a book like Stanley and Janice Berenstain's *The Berenstain's B Book* in which every word in the book begins with *B*. The book tells a nonsensical cumulative story that amusingly reinforces the sound of the letter.

Most books illustrate the entire alphabet, using nouns that label one item per page and letter. Rosalinda Kightley's *ABC* clearly prints the uppercase and lowercase letter and labels the two-dimensional, large, brightly colored pictures of familiar objects. Mary Azarian's *A Farmer's Alphabet* also provides the uppercase and lowercase letters and the label of an object (in a bright shade of red), but in contrast to the simple toylike pictures in the Kightley book, Azarian illustrates her alphabet with sophisticated, detailed, black-and-white woodcuts of life in rural Vermont. The illustrations are of such aesthetic quality that they are sold individually as prints to be framed. Azarian studied art with Leonard Baskin, and it might be worthwhile to compare her book to *Hosie's Alphabet* by the Baskin family. Yet another aesthetically outstanding book is *Animal Alphabet,* by Bert Kitchen. The book is large (10 by 13 inches). Each page contains a gigantic matte black letter in which is entwined a textured and realistically colored animal. At the end of the book a list is provided of the names of each of the animals.

The design of an alphabet book is important to its success. Two books that play with the shapes of the letters are Suse Mac-Donald's *Alphabatics* and Marty Neumeier and Byron Glaser's *Action Alphabet.* The first uses bright strong colors against a white background to take pieces and shapes of each letter and insert them into the pictured object. The *m,* for example, becomes transformed into a wiggly mustache; the *n* is curved and inverted to become a nest. In the second book, the letters and pages are all in black-and-white. Each letter is humorously used to demonstrate the idea of the key word. For example, *M* is illustrated by a large block letter *M* that has a smudged right leg. This illustrates the word "Mistake."

Also in black-and-white is Tana Hoban's *A,B,See!* Through the use of photograms (a process of laying objects of photographic paper and shining a light on them so that the background is black and the object is white) the author highlights a number of objects with distinctive shapes to illustrate each letter.

Some alphabet books rhyme. In *Alphabet Dreams* Judith Gwyn Brown adapts "A, My Name is Anna," capitalizing on the nonsense, and the pattern, rhythm, and alliteration of the familiar jump rope rhyme. *All in the Woodland Early,* by Jane Yolen and illustrated by Jane Breskin Zalben, sounds like a traditional song, but the lyrics and music were invented by the author. Each verse presents as many as eight new characters beginning with each successive letter of the alphabet. The story-song invites interaction between the reader and audience.

Some alphabet books contribute to a child's store of knowledge about other cultures. *Jambo Means Hello: Swahili Alphabet Book* by Muriel Feelings, illustrated by Tom Feelings, goes through the twenty-four-letter Swahili alphabet, explaining each of the twenty-four key words related to East African culture. The book's illustrations earned a Caldecott Honor Award in 1975. Jill Walker's *A Caribbean Alphabet* was originally created to provide local children with an alphabet based on their own culture and experience. The author portrays objects common in the Caribbean, in a series of clear pictures, in alphabetical order.

Because there are so many alphabet books available, you and your children will never run out of fresh new approaches to making the names of letters and what they represent a part of the child's storehouse. When the letters are learned in an enjoyable, rather than threatening or pressured context, children are more successful in their reading and writing attempts.

Children can use *My First Book* and other books that give them an opportunity to write for themselves. This book provides a small flap on each picture. The flap has blank spaces for the child to fill in. For example, the book says: "I first smiled on _____ at _____." The child writes on the inside of a crib blanket that flaps open.

Another satisfying activity that makes good use of imaginative powers is taking a wordless book and narrating it. In *Ah-Choo,* by Mercer Mayer, pen-and-ink drawings tell the story of an elephant whose sneezes knock down a house. A police officer takes him to court, where another of his great sneezes blows the judge away. After another prodigious sneeze frees him from his jail cell, the elephant finally meets his match, an umbrella-carrying hippo in a very short skirt whose sneezes are as powerful as his own. *Pancakes for Breakfast* by Tomie dePaola, Raymond Briggs's *The Snowman,* Kjell Ringi's *The Winner,* and Peter Spier's *Noah's Ark* are other wordless books for which children can invent a narrative. (See the list of wordless books in appendix E.)

Knowledge and Information

Besides going through stages when they take pleasure in using and stretching their imagination, children between the ages of three and six often have an increased awareness of the world around them. Their consciousness expands beyond themselves and their imagination, and they become increasingly fascinated with accumulating information about the larger world. Some three- , four- , five- , and six-year-olds show an insatiable appetite for information, knowledge, and understanding. Since children at these ages have experimented with many fundamental concepts through their physical experiences, and because their language skills have expanded greatly, they are ready to learn about the world more abstractly, through well-written and well-illustrated books.

All sorts of large mechanical vehicles are of great interest to children, and books have appeared over the years using them as the focal point. Most books about machines and trucks give the machines human, usually childlike qualities and use them to communicate a message about perseverance, courage, and other virtues. The emotional value of famous books like *Little Toot, Katy and the Big Snow,* and *Mike Mulligan and his Steam Shovel* are discussed in chapters 1 and 6. More recently, however, children's books have appeared that acknowledge the eagerness many children have to attain a close-up view of large vehicles and a chance to view them more thoroughly than is possible from the seat of a stroller or moving car.

Donald Crews has written many popular books about large vehicles. In *Truck,* a Caldecott Honor Book, Mr. Crews takes one huge red truck and draws it from many angles, in many places, in different weather and at various times of night and day. It is not until page sixteen that the full form of the truck is shown, an unusually effective strategy for giving the reader a sense of the vehicle's largeness. The pictures speak paragraphs, which is important since the book is wordless except for the signs painted on the sides of trucks and on road signs. The book conveys information through illustration, and the last page adds some content for further speculation: In this picture we see through the open rear doors that the vehicle's cargo is tricycles.

In *Freight Train,* another award winner, the same author/illustrator gives readers a close-up view of a still larger and much less frequently encountered vehicle. A sense of the train is created through pictures and simple words, while concepts such as daylight and darkness are also being developed. *School Bus, Carousel,* and *Harbor* are all equally informative, communicating respect for the child's intelligence as well as his aesthetic sense. A recent Donald Crews book is *Flying,* which takes the reader on a flight over the airport, over highways, rivers, and cities, across the country, over mountains, into and over the clouds, through the sunset and back to the well-lighted city and airport in the night. Careful "reading" helps children see familiar things from the rare perspective of "above."

Gail Gibbons has also written a number of outstanding books providing the slightly older reader with detailed information about inanimate objects. Her recent book, *Trains,* uses realistic linear drawings, filled with blocks of strong color, coupled with clear, specific, factual language. She gives young readers a full, but not overwhelming, overview of trains, past and present. Steam engines, diesel engines, passenger trains, freight trains, and electrically powered trains are described in pictures and words as are the different kinds of cars and their uses. The book closes with a colorful rendering of the signs and signals related to trains.

Gail Gibbons has authored many other informative books. Three of the most unusual are *Tunnels,* which describes the construction and use of many different varieties of tunnels, including ant, mole, and chipmunk tunnels as well as four different kinds of tunnels made by human beings; *Up Goes the Skyscraper,* a thin tall book that tells about the building of a skyscraper from the planning, acquisition, and core-drilling stages through each phase of construction and furnishing of the building; and *From Path to Highway,* a small book that traces the history of the Boston Post Road. In each of these books, the author achieves a clear, detailed picture of the subject in a manner that communicates understanding and respect for the young child's interests and intelligence.

Ali Mitgutsch is an illustrator of reknown and a world traveler who has a passion for explaining processes that we tend to take for granted. He has produced a series of "start to finish" books that curious youngsters will enjoy. In *From Blueprint to House* children see the construction from blueprint and surveying to wiring and final painting. In *From Paper to Wood* they see the process of paper-making from forest, through paste-maker, sieve, rollers, giant irons to heavy paper rolls ready for cutting. *From Lemon to Lemonade* and *From Rubber Tree to Tire* are part of this series. Each book gives the reader the sense of being part of each stage of production.

Many factual books bring us closer to nature. *Hide and Seek*, a National Geographic Action Book, uses subtly colored, delicately detailed pictures. The book contains many pop-up multidimensional layers of forest, woods, jungle, plain, and polar vegetation to camouflage animals that either appear when the reader pulls well-marked tabs or that pop up when the page is turned.

In 1948 Berta and Elmer Hader wrote *The Big Snow*, a nature story that won the Caldecott Medal. It tells the story of the woodland animals' autumn preparations for winter. When the big snow comes, an old man shovels a path so that his wife can scatter seeds, nuts, and bread crumbs for the hungry forest animals. Through story and picture the authors bring children close to animals that children today rarely see for themselves.

Look for books that neither exaggerate nor demean their subject matter, that stimulate questioning and provide satisfying answers, which respect and challenge, but do not overwhelm the reader. Seek books that provide aesthetic as well as intellectual satisfaction, which move children beyond themselves and bring the unfamiliar closer.

When children are confronted by new situations, books providing information and knowledge about those situations are often very useful. Prepare your child for going to the doctor with Fred Rogers's *Going to the Doctor*. Books can also prepare for visits to the dentist (Harlow Rockwell's *My Dentist*) or for hospital stays (H. A. Rey's *Curious George*).

Through the years many authors have written about the first day of school. In the past, most introductions to school were fictional accounts, but recently a number of realistic documentary books have appeared. All use large color photographs and allow the reader to see children who are productive and content in their school environment. For preschool children, Harold Roth's small board book, *Nursery School*, depicts nursery school as a happy, busy place where children draw with crayons, or "try a sponge painting," bake, exercise, have lunch, do chores, build with blocks, listen to a story, play outside, and go home.

Not many books have appeared about the experience of staying with a baby-sitter, yet this is something that most children face even earlier than going to school. Shirley Hughes has written an informative and amusing book called *George the Babysitter*. George is a young man who comes to stay with Mike, Jenny, and baby Sue during the day. "He looks after the children, and together they look after the house," clearing the table, sorting out toys, shopping, and even washing the baby. The routine of the day is described, complete with a walk, lunch, nap, shopping, a playground visit, a game that gets too wild and makes George "cross," and a time watching television together. The children are shown to be cheerful and at ease, as is the sitter.

In Anne and Harlow Rockwell's *My Baby-Sitter*, the sitter, Martha, is a fifteen-year-old whose charge is age five. When the parents go out for the evening, Martha plays with the child, helps him prepare for bed, reads him a story, and tucks him in. Martha is then shown working on her homework, talking on the telephone, having a snack, knitting, getting paid, and being driven home. The sense of calm and routine are reassuring. For the child who has never had a sitter it is useful to "walk through" the evening with a book that mirrors the upcoming situation. This book does that well.

The Telephone Book, by Nancy Hannah Glazier, is another useful resource for child and baby-sitter alike. It is a board book in the shape of a telephone with a separate illustrated page for the phone number of mother, emergency operator, police, fire, doctor, hospital and ambulance, neighbors, grandparents, family, and friends. An excellent feature of the book's design is a space for the photographs of friends and relatives so that a nonreading child can identify the person. At the end of the book there is space for parents to write essential health information: allergies, medication, and blood type as well as important numbers for the baby-sitter.

Children love to hear the ring of the phone and enjoy conversing with people at a distance, but they should be taught that the telephone is not a toy and has life-saving potential if it is used properly. Although preschool children should not be left alone and will probably not be able to use this book by themselves, it engenders a sense of security to know that people who are important to them can be reached by telephone.

Books can also inform children about what adults are doing while they are away at their jobs. In *People Working*, each double-page spread shows a different working environment: city, country, in a boat, at a construction site, in airplanes, underground, in offices, and at home. People are shown working with their hands, with tools and machines, with animals, with plants, alone and together, day and night. Both men and women are depicted in most illustrations. Take care to find books that show equality of the genders when you are instructing your youngster about the world of work. A number of books such as *Mommies at Work*, by Eve Merriam, and *Mothers Can Do Anything* by Joe Lasker, show an awareness concerning this important issue.

For children whose mothers are away a great deal, *My Mother Travels A Lot* by Caroline Feller Bauer can provide the comfort of knowing that other children also experience this situation. The pros and cons are presented on alternating pages: getting to go to the airport is good, getting only one person's nighttime kiss is bad; receiving long-distance calls is good, having mom miss the puppies' birth is bad; getting lots of postcards is good, mom's missing the school play is bad, and so on. In this book, although the father is shown as being present all the time, his importance as a parent is in danger of being diminished in the light of the focus on the mother's absences. (Fathers' absences are rarely mentioned as long as mothers are present.) Nevertheless this book provides children with a rarely discussed situation that can be helpful to them.

Joshua Horwitz's book *Night Markets: Bringing Food to a City*, illustrated with black-and-white photographs, informs readers that five million pounds of bananas and pineapples arrive at a pier in New York on the East River. The book continues to give fascinating information about where the produce comes from and describes the night markets and people who prepare and sell food for the coming day. This book raises the reader's awareness of a working world that is generally unfamiliar to adults as well as children.

The lives of workers and animals on a farm are also unknown to many children, particularly those who live in urban and suburban areas. So, too, is the reality of how farm animals provide us all with necessary materials. *The Sheep Book* by Carmen Goodyear tells the story of one little black lamb and how she grows. It continues with the process of how wool becomes a garment and ends with the birth of a new lamb.

Information about the life cycle and reproduction can be communicated to children early and naturally through well-designed books. In *My Puppy Is Born*, Joanna Cole's text and Jerome Wexler's black-and-white photographs tell the story of the birth of puppies. It shows the dog straining her muscles to push the puppies out, the first puppy emerging in its sack, the mother opening the sack, biting the cord and licking the pup. The puppy is very small, its eyes are closed and its ears are plugged. It can crawl and bawl, but it cannot walk or eat food. It can suck and it will grow increasingly strong and independent. Other fine books about reproduction and birth include not only descriptions of animals but also stories and information about human beings.

Wind Rose, by Crescent Dragonwagon, illustrated by Ronald Himler, is a poetic book conveying a happy feeling about the product of a loving relationship between a man and a woman. The mother tells her daughter, Wind Rose, all of the details of her conception and birth that are appropriate developmentally for a four- to five-year-old to understand. It is important to find materials that you are comfortable with to read with your children about sexual information and any other emotional or value-laden topic.

A storehouse of books can go a long way toward fostering intellectual curiosity and cognitive development. The greater the variety of books, the more valuable the learning, since there are always different methods of presenting ideas. Accompanied by the responsive, selective, and enthusiastic adult, and coupled with the child's active involvement and direct experience, they form a partnership in the process that serves as a foundation for future learning.

5

Whistle While You Work

The responsibility of caring for young children in the home is an awesome one that requires great effort, creativity, and knowledge on the part of the caretaker or parent. The preschool years are the time when a young child's attitude and patterns of behavior and thought are being formed. Many parents of preschoolers understand that true learning, the lasting sort, begins when the children are in a situation that respects their feelings, piques their curiosity, and invites them to listen and look carefully. They know that it is the child's own interests and questions that stimulate and sustain investigation and thought.

In the years from two to six, although children's physical development is not as dramatic as it was in their first few months of life, they are increasing their speed, balance, and dexterity. Two-year-olds are learning to run, climb stairs, hop, throw, kick, start, and stop. Although a lack of sophisticated spacial relations may lead to frequent frustrations and accidents, children this age are seldom daunted. In fact, when this physical growth is coupled with their new emotional readiness to be more independent of their caretakers and with the powerful motivator, curiosity, the stage is set for a time of exploration and learning.

This is the age of what has been called the "supersnooper," the junior detective whose early learning moves along in three stages.

First, the child is hungry for information about the immediate environment. Children of this age need the opportunity to explore endlessly, to gather information. In fact, the sensory pleasures of the world are often so compelling that children resist sleep even when they are exhausted because the world is so enticing and exciting.

As they grow older, children work with the data they have gathered. They manipulate, sort, and compare it, hoping to find crucial clues in their search for understanding what the world is like, how it is organized, and how it fits together. At no age is it clearer that learning is something that children do, not something that is done to them.

Although well-designed toys may hold their interest for a while, children often prefer ordinary materials that are related to the adult world. At this point, parents and caretakers may find children are ready to help with work around the house. Many of the supposedly "simple household tasks" for which homemakers are responsible are not so simple at all. They require a considerable array of skills that are usually taken for granted, not only by the people for whom they are being done, but also by the person doing them. When household tasks are done in collaboration with a preschool child, they can provide a rich opportunity for many kinds of learning.

Children can build a positive sense of themselves with the accomplishment of real and necessary tasks. George Ancona has written a book called *Helping Out*. It has large black-and-white photographs showing children helping adults in various tasks. They hand a tool to someone who is building, help plant seeds, wash cars, rake leaves, sort mixed-up nails, gather eggs, bale hay, feed the baby, push a wheelchair, and sweep a classroom. The author says that he wrote the book because some of his happiest times when he was young were when he was helping a grown-up. He concludes by telling the reader that one of the best things about helping out is that it brings two people closer together, an important message.

For the child who is feeling unacknowledged, whose "help" does not seem welcome, the book *Sam* by Ann Herbert Scott, may be timely. Sam is the youngest child in a busy household. Each time he approaches an older family member, he is rebuffed because they are busy at their own tasks. When Sam touches his father's typewriter and his father yells at Sam, it is the final straw. Sam's tears bring everyone running and they become aware of the cumulative hurt they have inflicted. When Sam's mother finds a meaningful job for him in the kitchen, Sam feels much better.

Meal Planning and Shopping for Food

Most people eat at least three times a day. Homemakers plan ahead for a number of days' meals and snacks and most parents try to serve a variety of foods from the nutritionally advised food groups. But this is an adult perspective, and it involves the adult ability to take the needs of others into account. Young children think egocentrically. Since their only real point of reference is their own feelings, desires, and needs of the moment, children may enjoy hearing *Bread and Jam for Frances* by Russell Hoban. It details a young child's progress from wanting only to eat bread and jam, to her final willingness to add variety to her diet. The parents' role in this book is a good model.

The task of planning for the whole family over a period of time constitutes an opportunity for enlarging children's perspective. One way to start this planning is to begin with breakfast and progress through the other meals of the day. This helps children to develop their senses of sequence and time. It also imparts an understanding of how a day can be regulated and organized. Sequencing is a skill that is essential to the comprehension of written material, particularly the logical development of plot. Help your child to name items that are appropriate for breakfast. A child with only a very rudimentary speaking vocabulary but with a fair-size receptive vocabulary, can be asked to point to the things he or she eats for breakfast. Then you can provide the words.

Together with the child, compare, describe, or classify the items. Milk cartons can be picked up to see how heavy or light they are, how full or empty. Egg cartons are perfect for counting and grouping. The older child can count each family member, determine the number of eggs he or she consumes, and calculate the number of eggs required. Most breakfast foods lend themselves to this process.

The best activities are initiated because of the child's interest in a real task rather than an invented exercise. Producing a shopping list for an actual shopping excursion provides more motivation and learning than compiling a list for a pretend trip. Whenever learning occurs in a real context it is more powerful and long-lasting. Try to keep these activities light and entertaining. If children are pressured they will react negatively and the idea of future learning may become unattractive to them.

As you write an item on the shopping list, say the word aloud. Your beginning talker may repeat the word. On occasion, you may want to ask your older child what letter the word begins with or what other words she knows that begin with the same letter. Ask for other foods beginning with that letter. If the child shows interest in doing the writing for herself, she can try to form the letter. If she wants to learn more of the letters of the alphabet, there are many colorful and entertaining books that can help accomplish that purpose. Don't push these activities on your children. Activities should spring from interest they have shown and end when they seem to have had enough. A number of these books are described in chapter 4.

It might be fun to set aside a special day for one letter, then plan the day's foods and activities around that letter. For example, on *m* day children might eat macaroni, milk, and muffins. They could engage in movement and music and pretend that they are monkeys and magicians. You might read a book to them about a mighty mountain or marvelous magnet. Your child can be asked to design a meal that includes only words beginning with the first letter of his name, a monochrome meal, or a meal exclusively consisting of squares and rectangles (a fine excuse for making brownies).

Children are naturally egocentric, but thinking of other people is an attitude and skill that can be encouraged. Begin by asking children to think about the people closest to them. In the process of meal planning, for example, ask your child to recall what other family members like and eat for breakfast. Adults in the home may drink coffee or tea; older children may have specific preferences. This simple stretching of children's thinking beyond egocentric boundaries is another skill that will be necessary the more they play with other children and must learn to take the feelings and needs of others into consideration. It will also be helpful when they start to enter new worlds through the characters in books read to them or they later read for themselves.

Since young children love animals, Roy Campbell's *Pet Shop* may be ideal. It is a small board book that opens like an accordion. The first page is a "cupboard" of foods for the pets. A different food is found in each of its six slots. The child is asked to take each food out of its slot and slip it into the slot in front of the animal who will eat it. Children can give the kittens milk, the puppies a bone, and so forth. (See "The Bookshelf" for more books about animals.)

As you move through the day, planning for snacks, lunch, and dinner, you can introduce additional skills. As you plan the shopping list you can also introduce scientific concepts, considering the food groups, nutritional values of individual foods, and the functioning of the body. You also build speaking, comprehending, categorizing, sequencing, writing, remembering, observing, and organizing skills, but by considering the child's likes and dislikes, you can help develop a sense of self, an individual who is listened to and respected. This provides an important model of how all people should be treated.

In this context an amusing book to introduce is Eric Carle's *What's for Lunch?* The monkey in this book politely refuses one fruit after another. The monkey, who dangles from a string, can be passed or swung through a slot in each page until, at the very last page, he stops at a banana tree. You can ask your children what fruits they would like to skip over and where they would like to stop. The book invites counting, the naming of colors, identification of objects (fruits), manual dexterity, and simple picture reading. It may be particularly interesting to children who are beginning to recognize and assert their own preferences.

When you want to introduce aesthetic considerations, you can discuss how different colors and textures of foods would look in combination. Another Eric Carle book is appropriate to consider here. In *The Very Hungry Caterpillar* a caterpillar eats his way through an apple, two pears, three plums, and so on. Each fruit is colorful and each has an actual hole bored through it. On the seventh day the caterpillar gorges himself on a riot of nonfruit foods, gets a stomach ache, eats a leaf, and retires to his cocoon until he emerges as a gorgeous butterfly.

You can also prepare for your trip to the supermarket by reading books about fictional characters who go shopping. Younger children can "read" Harriet Ziefert's *Bear Goes Shopping*, illustrated by Arnold Lobel. On each page of this book the main character, a big brown bear, goes to different stores: a bakery, a fruit store, and so forth. Each time, the reader is asked which of four pictured items bear will buy. Only one item is appropriate. The book affords children an opportunity to work at classifying while at the same time having fun.

Three-year-olds and up can construct a set of colorful cards with pictures of items they want to purchase at the store. They can do this by cutting pictures out of magazines and flyers or drawing the pictures. In either case, the preparation of the cards involves the important skills of noting, matching, and reproducing similarities and differences, skills that are basic to both reading and writing. This activity also helps children to practice the difficult conceptual task of relating pictures of an item to the actual item in the real world. When you take the cards to the grocery store they become an illustrated shopping list, a sort of treasure hunt.

For four- and five-year-olds, ready for even further stimulation, you can construct a set of cards with words as well as pictures. The association of word labels with pictures is an effective way to build a reading vocabulary. A child can find an item and bring it to the cart. The child's motivation will be particularly high if the item happens to be a favorite food.

The supermarket is an excellent place to enlarge a child's vocabulary and understanding with a discussion of comparative size. The child and adult together can consider which box is the largest and they can play with various synonyms for large: huge, gigantic, humungus, enormous, king-size, immense, stupendous, or colossal. They can do the same with comparisons: small, medium, and large, or opposites like tiny, miniature, wee, and minute. Many of the books about opposites, described in chapter 4 and listed in "The Bookshelf" will be useful for these activities. For a child who is beginning to show an interest in categorizing and sorting information, the overhead signs in the grocery store will provide some help.

Children love having the chance to buy something for themselves. You may want to let your children hold some money and make a special purchase for you, a pet, or themselves. In conjunction with this activity you might read Kathy Caple's *The Purse*. In this story Katie's sister convinces her that she should replace her Band-Aid box with a purse to hold her money. Katie complies, and buys a yellow purse for herself, but when she puts her money in it she misses the clinking sound the coins made when they were in the metal Band-Aid box. She does odd jobs to earn more money and works out several transactions so that she can have both the purse and the box. Using this book with children will give you the opportunity to help them think ahead about purchases they would like to make and the possible consequences of those purchases.

In John Burningham's *The Shopping Basket*, a young red-headed lad wearing spectacles is asked to take a shopping basket and go to buy provisions for his family. He does his shopping, but on the way home he is surprised many times by animals that do not inhabit the streets of a country town. Children take pleasure in joining in this fantasy and in trying to make sense of what really happens along the way.

Food Preparation and Cooking

Preparing and cooking foods are daily activities in which children can beneficially participate. Talk to your children about clean and dirty, cooked and raw, hot and cold, heavy and light, large and small, smooth and rough, wet and dry, bitter and sweet, coarse and fine, hard and soft. Children learn through sensory paths, so it is advantageous to let them smell, taste, listen, and touch. They can measure ingredients, combine them, stir them, and observe the changes. They can watch the heating of foods, hypothesizing and observing the changes that heat can bring. New vocabulary can be introduced. Many children will show interest in learning the distinctions among boiling, simmering, melting, creaming, and blending, especially if they are directly associated with a desired product. And, of course, they love licking the spoon.

To extend the learning you can introduce any of a number of enticing books relating to food. *Chicken Soup with Rice* by Maurice Sendak is a good book to share with children to help them develop their appetites for reading. It is a humorous song about characters who find chicken soup with rice the perfect food to eat in each month of the year.

Your child can get involved in helping to set the table. This activity can build vocabulary: a placemat goes "in front of" each chair; a plate can go "on top of" the mat, a fork "to one side" and a spoon "on the other side." Something else can go "in the center" of the table, perhaps the condiments or some flowers. The activity can be turned into a guessing game or silly suggestions can be made for each place, for example: "What goes in the middle of the table. Is it a musical mouse, a mudpie, or the muffins?"

A book by Phyllis Hoffman, called *Baby's Kitchen*, is designed for children to manipulate finger-size vinyl stickers of familiar kitchen objects such as an apron, a broom, a cookie sheet, a can, a measuring cup, and a tea kettle. These objects can be stuck in the appropriate spaces of the kitchen scenes that follow. In this way the youngster can learn the vocabulary and the function of kitchen utensils along the way. Be sure to supervise this play, or make certain that the children are old enough not to want to put the little vinyl stickers in their mouths.

As for kitchen clean-ups, they are seen as a burden by most adults. But children do love bubbles, and a lot of scientific experimentation occurs during water play. Give children plastic measuring cups and a number of different-size containers. Let them explore comparative size by pouring from one vessel to another. Or give children an assortment of items and ask them to predict which ones will float. The activity provides a good opportunity for ongoing dialogue. Straws can stimulate bubble making, and sponges are instruments for miraculous transformations from dirty to clean.

A book with a parallel theme, Andrzej Krause's *Christopher Crocodile Cooks a Meal*, presents a crocodile who shops and cooks for his cousins who are coming to dinner. The meal consists of pancakes and chicken soup with lots of vegetables including onions, which make the chef cry. He and his guests eat, wash up, and then relax with a board game. This book can be used to reinforce the family clean-up, and can help youngsters recall the sequence of events in preparing a meal.

Many books relating to preparing and eating food exist. You may enjoy *Cookies and Breads: The Baker's Art*, written by Ilse Johnson and Nika Standen Hazelton, based on an exhibit at the Museum of Contemporary Crafts. It presents the reader with the culinary inventions of some of the most imaginative artist-bakers of our time. Bread is shaped into flowers and vases, animals, houses, saint and peasant figures, and even the molding for "stained glass" made of colored candy. This book is food for thought and impetus for explorations using either colored Play-Doh or real dough.

Stories about food vary from Tomie dePaola's *Strega Nona* with its magic spells and unstoppable, overflowing pot of spaghetti; *The Dutchess Bakes a Cake* by Virginia Kahl in which a bored dutchess has to be rescued from the top of an enormous cake by a kingdom of hearty eaters; or stories like the beautifully illustrated *The Hedgehog Feast* by Jill Barklem about a hedgehog family getting ready for a prehibernation feast, to the many children's cookbooks now on the market.

Cookbooks

Cookbooks for children are plentiful. If your child already knows and loves Pooh Bear and is a lover of honey, *The Pooh Bear Cook Book* by Virginia H. Ellison will be a good choice. It includes recipes for breakfast, lunch, and dinner and, of course, "smackerels." The author points out that it is useful for special events, real or imagined. With a little imagination the smallest dish can be turned into a party dish.

Stuffin Muffin: Muffin Pan Cooking for Kids by Strom Scherie is written for muffin lovers who are concerned about avoiding "sweet, salty, processed, and artificial foods." The book contains thirty "child-tested" recipes and gives information about using the muffin pan, choosing ingredients, increasing recipes, freezing foods, safety, measuring, and more. It also has a section on making your own variations on recipes as well as how to create new ones.

If you and your family have an interest in the out of doors, you will find *Foraging for Dinner: Collecting and Cooking Wild Foods* by Helen Ross Russell intriguing. The author grew up on a farm and learned about foraging from her parents and grandparents. She lists edible plants found at different seasons, in different "environmental niches," and in different climates.

If you are ready for engaging in some research, ask children to think about the food they eat and where it comes from, both its natural and geographical source. Children may be startled to realize that peanut butter comes from the meat inside a peanut shell, that flour is made from something that grows like grass, that cotton grows on a bush, or that milk comes from the udder of a cow. Children may be motivated to find out how the food got from its place of production to the market. A cross-cultural investigation, considering what people in different parts of the world eat and why, can inform children in many ways. Science and information books for children abound. One series of four books that parents and caretakers may find useful because of the concise and clear information it conveys is *Tell Me Why*, by Arkady Leokum and illustrated by Howard Bender. A number of children's encyclopedias are also available. One of the good reasons for consulting reference books in response to children's questions is that the model of seeking answers from books is an excellent one for children to observe.

In addition to food purchasing and preparation, the other daily household tasks that many caretakers perform while with their preschool children can be engaging and beneficial. Cleaning house, making repairs, caring for pets, and doing laundry are some of the most common. All are activities in which children can be participants rather than bystanders. In the process they will find the satisfaction that comes from doing meaningful tasks and from having their minds and bodies challenged. Children's interests and level of development should be considered. Are they in the stage of avidly gathering every scrap of visual, auditory, and tactile information? Are they compelled to label every precious item they have come upon? Are they fascinated by how things are categorized and organized? Are they now experimenting with using objects, applying material learned in previous stages to what is currently at hand?

The Laundry

If there are dirty clothes scattered around your child's room you can play a game of hide-and-seek. Pretend that dirty clothes are hiding and your child has to find as many as possible in two minutes time. Or you can challenge your child to a race and at the end count who has found more articles of soiled clothing. When the game is complete, ask the child to deposit the clothes in the laundering area of the home.

When everyone's laundry has been gathered, the next task is to divide it into manageable loads. Dividing by color is the most conventional, starting with dark and light. Since children enjoy learning by doing, let them do the sorting. Or ask your child to gather together all things that fall into the category of underwear. Do not be surprised if this is a rather difficult task. Underpants and undershirts have a very different appearance. Young children may well take some time to understand what common attributes they have. You may have to help your child understand what characteristics a piece of clothing must have to be included in this category.

To supplement the learning activities and conversations related to laundries, you may want to sit down with one of the varied books that relates to the subject. *Theodore* by Edward Ormondroyd tells of a stuffed bear who is accidentally washed and dried and is unrecognizable to his mistress until dragged in the dirt by two fighting tomcats. It is a story that invites personal comparisons. *Soo Ling Finds a Way* by Judy Behrens is the story of a Chinese-American child who rescues her grandfather's laundry business when it is threatened by the installation of a laudromat across the street. *Washday* by Susan Merrill is the story of a little girl who loved washdays when she was growing up on a farm. Everyone in her family worked together, and the little girl experienced the pleasures of companionship, cleanliness, and the beauty of the countryside around her.

In a fantasy vein is Laura Geringer's *Molly's New Washing Machine*, illustrated by Petra Mathers. In this story a woman receives an unexpected washing machine. Bongo Bear and other fantasy friends arrive, contribute articles of clothing to the wash-load, and join in spirited dances in rhythm with the different cycles of the washing machine. When the cycles of wash and dance are complete, the creatures who delivered the machine return to repossess it.

Housecleaning

Though the work may take longer, children can begin helping with the housecleaning when they are over the age of two. A book like Kate Duke's *Clean-Up Day* may be a good way of introducing the topic. In this board book a little guinea pig is pictured holding a dustpan for his mother, emptying a wastebasket, and helping make a bed. The youngster is also shown riding on the vacuum cleaner and hiding under a sheet.

Dusting flat surfaces is perhaps the easiest task for very young children. It allows them to practice small motor control, to use fine visual discrimination, and to learn about the shapes and textures of different household items. The adult can help by asking stimulating questions. This activity can also provide an opportunity for labeling, developing a vocabulary of nouns, verbs, and adjectives for making comparisons, understanding the functions of things, examining things from different perspectives, seeing the relationship of parts to the whole, and for an endless variety of word and counting games. In *All of a Kind Family* by Sidney Taylor the mother places a button in every location she wants dusted. Then she asks her children to find all the hidden buttons, dusting each area as they remove and pocket the button. Even for children who cannot yet count, this hunt can be fun.

Children are usually highly motivated to read things that are written about themselves. A sign or banner declaring, "Sam dusts and finds 32 buttons!" is likely to be remembered by Sam, word for word. If you are too busy for such diversions simply praise the child, acknowledging what he has done before asking him to undertake a new job.

Teaching your children the place for each kind of object is also a useful endeavor. When you tell them to put all dirty dishes in the sink or all crayons in the empty coffee can, it allows them to practice generalizing. Once things have been gathered and put in their proper place, surfaces in need of cleaning may reemerge. Young children are fascinated with the power of sponges, so you can set them to work cleaning tabletops and countertops. From time to time it is useful to review previous events with children even when they have become part of your routine. Ask them to remember what you have accomplished this morning, or to try to remember the sequence of your cleaning routine. Memory is an important component of reading, and it should be practiced informally. So too is the ability to predict, so you might discuss what will happen next. Perhaps the children can guess what item each family member will deposit in your recently neatened space. Involve them in thinking about what you will have to do again to clean up the room. Or if you want to motivate children to join in some problem solving, ask them to think of ways everyone could prevent the mess from reoccurring.

Repairs

Repairs around the house often call upon our adult problem-solving capacities, and children can be invited to listen to our thinking out loud about possible diagnoses of a problem, hypo-thetical causes, and worthwhile solutions to a problem. Although the actual details may be beyond their comprehension, by think-ing a problem through you are providing a model that is invalu-able. Sometimes, when mechanical items break down or a con-struction project is undertaken, you can model consulting a book for ideas or instructions.

When you do repairs, let your child participate as much as possible. Even if children are too young to use a screwdriver, nail, or hammer, they are probably not to young to learn the names of these objects. Check their receptive language, and let them be involved in helping you by laying out your tools. Have them act as assistants, handing you the necessary tool when it is requested. Explain each step along the way. Do not underestimate the value of doing this. Although they may not follow every why and where-fore, they will understand the respect and interest you are show-ing in them.

Depending on your child's age, there are two books now avail-able for children about adult tools. One, by Gail Gibbons, called *Tool Book* uses brightly colored, clearly drawn pictures of labeled tools in use to teach children what each tool's function is. The other, *Christina's Toolbox* by Dianne Homan, shows a skilled child of about nine or ten using her tools to build a bird feeder, stilts, and a tree house. She is also shown repairing her bike and moving a metal bookshelf by herself.

When you cannot do a repair by yourself and have to call in a professional to do it, use the occasion for a lesson about personal safety. Before you permit a serviceperson to enter the house, ask the stranger for an identity card with an identifying picture on it. This need not frighten your child. Instead it can be another lesson in making comparisons, a task for the child to see if the face and the picture match. It also models good preventive measures.

Not every day is punctuated by an interesting visit from a repair person, a delivery van, or from friends or neighbors. Do your errands with your child, but take your time. Often children feel themselves being dragged from place to place. They may find themselves being punished for their curiosity and interest. It is not unusual to see a young child being pulled away from a display that has caught his interest but has no appeal to his caretaker.

If you realize that many of the places you go on your errands are valuable sources of learning for your children, the process may become more enjoyable all around. For example, take a trip to the post office. Begin by writing one of your letters in the presence of your child, preferably a letter to someone he knows. Invite your child to add something to the letter, a scribble, a drawing, a name, whatever your child is ready for. As you put the letter into an envelope, explain why the envelope needs an address. Permit your child to carry this letter when you go to the post office together.

When you get to the post office it might be the perfect opportunity to explain to the child a little about how letters get to their destination. You may want to add that people get paid to do this work and that a stamp helps pay for the services provided by the post office. Let your child put the stamp in place.

If the stamp piques your child's interest, you can examine the face of the stamp together. There is often rich opportunity for learning there; an historic event or person, a worthwhile cause or an upcoming celebration may be depicted. Design and color may also be of interest. Capitalize on this at home by having your child design his or her own stamp. The child might choose to draw his or her own portrait, or one of you, a favorite stuffed animal, or even food. Perhaps your child would like to send this design to the offices in Washington where stamps are designed.

Receiving letters is a very exciting, special, and stimulating experience for a young child. Nothing is more enticing than a personal message to the prereader. If you have no relative, baby-sitter, or friend who would ordinarily write to your child, mail a letter or postcard yourself. Many children begin reading with their own names. Show your children their names and let them read them back to you. If you have sent a card, read the message aloud. They will probably ask you to do so over and over until they have memorized the message and can "read" it back to you. Although you may not recognize this as reading, it is. Your child is beginning to associate the written word with the sound of the word and with its meaning. Let your child "read" to you in this way as often as possible because this is how the child builds a sight vocabulary.

Finally, you can read to your child about the post office. There are many books available. One is part of the *People Who Help Us* series published in England by Ladybird Books Ltd. In this book, *The Postal Service*, the author, Ron Edwards, explains how the postal system works in a step-by-step text and numerous color photographs.

Janet and Allan Ahlberg's *The Jolly Postman or Other People's Letters* follows a fictional postman along his route. He delivers his first letter to Mr. and Mrs. Bear at the Three Bears Cottage. The page on which the address is written is a folder. It looks like an envelope and is open at the top. The child can reach in, pull out the letter and listen to an adult read it. In this case the letter to the Three Bears is an apology from Goldilocks. Other deliveries go to The Witch at Gingerbread Bungalow, Mr. V. Bigg at Mile High House, Beanstalk Gardens, and to other fairy tale characters. Since this book is sure to be read again and again, it would be wise to cover each of the letters with clear contact paper. The format of the book motivates children to invent more communications to other fictional characters.

My Mother the Letter Carrier by Inez Maury and illustrated by Lady McCrady is a bilingual story in which a five-year-old tells about his mother who is not only a mail carrier, but also a very caring parent. It is useful to show children women employed in formerly all-male jobs and to help them learn something about the work that women do outside of the home.

Harriet Ziefert and Richard Brown have collaborated on *Birthday Card Where Are You?* In this story Sam mails a birthday card to Sally. The card moves from the blue collection box, into the post office jeep, then the post office itself, and so on until it is delivered. The drawing of each place the letter is deposited has a flap that children can open to find the letter. After reading this book, or visiting the post office, it would be helpful to provide some paper, envelopes, pencils, old ink pads, and other materials for children. By making their own letters, by playing out how the tasks of postal employees are done, by imitating or inventing sorting systems, children integrate and make use of what they have learned. Questions that did not occur to them as observers or listeners will crop up as they try to cancel, sort, and deliver their pretend mail. Further learning will occur, since young children learn best through tangible, hands-on experiences, and move from the concrete to the abstract. Allowing children to move freely back and forth from the real world to their play re-creation of it gives them an opportunity to check their understanding.

An errand to a sewing or knitting store can be an invitation to explore color, texture, patterns, and sizes. To build on your experience in the store, you might consider having your child begin a sewing project while you are doing yours. A piece of felt and a very thick needle with bright woolen thread works well. If your child is not ready for a slightly sharp needle, substitute a piece of the very largest gauge needlepoint plastic and a completely blunt needle. Lovely patterns can be made by a young child, and fine motor coordination will be developed as the child struggles with the in-and-out movements required in sewing.

It's possible to construct a very simple skill book of the sort frequently found in book stores. Children can stitch together four or five squares of colorful felt or muslin to make a book. Then they can draw on those pages or attach objects such as a shoelace to practice bow tying and a zipper to practice zipping. Other pages can be used to practice buttoning, using velcro, snapping, and hooking. Stringing beads is an old and still popular "sewing" task. Whatever the specific project, the pride children will feel from mastering a real and useful skill is worth the time spent helping and directing them. In *Peter Learns to Crochet* by Irene Levinson, Peter wants to learn to crochet but can't find anyone to show him how. It is his male teacher in school who teaches him and provides an excellent model.

Other errands can be made equally productive for children. Whether it is a stop at the dry cleaners or a trip to the hardware store, eyeglass repair shop, computer store, stationery store, car wash, furniture store, flower store, fish shop, or camera store, children can be involved in a way that will keep them happily and constructively occupied.

Each of these experiences can usually be reinforced with a carefully chosen book. For example, after a stop at the dry cleaners, you might want to go to the library and pick up Susanna Gretz' colorful story *teddy bears 1 to 10*. It is a counting book about ten charming but dirty and patched old teddy bears who are washed, dried, and then sent to the dry cleaners. There they luxuriate in separate color baths that dye them a glorious new color. Once dried and fluffed, the bears proceed home on the bus and arrive in time for tea. You too may want to pretend that you are newly cleaned teddy bears, returning from town in your new colors, looking forward to a little something, a bearlike snack, as Pooh would say, when your errands are done.

A good idea might be to take the time to observe other children as you are walking in town. One strategy can be to focus on their facial expressions, helping your child to infer people's inner state. If you have had an argument about what clothing was appropriate for the day, a survey, at whatever level of sophistication is possible for your child, of what other children's mothers made them wear might be fun and another good way to build those important observation and discrimination skills. If your child loves animals, ask him to find four different kinds. You can make seasonal observations. Can your child find ten signs of winter/spring/summer/fall on your walk? Once again, the opportunities are there and such focusing can make a very routine path that seems to hold little fascination a place of great interest.

Learning to read signs is another valuable endeavor. Children often begin by noticing the STOP sign because it has such distinctive characteristics. It can be identified by color and shape as well as by its letters, as can other simple signs. Many children use configuration clues when first learning to distinguish one word from another. They may remember that *Dan* and *Dad* are different because *Dad* ends with a tall letter. Children will also have fun on their walks if you ask them to play detective, reading the signs and telling you what you should do.

Many other areas of routine in and around home provide children with channels for learning, involvement in real life work, and enjoyable companionship with their caretaker. One such area is the care and understanding of pets. The other is the design and maintenance of an indoor or outdoor garden.

Whether you live in the country or city, as long as you have a window, you can become a benefactor of birds. Some of the least expensive and most exciting feeders are small platforms that attach to the window with suction cups. They can be sprinkled with different sorts of seed depending on what kind of birds you are trying to attract. Another simple way to make a feeder is to fill an onion bag, the kind made of stringlike nets of colored plastic, with fat or suet from the market. Rolling it in seed will add to its appeal. This kind of feeder can be hung from a string.

You can talk about what causes the birds to come to your feeder. The discussion can range from "because they are hungry," to the seasonal nature of food sources or the migratory patterns of different species. Formulating answers and giving reasons for them are important skills for children to acquire. You'll find here another opportunity to consult reference books.

Children may enjoy looking very carefully for the unique characteristics of the birds that come to the feeder. Equip yourself with a guide to birds. Together you and your child can attempt to match the real birds to the pictured ones. Fine visual discrimination is necessary for accurate reading and it is also used in writing. Remember that one wonderful way to start writing is with drawing. Ask your child to draw the bird he or she is observing. This in itself is very much like trying to reproduce a letter. Once your child has drawn the picture (even if it is at the "scribbling" level), ask your child to describe the drawing. Write exactly what the child says on the paper and then read it back. Perhaps, as with the postcard, your child will "read" the writing back to you.

If your child's interest persists there are many simple fiction and nonfiction books about birds. *Casper and the Rainbow Bird* written by Robin and Inge Hyman and illustrated by Yutaka Sugita is the story of a country crow who ventures to the city and meets a beautiful, but caged, rainbow bird. Casper befriends the rainbow bird, brings it a flower from the meadow, and finally frees it. The book is rich in opportunities for thinking and learning. Its illustrations stimulate questions about color, texture, and shape. Its story invites the readers to wonder about the life of a bird in different habitats. Children can work on skills of understanding sequence, interpreting feelings, getting the main idea, predicting outcomes, and drawing conclusions. Or they can simply sit back and enjoy listening to the story or even sit "reading the pictures" by themselves.

The list of daily tasks and routines that can be shared with young children is long. The content of the task is not as important as the attitude of the adult who invites the child to join in useful everyday pursuits. At a time when young children are eager to participate in the real world you can help them to gather information about how to operate effectively in it. Look for books that relate to any household task or hobby that can be shared with children. Allowing them to join you can develop skills and might make the time you spend in and around your home more rewarding for you as well. You may find yourself whistling rather than grumbling while you work.

6

The Beginning Book Bag: Books That Touch the Heart

In the earliest months of life children use their eyes, ears, noses, skin, and mouths to gather data about the world around them. They need a well-orchestrated environment that provides them with stimulation that is interesting and even exciting, but not overwhelming. Both boredom and overstimulation are causes of infant distress. Caretakers learn from observing the child in their care what level of stimulation is pleasant.

During these earliest months children do not differentiate between themselves, their mother or primary caretaker, and their surroundings. The child is "one" with them. There is no concept of the "self" that is separate. Children feel good about the world and themselves when their need for food, warmth, dryness, affection, stimulation, and rest are met by their caretakers. At this developmental level children are not aware of books as the source of emotional or cognitive material. Reading aloud is certainly an important and comforting experience, but the books themselves do not yet interest the child.

Many theorists and researchers agree with psychologist Erik Erikson who asserts that it is during infancy when children are very dependent that they establish their fundamental attitude toward life. He believes that if children experience consistent, need-fulfilling caretaking they will build a basic attitude of trust toward the world around them and the people in it. If their caretakers can be counted on to provide them with physical and emotional necessities; if they are fairly quick in responding to signs of discomfort and distress; and if they can be relied upon to return after brief absences, then the children will come to feel that the world is a secure, satisfying place. If their caretakers are ineffective, unresponsive, or frequently absent for long periods, the children may develop a basic feeling of distrust toward the world and the people in it. Abraham Maslow, another psychologist, studied people who led unusually productive and happy lives. He concluded that before they can move out and satisfy their needs for self-esteem and self-actualization, children must have their early needs for safety, a sense of belonging, and love fairly well met.

Six Months to One Year

Many stories for children who are very young speak to their earliest needs, those of security, belonging, and protection. In Platt & Munk's board book *My First Book of Animal Babies* a sense of caring and connectedness is conveyed. The baby chimpanzee and baby panda are nestled close to their mothers. The mother of the baby hippopotamus watches over him when they swim together in the river. The baby giraffe shows his pleasure at being licked by his mother. The mother elephant teaches her calf how to stay cool in their hot environment. Children love books that mirror the security, protection, and oneness they feel with their mother.

Children may also enjoy Debby Slier's *Whose Baby Are You?* In this book children can turn the split pages and play a game of finding which baby animal goes with which animal mother. In the classic *Where's My Baby*, by H. A. Rey, children can participate with the animal mothers in finding their babies by opening a flap on the right-hand page.

One Year to Eighteen Months

Somewhere between just under the age of one and continuing to about the age of two (depending on the child and depending on the theorist you read), children begin what Margaret Mahler calls "the hatching period" or the stage when they begin to separate themselves from their primary caretaker. Prompted by their own developing physical powers, children begin to creep and crawl and then to stand upright and walk on their own. At the same time they are also powerfully drawn into the world around them by a compelling curiosity. During this exploratory period, children need to know that their caretaker will watch over them.

Make Way for Ducklings, by Robert McCloskey, assures readers that the mother duckling will go to great lengths to protect her babies. She is confident, competent, and clever enough to do so despite the setting of a busy city. The mother duck teaches her children not only how to swim and dive but also "to walk in a line, to come when called, and to keep a safe distance from bikes, scooters, and other things with wheels." Adding to the ducklings' security is the evidence that humans will also cooperate in the challenge of seeing to it that the ducklings remain safe. When the duck family reaches a busy intersection, Michael, the traffic officer, halts the traffic so that they can cross safely into the garden. In a world where cars and trucks threaten children, this tale is particularly comforting.

At the age of about one year when they begin to walk, if they have the security of knowing there is a mother or primary caretaker to whom they can always return for reassurance and affection, toddlers will be free to enjoy a period some developmentalists refer to as their "love affair with the world." Just as in infancy when they felt that they were "one" with their mother, now they feel "one" with the sensory world they are entering and exploring. Toddlers are fascinated by the textures, colors, sounds, and shapes of all that they encounter on their excursions away from mother. Rachel Isadora's illustrations in her book *I See* convey children's experiences when they touch a cat, slip down a slide, throw a ball, and engage in new, fresh, and thoroughly absorbing experiences. In later stages, when children seem to have moved away from this sense of exhilaration with the ordinary, a book like *Time of Wonder*, by Robert McCloskey, may help them to recover some of what they have lost. Chapters 3 and 4 contain detailed discussions of many early books that reflect the child's delight in the world as discovered through the senses.

When children move into new stages, they are not usually

finished with the challenges or behaviors of a previous stage. It is therefore important to find books that reflect and respond to the content of early developmental stages. The famous classic *Curious George* is just such a book, delighting older children who also occasionally become intoxicated with their explorations.

Striving for competence is a drive that occupies much of the time and energy of toddlers. "I want to do it myself!" manifests itself in behavior even before the child is able to express it verbally. For example, children often insist on feeding themselves before they are coordinated enough to use a spoon with any accuracy. They will take the spoon from a parent's hand or refuse to open their mouths to be fed. They may also develop strong opinions about clothing and struggle to dress themselves despite the fact that they lack the coordination to negotiate the placement of five toes in one sock. At around a year of age, early talkers may begin using sounds or single words to try to communicate their wishes. A number of books depict very young children developing competence without negating their need for belonging and security. Reading these books with your children will communicate that you approve of their efforts to do things for themselves.

Some authors portray the toddler's compulsion to become competent and independent with such freshness and sensitivity that young readers are certain to think that the author has read their minds. One board book designed for the hands of a toddler, *I Can* by author and illustrator Helen Oxenbury, shows a round-faced toddler thoroughly pleased with himself and his abilities to sit, crawl, jump, stomp, dance, run, slide, bend, stretch, kick, wave, and even fall. Each page is white except for a single action-word and a simple picture in which the pose and facial expression of the toddler reveal both his effort and his delight.

In a story for somewhat older children, Shigeo Watanabe's *I Can Build a House*, a little bear is pleased when he builds himself a small house out of blocks. When it tumbles down around him, he constructs a somewhat larger house from larger blocks. When this too collapses, he finds a large carton, experiments with it, and is rightfully satisfied when it stands the test the others failed. He declares happily, "Now I've got it./I did it all by myself!" The story accurately depicts the joy of the challenge and the toddler's pleasure in accomplishing a task on his own. It is somewhat less realistic about the frustrations of temporary failure. Many tod-

dlers would have a difficult time facing two collapses with as muc
equanimity as the bear in this story does, but he provides a good
model of perseverance.

The Older Toddler: Eighteen Months
to Three Years

For the older toddler there is also Christa Chevalier's funny book,
Spence Makes Circles. In this story a little boy is very busy with
pencils, glue, and scissors. Whenever his mother asks whether she
can help, Spence says, "NO, I can do it myself." In the course of his
project, Spence gets glue in his hair. He "solves" the problem by
cutting his hair. The hair falls into the glue. Spence retrieves the
hair from the gluepot, scratches his nose, and creates a moustache.
Spence's mother reacts to his appearance with surprise, a mirror, a
laugh, and the comment, "Just think, you did it all by yourself."
Then Spence laughs too and his mother takes him to the bathroom
and cleans him up. They both seem to feel that the price of
Spence's independence wasn't too high.

Both Piaget and Mahler have noted that between eighteen
months and two years of age the quality of children's experience of
the world begins to change. The sensory exploring and experiencing of the world is now supplemented with the beginnings of
complex thought. Children now can be observed pausing, ponder-
ing, thinking. They begin reflecting, experimenting, trying to
understand how the world works, and what happens when one
treats objects in a certain way. When something is dropped, does
it always move in the same direction? When different objects are
thrown into the bathtub, which ones will stay on the top and which
ones will sink to the bottom? In short, children now realize that
the world is separate from themselves. They want to gain some
degree of understanding, and using their minds they now *can* gain
some degree of understanding and control. They discover the laws
of physics, chemistry, mathematics, relations, and patterns in the
physical world. Books relating to these cognitive explorations,
discoveries, and consolidations of understanding are discussed in
chapter 4.

Emotional changes are also occurring in the child in conjunction with cognitive growth and change. The laws of human relationships are also being explored. Children now have learned that

their mother is not an extension of themselves. They know that she can go away from them and they learn not to fear her absence when she returns promptly and consistently. They are beginning to be able to hold a mental image of their mother, an inner sense of her which makes separations less difficult. Children also test what will happen when they move away from their mother and become preoccupied with something else. They come back to her frequently, checking whether she is still where they left her, still available as a secure beacon. When you read books to your child about animals or children who move away from their caretakers and enjoy themselves, you are communicating that you understand and approve of their burgeoning independence. You are also reassuring them that their feelings are shared.

Children at this stage engage in many forms of the peek-a-boo game. Books respond to this interest. In peek-a-boo games the child is playing with the issue of separation. When children cover their faces they are playing with both the excitement and anxiety that come with separation and independence. The beauty of the game is that they are in control. While at an earlier age children may have played this game, and even enjoyed these books, the same level of understanding was not achieved.

Moo, Moo, Peekaboo by Jane Dyer is a well-designed board book for young children. On each page of the book a large animal is shown in a farm environment and the reader is asked, "What else can we see?" Each page has a tiny slot, hole, or window through which an animal on the next page can be viewed. Children enjoy glimpsing the piglet through the hole in the cow's stall, and then turning the page to see the same piglet in the company of his huge mother and tiny siblings. They can then look through the slot in the door of the pig's stall to see a foal's face. When they turn the page, they can observe the bucolic contentment of the foal and its mother and then discover a tiny chick who is seen through a hole at the bottom corner of the page. In no case is an animal pictured without its parent.

Many other board books have recently been published that allow young children to see peek-a-boo games being played on the printed page. They will be found in "The Bookshelf." It is no coincidence that one of the most popular and enduring books for toddlers, *Pat the Bunny*, includes a peek-a-boo page. Though

times may change, many of the fundamental challenges and preoc-
cupations of young children have not.

My Blanket Burt is a more recently published participatory
book similar in format to *Pat the Bunny*. On every page there is
something for the reader to do, a flap to lift, a texture to feel, a part
to move. Children, and perhaps parents too, will be surprised and
amused when they find a bag of nuts under the father's cloth tie. As
in *Pat the Bunny* there is a peek-a-boo page. In this story a little
red-headed boy has a soft yellow blanket named Burt that he takes
everywhere with him. Burt is his security blanket. Many children
carry such security objects at the stage when they are moving
toward independence and are somewhat anxious about their separations from their caretaker. In this story the boy loses his blanket
and searches for it. The boy is bereft for a while, but he soon finds
his blanket in the washing machine and celebrates his reunion
with it.

In Robie Harris's *I Hate Kisses*, a little boy declares that he is
ready to give up his security object, his stuffed dragon, Nellie. He
says he's also ready to give up kisses. At the end of the day, when
Peter is tired, he trips over one of his toy trucks and falls on the
sharp edge of his toy robot. Dissolving into tears, Peter calls for
his parents and his Nellie. He also accepts a kiss on his hurt knee.
In bed later that night he once again rejects his parents' kisses, but
is willing to hug them and falls asleep hugging his Nellie. Just as it
is sometimes difficult to be away from mother or caretaker, so too
the transition toward independence from security blankets and
stuffed animals is rarely a smooth or complete one. (Note the
number of adults who are infatuated with teddy bears.) Slowly,
however, with the help of consistently returning caretakers, security blankets, peek-a-boo games, stuffed animals, and books
such as the ones above, children make the mental changes necessary to endure separations and enjoy a little independence.

In *Geraldine's Blanket* author Holly Keller recognizes the love
and sense of security that can be invested in a blanket. When
Geraldine Pig's mother and father insist that she give up her
flowered pink blanket, a constant companion, Geraldine invents a
solution: she dresses her doll, Rosa, in a piece of it and continues to
play with Rosa. Here is a child moving toward autonomy, designing strategies to ease her transition.

In Margaret Wise Brown's *The Runaway Bunny* most children readily identify with the bunny who simply wants to experience a little freedom. No misbehavior or incident of conflict stimulates this desire. It is there, as it is in most youngsters. The book opens with his announcement, "I am running away." Wisely, his mother does not reprove him. She simply states that she will go after him. And so begins a fantasy game in which the bunny tries to hide, and his mother finds him. The bunny becomes a trout; his mother goes fishing for him with a carrot as bait. The bunny becomes "a crocus in a hidden garden"; his mother pursues him, watering can, hoe, and basket at the ready. When he takes flight as a winged bunny she becomes a leafy tree for him "to come home to." The message is clear: mother is always there with nourishing food and sustaining love.

It is noteworthy that in this case it is the child who leaves, not the mother. The child is the doer and not the person being left. This parallels the situation of the young child who is beginning to move out on his own. For the first time he is in control of the separation process, while in the past it was the mother who came and went.

While *The Runaway Bunny* addresses the issue of physical separation stemming from the child's choice, few books help children confront the issue of the caretaker's leaving the child. In 1949, Dorothy Kunhart included the story of *Mrs. Sheep's Little Lamb* in her series of tiny books. In this story a lamb gets separated from her mother at the grocery store. A friendly manager finds the child in tears and she is soon reunited with her mother. Although the very small size of the book and animal characters are used to lighten the story, the situation is a realistic and frightening one. The story is well enough resolved to make this a very useful book to read with young children. It can help them acknowledge their fears and help them think about what they would do if they were lost.

Are You My Mother? is an amusing fantasy about a little hatchling whose mother has gone in search of food just before he hatched. The baby bird goes to look for her and asks many different animals if they are his mother. He also asks a few mechanical creatures, one of whom is a steam shovel. The shovel transports him back to his nest where he is reunited with his mother. When seriously disturbing issues, such as abandonment, are presented humorously but respectfully in literature, they provide an opening for discussion of topics that might not otherwise be broached.

A recent, and valuable, addition to the short list of books dealing directly with young children's fears of separation is Dorothy Corey and Lois Axeman's story *You Go Away*. This well-constructed, developmental story begins with a child playing peek-a-boo, going "away" by hiding her mother behind a pink blanket, and being reunited with her simply by dropping the blanket. Next we see a father throwing his baby son in the air ("Away") and catching him ("Back"). Third, we see just a mother's feet going out the door and a sad-faced toddler watching her leave. The picture is captioned, "You go away." On the following page the delighted child greets his mother on her return, ". . . and you come back." In subsequent pages there is a variety of coming and goings of both children and parents, focusing on the consistency of the return. The book's effect is cumulative and useful. Some of the added advantages of this book are its avoidance of gender stereotypes and its inclusion of many races.

Wesley Dennis's story of *Flip*, which has stayed in print for more than forty-five years, also concerns issues of separation. In this case Flip's mother separates herself from her foal by jumping over a stream. She does so because she is fed up with his antics. Flip exhausts himself whinneying and trying to get across the stream. When he falls asleep, he dreams that he has wings and can fly over the fields and over the barn as well as over the brook. When he wakes he feels as though he still has wings, takes a long running start, and soars over the brook to join his mother. When he looks over his shoulder, he realizes that he has no wings but has the newfound ability to control his own behavior. Children readily identify with Flip and his mother and seem to understand the feelings of both characters.

Toilet training can be experienced by some children as confirmation of their autonomy and an exciting move toward independence. The process is more likely to go smoothly if the child feels that he is in charge of himself, learning a skill that is important to him, rather than if the child feels that he is doing something for his parents alone. Mr. Rogers has written a straightforward book for children called *Going to the Potty*. The book is illustrated with photographs of fathers and mothers of different races, all of whom model an awareness of the children's feelings and needs at this sensitive stage. Other books on this topic are listed in "The Bookshelf."

Toilet training, like most tasks, develops in stages. In *All By Myself* by Anna Grossnickle Hines, Josie and her mother review the many things that Josie has learned to do by herself since she was a baby. Josie then announces that she is ready to sleep through the night without diapers. Her mother respects her statement of readiness. For a number of nights Josie stays dry. One night Josie's mother forgets to leave the light on in the hallway, and Josie has to overcome her fear of the dark in order to get to the bathroom in the middle of the night. When she succeeds in doing so she is delighted with her new competence.

Unless the process of toilet training has proceeded with unusual self-direction, with no pressure, and with tolerance for occasional lapses, it sometimes seems to the young child that the primary caretaker's love is no longer unconditional. In order to stay loved by mother the child feels he has to use the toilet as requested. Acquiescence results in smiles and praise while failure, forgetting, or refusal result in disapproval. Books about other children who are learning to use the toilet, who make occasional mistakes, and who feel occasional ambivalence about this new sign of growing up and taking control of themselves can be very useful to young children struggling with the same issues.

At around the same time, though it may have started earlier in small doses, parents and caretakers also begin expecting children to resist touching certain things and to be able to postpone some sorts of gratification. Instead of moving breakable objects out of a baby's reach or distracting the young child from certain objects or activities, caretakers are increasingly likely to say "No" and expect toddlers to control their impulses. It is essential for young children to be given firm limits that they can slowly make their own. This process can sometimes be a great strain for the toddler who still wants desperately to maintain his caretaker's approval.

In Anne Sibley O'Brien's carefully written and realistically illustrated board book *Don't Say No!* children will find evidence that someone understands their struggle and the pain that can come with too many no's. Little Jessie is told by her father that she may not have a cookie before lunch. Then she is told that she may not go outside to play because it is time to eat. Finally she is told that she may not look at another book because it is time to come to the table. She dissolves in tears of anger and frustration, screaming, "No, no, no! Don't say no!" A hug from her mother and the question acknowledging understanding, "Have we been saying no too much?" enables Jessie to say "yes" when she is invited to join the family at the lunch table. Although the limits have not been removed, her parents' understanding of the difficulties of living with new demands helps Jessie to feel happy again.

In Miriam Schlein's book *The Way Mothers Are* a little kitten struggles hard to understand why his mother loves him. When he concludes that it is because he is nice more often than he is disobedient, she says that that is not the reason that she loves him. He is loved, not because of his charms and accomplishments, but because he is her little one. She does not stop loving him when he is loud or naughty. She loves him all the time because that is the way mothers are.

Children want to know that they are unconditionally loved, that even when they do something naughty, something explicitly prohibited, the result may be that they are frightened, uncomfortable, and/or punished but they will retain their parents' love and not be rejected. Perhaps this acknowledgment accounts for the lasting popularity of such books as *The Tale of Peter Rabbit* by Beatrix Potter, *Where the Wild Things Are* by Maurice Sendak, *The Story About Ping* by Marjorie Flack, and *Harry, the Dirty Dog* by Gene Zion. In each of these books the child misbehaves and although he must suffer some of the consequences of that misbehavior, he is welcomed back into his family, and their love for him is not impaired. When love withstands this sort of test, it is often strengthened. Children learn that they can venture forth, try their wings, make mistakes and still be loved. For example, in *Where the Wild Things Are* Max not only tames the wild things in his dreams, he tames the wild things in himself and has the strength and competence to rid himself of these monsters.

Edna Mitchell Preston's *The Temper Tantrum Book* presents children with seven animals, each of whom is having a temper tantrum. Lionel Lion is "hopping, roaring, raging, and crying." Why? Because he hates it when his mother insists on combing out his tangled mane. Elizabeth Elephant is "kicking and hitting and howling/And screaming with all her power." Why? Because her mother is getting soap in her eyes while giving her a shower.

Persnickety Pig is in a state because someone else got the biggest piece. And so it goes. The use of animal characters allows children the dignity and safety of a certain distance from the characters, yet in colorful, specific language the author describes situations with which many toddlers and their parents can readily identify.

In many cases a tantrum is set off by frustration that threatens the toddler's just-developing sense of independence, ability, or autonomy. You may be in a hurry and ask her to move at your pace rather than hers. Or you may simply be insisting on her doing something that is essential for her health and safety. Whatever the case, it is important for both of you to know that emotional fuses can be blown and reset, that a tantrum can be endured and will not damage your relationship. *The Temper Tantrum Book* ends with a mother hippopotamus and child happily wallowing in the mud together. Children need to know that although they may rage against their caretakers, the caretakers will continue to love them and affirm their moves toward independence whenever possible.

In Susan Marie's *I Will Not Wear That Sweater* a little girl recites a list of the numerous pieces of clothing that she will wear as well as the one sweater that she will not put on. Many of the clothes that are acceptable to the child may seem to the reader to be far less attractive than the rejected sweater. This adds to the reality of the situation. Sometimes children have an inexplicable aversion to a piece of clothing, an activity, a person, or a food. Unless the rejected thing is essential to the child's welfare, it may not hurt to accede to the child's wishes and bolster the child's developing opinions. In the long run the goal is to have children make constructive choices for themselves.

Sometimes children handle their conflicts in a defensive fashion. Instead of daring to speak out about their frustrations, their wishes, or their choices, they cover them over with seeming indifference or statements of not caring. Maurice Sendak has captured this situation in the story *Pierre*. When Pierre's mother tells him that he is her only joy, he says he doesn't care. When she asks him what he wants to eat, his reply is "I don't care." When she tells him that he is acting like a clown, his retort is the same. Finally, when she and Pierre's father ask Pierre if he wants to go downtown, Pierre repeats the same refrain and is left behind. When a hungry lion comes to the house and asks whether Pierre would mind being eaten, Pierre once again declares that he doesn't care. So he is eaten. When Pierre's parents return home they find Pierre gone and a sick lion in bed. Putting two and two together, they take the lion to the doctor and Pierre is extracted. Pierre emerges, rubs his eyes, and when the lion asks if Pierre would care to be given a ride home Pierre readily changes his tune and shouts, "Yes, indeed, I care."

According to Mr. Sendak, the moral of his "cautionary tale" is "care!" While some readers may feel that Pierre's indifference to his parents is in need of change, others may believe that it is Pierre's parents who need to learn about caring. Some young children affect indifference when they feel that their wishes are overwhelmed by the strength of their parents' opposition. The conclusion is less important than the opportunity the book provides for children and their parents to discuss Pierre's attitude.

Beyond the fear that tantrums and naughtiness will undermine the security and belonging children long for, other fears challenge young children. Many of these fears arise from situations that are completely outside the child's realm of control. Books can help them know that other children share their feelings. Separation and the move toward competence and autonomy are difficult steps. There are few children who progress in a straight line. Ambivalence and anxiety are the norm.

Even children who seem confident in their daytime venturing forth, who seem to be unafraid of short separations and becoming increasingly competent and independent, often find nighttime separations from their caretakers very difficult. One book that reflects this process is *Goodnight Moon* by Margaret Wise Brown. The author and illustrator exhibit a profound understanding of how difficult it is for many young children to let go of the familiar and secure daytime world and go alone into the night to sleep.

Margaret Wise Brown has also written *The Child's Good Night Book*. In this story she devotes one page to each of nine different animals, each of which is described as ceasing its daily activities and going to sleep. The cumulative effect is serenity and slowing down, a perfect ending to a busy day. The book closes with a prayer.

John Graham and Tomie dePaola have collaborated on *I Love You, Mouse*. On each of twelve double-page spreads, a small boy tells an animal that he loves it and that if he were its caretaker, he would provide it with an especially appealing home and join it in

143

an especially enjoyable activity. On the last pages, the child's father picks him up and carries him into the house. When we hear the father telling the boy he is loved, has been given a house, a bed and warm quilts, a cool drink of water, a kiss on the nose, and a quiet good night, we realize that the child has learned his loving ways from his caretaker. Their patterns of reassurance are identical.

Wake Up and Goodnight written by Charlotte Zolotow and illustrated by Leonard Weisgard is another good-night book of great appeal. Although one small section of it is reminiscent of *Goodnight Moon* it adds another reassuring element, the cycle of day and night. The simple text and illustrations begin by depicting a number of daytime events. The illustrations are bright and cheerful. The book then moves to the night, describing first the world outside and then the world inside. Grown-ups downstairs are talking quietly and playing checkers. The children upstairs come warm from their baths, read in their beds, say good night to their dog. Then the light is turned out and familiar items are barely visible in the "friendly dark."

Bedtime for Frances by Russell Hoban is the story of a warm and loving family that has a great capacity for patience with all of little Frances's stalling tactics at bedtime. After many reassurances and indulgences, Frances's exhausted father helps her end her procrastinations in an effective manner. The story is told with humor and good sense.

Cynthia Rylant's recent book, *Night in the Country*, illustrated by Mary Szilagyi, helps children accept, and even listen for, the sounds that stand out in the dark country night. She enables children to make friends with "the night and nighttime things" by presenting them one by one: great owls who swoop, night frogs singing, dogs' chains clinking, apples falling, houses squeaking, groaning, and thumping. Without denying their potential to frighten, the author and illustrator encourage children to overcome their fears.

Many good-night stories are among the most aesthetically pleasing of picture books. Paul Zelinsky has won numerous honors for his illustrations. His recent *The Sun's Asleep Behind the Hill* is adapted from an Armenian song by Mirra Ginsburg. The book presents a progression: the sun, the breeze, the leaves, a bird, a squirrel, and a child each grow tired and go to sleep. The illustrations appear increasingly veiled, until at last the moon rises and illuminates the sky and the child's room.

On Mother's Lap by Ann Herbert Scott is another book that speaks to any young child whose security is threatened. In this story the threat is not due to any act of defiance or independence seeking on the child's part. Nor is it due to something like the coming of night over which no one has control. This well-constructed story tells of a little boy who is afraid that he will be supplanted by his new baby sister in his mother's affection as well as on her lap. The mother's loving behavior demonstrates both to Michael and the child-reader that the mother has room and love enough for all. Both the text and the illustrations convey the message. The figures of the child and the mother meld into each other suggesting a oneness. The mother's figure is ample, and her ampleness of spirit also speaks deeply and sensitively to any young child. While young Michael rocks on his mother's lap, adding his favorite toys, one by one, the language rocks too; cumulative lines alternate with a sort of chorus about rocking. "Back and forth, back and forth, they rocked." When the baby's cry breaks the pattern both the pictures and language reflect Michael's anger and distress. But mother suggests that the baby can be accommodated, just as Michael's toys were. The last illustration in the book shows Michael, baby, and possessions happily ensconced on mother's lap. Young children need many demonstrations that their security will not be impaired by the birth of other children and that there will continue to be enough love to go around. The adult in this story can serve as a model to parents.

Children appreciate support during times of stress and anxiety. If you choose books that reflect your understanding of their feelings and discuss them with children, they will feel reassured about their closeness to you and will feel able to move out and explore freely once again.

Three-Year-Olds

The balance changes frequently between the need for nurturing from others (whether in the nighttime or the day) and the need to do things independently. Children have spurts of creativity, initiative, and mastery and they have periods of consolidation and reflection, using the knowledge, skill, and understanding they have acquired. There are times when they move out confidently to observe, experiment, or explore, and occasions when they are more timid, reluctant, and even afraid. Sometimes there is an obvious connection between what challenges them, fascinates them, or compels them and the things that frighten them. Sometimes there seems to be no apparent reason for their fears.

During children's periods of fearfulness it is important for parents and caretakers to focus on competencies already attained and to remind children that they can return to their caretaker for reassurance, affection, and "refueling" whenever they feel the need. Books can help in this process.

The three-year-old's behavior is often dominated by taking initiative, a drive toward personal efficacy or mastery, trying hard, and persisting. These behaviors are all part of the move toward competence. So is the courage to overcome fears. Children are attracted to characters who manifest these qualities without jeopardizing the security of being able to return to their family's protection, love, and guidance. As Abraham Maslow points out, needs are hierarchical. Without knowing that the basic needs for safety, belonging, and love will be met, children cannot move forward and seek to fulfill their needs for esteem and recognition.

Madeline (and the other books in this series) describes a feisty girl whose adventures in Paris are depicted by author-illustrator Ludwig Bemelmans. Madeline is the smallest of the children in Miss Clavel's charge. Madeline is permitted to test her powers (and at times, the limits), but she never steps so far out of line that she cannot return and resume her place among the other children under Miss Clavel's care.

The Little Engine That Could, by Watty Piper, conveys to children the efficacy of perseverance and a positive self-identity. The famous rhythmic refrain "I think I can, I think I can" touches a chord in everyone, young and old, who has struggled with a seemingly impossible task. This chant of belief in oneself may seem superficial, but it is clear to researchers that *believing* oneself to be capable often makes it so. Parents need to help children to take on tasks that will challenge but not overwhelm them, tasks that require a full investment. Children need to experience the satisfaction of persevering when success is not certain, immediate, or easy.

Mechanical creatures in literature are often imbued with human characteristics so that children can identify with them. The book *Little Toot* by Hardy Gramatky is a story of maturation. Little Toot wants very much to make his father proud of him and to be perceived as a competent tug boat. On the other hand, he is afraid of the large ocean. He also loves to spend his time just fooling around. In the story he overcomes his self-centeredness as well as his fear when he rescues a ship in distress. Most children identify strongly with his struggles.

Virginia Lee Burton's two famous female machine-characters, Katy, the snowplow, in *Katy and the Big Snow* and Mary Anne in *Mike Mulligan and His Steam Shovel,* have spoken to children's wish for competence, power, achievement, efficacy, and respect for more than forty years. Although Mike Mulligan's beloved steam shovel, Mary Anne, lives up to Mike's boast that she can dig in one day what would take one hundred men a week, the tale is cautionary, because she has literally dug herself in. The story of *Katy and the Big Snow,* written four years later, has fewer problems. The energetic, colorful, information-packed pictures and borders help to tell the story of this strong, determined character whose beauty is not stereotypic, but is, nevertheless, notable. Katy digs out the entire town of Geopolis when all of the other vehicles have broken down under the pressure.

Despite the high achievement of the characters in these classics, children also need to know that to have a sense of competence and to be accepted by others, they do not have to be heroic. Too often, perhaps, our society stresses upward mobility and achievement. Too often parents find themselves comparing their children to other children and wondering if their child is doing "well enough." In the course of worrying and comparing, they fail to appreciate the many small but significant accomplishments of their children.

Don't fail to recognize and appreciate qualities that are as important as first steps, first words, toilet training, feeding themselves, counting to ten, learning colors, running fast, and the like. Try to notice and comment on children's development of the ability to wait and the ability to think about the needs and agendas of others. Demonstrate that you appreciate this quality as you run errands and impose your pace on your children. Praise your children for playing contentedly on their own or with siblings and friends rather than requiring you to provide them with help or companionship. Comment on their small acts of kindness. When they admit to doing something naughty, focus on their honesty. In short, recognize the development of those skills that make them people whose *character* as well as achievement you admire.

In Charlotte Zolotow's *One Step, Two* a little girl goes for a walk with her mother. Along the way the child stops to point out a yellow crocus, a blue jay, a very round white pebble, and other "common" sights. When they return home the mother thanks the little girl for showing her these things. The implication is that the child enriched the adult by sharing her wonder.

In Eve Rice's story *New Blue Shoes* a girl and her mother go to the shoe store to get the child new shoes. The child insists that she wants plain blue shoes while her mother states a strong preference for brown. The little girl insists on getting plain blue shoes and on the way home suddenly has an attack of self-doubt. Once home, the mother suggests that the little girl wear her blue shoes around the house. Slowly the child regains confidence in her choice. While the mother could have tried to save the child from her discomfort either by returning the shoes for brown ones or by quickly reassuring the child about her choice, she allows the child to resolve the dilemma on her own. The message she conveys is "You can do it, you can make good decisions for yourself." You can consistently help your child develop a sense of autonomy and confidence in his or her own abilities by giving small, safe choices to make.

Another worthwhile book with a similar theme is Vera Williams's *Something Special for Me*. Rosa, a young girl, finds it difficult to make up her mind about what she wants for her birthday. The gift will be paid for with the change from the money jar that her mother and her grandmother have slowly filled. On a shopping trip with her mother she is tempted several times to select something, but each time her doubts make her change her mind. Her mother patiently empathizes with her indecision, but leaves the choice entirely in the hands of the child. Finally, on the day of her birthday, she makes her choice and has no regrets. The details of the family's economic situation as well as their palpable caring for one another add to the quality of the story's message.

Stories like Ezra Jack Keats's *Whistle for Willie* and Robert

McCloskey's tale *Lentil* celebrate children's ability to persevere. In the former, little Peter wants very much to be able to do something he has observed other people doing. He wants to be able to whistle with authority so that his dog, Willie, will pay immediate attention and run straight to him. He sets this goal for himself. After many tries, when Peter finally succeeds in learning to whistle, the reader shares in his delight. So do his parents. They recognize and acknowledge his growing up by sending him to the store alone on an errand.

Whistle for Willie is set in an urban environment. The equally popular book *Lentil* is set in a small Ohio town. Lentil wants to be able to sing, or at least whistle, but he can't. He persists in wanting to make music and finally resolves his dilemma by purchasing a harmonica. Lentil's playing gains the attention of the whole town. The pride Lentil has in his everyday playing is noteworthy and satisfying. Children who are struggling to gain mastery sometimes find that what they have undertaken is not possible for them. When they find alternatives they will not be devastated by their failures.

Sometimes children are much slower than their peers in gaining certain basic competencies. Or they are simply slower than "the charts" say they should be, or than their siblings were, or than their parents wish they would be. In Richard Kraus and Jose Aruego's book *Leo, the Late Bloomer,* Leo, a small sad-faced tiger, cannot read, write, draw, or eat neatly, and he does not say a word. When Leo's father asks Leo's mother what is the matter with Leo she says that he is a late bloomer. When Leo's father watches him for signs of "blooming," the mother declares that "A watched bloomer doesn't bloom." After a number of anxious seasons, Leo suddenly flourishes. He can read, write, draw, speak in sentences, and eat neatly. The story closes with a smiling family portrait and Leo's statement, "I made it." The sense of relief, relaxation, and affection are palpable. It is important to realize, however, that Leo was never the problem; his parents' unreasonable expectations were, and could have caused problems if they had not been content to wait.

Sometimes children are challenged by the adults they live with to take on responsibilities they feel they could live more happily without. In *The Terrible Thing That Happened at Our House* by

Marge Blaine, a different sort of situation prevails. The young children in this story are accustomed to their mother's performing all sorts of services for them, including finding their underwear and socks. When the "terrible thing" happens, and their mother takes a teaching job outside their home, the children are miserable. They have enjoyed being waited on, and it is difficult for them to understand that they are better off doing things for themselves. They finally learn that if they share in doing laundry, dishes, and other household chores, their parents will have time to read to them and pay attention to them. The lesson that everyone must cooperate and take responsibility if the family is to be harmonious and cohesive again is brought to readers through very amusing illustrations of a realistic series of incidents.

Sometimes children are afraid that in growing up, in becoming more competent and independent, they will lose something very precious. Occasionally children show reluctance to read because they are afraid that they will lose the deep satisfactions that come from sitting in a loving adult's lap and being read to. Ruth Bornstein has captured the fear of growth and change in her story *Little Gorilla*. When the story opens, a tiny, sweet, fluffy baby gorilla is shown being adored by his mother, his father, his grandparents, and each of the many creatures in the forest. Each page communicates the affection, warmth, love, and acceptance the little gorilla receives.

Then the little gorilla begins to grow. Now the animals who adored him in the past seem to be standing at a distance from him. He has now become a very large, melancholy gorilla. His sense of being loved, despite his size, is reestablished when all the animals come running, singing and carrying a cake with five candles to Little Gorilla's birthday party. The book closes with the same picture of Little Gorilla's face that was found on the opening page. The only difference is that it is greatly enlarged. Beneath it are the words "And everybody still loved him."

Although all growth and change may involve giving up something as well as gaining something, adults can help children appreciate and feel confirmed in the gains. Read this humorous yet deep book with your children if you have the feeling they are concerned that they will lose some connection with you because they are growing up quickly. It will be evidence of your understanding and of your continuing closeness.

Four-Year-Olds

In addition to building an increasing repertoire of skills and competencies about which they can feel proud and that enable them to feel confident in their increasing independence, children also feel a special kind of power when they are able to give to their parents and to those whom they love. Although it is enjoyable, it is also somewhat diminishing to always be the recipient in a relationship. It feels good to be able to give. A number of books for young children reflect this.

In *Mr. Rabbit and the Lovely Present* by Charlotte Zolotow, illustrated by Maurice Sendak, a little girl gets help from a large rabbit in her search for the right present for her mother's birthday. There is a pattern to their search: the little girl names a color that her mother likes; the rabbit declares that you cannot give someone a color and then suggests a number of items of that color, including some things that are impossible to give, but each time ending with the suggestion of a specific fruit. This delights the child because fruit is possible for her to give and is something her mother likes. Together the small girl and the large rabbit make a lovely present, a basket of many colored fruits. Children who are learning to classify by color and who are learning that giving is a part of loving may enjoy this simple story.

In *A Chair for My Mother*, by Vera Williams, a Caldecott Honor Book, a little girl, her mother, and grandmother all find ways to save coins to put in their large glass jar. When it is full, they plan to buy a chair, "a wonderful, beautiful, fat soft armchair . . . covered in velvet with roses all over it . . . the best chair in the whole world." The chair is for Mother, who returns each evening with aching feet from her work at the Blue Tile diner. The pleasure the little girl takes in contributing to saving for this chair, anticipating it, selecting it, watching her mother and grandmother using it, and in sometimes sharing it with her mother provides a model for young readers.

Zamani Goes to Market, written by Muriel L. Feelings and illustrated in earth tone drawings by Tom Feelings, tells the story of Zamani, a young East African child, and his first trip to market with his father and older brothers. At the end of the day, having done his share of work, his father hands him two coins. Zamani has a difficult time deciding what to buy. After much inner debate,

Zamani thinks about how his mother always remembers to buy him sugar from the market. He resists buying a beautiful shirt for himself and spends his first money on a necklace for his mother. This story is especially valuable because it gives a picture of family life in a different culture, yet the protagonist is one with whom many young children can identify.

Learning within the parent-child relationship that give-and-take is more satisfying than just taking lays the groundwork for good sibling relations and friendships. After forming strong ties with parents, children often form their second most important relationships with their grandparents or other close relatives whose love is often very deep, freely given, and special. It is good for children to expand their understanding of people and of themselves and their roots by listening to and associating with their grandparents or other older people. Cynthia Rylant's Caldecott Honor Book *When I Was Young in the Mountains* is a mother's recollection of her own mother and father and their life together in the mountains. It is the story of kisses from her coal-covered father, of corn bread, pinto beans and okra, of swimming in the dark, muddy swimming hole after walking through the pasture and many other simple pleasures. It is the story of love of people and love of place, and of a way to share it with the next generation.

Patricia MacLachlan's *Through Grandpa's Eyes* is but one of many books depicting the special sort of love that grows between children and their grandparents when there is mutual consideration and respect. In this story the grandfather is blind, but the little boy recognizes that his grandfather sees in very special ways. The grandfather is not superhuman; he is quintessentially human. The grandmother, too, is a special person because of her talents and her view of the world. The three characters form a strong, loving unit that serves as a model for young and old. Look for other books by this author; she is sensitive and respectful, and her writing is always deep and humorous.

Granpa, by John Burningham, describes the special relationship between a little girl and her grandfather. The author is careful to present not only the times when the child and her grandfather agreed with each other, but also the times when they differed. In all cases, the sense of mutual appreciation and affection they have for each other is communicated through simple and even commonplace activities that are raised to a higher level because of the emotional tone. The final two pages show the grandfather's empty chair and the little girl going alone for a walk.

Cynthia Rylant's recent book, *The Relatives Came*, is a warm and funny book about a large group of relatives who pack themselves, lots of food, and suitcases into their old station wagon and come for a summer visit. They are a hugging, crying, laughing, talking, eating, helping group. After a time they leave and the house seems too big and too quiet. They are missed, but the book ends with the statement that they will return. This is a story about people who open their homes and hearts to one another, share fully, and then say good-bye. With relatives the ties are often strong, and memories can seem almost as tangible as the people's presence.

Four- to Five-Year-Olds

Books describing relationships with adults beyond the family can serve as models for children in their later attempts to engage in loving peer relationships. They reflect a readiness for independence of a new sort, a moving beyond the family, and tapping other sources for belonging, security, and fun. Until about age three, peers tend to engage in parallel play, but books describing friendships can lay the groundwork for later relationships.

Mushy Eggs by Florence Adams tells of David and Sam who live with their mother, a computer operator, and Fanny, their housekeeper. The children have become very attached to their wonderful caretaker. When she leaves to go back to her native land, the children mourn her absence. Because they have had the experience of friendship with an older person, the indications are positive that they will also become fond of the new caretaker their mother engages.

Hold My Hand by Charlotte Zolotow and illustrated by Thomas di Grazia is the simple story of two little girls who share both the darkness, cold, and wind of a winter's day and also the light and pleasure when the sky fills with silence and falling snow. The quality of the pictures can evoke sensory experiences in the young child and so does the warmth and reassurance that the hand of a friend can provide.

Winnie the Pooh by A. A. Milne combines the love of the protector, Christopher Robin, for all of his forest friends, and the more equitable friendships among the famous Piglet, Rabbit, Owl, Tigger, Kanga, Little Roo, and Eeyore. Each character's foibles and strengths emerge as integral parts of their escapades. For many children these characters do become friends to whom they can relate. The models of friendship and gentle and loving acceptance of weakness can be very reassuring to young children.

Acceptance and responsiveness are qualities that pervade all of the *Frog and Toad* books, written and illustrated by Arnold Lobel. This series of books and stories touches the hearts of adults as well as children with its wry but sympathetic look at relationships and the human condition through these two amphibians. Each of the episodes involves an example of the different faces of friendship as a process of affection, understanding, and accommodation.

In another series, written and illustrated by James Marshall, George and Martha are two hippopotamus friends whose relations are not always free of conflict. However, their honesty with each other, their warm and caring reactions to each other's fears and feelings, their fun together, their willingness to respect each other's limits and privacy are models of friendship humans would do well to emulate. For example, in the first story of *George and Martha Encore*, the protagonists are having a disagreement. Martha tells George that even though he thinks dancing is dumb, she will be hurt if he doesn't come to her dance recital. George goes, thinking that he will hate it. Instead, he loves Martha's performance and goes to dancing class himself the next day. Soon he is performing too.

Both characters are open to each other and to their own feelings, which can change if given a chance. In another story from the first book, *George and Martha,* we learn that Martha loves making pea soup and although George hates it he is reluctant to tell Martha. After George pours the soup into his shoes one day, Martha notices and George admits that he hates the soup but does not want to hurt his friend's feelings. Martha surprises him by telling him that friends should be honest with each other and that she too doesn't like the taste of the soup, she only likes making it.

The White Marble by Charlotte Zolotow is the story of a brief friendship. Taken to the park by his two tired parents, John Henry is the only child at the park on a very hot summer night. Then he sees Pamela, a little girl from school, and the mood of the evening changes magically. "Like two small things, intoxicated with the cool smell of rain about to come, they ran together." They share a cool drink, a quiet moment in the grass surrounded by the murmuring voices of the distant grown-ups, and cool ice sticks. When it is time for them to leave with their families, they separate. Suddenly Pamela breaks away from her family and runs to say good night to John Henry. He pulls a treasure from his pocket, a beautiful marble he found at the beginning of the evening, and gives it to Pamela. One finishes the story sensing that they may never again share or even acknowledge the wonderful connection of the evening, but that they have each experienced a moment of friendship that will be with them for a long time.

In Eric Carle's almost completely wordless book *Do You Want to Be My Friend?* a little mouse searches for someone to be his friend. He asks a number of large creatures, but animal after animal shows no interest in befriending the mouse. In the last page, however, a like-size friend has been found. To a young child, the search for a friend may seem equally arduous. The quality of illustration and the sophisticated design add to the appeal of this story.

Will I Have a Friend? by Miriam Cohen and illustrated by Lillian Hoban poses the question in a more realistic setting. A little boy walks to school for the very first time with his father. While walking he asks his father, "Will I have a friend?" His father answers, "I think so." Upon arrival the little boy sees all the noisy, laughing children and wonders where his friend is. One child is busy pretending he is a rocket, one child is busy with blocks, and others are deeply involved with clay. The little boy joins the clay pinchers, makes a man, but has no friend to show it to. It is not until nap time, a number of exclusions later, that the little boy feels another child reach out to him. By the time he goes home, he feels he has a friend. This book will serve you well if you have the sense that your child may be having a difficult time connecting with other children or has experienced some unintentional rebuff from other children whom he wishes to befriend.

The fear of not having or losing friends is certainly only one of the fears that challenges young children. Whatever the fear, books can help them know that they are not alone. The responses of adults in these stories can serve as models to parents.

In Muriel Stanek's *Who's Afraid of the Dark?*, Kenny is a generally competent child who has a deep fear of the dark. Kenny's sister and father each think of a special way to help Kenny over-come his fear. But Kenny's grandfather is most helpful. First, he tells Kenny that everyone is afraid of something, and this truth is confirmed by each member of the family. Second, he gives Kenny a small flashlight. Kenny uses it at home and also uses it at school when he discovers that the new child in the class is also afraid of the dark. No simple solution to fear is offered in this story, but the validity and universality of fears is acknowledged.

In *Willy Bear,* by Mildred Kantrowitz, the little boy who is the protagonist of the story transfers his fear of going to school to Willy, his teddy bear. The night before the first day of school, Willy is unable to fall asleep. After a drink of water, the rekindling of the light, and other accommodations, Willy is allowed to sleep in bed with the little boy. Morning finds the little boy rushing around in preparation for school. He sets Willy on a high stool in front of the window and tells Willy that he will go to school for him, meet the teacher, and try the cookies. He promises to return when school is over and tell Willy all about it. Children who share the little boy's apprehension may respond warmly to this humorous and wise story.

The more a child's fears are accepted openly and talked about with a caring adult, the more children will feel that they have the strength and ability to overcome their fears. Sometimes, when direct conversation seems too difficult, carefully chosen books can help you and your child look vicariously at the issue. There may well be periods when children seem to retreat from their in-creasingly competent and confident selves as well as times when they revel in their strengths and seem to be growing more aware, understanding, and competent by the moment. Most children learn cognitive, physical, social, and emotional strategies through an uneven process of experience, experimentation, hypothesiz-ing, assimilating, consolidation, and often reevaluating and re-learning at a more sophisticated level.

The goal, the balance to be hoped for, is to help children appreciate their strengths, to accept, and not feel undermined by, their weaknesses, and to feel that it is within their power, with the help of adults, books, and other resources, to solve their intellec-tual, social, and emotional dilemmas. Furthermore, it is very important that young children believe in the rightness of their own experiences, judgments, and conclusions, while remaining open to new information. If they develop an inner security and deep self-acceptance, they will be able to resist peer pressure and the pressure to conform to any voice, live or in print, that they believe to be wrong. Once again, there are some fine books that model this kind of inner strength and the willingness to be "different" if necessary.

In *Frederick,* by Leo Lionni, a small field mouse insists on gathering sun rays, colors, and words while the rest of his family gathers food for the winter. When the snow falls, the mice take to their winter home. After a time, Frederick sustains them with his description of the sun, brightens their spirits with his verbal pictures, and moves them to applause with his poem about the seasons. The recognition the mice give Frederick of his being a poet affirms his understanding of himself. He knows that his unique contributions are valuable.

William, in *William's Doll* by Charlotte Zolotow, wants to have a doll. His father wants him to play with trains. He also wants William to play basketball. William acquiesces, plays well, but still wants a doll. Even when he is teased by his friends, he holds fast to his wish. It is William's grandmother who buys him his doll. She clearly respects and understands William's wish to practice being a nurturing person like his father.

In *Max,* by Rachel Isadora, the protagonist is a "great baseball player." One Saturday morning Max walks his sister to her ballet class, is invited to join in, and loves dancing. From then on he warms up for his Saturday ball games at dance class. Max meets no opposition to his wish to dance. He is confident in his sense of himself and allows himself to enjoy participating with his sister and her friends.

Alice, in Barbara Cooney's award-winning *Miss Rumphius,* is a little girl who tells her grandfather that she wishes to go to faraway places and, later, live by the sea, just as he has done. He tells her she must add one goal to her list: she "must do something to make the world more beautiful." Miss Alice Rumphius travels, sees faraway places, and later settles by the sea. It is not until she is old that she thinks of a way to achieve her most difficult goal. With pockets full of seeds, Miss Rumphius, sometimes now called "that crazy old lady," scatters lupine seeds all summer long. Years later, when the land is filled with the beauty of lupine flowers, the very old woman, now known as "the lupine lady," tells the children who gather around her of her travels to faraway places and of her grandfather's words. Like the characters of William and Max, she has trusted herself, done the unconventional, and been happy because of it.

Golden MacDonald and Leonard Weisgard's story *The Little Island* has been enjoyed by children for more than forty years. In the story, a very little island has many life forms on and around it: the fog, the wind, the tide, spiders, lobsters, seals, and kingfishers, each in their season. Occasionally boats visit the lovely little island. One day a boat comes bearing a small black kitten.

The island and the kitten engage in a philosophical conversation about their identification as individuals as well as their connectedness to the larger world. Although the kitten leaves the island the reader understands that the two "friends" will retain their connection. The message is that with a sense of self-acceptance, people can be comfortable when they are alone, and can meet others and be enriched. People can find great beauty around them and understand that they are part of a larger whole.

7
Mirrors
and
Windows

Books can serve as mirrors for children, reflecting their appearance, their relationships, their feelings, and thoughts in their immediate environment. And books can also act as windows on the world, inviting young readers to begin to look beyond their most immediate surroundings. When literature is most effective, children are able to look beyond themselves and form a bond with characters and circumstances they could not otherwise encounter.

Mirroring is one process by which children begin very early in life to form their self-concepts. At first, these are derived from the reactions of the people around them, particularly those of their primary caretakers. The infant does not distinguish between self and other, internal and external. When caretakers respond to children lovingly, consistently, and promptly; when they orchestrate the infants' immediate environment so as to make the babies physically and emotionally comfortable; and when they reflect their joy and delight at the mere presence of the infant, the children come to see the world and themselves as good.

Studies have demonstrated that success in personal relationships and accomplishments at school and work depend very strongly on how one feels about oneself. Responding to our children so as to help them build a positive image of themselves is a challenge that continues well beyond their infancy. A book such as

Miriam Schlein's *The Way Mothers Are* can help by providing an example of a child who is constantly reassured that it is not his behavior that governs the mother's love, it is the simple fact of the child's *being* that makes the mother love and accept him.

As children grow older, the process becomes more complex. Although toddlers still have a deep need to be cared for by responsive, loving adults, they also need to begin developing a sense of their own competence. Their inner sense of worth is confirmed when they are permitted to begin to develop and exercise their own abilities to do things for themselves. It is important to support children's growing desire to increase their repertoire of behaviors and abilities.

For example, as has already been pointed out in chapter 3, babies should be encouraged and permitted to feed themselves. Their attempts in this act become more important than the adults' burden of cleaning up the mess that ensues. Keep reminding yourself as you comb cereal out of hair and encourage the cat to lap up the pools of milk on the floor that your child's sense of pride in self-management has fed more than his or her stomach. Clothing selection and dressing oneself are other tasks that cause consternation for parents and children. Clothes put on backwards or inside out or socks that don't match can be sources of embarrassment for parents, but in every case this needs to be weighed with the consideration of the child's feelings of satisfaction as he or she begins to take care of his or her own routine.

Even toddlers need to begin to feel self-confident and to recognize their own powers. Sometimes the process of making the transition from dependence to autonomy is a painful one. Books can help children acquire a healthy perspective on this process. In Anne Sibley O'Brien's *Come Play with Us* a toddler named Rachel is upset when her father leaves her after dropping her off at nursery school. Eventually, she joins the other children and the illustrations trace her shift from shyness to pleasure. This simple board book ends with her delight at her father's return and her triumph over her fear. Another book that deals well with the issue of a child's sense of confidence when faced with temporary separation is *Ira Sleeps Over* by Bernard Waber. Young Ira is reassured when he discovers that his friend, too, sleeps with a stuffed animal.

For the slightly older child, the book *The Terrible Thing That*

Happened at Our House, by Marge Blaine, is a humorous recounting of the negative feelings a young child has when her
mother goes back to work outside the home. The book can serve as
an entertaining catalyst for discussion and evaluation to tackle the
issue of taking responsibility, and becoming a member of a cooperative family. The girl in this book is also unhappy because her
mother has now begun to respond less sympathetically to her
stories about the teacher's reprimands. Parents must tread a fine
line between exhibiting loving and uncritical understanding and
helping their children bear the consequences of their own behavior. This is but one of many books that can be used as a basis for
conversations between parents and children, to help them guide
their struggles with the issues of independence and responsibility.

Whatever the challenges we may provide or life may set before
our children, one need remains constant: The need to have their
positive and negative feelings perceived, acknowledged, cared
about, and responded to appropriately. A helpful little book, *No
One Is Perfect* by Karen Erickson and Maureen Roffey, describes
in simple terms and cartoonlike pictures, a child who makes many
errors while striving to be perfect. Both the father and child in this
book continue going about their business without letting the
mishaps upset them unduly.

Books can provide a loving model for parental response to children's attempts to find their own style and manage their own
behavior. In *I'm Terrific*, by Marjorie Weinman Sharmat, Jason
Everett Bear, an only child, enjoys his mother's total attention and
approval. When the time comes for Jason to start being his own
person his mother does not interfere, but responds to his feelings
and his behavior with consistency and humor. In Russell Hoban's
Bread and Jam for Frances, the little badger's parents respond to
her refusal to eat anything but bread and jam with support and
acquiescence to her food preference; they feed her *only* bread and
jam for a few days until she herself finally tires of this diet. Children can see themselves reflected in these books and enjoy the
escapades as well as the resolution of the characters' dilemmas.

Most children love to hear and see in print stories that relate to
familiar feelings and experiences. They gravitate to characters
with whom they can identify, whose responses are akin to the
children's own. They seem particularly interested in those stories
that speak to those emotions that they are grappling with. These

need not be of a traumatic or catastrophic nature; they may be the ordinary day-to-day needs and interactions that occur without anyone's really thinking about them, but that make up the fabric of a child's life. Numerous books have been written and are continuously being published about such universal themes as moving away from one's familiar neighborhood; going to a doctor or a dentist's office; fears of the dark; power struggles between parents and children; fear of new situations; quarrels with friends and family; or being the "different" one because of looks, temperament, or ability. Good authors understand the worth of communicating that no person or world is perfect and that young readers need to see characters who grapple with the challenge of growing up.

Equally important for parents and concerned adults is to amass a number of books reflecting and extending children's feelings and behaviors, containing protagonists of both genders. Books such as *William's Doll* by Charlotte Zolotow and *Girls Can Be Anything* by Norma Klein can underscore the movement away from stereotypic gender roles. Publishers are increasingly aware of the need to provide balanced models for young boys and girls. They recognize that children form their role images from a variety of models, including those they see in print.

A positive feeling about oneself is one of the key factors in learning, in relationships, and in behavior. When children feel that they are lacking in some way, they react negatively. When they sense that they are not valued, or that the important people in their lives are withholding attention and affection, they become confused, hurt, and sometimes angry enough to misbehave. A number of books contain situations that parents might well use to help children recognize that they *are* valued and loved even when their behavior is not acceptable. In Rosemary Wells's book *Noisy Nora*, a tiny mouse who is a middle child, resentful of the notice her siblings are receiving, tries to capture attention in numerous unacceptable ways. She dumps silverware on the floor, slams doors, disrupts games, and flies her brother's kite down the stairs. When she withdraws from their sight and hides in a closet, they at last sense her unhappiness and search for her. When she emerges from the closet "with a monumental crash" her entire family lovingly welcomes her. Another character, in Judith Viorst's *Alexander and the Terrible, Horrible, No Good, Very Bad Day*, wakes up with bubble gum in his hair, he trips over a skateboard, his school day goes badly, his best friend lowers him to "third-best," his dentist informs him of a cavity, and he spills the ink on his father's desk. He has to, and does, cope on his own. But when he speaks up at the end of the day and says, "It's been a terrible, horrible, no good, very bad day," his mother empathically replies, "Some days are like that." The book makes it clear that the child is not rescued, blamed, or judged. Young readers are assured that life goes on even after a plethora of minor disasters.

Although authors have acknowledged the challenges of daily living, some themes have, until recently, been conspicuously absent from literature for young children. Children of heritages and cultures different from the majority rarely found themselves in print, and consequently felt either invisible or rejected. Until even more recently, books with characters having physical or mental abilities different from the "average" rarely appeared. Children with learning disabilities, slow learners, children with unusual talents, children with visual or hearing difficulties, children with illnesses or physical disabilities should, along with all of the rest of the child population, be able to see themselves in books as accepted members of their families and peer group.

Another sensitive area is the whole topic of death and dying. Perhaps because this issue is such a difficult one for adults to deal with, our society discourages us from even mentioning it to children. Or perhaps there was some notion of being able to protect our youngsters. But this avoidance has a detrimental effect, particularly on those unfortunate children who experience the loss of a loved one. They are excluded from the comfort of having open discussion about their loss, and are also deprived of the resource that books can provide for dealing with this massive trauma.

Divorce is another topic that society has been unwilling to examine in print for young children. While not happening to every child, it merits inclusion in the literature so that those ever-growing numbers of children whose parents have separated or divorced can derive solace and advice as well as develop coping strategies through seeing models of how children and adults in literature handle the situation. Children can also identify with the characters in these books and have their self-image bolstered by the fact that other people in the world have the same reactions and inclinations.

Books acknowledge that there is a basic need for children to have their unique physical, cultural, and familial identity confirmed. Books can affirm children's need to feel that they belong and are accepted by others. Through books children and adults can be helped to understand and overcome fears about everyday as well as calamitous concerns, loss, disability, and conflict.

Heritage

In the past fifteen years, publishers, authors, and illustrators have recognized that as an aid in developing a positive self-image children should encounter in print characters who not only behave and feel as they do, but also characters who look like them and whose culture and heritage are similar. Current books have affirmed the reading public's diversity and have included characters of different heritages, socioeconomic backgrounds, abilities, and life-styles. It is important to try to read books that expose your child to many groups, just as it is important to provide them with the understanding that every group contains a variety of personalities, life-styles, and values.

Books can be found that include multicultural populations as part of the story; the illustrations reflect society realistically, and a variety of cities, suburbs, rural areas, and small towns are used as settings. Characters are depicted as individuals, evidencing a sincere attempt on the author's part to avoid stereotypes. Even very young children can benefit from board books such as *What Do Babies Do?* and *What Do Toddlers Do?* with photographs, selected by Debby Slier, showing babies of different races engaged in ordinary activities. Lois Lenski's *Sing a Song of People* is another book that demonstrates the variety of races and ages of people coexisting in a city. Not every book can contain a variety of ethnic characters, but if, for example, a book is about city life, it would be helpful to a child's understanding to reflect the ethnic diversity of a typical city.

In addition to reflecting and reinforcing positive feelings about heritage, books can be instrumental in building accurate portraits and guarding against stereotyping. Children often garner bits and pieces of information that may not be accurate or that they may have heard out of context and misinterpreted. When they have books that contain authentic descriptions imbedded in stories about diverse people, the erroneous material is counteracted, and the young reader or listener can add the new information and begin to question the old.

Books such as *American Children* by Susan Kismaric, which uses photographs from the collection of the New York Museum of Modern Art, picture the changing concept of childhood over a period of more than one hundred years. The children come from different social, cultural, and economic backgrounds and from different geographic locations. Widening the circle is Dorka Raynor's *My Friends Live in Many Places*. This book depicts contemporary children from twenty-three countries and five continents who are engaged in everyday activities. Both books celebrate diversity while at the same time underscoring commonalities.

Designed as a step toward world peace, *All in a Day* contains the work of nine of the most prominent international illustrators of children's books. This book takes the reader through a twenty-four-hour period celebrating one New Year's Day, demonstrating both contrasts and similarities of children in Brazil, England, Japan, Kenya, China, Japan, Russia, Australia, and America. Designed for adults, *The Family of Man*, a collection of photographs of people from all over the world, conveys the same message: that people share universal concerns, activities, and emotions.

Perhaps the greatest gains have been made in the publishing of books containing characters whose heritage is Afro-American. Black families with many different characteristics are portrayed in various books. Children of any heritage can identify with these stories since the themes, situations, feelings, and responses are universal.

John Steptoe's books are good examples of the above. *My Special Best Words* and *Daddy Is a Monster Sometimes* particularly speak to young children and their concerns about toilet training, sibling interaction, and managing in a single-parent home. The children in these two books argue, care for each other, get into trouble, resent some of their father's restrictions, and resolve their differences. The father is portrayed as a loving human being whose behavior is not at all times exemplary, but *is* at all times caring.

Eloise Greenfield is another author whose books depict black characters in situations children will recognize and respond to.

Honey, I Love, and Other Love Poems, a book of poetry illustrated with realistic portraits of black children, reflects the experiences and perceptions of a young black girl. The child takes us with her in her play, her relationships with people, and her view of the world. One poem describes the child's appreciative response to the gift of a nickel that a woman has bequeathed her. Another talks of the transient nature of "things" and the enduring nature of poetry. All of the poems are in language very young children can understand.

If books are needed to help us see ourselves reflected and respected in the literature, it is important to provide material that helps our children acknowledge that there are many different people from many backgrounds. When you are looking for an alphabet book you may want to include *Ashanti to Zulu* by Margaret Musgrove, a book that goes through the alphabet while at the same time instructing the reader in various African traditions. In the same vein, *Moja Means One: A Swahili Counting Book* by Muriel Feelings, provides much more than the opportunity to count from one to ten. When you are looking for concept books, collect some like Tana Hoban's *Is It Red? Is It Yellow? Is It Blue?* It contains children of different races in vivid photographs.

Certainly the greater the variety of books, the more likely it is that young children will appreciate and expect diversity in the world. Remember that until age five children see everything in the outside world as part of themselves. They are building a sense of themselves that includes the rest of the world. This time is our golden opportunity to help them extend their sense of themselves into the greater family of humanity.

The Native American population is small compared to other groups, and it is not likely that all children will encounter in everyday life many representatives of this heritage. There are certain states that have many Native Americans, but this heritage is one that most children learn about through literature and media. Although much of the information contains negative stereotypes, a few Native American authors have contributed authentic reflections of their life. You might look for such books as Jamake Highwater's *Moonsong Lullaby*, which contains photographs of the activities of a Cherokee camp. The lullaby that forms the text is an affirmation of the positive quality of the Cherokee way of life. Another book full of chants, songs, and poems of Native Americans across the country is *The Trees Stand Shining: Poetry of the North American Indian* edited by Hettie Jones.

Native Americans figure in storybooks as well. *Salt Boy* by Mary Perrine is a classic tale of a young Navajo boy who wants his father to teach him how to rope a horse. The father will not teach the young boy until the child proves that he can be more responsible about performing his assigned tasks. The happy ending occurs when the boy does, indeed, prove himself responsible. Four- and five-year-olds can easily understand and enjoy the story. Two other stories especially for young children are *The Legend of the Bluebonnet*, written and illustrated by Tomie dePaola, based on Comanche Indian lore, and featuring a young orphaned girl who saves her people by giving up what she loves most. Jean Fritz is the author of a book adapted from a collection of Wampanoag Indian tales called *The Good Giants and the Bad Pukwudgies* illustrated by Tomie dePaola.

Children need to know that Native Americans still exist, and that they are like other people, and not as they are often portrayed in movies and television. Parents can help by searching for stories and books that treat Native American heritage and customs in a respectful and accurate way. One such contemporary book is *Child of the Navajos* by Seymour Reit. The story is illustrated with black-and-white photographs that show a young Navajo boy at home and at school.

First Snow by Helen Coutant demonstrates a young Vietnamese-American child's respect for her grandmother who helps the child understand that death is part of the cycle of life. Another book that helps young children to value differences of heritage (the story takes place in Japan) is *Umbrella* by Taro Yashima. The book portrays Japanese characters in an appealing fashion. Yet another such book is *A Pair of Red Clogs* by Masako Matsuno. In this book a grandmother and granddaughter enjoy sharing an age-old tradition. The book provides a close look at a small piece of Japanese-American heritage. Most parents and educators would welcome more good books that accurately portray the Asian-American populations. Currently, there are a few board books for very young children, notably those illustrated by Anne Sibley O'Brien, that include illustrations of children of Asian heritage.

The same is true of Hispanic characters. It is difficult to find books depicting the Hispanic heritage. *El Circo Magico Modelo/*

Finding the Magic Circus by Macduff Everton recounts a real-life trip the author and his son took to Mexico where they visited the Yucatan Circus. The book is written in both Spanish and English, and the illustrations are done in the style of the Huichol Indian yarn paintings. Another book in both Spanish and English which appeals to young children is *The Cuckoo's Reward/El Premio del Cuco* by Daisy Kouzel. This story is an adaptation of a Mayan legend.

In a more realistic vein, a book worth finding is *Yagua Days* by Cruz Martel. The photographs of contemporary Puerto Rico and Puerto Ricans illustrating the story help to dispel many stereotypes about the land and people of Puerto Rico. Peggy Christianson does the same for one bit of Hispanic tradition in *Carla's Surprise*. In this book Carla's classmates do not know what a tortilla is until Carla makes a batch and gives one to each child. (The book even includes a recipe for tortillas.) Carla is clearly in control of a situation that reflects her classmates' lack of information about her culture and no adults intervene. The incident can be used as a model for other opportunities for children to learn about one another.

A number of publishers have recognized the growing Hispanic population and have printed Spanish translations of popular English-language books, retaining the original illustrations. P. D. Eastman's *Are You My Mother?* is one such story that young children enjoy. Others are the entire *Clifford, the Red Dog* series by Norman Bridwell, and the *Little Bear* series by Else Minarik. Scholastic Book Services publishes the largest number of these translations, in inexpensive paperback editions. Some books were written originally in two languages. One such book, *My Mother the Mail Carrier/(Mi Mama La Cartera)*, by Inez Maury, shows a woman who is a single parent, in a nontraditional occupation. Throughout the story, it is clear that her son, Lupita, loves his mother very much and is very proud of her.

Jewish Americans represent yet another group that is subject to stereotyping. Religion, culture, life-style, and history make up the Jewish experience. The *Hannah* series of books by Mindy Warshaw Skolsky describes Hannah and her cohesive Jewish family. Hannah and her family own a diner in rural New York in the 1930s. All children can identify with Hannah's adventures and with her feelings. Jewish foods and customs are sprinkled

168

throughout the stories, forming the setting for the unfolding of the plot; the customs are presented in a natural and positive manner.

Hannah's close relationship with her grandmother provides the reader with much of the substance of the stories. Hannah's grandmother is a feisty, somewhat traditional woman who, nevertheless, is eager and willing to learn from her granddaughter. The treatment of Jewish grandparents in children's literature shows that each one is an individual, just as every grandparent in the world is unique.

Children might enjoy comparing the grandfather in *The House on the Roof* by David A. Adler with the grandfather in *Jesse and Abe* by Rachel Isadora. In the first book the children's grandfather surprises them by building a Sukkah (a houselike structure laden with fruits) on their roof in order to celebrate the holiday of Succoth, the harvest festival. This grandfather helps the children to maintain an excitement and joy in traditional rituals. In the second book, the grandfather is a stage door attendant, and with his grandson, he shares a very special relationship that helps each of them to reinforce his own worth.

In *A Mitzvah Is Something Special* author Phyllis Rose Eisenberg introduces us to two very unusual and very dissimilar grandmothers. One is conventional and the other is a modern single woman, but each reinforces the traditional Jewish value placed on doing a *mitzvah* (a good deed). What is embodied here in these stories of children interacting with their various grandparents is the basic value of love and respect for older people and for family ties. Children of any heritage can recognize and relate to the special bonds between these grandparents and grandchildren.

One genre that helps children see themselves and their heritage depicted in a positive light is that of the folktale or fairy tale. At the same time, these tales lead young readers to make connections with other cultures. *The Tale of Meshka the Kvetch* by Carol Chapman is an amusing story written in folktale style, in which an old woman learns an important lesson about the value of focusing on the positive rather than always complaining. With a little research, you'll discover other cultures that have tales with the same or similar lessons.

Some themes are so powerful that they appear in the tales of many cultures. *Yeh-Shen,* the Chinese Cinderella, retold by Ai-Ling Louie and illustrated by Ed Young, is a retelling of the very first Cinderella story the world has known. In the Vietnamese version, *In the Land of Small Dragon* by Manh Kha Dang, the story is basically the same. These are books to have on hand in order to help children see the universality of themes. Any of the more than five hundred additional versions of *Cinderella* that are part of every world culture can be used to entertain children while at the same time reinforcing the fact that folk themes are a part of the entire human experience.

Special Needs

Diversity includes more than heritage. Anyone who looks or feels different from the majority needs to be acknowledged and included as a full member of society. Since 1981, the International Year of Disabled Persons, the public has been more conscious of the presence and needs of disabled people. Many buildings and streets have been renovated to provide accessibility to wheelchairs; more and more elevators and public buildings contain special signs, written in Braille, so that people with visual impairments can manage to find their own way; some programs on television are interpreted simultaneously by people using sign language so that viewers who have a hearing disability may enjoy the presentation. Since 1978, when the federal law was enacted requiring that disabled children remain as much as possible in a regular classroom setting, more children have been mainstreamed, permitting children with a variety of physical, mental, and emotional abilities to interact with one another. This enables children to experience their similarities as well as their differences.

Although giftedness should not be viewed as a disability, our society sometimes imposes handicaps on children with advanced abilities. Books that invite empathy with people who have talents should be among those acknowledging the necessity for valuing differences. One such book for young children is *Crow Boy* by Taro Yashima. In this story set in Japan, a child who is very different from the rest of his classmates is finally acknowledged because of his abilities. You can use this story and others like it to invite children to see beyond the immediate differences of a person, and to look for giftedness in everyone. The story also brings out the fact that even people with special talents have feelings, needs, and common interests that bind them together with people whose talents may be in other domains.

Before 1980 it was difficult to locate any literature that dealt fairly with characters who had disabilities. As a matter of fact, if a character had a disability it was probably a signal that this was either an evil person or a saint. Canes and eye patches indicated deformities and were used as literary devices to reflect an impaired personality; wheelchairs often indicated that the character would die young. In any case, the character was usually described by what he or she could *not* do, rather than what he or she *could* do.

Partly because of the absence of accurate descriptions and inclusion of characters with disabilities in literature, disabled people have found it very difficult to develop a positive self-concept and gain their appropriate status in our society. They have been required to prove that they are superhuman in order to gain ordinary acceptance. Another consequence is that "normal" children are also victims of the myths that surround the topic of special needs. They are often afraid to talk to or even approach people with disabilities. They fear people who look different and sometimes assume that they will be harmed in some way by the disabled person.

There are now a number of books for young children that include characters who have disabilities, or who have other distinguishing factors such as giftedness or talent, who are abused, or who suffer from the results of an adult's substance abuse. There are also books about children who are obese or whose appearance is in the extreme range of development, that is, they are taller than average or very small. When these books treat the characters as people whose feelings and responses are comparable with those of the rest of the population, and when they are respected as individuals and not paraded as abnormal, then young children will be treated to well-balanced stories and to messages that they can carry with them to life experiences.

Young children can appreciate a book like *The Balancing Girl* by Bernice Rabe, a story about a clever and talented child who is excellent at balancing things. Margaret has feelings: she becomes angry and she herself demonstrates empathy for another child's feelings of inadequacy. The fact that she must use a wheelchair to get around is only one of her attributes. The story focuses mainly on what she *can* do and how she uses her talents to help another child in the story to resolve his problem. Another book, *He's My Brother* by Joe Lasker, written from the perspective of a young child's older brother, describes the problems the younger child has (he is a slow learner) but focuses on the positive aspects of the child's behavior and abilities. Nevertheless, the older brother's feelings are respected and accepted even when those feelings are negative. When you find books that do not do this, you can help your youngsters put the character in perspective by talking about what you think the disabled person is capable of.

Since young children often will stare at a person with an artificial arm or leg, or someone who is in a wheelchair, books that provide the opportunity for children to satisfy their need to stare and to be given accurate information are helpful. *Don't Feel Sorry for Paul* by Bernard Wolf provides graphic photographs of a child's prostheses, two for his legs, one for his right arm, and particularly the one that is his artificial hand. The close-up photos show how Paul attaches the devices to his body and how he uses them. The story focuses on what Paul *can* do. And the clear text provides additional information about Paul and his life.

Another book that affords young children the experience of accurate observation of a prosthetic device is *About Handicaps* by Sara Bonnett Stein. This book is one of the *Open Family* series for young children and their parents. Accompanying the simple text for children is explanatory material for adults. The story tells of a young boy, Matthew, whose friend Joe has cerebral palsy. Matthew's fears and overtly negative behavior are explored in the story, and Matthew's father helps him to come to terms with them in a positive and nurturing way. The illustrative photographs demonstrate the working of an artificial hand and arm.

Other disabilities, such as Down's syndrome, are also portrayed in several books for young children. *Like Me* by Alan Brightman is a photo story narrated by a child who has this condition. It invites sympathetic understanding from the young reader. Miriam Cohen's *See You Tomorrow, Charles* represents a first-grade class and its response to a new child who is blind. Charles and the children learn a great deal about one another, come to respect one another's abilities, and end up liking one another. It is noteworthy that all of the books in this series describe a diverse group of children who are also racially integrated. The author clearly cares about societal values and presents them in an entertaining and engaging style.

The opportunity for greater interaction in the classroom among all children, those with disabilities and other special needs and all other children, is now reinforced in books. Much more should be done, but at least there has been a start in the ongoing effort to bring the issues to parents' attention and to help children confront their own discomfort and fears.

Death

Until recently our society has encouraged us to protect our children from any encounter with, or knowledge of, death. Children were excluded from attending funerals; life-threatening diseases were spoken of in hushed tones; funeral and burial plans were revealed only in wills. Even dead pets were quickly removed and disposed of. Yet death comes to every one of us; it is part of our lives and our children's. Grandparents, relatives, and friends fall ill, have accidents, age, and die. While you might shield children from human death, they cannot be shielded from encounters with death in nature: the death of trees, flowers, leaves, insects, roadside animals, and pets.

It is important that children be permitted to experience and share their feelings about loss and death, and be encouraged to question and to mourn. Books can help give children the information and the support they need. One book for very young children, *The Dead Bird* by Margaret Wise Brown, tells children straightforwardly about death. When four children find a dead bird in the woods they learn about the cessation of heartbeat and the body growing stiff and cold. The book acknowledges the importance of the children's feelings through their participation in a funeral ceremony. The book ends with the act of mourning and the suggestion of reawakening to life. "Every day, until they forgot, they went and sang to their dead little bird." The book is a simple one. It invites the child to reflect, ask questions, and express feelings. It gently opens the door to a potentially uncomfortable topic.

Two excellent books about the death of pets can prepare children to deal with the issue of an impending death or be used to help children with their feelings after experiencing loss. Sara Bonnet Stein's *About Death* openly acknowledges the death of a beloved pet and provides a physical description of what death is. It presents a good model for helping children cope: a funeral is held (showing some ways we have to let go) and memories are invited (showing other ways we can hold on). Later in the book when a grandfather dies, feelings are again allowed to emerge, ritual is provided to help people mourn, and fantasies and wishes are acted out by a child and addressed by his parents.

My Grandson Lew by Charlotte Zolotow demonstrates the power of happy memories to counterbalance the sense of loss. The child in this story shares his remembrances of his loving grandfather, Lew, with his mother and the reader. The child's memories revive the mother's and we are shown how their grief is mitigated by their sharing. Once again, this is a positive model. Both children and adults experience a variety of feelings when someone they love dies, but these are less painful when accepted and shared.

Grief is acknowledged on the very first page of Judith Viorst's book *The Tenth Good Thing About Barney*. The child whose cat has died is so unhappy that he cries and cries and cannot even eat chocolate pudding. His family responds with understanding hugs, the statement that they will have a funeral the next day, and the suggestion that the child prepare himself by thinking of ten good things to tell about Barney at the funeral. At the funeral the child can only think of nine good things about Barney and he tells those. In this book, mourning is quite realistically depicted; it does not end with the funeral but some of the pain is lessened when the boy realizes that the tenth good thing about Barney is that he has become a part of nature and will nourish other living things. The inference is that in this way Barney will stay a part of life and enrich it.

Another book that acknowledges the loss and sadness of death while celebrating the power of memory is Nancy Jewell's *Time for Uncle Joe*. At each season a young girl is reminded of her beloved uncle and misses something specific, his jokes, his way of shaving, his contributions to the garden, his richly textured times with her. At first, she holds on to a box of his things that were stored in the attic. Then she moves slowly from the comfort of the tangible to the comfort of the intangible. Denial, anger, guilt, fear, and grief constitute the developmental pattern most of us go through when we mourn someone we love and its sensitive depiction here may help young readers and their parents better understand themselves or other mourners.

Divorce

Divorce is another fact of life for children growing up in our society today. As many as half of American children will experience it directly. Authors have realized that these children can be helped to feel less frightened, different, and alone by seeing their situation mirrored in print. Children can experience a sense of relief and confirmation of the legitimacy of their feelings when they see people in books who are also angry, sad, or confused. Authors know that children can be reassured when the printed page addresses their fears and fantasies, when, for example, fictional children are told that they are in no way responsible for their parents' separation and that they cannot change it by being unusually good or bad. Many authors acknowledge that children need to build a new vocabulary to understand what is happening and will be helped by learning the definition of words like *separation, lawyer, custody, visitations,* and *divorce.*

Parents can assess which kind of story their children might benefit from and choose from the many available. Most important is the opportunity these books provide for initiating conversations between parent and child, for sharing feelings, for asking and answering questions, and for being close at a difficult time.

Books about divorce are intended not only for children of divorced or divorcing parents but also for their friends, schoolmates, relatives, or neighbors. Stories about divorce vary greatly in style, but most of them begin by acknowledging that children whose parents are divorcing may be inundated with a variety of feelings: fear, confusion, guilt, anger, embarrassment, helplessness, loneliness, and sadness. Earl Grollman's classic book *Talking About Divorce: A Dialogue Between Parent and Child* is designed to help parents begin a family dialogue. Recognizing how difficult this may be at a time when parents may be confused and distressed, Grollman provides a thirty-page guide for parents at the end of his book in which every line of the carefully worded children's text is enlarged upon for the receptive adult.

Suzanne Sedgewick's *A Look at Divorce* gives insight into divorce through another medium, black-and-white photographs.

The photographs first depict children with both parents, then concerned-looking children alone with one parent. The book ends with photographs of children working cheerfully together or with one parent on basic chores. Although the simple text gives children such verbal messages as parents may be happier apart or that nothing can break the relationship between parent and child, the pictures tell the tale: families sometimes separate, but, in time, children can find contentment with the changed and new relationship they have with each parent.

In Beth Groff's book *Where's Daddy: The Story of a Divorce* the reader moves with a wide-eyed toddler named Janeydear through the stages leading up to the divorce of her parents. First Janeydear feels Daddy's change in mood, then he isn't home in the morning and her upset Mommy does not know when he is coming back. Finally he returns, takes her to the beach alone, and tells her that Mommy and Daddy are going to live apart. At each stage, the actions and feelings of each character are true to life and easy to identify with. After the divorce Janeydear, her beloved dog, Funny, and Mommy live with Grandma and Mommy goes to work outside of the home. This situation builds to a crisis that finally culminates in Mommy's understanding Janeydear's deepest fear, and to her responding with a new kind of reassurance and acceptance.

Lucky Wilma and *Daddy* are two books showing how children cope with the once-a-week visits of their fathers. *Lucky Wilma*, an almost wordless book by Wendy Kindred, shows a young girl and her father learning to be alone together on Saturday afternoons. *Daddy*, by Jeanette Caines, features a black family in which the child and her father establish new routines that include the father's new partner. In this book, the child's anxious feelings are acknowledged as well as her pleasure when her father pays special, loving attention to her.

Mushy Eggs, by Florence Adams, models another kind of adjustment. In this story two young boys have to say good-bye to a beloved housekeeper and come to accept and appreciate another. For children whose custodial parent is employed, this can be a helpful text. It is important that the mother is depicted as a competent and understanding person who empathizes with her sons, and at the same time manages the business of engaging a new person to look after the house and children while she is at work.

Two books worthy of note are *Your Family, My Family* by Joan Drescher and *Families* by Meredith Tax. They both point out through text and illustration that families come in many shapes and sizes. They convey the message that a family is defined as people living together, caring, and sharing. Small families, large families, families headed by grandparents or foster parents, with one parent, with two parents, with same-gender parents, with adoptive parents, all are acknowledged and accepted.

Both mirrors and windows are necessary devices. Seeing, knowing, respecting, and liking ourselves form an important basis for doing the same with other people, and books can help us to provide ourselves and our children with the opportunity for building understanding and acceptance of ourselves and others.

8

The
Enduring Bond:
Exploring Sibling
Relationships

Sibling relationships can be packed full of pleasure and pain, love and hate, fulfillment and disappointment, understanding and misunderstanding, appreciation and bitterness. Many psychologists believe that these interactions can shape how people feel about themselves long after the childhood years. Some also believe that patterns of behavior among brothers and sisters serve as important models for how people will relate to their future friends, mates, and children. It is startling to realize that the sibling relationship can continue for as long as seventy or eighty years, longer than with parents or partners. One amusing children's book, *Two Sisters and Some Hornets* by Beryl Epstein and Dorritt Davis, demonstrates that some siblings continue to quarrel and make up even when they are old.

Whether the relationship between siblings is one of support, sabotage, friction, or fun, trends in our society suggest that siblings' need for each other will increase in the coming years. Since the size of the American family is decreasing, adults have fewer family members to connect with. Those few that exist therefore become more important.

Current research provides us with many theories about siblings. One of the most prevalent is the theory that sibling rivalry is the dominant dynamic among brothers and sisters and that this rivalry is best explained as competition for parental love. Another theory states that each child acts as a part of a subgroup within the family. This subgroup is "the children." "The children" are then perceived as being in compliance or in defiance of the other family subgroup, "the parents."

From the mountains of research on the influence of birth order, we learn that one's position within the family (first child, middle child, last child, and so forth) may have a heavy influence on future personality. The book *The Sibling Bond,* by Stephen P. Bank and Michael D. Kahn, explores why some siblings develop positive relationships and some more negative ones, and the theory that overly close and overly hostile relationships develop between siblings when parental influence is too minimal. The famous developmental psychologist Arnold Gesell tells us that fighting, bickering, and quarreling are to be expected and that we should be less distressed and more accepting of this behavior. On the other hand, after reviewing many recent studies, Judy Dunn points out that siblings can show great interest in each other, great understanding of each other, and take great pleasure in each others' company.

Fortunately there are a number of fine books for children that do provide strategies for coping with tensions between siblings as well as specific models and unobtrusive solutions. They create characters and situations that demonstrate empathy for young readers' feelings, both positive and negative. They acknowledge fantasies that children may invent in response to their difficulties in handling their feelings. They remove some of the fearfulness from these fantasies by showing adults responding appropriately. They help children avoid disappointment by indicating realistically what will happen when a new baby is born into the family. They recommend and model solutions that build on the child's own strengths. They hold out promise that positive interactions between siblings can and will eventually evolve.

Since the initial adjustment to a new sibling is seen by almost all theorists as a potential foundation for future relationships, parents might use the many books now available to help make this adjustment a positive one. With the birth of a second child the firstborn gains a brother or sister but loses the status of only child, the baby of the family. Many firstborn children show signs of stress when a second child joins the family: they may cry more often, demand and cling, revert to diapers, sleep less well, and play with less concentration. Although we may worry about these changes in behavior, careful unbiased observation of first children often reveals that firstborns show a great deal of interest in the new baby and are often friendly, affectionate, and actively solicitous and concerned when the baby is distressed. Parents would do well to encourage and nurture this interest, warmth, helpfulness, and concern while at the same time recognizing, accepting, and guiding the older child's feelings of frustration, anger, and jealousy.

Helping a firstborn to form a picture in his mind of what it is like to have a new baby in the house can be very constructive. *Betsy's Baby Brother* by Gunilla Wolde is a cheerful yet realistic picture of a three- or four-year-old's life with a new sibling. Betsy and her mother are good models. Betsy holds her baby brother and clearly is pleased. Her mother includes her in the caretaking and trusts her. The baby accepts her. Betsy learns a lot about the baby: he is very small; sometimes he is very quiet, sometimes very noisy. Only when Mommy spends time feeding the baby does Betsy respond with an angry fantasy: she wishes, as many children do, that her mother would give the baby to another lady so that she could have her mother all to herself again. But the fantasy is followed by a cooperative, helpful task on Betsy's part, making clear that in real life the baby is here to stay and will be accepted as part of Betsy's life. Betsy has learned that baby brothers are "funny," that they can be a "big nuisance," but that they are "mostly cuddly and sweet."

Roslyn Banish's *I Want to Tell You About My Baby* gives the young reader a first-person account of one boy's experiences during the period just before and after a sibling is born. He describes his mother who can no longer button her coat because the baby inside her is getting so big. He describes changes in his mother's behavior: her fatigue, her visits to the doctor, the exercises he does with her on the floor. He is shown with his grandparents who stay with him while his parents are in the hospital, and he is shown meeting his baby brother for the first time. The child narrator speaks to the young reader in an amiable tone. He presents a very positive picture of his experiences that may help the reader develop a feeling for what having a new baby in the family will be like.

Getting Ready For Baby: A New Feelings Activity Book tells the story of a little girl who observes that her mother is "getting fat." The mother says that she is pregnant and explains that means that she is going to have a baby. The book contains activities for children to engage in that reinforce the young reader's knowledge of good prenatal nutrition, the hospital, baby equipment, child-proofing the house, as well as other topics. The child reader learns about many of the changes occurring to her parents, her environment, and to herself before the baby is born, while it is being born, and after it has joined the family. The activities in the book are well designed and invite the reader to participate in the preparation process. Since we know that children learn best when they use the information they are given, this book may be an important addition to your collection.

The Baby's Catalogue by Janet and Allan Ahlberg uses pictures of five families to convey what it is like to live with a baby. Each page has a single label for a group of pictures. For example, one page, labeled "Dads," shows one bearded father brushing his teeth, one red-headed Dad sleepily reaching for his alarm clock, one father dressed rather formally powdering an infant's bottom, a black father making tea, and a father getting on a bicycle. Other headings include "Mornings," "Highchairs," and "Breakfasts," "Brothers and Sisters," "Toys," "Prams," "Swings," and "Accidents," to name just a few. The distinctiveness of each example lends freshness, and frequent touches of humor add to the enjoyment of the cataloging and convey a respect for differences among families and their babies.

Elaine Edelman's *I Love My Baby Sister (Most of the Time)* is another book that prepares children for life with a new sibling by telling a story about a preschool child with a positive attitude toward her baby sister. The child in the story sings with her new sister, cuddles with her, shares candy and blocks with her, and even wipes her nose and mouth. When small breaches of toddler etiquette are made by the infant (a pulled nose, a toppled tower) they are tolerated by the older child. This book adds a view to the future. The older child realizes that when the baby is bigger she will be able to teach her younger sister many more things, share bikes and skates. And in the future the baby may even be able to help her. You might try making the baby's future growth more concrete by showing your older children pictures of themselves at different ages. You can remind them of their own birth and what they were and were not able to do.

How You Were Born by Joanna Cole addresses the young reader directly and, with the help of full-page black-and-white photographs, tells the child what the womb was like and about different stages of prenatal growth. Careful sketches show how a baby moves through the birth canal. These are followed by many photographs of very young infants pictured with people lovingly holding and admiring them.

Children love to hear about themselves and to get the subtle message that when they were tiny they were treated just as the new baby will be. If you have kept a baby record book this would be a good time to take it out and look through it with your child. Perhaps you and your older child can construct a record book for the new baby. Some publishers have designed special formats for this purpose. Several are listed in "The Bookshelf."

Stretch your child's memory and make the stages of very early development more real by asking the child to pretend being different ages. Allow the child to be a baby again, crawling, bawling, cooing, and being fed. Allow your child to pretend to be learning to walk and to say a few words. Then ask the child to think about the baby at each of these stages and how the child will be able to interact with the new brother or sister. By doing this you will not only be helping your children develop a positive relationship, you will also be helping your older child build the important skills of perspective and empathy. One further activity parents can engage in is a discussion of the adults' present and past relationships with their own brothers or sisters. Looking through family albums, constructing new ones, and labeling the photos may help to reinforce the positive connections of kinship for your child.

The New Baby, by Fred Rogers, was designed as part of a series of books to help children face the fears and difficulties of new situations. It is illustrated with large, warm color photographs showing black and white families with both parents in nurturing roles. Its text is informative, direct, and reassuring. Its special point is that firstborns have "their own special place in the family—a place that no one else can ever take." It also states that the new baby needs the older child "for all kinds of times: happy times, sad times and lonely times" and that families are for needing and caring. The book acknowledges some of the frustrations a first child may have when a new baby joins the family.

A more complex and probing book, *Billy and Our New Baby* by Helene S. Arnstein, was approved by a panel of experts in child development. Billy's initial reaction to his new sibling is generous, but the tone of this book quickly changes. Billy is soon saddened and disappointed because the baby can't play with the toy car Billy wants to share with him. The baby is only able to sleep, eat, and cry. Billy is also angered because his mother is so involved with the baby that she is unimpressed with his ball throwing. And he is upset because she neglects old routines such as reading to him. These situations, described in print, afford the opportunity to invite children to discuss their similar feelings of hurt, anger, or frustration.

Listening to your children and asking them to listen to you are ways of building essential skills for future relationships in and out of school. Time together with your children to express thoughts and feelings is important in itself. Once feelings are expressed and grievances are aired, plans can be made for addressing them, for reading together, for creating new routines or reestablishing old ones. The regular nighttime routine of reading to a child should, in particular, be maintained. An abundance of books suitable for this routine are available, and "The Bookshelf" lists many fine ones.

That New Baby by Sarah Bonnett Stein is *An Open Family Book for Parents and Children Together*. Its large black-and-white photographs and carefully worded text are designed to provoke discussion with your older child about the birth of a new sibling. From the very first page, which reads "Before the baby was born, there was already no room for Charles," the book and its illustrations give expression to some of what the author concludes are many children's unspoken feelings, frustrations, and fears. She shows a little girl eating crackers and says that Melissa "hoped they would make a baby in her." A photograph shows a little boy named Charles putting a pillow under his shirt so his tummy would look big. She shows Darrell rocking his baby too hard and his Mommy stopping him. Charles plays out his anger with his toys and his Mother says, "I see you don't like babies very much today." The instances of children expressing their feelings continue. Alongside the large-print text for children is a small-print text for parents. It explains that many children feel the way the children in the story do and advises parents on how to respond to their own children. Your children may love this book because of the reassurance it provides them that their feelings are shared, understood and acceptable.

Children resort to thoughts and gestures of escape when no other path seems available to them. Because the feelings of anger that prompt a child to run away are so powerful, both the author of *A Baby Sister for Frances* and *Noisy Nora* have made their leading characters small animals. This allows the child who reads the story to identify with the main characters while still maintaining a safe distance. In Russell Hoban's *A Baby Sister for Frances*, Frances, a small badger, is generally supported by loving, responsive parents. Nevertheless, the birth of baby Gloria leads to small parental imperfections: a favorite dress of Frances's is left unironed and there are no raisins for Frances's lunch. Frances announces that she is running away (to under the dining room table where it's cozy and she won't run out of cookies). Both her parents declare loudly that they and Gloria miss her. Frances then emerges because she knows that she is wanted and that she is appreciated for who she is. Gloria cannot replace her.

The protagonist in Rosemary Wells's *Noisy Nora* is a tiny, yellow-smocked mouse with a big, angry frustrated feeling because her baby brother and her older sister seem to be getting all the attention. From the very beginning of the book, on the cover, Nora acts out her frustration. There she is shown tipping the table and all the silverware on top of it onto the floor. From then on her posture, behavior, and expressive eyes make her feelings of jealousy, frustration, and anger abundantly clear. When her acting out seems of no avail, she decides to run away. She is rigorously sought by her parents until she is found hiding in a closet.

Peter's Chair, by the popular author Ezra Jack Keats, contains a human protagonist, a young boy named Peter, who decides to run away after his parents have repainted his old cradle, his old crib, and finally his old high chair in pink. He runs away with his blue baby chair, his toy crocodile, a picture of himself as a baby, some cookies, dog bones, and his dog, Willie. The author is careful to have him run to a safe, contiguous place where his parents are near and aware. Once he is there he tries to make himself comfortable. He can't because he discovers that he is too big to fit in his old chair. When his parents invite him back into the house for lunch he has achieved a new level of understanding and acceptance on his own. He is ready to paint his old chair pink. This is a perfect book to share with a child who is jealous but is moving toward an acceptance of his new status as older sibling.

When reading these books with your children take note of their responses. Where is their attention most intense? Where do they smile? Where do they look uncomfortable? Gently ask them how they think the character in the book may feel and if they have ever felt the same way. This will help them find words for their feelings. Building a broad vocabulary of emotions will help make your young children less likely to need to act out their feelings. Once you know what they feel, you can help them by letting them know that their feelings are normal, common, and acceptable (though all their *behavior* may not be). Your expression of understanding will go a long way toward helping them cope.

Your response will be unique to your child and to your situation. The interactions in the children's books presented here may or may not be relevant to you. The books are merely a place to start, a means to open up the issue. But the fact that you have selected them for your children will, in itself, communicate to them that you want to understand how they are feeling. If the books are well chosen you will know it because your children may very well ask you to read them over and over.

In her recent book *Sisters and Brothers,* Judy Dunn reports that in families where the firstborn showed marked affectionate interest in the newcomer, a relationship of friendliness and affection continued over time. How do we encourage and support this initial positive interest that the research suggests is so important? Apparently the key is involving the firstborn with the mother or a primary caretaker in caring for the baby. Dunn reports that in some families the mother discussed the baby with the firstborn child, almost as an equal. She commented on what the baby might be feeling or needing, drawing the firstborn's attention to the baby's interest in the older sibling. These mothers often asked the first child, even those who were barely two years old, what should be done with the baby. They discussed the reasons why the baby was crying or smiling. An example of this is in *Betsy's Baby*

Brother when Betsy's mother explained to Betsy why the baby pulled her hair.

Beyond using conversation, it is often necessary for parents to think of concrete, physical ways to achieve this important initial bond between the siblings and to help the older child move from a sense of loss or exclusion to one of gain and involvement. Books that show families in which such a transition is achieved can serve as models or as conversation starters for finding your own specific ways of persuading your children to interact in a positive manner.

When Kevin, in Eloise Greenfield's *She Come Bringing Me That Baby Girl*, first meets his new sister he is disappointed and jealous. But when his mother places the baby right in his lap and teaches him how to hold her, he begins to feel that he has a role, and sees that both the baby and his mother delight in his being a "big brother." As protector, helper, entertainer, and understander, your child too can feel a new sense of intimacy, pride, and inclusion. Older children will gain a new sense of themselves as valued because of their unique abilities and roles.

In *Ometiji's Baby Brother* by Mary-Joan Gerson, an older child in an African village struggles with the exclusion and hurt he feels after his baby brother is born. A series of disappointing encounters with a number of important people in his life leave him feeling alone and useless, as many children do at such a time. But Ometiji comes to a solution by himself. When drummers come to play in the village, Ometiji finds an accompanying poem about the new baby forming in his mind. At first it is an angry rhyme, but he transforms it into a song of praise to be presented as his very special gift at his brother's naming ceremony. The gift brings joy to everyone at the ceremony. Most important to Ometiji are the pride and love he sees shining in his parents' eyes and directed at him.

Beyond these initial bonding experiences, mothers whose children develop early positive relationships often draw their first-borns into a continuing process of sharing in caring for the baby. They also encourage their older children to enjoy the new baby's achievements.

The key to this process seems to be the relationship between the older child and the mother. They are making the new baby into a shared endeavor. Rather than balancing the needs of each child and dividing their time between each of their children, these mothers spent hours with their older child, in the presence of the baby, caring for and discussing the new family member and attending to the older sibling at the same time. Look for books that reinforce this process of discussion. Such discussion, in addition to the emotional support it engenders, also builds the skills of observation, vocabulary, empathy, and communication that will serve your child well.

There are many ways to begin this process of making the baby a source of common interest and learning for your older child. You can begin by helping your child learn to read the baby's expressions. Labeling the baby's moods helps your child build a vocabulary to describe emotional states. The baby's body and movements can also be labeled and described.

Here is a rich opportunity to explore opposites and similarities. The older child can compare his body with yours and the baby's. Feet can be placed next to one another and marveled at. And abilities can be compared. At every turn you can invite your older child to observe carefully, make comparisons, develop concepts and explanations, make connections, build vocabulary, and enlarge understanding. In short, a lot of learning can ensue while you're establishing a sense of inclusion and participation.

An aid to this discussion is *My New Baby and Me* by Dian G. Smith. Its large fill-in-the-blank and multiple-choice workbooklike format invites children to describe and compare themselves to their new sibling in different ways throughout the first year of the baby's life. Children indicate how much they weigh and then choose whether this is "as much as a TV set, toaster, helicopter, baby carriage, or lamb." They are then asked how much their baby weighs and whether it is "as much as a rabbit, feather, telephone book, suitcase, or bag of groceries."

At the same time that it builds the age-appropriate skills, the book encourages a positive look at self and baby. It moves increasingly toward helping the older child take pride in the younger sibling's growing abilities. It ends on two interesting notes. First, it asks the child to draw or find a photograph of "me and my baby at my baby's first birthday party," and then it asks older children to imagine what they will learn in the next year and what the baby might learn in the next year. This again is a good model. People can often tolerate the praise and recognition of a potential competitor if they feel acknowledged and secure themselves.

Giving the older child some success-building responsibility will also help solidify the sibling relationship. It can help older children feel pride because their younger sibling appreciates, needs, and admires them. In *Go and Hush the Baby* by Betsy Byers the elder brother is repeatedly requested to entertain the crying baby while his mother finishes various other tasks. Both his inventiveness and his attitude of thorough involvement and caring are something from which an older child can learn.

Go and Hush the Baby could well be a stimulus for you and your child to let your imaginations loose. You could work together composing silly songs, staging puppet shows, and concocting edibles. Not only can these activities be fun and companionable, but they also may be educational. Song writing can build rhythm, rhyme, and memory skills; puppet productions can involve character, plot, and sequencing skills and develop hand coordination; and cooking involves new vocabulary, measuring skill, prediction, and understanding of what combining things and heating them will do.

Given this kind of encouragement, siblings tend to continue this positive attitude toward their sibling on their own. In John Steptoe's *My Special Best Words*, three-year-old Bweela helps her baby brother, Javaka, learn to use the toilet. When she succeeds (or he does), both children and their single-parent father are delighted with one another. The atmosphere in this book is both natural and cheerful, the relationships straightforward and cooperative without being the least bit goody-goody. The fact that the family is black is another plus.

My Brother Fine With Me is another book about two black children, this time an eight-year-old and a five-year-old. Johnetta talks as if she considers her younger brother Baggy more of a problem than a pleasure. But when he decides to leave home she immediately misses him, imagines being without him at night, alone in the park, and making sandwiches for herself and no one else. It becomes clear that Baggy has been rethinking his decision while sitting on the front step because he decides to stay after all. Although these two siblings are never depicted in the book to be actively enjoying each other's company, it is evident they do appreciate each other.

Martha Alexander's deceptively simple story *I'll Be the Horse If You'll Play with Me* illustrates another important aspect of sibling relationships. In this story, as the title suggests, a middle child engages her older brother in fantasy play. To get him involved she has to bargain with him and takes the less desirable role in their game. Even with this concession, he stays involved only briefly. When he quits and even her pets won't cooperate, the child manages to get her baby brother to be the horse for her.

Although the relationships among the children in this story are not a model of mutuality, they do suggest a potential area of sharing among young brothers and sisters. According to some studies reviewed by Judy Dunn, up to 60 percent of a two-year-old child's day may be spent in pretend, or make-believe, play. Here, then, is a golden opportunity for siblings to assume pretend identities and to play together. Using their own imaginations, children can become animals large and small, tame and ferocious. They can play house and safely try on new roles: mother, father, baby, elder. They can become pilots, bus drivers, train engineers, and astronauts. Or they can set up a make-believe store and become shopkeepers and shoppers. A basket of assorted hats will enable them to become grown-ups in different roles. When children are helped to move out of their usual roles, they can safely experiment with and change their perceptions, behaviors, and relationships.

In Charlotte Zolotow's *Big Brother*, an older brother derives great pleasure from teasing his little sister and enjoys it when she reacts each time with tears. One day, the little girl is sufficiently occupied with her own activities to refrain from reacting negatively to her brother's antics. She finally figures out that ignoring his behavior is more effective than crying. The book ends with the brother and sister playing happily together at *her* activity.

A book depicting mutuality and sharing is *Let's Play* by Satomi Ichikawa. On the opening pages two youngsters are shown trying to stop a baby from crying. On each following page the children are shown enjoying activities together, including the now-delighted baby. They play with blocks and with a ball. They play with dolls, with tambourines, a rocking horse, and balloons. The book demonstrates how boys and girls of different ages can engage harmoniously in imaginative, collaborative activities.

Baby and I Can Play, a book by Karen Hendrickson, teaches older siblings specific activities and responses to try with their baby brother or sister at different stages of the baby's development. It also acknowledges that babies are not always fun, and it teaches children what to do when they are feeling bad about having a new baby in the family. *Fun With Toddlers*, another *Getting Along Together* book, takes the same approach, teaching an older sibling how to play with a toddler and what to do when life with the toddler is unpleasant. These books are well written and nicely illustrated. They contribute useful strategies for the child who needs to find more positive ways of playing with a younger sibling.

In a much lighter tone, free of didacticism, mutual enjoyment is humorously illustrated in Fran Manushkin's *Bubblebath*. Two grubby little sisters decide that they need a bubblebath. With double bubbles, rubber duck, tickles, hugs, and some minor power struggles, they manage to make each other very clean and equally happy.

In Judith Viorst's *Sunday Morning*, two brothers, who have promised their parents that they will be quiet until nine forty-five one Sunday morning, enjoy each other's company thoroughly. One arises very early, gets lonely, and wakes his brother. Then the adventure begins. The two boys invent all sorts of hilarious games and get involved in all sorts of mishaps, problems, and solutions until the designated time when their parents arise to find chaos. In both these stories the children are presented as a team, working together. Theorists who ascribe to the systems approach often analyze sibling and family relations in terms of the alliances within the family. They frequently see "the children" relating as a team and "the parents" acting as another team. These stories suggest that such alliances do occur and present them in a positive light.

All of these stories provide models of siblings who are companions and friends. Whether fueled initially by the need to please parents, by pride, generosity, fear of loss, loneliness, or by parental wisdom or neglect, the relationship between siblings can be as satisfying and enduring as any in our lifetime. It is, therefore, important that parents encourage, emphasize, praise, and reward all positive interactions among brothers and sisters.

This is not to deny that sibling relations, like all intimate ones, can be most troublesome, involving comparison, competition, and jealousy well beyond the stage of the youngest's infancy. Many books for young children focus on these dynamics and give the reader an opportunity to identify with the main character. Two books by Judith Viorst make a contribution simply by showing that it is very usual and normal to achieve less than perfect harmony with one's siblings. *Alexander and the Terrible, Horrible, No Good Very Bad Day,* and *I'll Fix Anthony* make this point over and over in a very humorous way. So does Crescent Dragonwagon's *I Hate My Brother Harry.*

The fictional characters, their situations, and their lists of grievances can provide an opening for your children to express their feelings and to let you know what is bothering them about their relationships with their brothers and sisters. Sometimes their complaints will be ones you were aware of. Often they will not.

Beyond building an open relationship between you and your children, these books also provide an opportunity for you to help your children's discussion and listening skills. Furthermore, you can use them to teach the process of brainstorming by inviting them to think of as many solutions to the characters' problems as they possibly can. Tell them that no idea will be rejected. What you want is as many solutions as possible.

In addition to telling children that rivalry is normal, a number of practical antidotes to rivalry appear in books written for young children. One is suggested in a number of books, several of which have already been discussed. It is the gradual encouragement and conscious building of the ability to understand and empathize with another person, in this case a sibling. In *Fun with Toddlers,* Karen Hendrickson explains that toddlers "sometimes grab what you are playing with just because you have it." She goes on to recommend that the older sibling replace the disputed toy with another attractive item. In *If It Weren't for Benjamin* by Barbara Shook Hazen, the younger brother is at first terribly jealous of his older sibling but comes to understand that there are disadvantages to being older too. Although it is very difficult for young children to put themselves in the place of another person, their seeing children in books who are beginning to practice empathy will be helpful.

You can build a positive self-regard by recognizing, acknowledging, and encouraging the moves your children make toward competence and independence. Though letting go of old ways of getting attention may involve some risk and ambivalence, you can and should reinforce your children's drive to change and grow. With color pictures and a simple text, June Behrens's *Can You Walk the Plank?* shows children walking a balance beam, throwing a ball, stretching, galloping, jumping, and crawling. Sit down with each of your children and a book like this one. Make a list together of all the things that your child can do. A good way to stimulate interest in reading and writing is to take index cards and write down each ability, one to a card. Then read the list back to him of all the things he can do.

It has been shown that children remember words that they care about, words that they have chosen, much more readily than those that have been provided for them. Write your child's word, praise his or her ability to do what it says, then ask him or her to read it back to you and illustrate it. If you bind these cards together you will have a book of your child's skills. Equally exciting is the fact that you may very well have a book that your child can and wants to read. Ask your child to read it to someone else. Now the child has something else to be proud of, a personalized book. Or make a book together using photographs or magazine pictures of the things your child is good at and is learning. Be sure to include things like cooperation, friendliness, and helpfulness along with physical skills.

Love and inclusion for nothing more or less than being oneself are particularly important for the child who is feeling jealous. As Carole and Andrew Calladine say in *Raising Siblings,* "letting a child know that there is more than enough love to go around will help lay a healthy foundation for sibling relationships in your family." An unusual book for young children which makes this important point is Ann Herbert Scott's *On Mother's Lap.* The book begins with little Michael on his mother's lap. His doll, boat, and reindeer blanket join him. When baby wakes and cries, mother suggests that the baby would like to cuddle too. Michael immediately declares that there isn't room, but mother feels that they should give it a try. Although your attempts to include everyone may be somewhat less easily accomplished, this book, accompanied by discussion, may open the way for your child to learn that there is enough room in your heart, if not on your lap, for all the children in your family.

In *It's Not Fair* by Robyn Supraner an older sister is offended because the baby always seems to get what she wants. The older child feels that it is grossly unfair when her mother says "you should know better because you're the older." But the unfairness is reversed when the older child has a day out alone with her parents. Then the older child wants the baby to understand that "things cannot always be *that* fair." Though the implication in this book is that unfairness is okay when things go your way, the book can be used constructively with an aggrieved child. It provides an opportunity for you to explore children's feelings and for you to explain that you will respond to each child's needs as they arise. The book reflects both siblings' perception of their mother's unfairness. It also may help children to see that at different age levels different parental responses are appropriate.

More books are needed that teach children specific ways to resolve conflicts in a way that is satisfactory to each of the siblings involved. In P. K. Roche's *Webster and Arnold and the Giant Box,* two mice who are brothers are shown having a marvelous time together until Webster decides to quit. When Arnold asks Webster why he is quitting, the retort is "because you are a big boss." Just this small interchange is a model. Arnold does not retaliate; he does not, for example, pretend that he also wants to quit or deride his brother in any way. Instead, he acts as a constructive problem solver. He asks why his brother wants to quit. Webster's reply is equally direct, specific, and useful. He describes Arnold's unacceptable behavior, providing his brother with the information he needs to solve the problem. Arnold sits down and thinks about what he has been told. Then he comes up with his solution, a new game that has an active role for each of them. In ten sentences children have been provided with a pattern they can use to resolve their differences.

Elizabeth Crary's four books in her *Children's Problem Solving* series are specifically designed to help children learn to solve social problems. In *I Want It,* two children who usually have fun playing together have trouble because they both want to play with the same toy dump truck. The adult asks what Amy can do so that she can have the truck. After the child answers, a list of seven solutions is provided. Then the reader can turn to a given page to see the scenario for how each solution may work. The results of grabbing for the truck, asking for it, trading for it, making a deal, waiting for it, threatening, and getting help are all spelled out. This book's strength lies in its combination of responsiveness to the reader's input and the clarity and extent of its content.

Another often neglected solution to conflict is solitude. To enjoy one's own company is a resource and a gift. Developing hobbies and interests in which one can become deeply absorbed and to which one can regularly return is important. Being alone can be a pleasure and an antidote to irritation and rivalry. *Bear By Himself* by Geoffrey Hayes is a book for young children about a charming little bear who truly enjoys time "alone with himself" to think his own thoughts, sing, and enjoy a host of solitary pleasures. This book provides children with a good model.

Finally, building friendships beyond the family is an excellent way of lessening tension between siblings. Books like *Frog and Toad Are Friends* by Arnold Lobel show animals enjoying each other's presence, empathizing with each other's feelings, sharing the pleasures of the world around them, and solving problems whenever necessary. Encourage your children to play with other children and to visit with grandparents and other adults who are fond of them. Chapter 6 contains more discussion and recommendations for books that can help children deal with their emotions and behavior.

Books cannot solve problems or change behavior. They can, however, serve as catalysts for growth and change. They can help in the quest for stronger and more satisfying interactions with the birth family, acquired families, and other people. And books can certainly help you and your children see that the sibling relationship can be a deep and enduring bond.

9

Taming
the One-Eyed
Monster: TV

Television can be a resource for encouraging children to think, read, and write. Most parents are aware of the overuse and abuse of television. Startling studies report that two-and-a-half-year-olds regularly look at television, and that four-year-olds spend one third of their waking hours in front of the TV set. Some parents limit their children's viewing time and censor what they watch, but these strategies are often occasions for bickering and disobedience on the part of the children. Some experts believe that children view television only when they have nothing else of interest to do, and they recommend supplying children with other entertaining or absorbing activities to augment television viewing.

It is important to remember that even when children are "watching" television, they may also be engaging simultaneously in other activities such as eating, playing a game, reading, creating some crafts, or participating in social conversation with peers or family. Often when children appear to be doing nothing but viewing the TV set, they pay sporadic attention to it, and even leave the room for varied intervals of time. It has been determined that most young viewers actually pay attention to no more than two-thirds or less of any show. Of course this varies from program to program and from child to child. Babies up to the age of thirty months have been found to be far more interested in playing with toys or engaging with their caretakers than in watching a television set.

Before resorting to punitive measures or scrambling to find distractions from television, it would be wise for parents to understand better what happens when children watch television. Dr. Daniel R. Anderson has conducted numerous studies over the past fifteen years examining young children's viewing behavior. He and other researchers have found that children view television actively. Children generally do not spend time looking at what they do not understand. They make decisions about what to pay attention to and what to ignore. When they watch with their peers, they engage in lively commentary with each other about the content of the program. This suggests that adults can learn much about what interests and informs their children if they will observe their children's television-watching habits.

From age two and a half on, youngsters become more attracted to the TV. A number of researchers have concluded that preschool children direct their visual attention to the TV screen actively and strategically in order to comprehend what they see. They are able to use what they see to develop more and more language comprehension, and they acquire the ability to understand sequencing. They prefer children's programs to the ones that their parents are watching, such as the news. They can name their favorite programs, and further, they can recognize their favorite characters from pictures. They know the difference between programs and commercials. They regularly learn from what they view: they can often predict what will happen next, and they exhibit an excellent ability to demonstrate their learning of such academic information as the alphabet, counting, names for parts of their bodies, and other specific content that shows such as "Sesame Street" present to them.

In several of his studies, Anderson points out that "the child's approach to solving the problem of cognitive continuity in television viewing is active and unexpectedly sophisticated." Anderson demonstrates that TV viewing is a complex cognitive activity in which children perform the same sorts of mental activities that they do in reading, game playing, and social interaction. Anderson asserts that "young children are far more able to cope with the information-processing demands of television than they have generally been given credit." As young as two and a half years of age, they practice the ability to manage the demands, distractions, and information provided by the television program while at the same time taking advantage of the activities available to them in their homes. The more comprehensible television becomes to children, the more attention they pay to it. Since children do engage actively in watching television programs that are of interest to them, it is important to examine the content of the programs that are especially designed for children.

"Sesame Street" is the most popular of shows for preschool children. The producers engage in continuous self-study and keep abreast of the research others conduct. They have found that the show has a positive effect on children's acquisition of certain cognitive skills. The list is a long one, and includes such concepts as the recognition of letters and numbers, rhyming, parts-whole relationships, sequencing, and classification. The staff of "Sesame Street" is also careful to present in an age-appropriate manner such concepts as nutrition, career awareness, cultural diversity, differing perspectives, valuing the natural as well as the neighborhood environment, and conflict resolution. Programs deal with the issues of handling the emotions, reacting to death, coping with separation and divorce, and getting along in a family.

When the actor who played Mr. Hooper died, the "Sesame Street" staff consulted experts and examined research on the developmental level of understanding preschoolers have about death. They determined to do a show informing children about Mr. Hooper's death. They articulated three concepts that they wanted children to understand: Mr. Hooper died; he is not coming back; and we miss him. They agreed that they would use no euphemisms, and that they would avoid any issues that would confuse rather than help children understand. Thus armed, they produced an episode that is now a classic much in demand by day care centers, nursery schools, and college classes on death and dying.

The care and attention to detail that went into the creation of this episode are worth noting, so that you can look for evidence of this sort of care in other programs that treat sensitive issues. Because the aim was to communicate to children that Mr. Hooper would not return, the staff encountered a dilemma when they wanted to help children actively recall Mr. Hooper. If they showed flashbacks, children would think he was still alive, or had returned from the dead. They decided to use still photos so that the character would not be shown in motion.

"Sesame Street" produced yet another segment several seasons after Mr. Hooper's death in which a new child on the block asks about Mr. Hooper. Big Bird takes this question as an opportunity to recall his dead friend with love, acknowledging that it is sometimes painful to remember, but that in general remembering is good to do. Airing this sequel helps children to affirm that when someone dies they are remembered not only immediately after their death, but for a long time to come.

A series of books, peopled with the "Sesame Street" characters, deals with children's feelings. *It's Not Fair* by Deborah Hautzig helps children see that friends sometimes can be unfair to each other, but that if they care, they can restore the balance. *Grover and the New Kid* by Jennifer Smith acknowledges that the problems a new child in school faces may affect the child's behavior. Grover is seen as an empathic and sensitive friend in this story and in the others in which he is the protagonist. In one book, he suffers because his friends tease him, and then he finds that one friend can help heal the hurt; in another he wants so much to be liked that he negates his own personality and preferences until a friend helps him to understand that he can be himself and still be liked. Big Bird, too, encounters problems of homesickness, of belonging, of teasing, all of which are resolved by friends. Children may be attracted to these simple story books because of the "Sesame Street" characters. The books are not great literature but they are psychologically sound.

Other programs for the preschool child also take into consideration the needs and developmental level of these youngsters. "Captain Kangaroo," in its recently restructured format, contains a variety of presentations, among them films of children displaying unusual talents, such as a seven-year-old girl who is an accomplished rodeo rider. There are also several puppetlike creatures who inject some short, humorous segments into the show, and, of course, there is Mr. Moose, who serves as a comic foil. Since all of the programs are reruns, Mr. Greenjeans, one of the human characters on the set, still appears, even though the actor recently died.

The Captain visits interesting places, like the shark tank at the aquarium, and gleans interesting bits of information from the people in charge. He is careful to include people of color, males and females, and old people. His science segments respond to the statement, "Tell me how things work." The commercials warn against smoking or other harmful activities and are respectful of children. Captain Kangaroo also engages in little skits that, in a humorous context, present concepts to his viewers. One such bit of silliness involved the Captain's being the owner of a beanbag factory. He carefully instructed his crew on their particular duties, and in a somewhat slapstick fashion, he and the group demonstrated how an assembly line works. The segment would have benefited from a film clip of a real assembly line, or at least a comment about assembly lines so that children would have made the connection, but if you were to view something like this with a child, you could point out that this, in fact, is how an assembly line works. The program is pleasant, entertaining, and informative. The Captain clearly cares about young children, and his show contains much that is appropriate for their preschool level.

"Mister Rogers' Neighborhood" is another program for preschool children that demonstrates a careful plan for taking into account young children's developmental levels and their needs. Mr. Rogers himself is a model of a gentle, low-key, affectionate, and nurturing adult male. His guests, too, demonstrate these same characteristics regardless of their gender. Mr. Rogers takes great care to communicate to children that he respects them for who they are, that he empathizes with how they feel, and that he enjoys being with them. Mr. Rogers deals on an everyday basis with children's anxieties and concerns and his programs are informative and reassuring.

Mr. Rogers is careful to unobtrusively but consistently demonstrate the everyday rituals of cleanup, neatness, and good manners. He hangs up his jacket, cleans up any mess that he has made, and respectfully introduces all visitors to his viewers. The fantasy segments are introduced with the clear statement that this is make-believe. The transition to fantasy is made by use of a little trolley that rides into King Friday's kingdom. In this kingdom, nonetheless, people experience the same problems that real people do.

Mr. Rogers encourages young viewers to do some problem solving. He plays games with them and asks them to figure out how the games work; he raises issues such as the necessity to earn a living and sometimes postpones telling his viewers the solution until a subsequent program. He introduces new vocabulary and explains its derivation. ("Recirculate comes from circle.") And he reassures his audience that he likes them just the way they are. Although Mr. Rogers is most appropriate for children from age two to four, older children can appreciate the program as well.

Fred Rogers has written several books for children to help ease them into "first experiences." *The New Baby, Going to the Potty, Going to the Doctor,* and *Going to Day Care* are as respectful and knowledgeable of the child-audience as is his TV program. Illustrated with color photographs, each of these books is informative without overloading the child with excess information. They address the child's fears, but focus on what is positive about each experience. They are realistic enough and inclusive enough of all ethnic groups to provide an opportunity for the child to practice a potentially disturbing situation so that it becomes tolerable and manageable. These books are informational rather than storytelling.

One award-winning program that focuses on books that tell stories for children age four and up is "Reading Rainbow." Levar Burton is the able host of the show. He introduces the day's theme, narrates some of the segments, and participates as a co-learner with the viewer in some of the instructional sections of the show. Each of the shows revolves around a theme and presents a story that goes with the theme. Visitors who are experts on aspects of the theme come to the show, and viewers are also taken on various trips to sites where they can gain yet more information. When *Ox-cart Man* was presented, Levar Burton also took viewers on a tour through Old Sturbridge Village, a reconstruction of a colonial New England village, where people costumed in the style of the early nineteenth century perform the tasks appropriate to the time. Award-winning books such as *Ox-cart Man* and *A Chair for My Mother,* suitable for preschoolers, are presented on the show, with fidelity to their original illustrations and text. One attractive feature of the show is that children serve as book promoters, motivating young viewers to read the books they are recommending.

Bob Keeshan, better known as Captain Kangaroo, hosts "Storybreak," a half hour show that presents a story in cartoon form from a children's book. If you can get a listing in advance of what the story will be, you will be able to judge if it is suitable for your child's age and interests.

"Wonderworks" is a program generally for children older than five. It dramatizes good literature for children. But watch for the selections on this show; sometimes the story is appropriate for younger children.

Although the total number of programming hours for children has increased over the past few years, there is still not enough attention paid by the networks to young audiences. According to the National Cable Television Association, approximately 94 percent of the increase can be attributed to cable services. If you do subscribe to a cable service, the range of programs available to your children is greatly increased. National Educational Television supplies most of the quality. Nickelodeon, a subsidiary of MTV, airs a number of hours of fine programs such as "Pinwheel," suitable for young children as well, especially in the morning and early afternoon hours when older children are at school.

Even if you do not have access to cable, there are some good programs that your child can enjoy and benefit from. Since each local network as well as cable channel varies in the extent of its programming for children, the best way for you to be able to help your child design a viewing schedule is to consult your own local listings. You might also call each of your local channels and ask them to send you a list of their programs for preschoolers.

It stands to reason that programs created for public television networks will focus more on children's development and needs than will those that appear on commercial channels. Nevertheless, the commercial networks present some programs that enlighten and entertain with high quality. PBS/ABC sponsors "Project Literacy U.S.," NBC has "Books Make a Difference," and CBS produces special programs designed to utilize children's enthusiasm for television to help improve their reading skills and their motivation for additional reading, learning, and creative thinking. In conjunction with the airing of specials such as Lewis Carroll's *Alice in Wonderland* and *The Lion, the Witch and the Wardrobe* by C. S. Lewis, the CBS Reading Program distributes actual scripts of the shows, plus a teacher's guide to viewing, so that school children can act out the shows, and teachers and children can engage in a discussion about the shows. Most of the books that are televised for this program are aimed at older children, but some may be suitable for four- and five-year-olds.

As with reading, the more children view, the more they should be able to develop their taste and a sense of what it is they enjoy. It is productive to help them to verbalize their responses so that you can influence the acquisition of their taste for quality. Which TV shows usually avoid gratuitous violence? Which ones seem to care more about characters' feelings? Which of them respect the young viewer's intelligence? If they are based on a book, how faithful are they to the intent of the original work? How respectful of both content and audience was the presentation?

Even very young children can appreciate a story that is uncluttered by distracting special effects, one-dimensional characters, and inappropriate subthemes. The more closely a program follows a familiar book, the more likely the young viewer will watch the program and comprehend it. Viewing the dramatization of a book on television can often serve as an impetus for a child to want to read the book itself. Libraries report a surge of interest immediately after the airing of "Reading Rainbow" of the book that the program has highlighted.

Some of the most frequently viewed programs can cause parents the most worry. Saturday morning cartoons often serve as entertainment for children whose parents may not be monitoring what's on TV. Some of the cartoons are less violent than others; some provide greater clarity and quality of language; some invite children to think as well as watch; some have greater visual worth than others. In order to see a sample of what your children are watching while you aren't present, videotape one morning's offerings. You needn't tape more than ten minutes of each show; that will be sufficient to give you a flavor of the program. If you don't own a video recorder, you might want to rent or borrow one, just for this purpose. Or you could take turns with another adult, viewing on just one weekend morning. Or, just audiotape them; the sound track will give you some information, and your children may be able to fill in the rest.

There may be some shows that are sufficiently attractive and entertaining for you to want to watch yourself. (That is certainly true of the award-winning "Pee-Wee's Playhouse," whose fans probably number as many adults as children.) On the other hand, you may find some elements of some shows very disturbing. Some may be too violent, disrespectful of human dignity, misleading, or confusing. Some are insulting to specific minority groups, treating them in stereotypic and negative fashion. You should listen to some of the language that the TV characters are using. How clear is it? How continuous is the discourse, that is, is it choppy and unrelated to what previous characters have said? Or is it truly communicative and flowing? What sort of vocabulary is used? How respectful is the tone? Sometimes just listening to the tone of voice of a narrator will signal to us that he or she is talking down to the audience.

Even if you can't view all of these programs yourself, encourage your children to talk about what they have viewed. They can discuss their confusion or their positive reactions so that you will get a better idea of what influence the programs are having on your children's thoughts, feelings, and behavior. Sometimes cartoons present stereotypes that need to be counteracted. Sometimes they exhibit through their characters an absence of empathy, helpful behavior, and kindness. Sometimes their characters and situations are so one-sided and simplistic as to be bothersome. On the other hand, there are some cartoons that try to demonstrate attention to the important qualities of caring about others and valuing diversity.

In order to help control the quality of the programs children watch, make it a regular practice to consult your local *TV Guide* or the listings in your newspapers for details about what will air for your child's age level. Be sure to include your child in the search. It is important for children to understand as early as possible that they should plan their viewing rather than just turning on the tube at random. It is equally important to talk to your child about his or her choices of programs, asking that they articulate the reasons for their preferences.

To help children become thoughtful TV viewers, Action for Children's Television (ACT) has produced *The TV-Smart Book for Kids*. Although it is aimed at children age seven and up, it can be a resource for parents to use with younger children as well. Every other page is a blank calendar page on which children can note the days and times of the programs they intend to watch. The purpose is to get children to think about their choices and to plan their TV viewing. Sometimes, seeing a calendar page filled with program names may alert children and their parents to the fact that too much time is being spent in front of the set. Puzzles, games, activities, critical-viewing questions, and suggestions for enhancing the viewing experience are located on alternate pages.

Attached to the calendar is a pull-out guide that alerts parents to some of the potential problems of television. It also contributes good suggestions for activities that parents and children can do together. The book was written by Peggy Charren and Carol Hulsizer of the ACT advisory board. ACT is an organization that lobbies and advocates for better quality programming for children. It also publishes a number of handbooks that inform parents about how to make the most of television for their children.

ACT advises parents and caretakers on how best to talk to children about television. It recommends a number of ideas on how to combat stereotypes. They recommend that parents watch TV with their children and talk about the role models and stereotypes they see on the screen. They suggest that parents and children look for women who are competent in a variety of jobs, for TV characters who care about others, and for people from a variety of cultural and ethnic groups. They also encourage parents to try to coordinate TV viewing with activities in the home. ACT distributes literature recommending that parents talk about programs that upset their children, about ways that TV characters might settle problems without violence, about the differences between make-believe and real life, and about toys that are advertised on TV and break too soon. They annually award those shows that have made the greatest contribution to children's television. They publish a newsletter to which parents may subscribe.

Another organization that advocates quality in children's media is the Parents' Choice Foundation. It publishes *Parents' Choice,* a review of children's media, including books, television, home video, movies, recordings, toys, games, computer programs, and rock 'n' roll. The critics supply the criteria they use for judging any of the media. Dorothy Singer, an expert on critical viewing of TV, suggests that viewers ask themselves if the story was a good one; if the viewer was made to care about the characters in the story; if sensitive issues were handled in good taste; if the pace was such that the viewer had time to understand the show and if the information was accurate and comprehensible. It is also important that the show be appropriate to the child-viewer's intellectual, social, and emotional needs. Among the programs that have earned Parents' Choice awards are "Sesame Street," "Mister

Rogers' Neighborhood," "Pinwheel," "Faerie Tale Theatre," "Fraggle Rock," "Muppet Babies," "Walt Disney's Animated Classics," and "Reading Rainbow."

Not only do children watch programs created especially for them, they also watch adult programs when their parents are viewing TV. They see adults engrossed in the set and they note and mimic their behavior. This is an excellent time for you to model what you want children to do. Talk in advance about what programs you plan to watch for the evening, the weekend, the week. Look through the programming guides and talk out loud about how you are making your choices.

When you are viewing a program, comment on what you are seeing. Talk about whether or not you believe that the situation is realistic. Talk about the characters' behavior and conversation. Comment on the commercials and their accuracy, tone, and appropriateness. Guess out loud what will happen next in a story. Play along with the contestants in a game show and critique the players' strategies. Voice your thoughts and, in that way, your children will be able to see how thoughtful and responsive you are to what is occurring on screen.

Situation comedies afford excellent opportunities for discussion, especially those in which there are child actors. If, for example, you are viewing "The Cosby Show," and you see that Cliff is helping Rudy to get ready for going out of doors, you might make the observation that he is a good father who cares about his children. It is never too early to help children understand that men can nurture as well as women. When the children on the show bring their problems to their parents and their parents listen and respond firmly, but lovingly, you might point out how good it is that the children trust their parents enough to share their difficulties as well as their successes. Your children might also be reassured to hear you acknowledge that when "The Cosby Show" children argue, they are behaving in a normal, acceptable fashion, and that you know that all siblings argue with each other. You can help children to get the message that the program is presenting, that people can love each other and still disagree. During the commercials, you could probably point out that even though Bill Cosby (who is respected and admired, and who clearly cares about children) loves to eat a certain dessert, perhaps it is not *your* favorite, and your child need not feel compelled to love that dessert.

Some commercials for children's products can be particularly deceptive. The product may be shown without a referent for size, so that a toy car may appear to be three feet high when it is only three inches high. Look for commercials in which real children are shown handling the product so that you and your child will get a realistic picture of the size of the object. Teach your children to beware of those commercials that print disclaimers briefly and in small print at the bottom of the screen. For example, if a toy boat is being advertised, and is sailing the high seas in the child-actor's imagination, then the caption is briefly flashed on the screen, "Not a water toy," you can help your child to see how unfair the manufacturer is.

You can identify the language that some TV salespeople use to sell a product. It is usually carefully designed to convey a particular image, not only of the product, but also of the user. You can sometimes rephrase a sentence so that it is more factual, and see what difference it makes to the commercial. Commercials can have their uses beyond helping your children learn about propaganda and inflated language. Sometimes, when the commercial consists of a "test" (for the absorbent power of paper towels, for example) you can replicate that experiment with your children. This sort of action helps to show your children that people need not simply accept what is shown on television, but that they can conduct their own research, and come to their own conclusions.

With a book children can stop at any point, look back over what they have already seen, slow down, speed up, skip portions that do not interest them, and take the book to an adult or another child and ask questions about it. They can interrupt their activity at any point, and return to the same picture or episode again and again. One of the problems with making the most of television is the fact that unless a program has been taped, the viewer is not in control. That is, if a portion has been missed or misunderstood, there is no way to rewind the program and to view it again. It is difficult for a child to summon an adult for help with a small portion of a program that the child does not understand.

One suggestion is, if you have a video recorder, or can rent one, then the problem of lack of control is eliminated. Once a program is on tape, the viewer can fast-forward through the commercials, review what has happened before, view the program again and again, and, in short, treat the video as if it were a book. Parents can tape programs in advance for their children, and then, if they wish, edit out those programs that are inappropriate. You may also want to tape your own selections of "Sesame Street," "Captain Kangaroo," and "Mister Rogers" shows for repeated viewing instead of some of the less favorable cartoon shows on Saturday mornings. Hours of viewing time can be assembled on a tape for those times when nothing of value is airing in the regular programming sequence on television. Children can be taught to expect that their viewing will consist mostly of watching the tapes rather than the "live" programs, and they can acquire the skills of active and critical viewing by means of their operating the controls of the VCR. These viewing skills are analogous to critical reading skills and young children who develop these skills will make good use of them later on when they are readers.

An extensive library of videotaped stories produced especially for young children is available. The advantages of these tapes are numerous. The programs are not interrupted by commercials, so young viewers will get continuous rather than fragmented discourse. Good cassettes may be borrowed from the public library or rented at fairly reasonable cost from video stores. Some companies are particularly careful about the quality of their cassettes. They specialize in videotapes telling stories from popular children's books. The best of these use the illustrations from the original book. There are no gimmicks that distract from the story, and the story is presented in its entirety. The narrator does not talk down to the audience. The musical accompaniments preserve the tone as well as the setting and time of the stories.

CC Studios, a subsidiary of Weston Woods, has produced a series of cassettes, The Children's Circle, for home viewing of award-winning children's books. Each of these cassettes contains approximately thirty to forty minutes of entertainment; each of them presents several stories. *Doctor De Soto,* by William Steig, shares a cassette with *Curious George Rides a Bike,* by H. A. Rey, *The Hat,* by Tomi Ungerer, and *Patrick,* by Quentin Blake. Other well-known stories are presented on other cassettes, including *Strega Nonna,* by Tomie dePaola; *A Story-A Story,* by Gail E. Haley; *Make Way for Ducklings* and *Blueberries for Sal,* by Robert McCloskey; *The Story About Ping,* by Marjorie Flack; the lovable *Corduroy,* by Don Freeman; *Mike Mulligan and His*

Steam Shovel, by Virginia Lee Burton; *The Snowy Day,* by Ezra Jack Keats; and fairy tales such as Hans Christian Andersen's *The Ugly Duckling.*

Most of CC Studios' adaptations are suitable for very young children. One in particular is *Five Stories for the Very Young,* including *Changes, Changes* by Pat Hutchins, in which two little wooden dolls keep cleverly rearranging a set of building blocks to create different structures; *Whistle for Willie,* by Ezra Jack Keats, about young Peter and his attempts to learn to whistle so that he can call his dog; *Caps for Sale,* by Esphyr Slobodkina, the classic tale of a peddler and some mischievous monkeys; *Drummer Hoff,* by Barbara and Ed Emberley, a potentially powerful antiwar story; and Crockett Johnson's *Harold's Fairy Tale,* in which Harold and his magic purple crayon create a fantasy.

It is clear that there are a number of producers who respect children and children's literature. Their products lead children into the book rather than becoming substitutes for reading. Although Weston Woods was the first company to produce media for children derived directly from children's literature, other companies produce videocassettes as well. Scholastic's Blue Ribbon Storybook Video series presents stories, and then follows the stories with puppet characters who sing, ask questions, and recommend activities for young viewers. For some children this interaction with the puppets extends the experience of viewing the story and leads to a deeper understanding of the story. For others it may be a distraction that detracts from the story, and you would be better off fast-forwarding the tape until the next story begins.

Whoever the publisher is, look for stories you know you liked as a child, or stories that you and your child have recently enjoyed. Don't overlook the importance of the narrator; actors such as Meryl Streep, Katharine Hepburn, and Lorne Greene, and authors such as Arnold Lobel narrate some excellent videos. The same criteria hold for videos as for good literature. The entire production must be unified so that no one feature intrudes on the others.

Television viewing is analogous to reading and thinking, especially if it becomes more and more active. The process of interacting with you, with other children, and with the characters on the screen helps young viewers develop critical skills that carry over into reading, learning in general, and dealing with matters in real life. Your participation in the process and your encouragement of your child to become a critical and skilled viewer will enable you not only to tame the one-eyed monster, but also to convert it into a useful tool.

Appendix A

Selected List of Children's Book Awards

Each year a number of awards are presented by various organizations interested in promoting fine literature for children. It may be useful to you to look for books that have won these awards.

Boston Globe/Horn Book Awards: To authors and illustrators for outstanding work.

Caldecott Medal and Honor Books: Named for Randolph J. Caldecott, the noted English illustrator. Winners are selected by a committee of the American Library Association. The award is given to the illustrator of the most distinguished picture book published in the United States and illustrated by a citizen or resident of the United States.

Children's Book Award: Given to a fledgling author who is judged to have unusual potential by the International Reading Association.

Golden Kite Award: Presented by the Society of Children's Book Writers to fellow authors and illustrators for distinguished works of fiction and nonfiction.

Hans Christian Andersen Award: Given every other year to an author whose entire body of work is judged to be outstanding and memorable.

Laura Ingalls Wilder Award: Presented every five years to an author or illustrator whose body of work, published in the United States, has made a lasting contribution to children's literature.

Newbery Medal and Honor Books: Corresponding in prestige to the Caldecott Medal, these awards are presented for the most distinguished writing of American children's literature. They are selected by a committee of the American Library Association and named for John Newbery, the first British publisher of children's books.

Appendix B

Organizations Providing Parents with Useful Information

Action for Children's Television (ACT)
20 University Road
Cambridge, MA 02138
A nonprofit organization that advocates the presentation of quality and nonviolent, nonprejudicial programs for children. The organization reports on studies of television's effects on children. They publish a number of materials for parents and children.

The Children's Book Council
67 Irving Place
New York, NY 10003
A consortium of publishers, the Council maintains a library, open to the public, of the latest children's books. For a nominal, one-time membership fee, the Council distributes a newsletter containing articles and ideas for teachers, librarians, and parents. It also offers posters, bookmarks, and other materials, at low or no cost, promoting children's books.

Council on Interracial Books for Children
1841 Broadway
New York, NY 10023
The Council publishes a Bulletin that contains reviews and articles
about issues in children's literature such as racism, sexism, and
discrimination against people who are old, disabled, or in any way
different from mainstream America.

International Reading Association
800 Barksdale Road, P.O. Box 8139
Newark, DE 19714-8139
A professional nonprofit organization devoted to the improvement
of reading and reading instruction. The organization publishes a
number of free or inexpensive materials for parents.

Parents' Choice Foundation
P.O. Box 185
Newton, MA 02168
This organization publishes a newsletter that reviews all sorts of
media for children, including toys and books. They present annual
awards and advocate for high quality in children's media.

Reading Is Fundamental (RIF)
P.O. Box 23444
Washington, DC 20026
This national nonprofit organization supplies books free of charge
to millions of children across the country. Its aim is to motivate
children to read.

Appendix C
Children's Book
Clubs

Although most of these clubs focus on older children, they offer a number of picture books and easy-to-read books as well as read-alouds at a very discounted price. The clubs circulate monthly catalogs and order forms to schools. They are worth investigating. Ask a local kindergarten or nursery school teacher if you may place an order along with the school group. This may sound like a lot of extra effort, but the savings and selection are worth it. Or you may write to the companies and ask them if they will send you an order form. Specify the ages of your children.

Scholastic Book Clubs
50 West 44th Street
New York, NY 10036

Troll Book Clubs
320 Route 17
Mahwah, NJ 07430

Trumpet Book Clubs
Dell Publishing Company
1 Dag Hammarskjold Plaza
New York, NY 10017

Xerox Education Publications
245 Long Hill Road
Middletown, CT 06457

There are also a number of book clubs especially for infants and toddlers, which distribute cloth-bound books at a slightly higher price and offer direct ordering service.

Field Publications Book Club
245 Long Hill Road
Middletown, CT 06457

Grolier Book Club
Grolier Enterprises, Inc.
Sherman Turnpike
Danbury, CT 06816

Johnson and Johnson Brand
Child Development Division
Grandview Road
Skillman, NJ 08558
(catalogs of toys and books)

Parents Magazine Read-Aloud Book Club
685 Third Avenue
New York, NY 10017

Appendix D

List of Books by Age

For your convenience we have included a listing of books by age level. The age is the suggested time to introduce these books. This is, at best, an approximation. Certainly, the books may be read and enjoyed far beyond the age level at which they are first introduced. Use your own good judgment.

Infants

Aliki. *Go Tell Aunt Rhody.*

Atkinson, Allen. *Mary Had a Little Lamb and Other Favorites.*

Atkinson, Allen. *Simple Simon and Other Favorites.*

Bayley, Nicola. *As I Was Going Up—and Down—.*

Bryan, Ashley. *Walk Together Children.*

Caldecott, Randolph. *A First Caldecott Collection.*

Caldecott, Randolph. *A Second Caldecott Collection.*

Caldecott, Randolph. *A Third Caldecott Collection.*

De Angeli, Marguerite. *Book of Nursery and Mother Goose Rhymes.*

Frank, Josette. *Poems to Read to the Very Young.*

Frost, Robert. *Stopping by Woods on a Snowy Evening.*

Galdone, Paul. *Three Little Kittens.*

Galdone, Paul. *Little Bo-Peep.*

Hale, Sara Josepha. *Mary Had a Little Lamb.*

Hart, Jane. *Singing Bee!*

Highwater, Jamake. *Moonsong Lullaby.*

Jeffers, Susan. *All the Pretty Horses.*

Lobel, Arnold. *The Random House Book of Mother Goose.*

Milne, A.A. *When We Were Very Young.*

Moorat, Joseph. *Thirty Old-Time Nursery Songs.*

Opie, Iona and Peter. *The Oxford Nursery Rhyme Book.*

Prelutsky, Jack. *Read-Aloud Rhymes for the Very Young.*

Spier, Peter. *The Fox Went Out on a Chilly Night.*

Stevenson, Robert Louis. *A Child's Garden of Verses.*

Wescott, Nadine. *The Old Lady Who Swallowed a Fly.*

Wilburn, Kathlene. *The Pudgy Rock-A-Bye Book.*

Winn, Marie and Miller, Allan. *Fireside Book of Children's Songs.*

Winter, Jeanette. *Come Out to Play.*

Winter, Jeanette. *Hush Little Baby.*

Yolen, Jane. *The Lullaby Songbook.*

Yolen, Jane H. *The Fireside Song Book of Birds and Beasts.*

Six Months

Bruna, Dick. *Playing in Winter.*

Dubov, Christine Salac. *Aleksandra, Where Is Your Nose?*

Dubov, Christine Salac. *Aleksandra, Where Are Your Toes?*

Miller, J.P. *Little Rabbit's Garden.*

Piers, Helen. *Peekaboo Mouse.*

Platt and Munk, pubs. *My First Book of Animal Babies.*

Roth, Harold. *A Goodnight Hug.*

Schlesinger, Alice. *Baby's Mother Goose.*

One Year

Ahlberg, Janet and Allan. *Peek-A-Boo.*

Asch, Frank. *I Can Roar.*

Bradbury, Lynne. *On the Move.*

Brown, Margaret Wise. *A Child's Good Night Book.*

Brown, Margaret Wise. *The Country Noisy Book.*

Brown, Margaret Wise. *Goodnight Moon.*

Brown, Margaret Wise. *The Indoor Noisy Book.*

Brown, Margaret Wise. *The Noisy Book.*

Burningham, John. *Cluck, Baa.*

Carle, Eric. *My Very First Book of Touch.*

Duke, Kate. *Clean-Up Day.*

Dyer, Jane. *Moo, Moo, Peekaboo!*

Emberly, Ed. *Cars, Boats, and Planes.*

Fadiman, Clifton. *The World Treasury of Children's Literature (Vols.I, II, III).*

Fujikawa, Gyo. *Babies of the Wild.*

Ginsburg, Mirra. *The Sun's Asleep Behind the Hill.*

Goennel, Heidi. *Seasons.*

Goffstein, M.B. *Sleepy People.*

Gorbaty, Norman. *Baby Ben's Book of Colors.*

Gregor, Arthur. *Animal Babies.*

Hawkins, Colin and Jaqui. *My First Book.*

Hill, Eric. *Good Morning Baby Bear.*

Isadora, Rachel. *I See.*

Johnson, B.J. and Aiello, Susan. *My Blanket Burt.*

Krementz, Jill. *Lily Goes to the Playground.*

Kunhardt, Dorothy. *The Telephone Book.*

Kunhardt, Dorothy. *Pat the Cat.*

Kunhardt, Dorothy. *Pat the Bunny.*

Martin, Bill, Jr., and Archambault, John. *Here Are My Hands.*

O'Brien, Anne Sibley. *Come Play With Us.*

O'Brien, Anne Sibley. *Don't Say No!*

O'Brien, Anne Sibley. *I Don't Want to Go.*

O'Brien, Anne Sibley. *It's Hard to Wait.*

O'Brien, Anne Sibley. *I Want That!*

Ogle, Lucille, and Thoburn, Tina. *I Spy.*

Ong, Cristina. *Gymboree Jump Like Me!*
Platt and Munk, pubs. *Baby's First Counting Book.*
Rice, Eve. *Goodnight, Goodnight.*
Rockwell, Anne. *In Our House.*
Roth, Harold. *Summer Days.*
Scarry, Richard. *Richard Scarry's What Animals Do.*
Scarry, Richard. *Early Words.*
Schmidt, Karen Lee. *My First Book of Baby Animals.*
Slier, Debby. *Whose Baby Are You?*
Slier, Debby. *What Do Toddlers Do?*
Spier, Peter. *Gobble, Growl, Grunt.*
Voce, Louise. *My First Book of Animals.*
Welber, Robert. *Goodbye, Hello.*
Wells, Rosemary. *Max's First Word.*
Wheeler, Cindy. *Marmalade's Nap.*
Wingfield, Ethel and Harry. *A Ladybird First Picture Book.*
Wingfield, Ethel and Harry. *A Ladybird Fifth Picture Book.*
Winn, Chris. *Playing.*
Witte, Pat and Eve. *The Touch Me Book.*
Ziefert, Harriet. *Baby Ben's Busy Book.*
Ziefert, Harriet. *Clappity Clap.*

Eighteen Months

Brown, Margaret Wise. *The Runaway Bunny.*
Carle, Eric. *The Very Hungry Caterpillar.*
Carle, Eric. *The Very Busy Spider.*
Child, Lydia Maria. *Over the River and Through the Wood.*
Graboff, Abner. *Old MacDonald Had a Farm.*
Gretz, Susanna. *Hide-and-Seek.*
Rogers, Fred. *Going to the Potty.*
Roth, Harold. *The Playground.*

Two Years

Aardema, Verna. *Bringing the Rain to Kapiti Plain.*

Ahlberg, Allan and Janet. *The Baby's Catalogue.*

Andry, Andrew C., and Kratka, Suzanne C. *Hi, New Baby.*

Bang, Molly. *Ten, Nine, Eight.*

Blance, Ellen and Cook, Ann. *Monster Looks for a Friend.*

Boegehold, Betty. *Hurray for Pippa!*

Bornstein, Ruth. *Little Gorilla.*

Bradbury, Lynne. *My Day.*

Brown, Margaret Wise. *The Golden Egg Book.*

Burningham, John. *Wobble Pop.*

Burningham, John. *John Burningham's Colors.*

Burton, Terry. *Let's Go Shopping.*

Carle, Eric. *Let's Paint a Rainbow.*

Carlson, Nancy White. *Jesse Bear, What Will You Wear?*

Corey, Dorothy. *You Go Away.*

De Regniers, Beatrice Schenk. *May I Bring a Friend?*

Eastman, P.D. *Are You My Mother?*

Erikson, Karen. *I Can Share.*

Ets, Marie Hall. *Play With Me.*

Fowke, Edith (lyrics). *Roll Over! A Counting Song.*

Gillham, Bill. *Where Does It Go?*

Graham, John. *I Love You, Mouse.*

Gundersheimer, Karen. *Colors to Know.*

Haus, Felice. *Beep! Beep! I'm A Jeep!*

Hayes, Geoffrey. *Bear By Himself.*

Hoban, Tana. *Big Ones, Little Ones.*

Hoban, Tana. *Count and See.*

Hoban, Tana. *Push/Pull Empty/Full.*

Hughes, Shirley. *Alfie Gives A Hand.*

Ichikawa, Satomi. *Let's Play.*

Kalan, Robert. *Jump, Frog, Jump!*

Karn, George. *Circus Big and Small.*

Keats, Ezra Jack. *The Snowy Day.*

Keller, Holly. *Geraldine's Blanket.*

Kilroy, Sally. *Grandpa's Garden.*

Krauss, Ruth. *A Hole Is to Dig.*

Krauze, Andrzej. *Christopher Crocodile Cooks a Meal.*

Krementz, Jill. *Katherine Goes to Nursery School.*

Lacome, Julie. *My First Book of Words.*

Ladybird Series. *Let's Go Shopping.*

Lenski, Lois. *Sing a Song of People.*

LeSieg, Theo. *In A People House.*

Lobel, Arnold. *The Rose in My Garden.*

Lynn, Sara. *Colors.*

Marie, Susan. *I Will Not Wear That Sweater.*

McCloskey, Robert. *Make Way for Ducklings.*

Merrill, Susan. *Washday.*

Miller, J.P. *Yoo-hoo, Little Rabbit: A Peek-A-Board Book.*

Murray, W. *Talkabout Home.*

O'Donnell, Elizabeth Lee. *Maggie Doesn't Want to Move.*

Oxenbury, Helen. *Beach Days.*

Peppe, Rodney. *Circus Numbers.*

Petersham, Maud and Miska. *The Box with Red Wheels.*

Phillips, Joan. *Peek-A-Boo! I See You!*

Potter, Beatrix. *Cecily Parsley's Nursery Rhymes.*

Potter, Beatrix. *Meet Peter Rabbit.*

Preston, Edna Mitchell. *The Temper Tantrum Book.*

Price, Mathew. *My Daddy.*

Rey, H.A. *Where's My Baby?*

Rey, H.A. *See the Circus.*

Rogers, Fred. *Going to Day Care.*

Rogers, Fred. *Going to the Doctor.*

Roth, Harold. *Nursery School.*

Savage, Dorothy. *The Yellow Peephole Book.*

Scarry, Richard. *Richard Scarry's Best First Book Ever!*

Seidenn, Art. *Counting Rhymes.*

Shulevitz, Uri. *One Monday Morning.*

Silverstein, Shel. *Where the Sidewalk Ends: The Poems and Drawings of Shel Silverstein.*

Slobodkina, Esphyr. *Caps for Sale.*

Stevenson, Robert Louis. *The Moon.*

Tallarico, Tony. *Shapes: See and Say.*

Tax, Meredith. *Families.*

Tobias, Tobi. *Moving Day.*

Venables, Bob. *Jungle.*

Watanabe, Shigeo. *I Can Ride It!*

Watanabe, Shigeo. *Daddy, Play With Me.*

Watanabe, Shigeo. *I Can Build A House.*

Wildsmith, Brian. *The Island.*

Wolde, Gunilla. *Betsy and the Doctor.*

Wolde, Gunilla. *Betsy's Baby Brother.*

Wolde, Gunilla. *This is Betsy.*

Yolen, Jane. *The Three Bears Rhyme Book.*

Zolotow, Charlotte. *Hold My Hand.*

Zolotow, Charlotte. *I Have a Horse of My Own.*

Zolotow, Charlotte. *One Step, Two.*

Zolotow, Charlotte. *Three Funny Friends.*

Zolotow, Charlotte. *Wake Up and Goodnight.*

Three Years

Adoff, Arnold. *Black Is Brown Is Tan.*

Ahlberg, Janet and Allan. *Playmates.*

Alexander, Martha. *When the New Baby Comes I'm Moving Out.*

Alexander, Martha. *Out! Out! Out!*

Alexander, Martha. *Blackboard Bear.*

Allen, Robert. *A First Counting Book.*

Andry, Andrew C., and Schepp, Steven. *How Babies Are Made.*

Anno, Mitsumasa. *Anno's Counting Book.*

Asbjornsen, Peter Christen. *The Three Billy Goats Gruff.*

Baum, Louis. *One More Time.*

Behrens, June. *Can You Walk the Plank?*

Bemelmans, Ludwig. *Parsley*.

Bemelmans, Ludwig. *Madeline*.

Berger, Barbara. *Grandfather Twilight*.

Bonne, Rose. *I Know an Old Lady*.

Bonsall, Crosby. *The Day I Had to Play with My Sister*.

Brandenberg, Franz. *I Wish I Was Sick Too*.

Bridwell, Norman. *Clifford, the Big Red Red Dog*.

Brown, Margaret Wise. *The Important Book*.

Bruna, Dick. *The Apple*.

Bruna, Dick. *The King*.

Burningham, John. *John Burningham's 1 2 3*.

Burningham, John. *Mr. Gumpy's Motor Car*.

Burton, Virginia Lee. *Kathy and the Big Snow*.

Burton, Virginia Lee. *The Little House*.

Burton, Virginia Lee. *Mike Mulligan and his Steam Shovel*.

Byers, Betsy. *Go and Hush the Baby*.

Campbell, Rod. *Pet Shop*.

Caple, Kathy. *The Purse*.

Carle, Eric. *My Very First Book of Numbers*.

Chevalier, Christa. *Spence Isn't Spence Any More*.

Chevalier, Christa. *Spence Makes Circles*.

Clifton, Lucille. *Don't You Remember*.

Clifton, Lucille. *Good, Says Jerome*.

Cohen, Miriam. *Best Friends*.

Cohen, Miriam. *Will I Have a Friend?*

Crews, Donald. *Carousel*.

Crews, Donald. *Flying*.

Crews, Donald. *Harbor*.

Crews, Donald. *School Bus*.

Crews, Donald. *Truck*.

Crowther, Robert. *The Most Amazing Hide-and-Seek Opposites Book*.

Daly, Niki. *Look at Me.*

De Regniers, Beatrice Schenk. *Waiting for Mama.*

DePaola, Tomie. *Nana Upstairs and Nana Downstairs.*

DePaola, Tomie. *Pancakes for Breakfast.*

DePaola, Tomie. *Strega Nona.*

Dragonwagon, Crescent. *Wind Rose.*

Edwards, Ron. *The Postal Service.*

Eichler, Margrit. *Martin's Father.*

Erikson, Karen. *No One Is Perfect.*

Ets, Marie Hall. *Just Me.*

Ets, Marie Hall. *In the Forest.*

Felt, Sue. *Rosa Too Little.*

Ga'g, Wanda. *Millions of Cats.*

Galdone, Paul. *Henny Penny.*

Galdone, Paul. *The Little Red Hen.*

Galdone, Paul. *The Teeny-Tiny Woman: A Ghost Story.*

Galdone, Paul. *The Three Bears.*

Geringer, Laura. *Molly's New Washing Machine.*

Gibbons, Gail. *Boats.*

Gibbons, Gail. *Tunnels.*

Gillham, Bill. *Can You See It?*

Gillham, Bill. *What Can You Do?*

Gillham, Bill. *What's the Difference?*

Gillham, Bill and Hulme, Susan. *Let's Look for Opposites.*

Gillham, Bill and Hulme, Susan. *Let's Look for Shapes.*

Girard, Laura Walvood. *You Were Born on Your Very First Birthday.*

Goff, Beth. *Where Is Daddy? The Story of a Divorce.*

Goodall, John S. *The Surprise Picnic.*

Gray, Genevieve. *Send Wendell.*

Griffith, Helen V. *Mine Will, Said John.*

Gundersheimer, Karen. *Shapes to Show.*

Hader, Berta and Elmer. *The Big Snow.*

Hadithi, Mwenye. *Greedy Zebra.*

Harper, Anita. *It's Not Fair.*

Hautzig, Deborah. *Why Are You So Mean to Me?*

Hazen, Barbara Shook. *Gorilla Wants to Be the Baby.*

Hazen, Nancy. *Grownups Cry Too/Los Adultos Tambien Lloran.*

Hedderwick, Mairi. *Katie Morag and the Tiresome Ted.*

Hellard, Susan. *Billy Goats Gruff.*

Helmering, David Wild, and Williams, John. *We're Going to Have a Baby.*

Hines, Anna Grossnickle. *All By Myself.*

Hoban, Russell. *Bedtime for Frances.*

Hoban, Russell. *Bread and Jam for Frances.*

Hoban, Tana. *Is It Red? Is It Yellow? Is It Blue? An Adventure in Color.*

Hoban, Tana. *Over, Under & Through.*

Hoban, Tana. *Round & Round & Round.*

Hoffman, Phyllis. *Baby's Kitchen.*

Holden, Edith. *The Hedgehog Feast.*

Hou-tien, Cheng. *Six Chinese Brothers.*

Hughes, Shirley. *All Shapes and Sizes.*

Hughes, Shirley. *Bathwater's Hot.*

Hughes, Shirley. *Lucy and Tom's Day.*

Hutchins, Pat. *Changes, Changes.*

Hyman, Robin and Inge. *Casper and the Rainbow Bird.*

Jewell, Nancy. *The Snuggle Bunny.*

Johnson, Ilse, and Hazelton, Nika Standen. *Cookies and Breads: The Baker's Art.*

Kahl, Virginia. *The Dutchess Bakes a Cake.*

Karn, George. *Circus Big and Small.*

Keats, Ezra Jack. *A Letter to Amy.*

Keats, Ezra Jack. *Whistle for Willie.*

Kellogg, Steven. *Chicken Little.*

Kightley, Rosalinda. *Opposites.*

Kightley, Rosalinda. *Shapes.*

Krahn, Fernando. *Who's Seen the Scissors?*

Krasilovsky, Phyllis. *The Very Little Boy.*

Kunhart, Dorothy. *Mrs. Sheep's Little Lamb.*

Lakin, Patricia. *Don't Touch My Room.*

Lasker, Joe. *Mothers Can Do Anything.*

Lear, Edward. *The Owl and the Pussy-Cat.*

Lenski, Lois. *Lois Lenski's Big Big Book of Mr. Small.*

Lewin, Hugh. *Jafta.*

Lionni, Leo. *Fish Is Fish.*

Lynn, Sara. *1 2 3.*

Mack, Stan. *10 Bears in My Bed.*

Manushkin, Fran. *Bubblebath.*

Mayer, Mercer. *Ah-Choo.*

Mayer, Mercer. *A Boy, a Dog, and a Frog.*

Mayer, Mercer. *Hiccup.*

McCloskey, Robert. *Blueberries for Sal.*

McMillan, Bruce. *Becca Forward, Becca Backward: A Book of Concept Pairs.*

Merriam, Eve. *Mommies at Work.*

Miller, J.P. *Little Rabbit Goes to the Doctor.*

Miller, J.P. *Big and Little.*

Milne, A.A. *Pooh's Counting Book.*

Mitgutsch, Ali. *From Lemon to Lemonade.*

Moss, Elaine. *In the Garden.*

Ong, Cristina. *Gymboree Back and Forth!*

Ormerod, Jan. *Moonlight.*

Ormerod, Jan. *Sunshine.*

Ormondroyd, Edward. *Theodore.*

Oxenbury, Helen. *Playschool.*

Peek, Merle. *Roll Over.*

Piper, Watty. *The Little Engine That Could.*

Pomerantz, Charlotte. *The Half-Birthday Party.*

Potter, Beatrix. *The Tale of Peter Rabbit.*

Pryor, Bonnie. *Grandpa Bear.*

Rey, H.A. *Curious George.*

Ringi, Kjell. *The Winner.*

Roberts, Sarah. *I Want to Go Home!*

Roche, P.K. *Webster and Arnold and the Giant Box.*

Rockwell, Harlow. *My Dentist.*

Rockwell, Harlow. *My Nursery School.*

Rogers, Fred. *The New Baby.*

Scheffler, Ursel. *A Walk in the Rain.*

Scott, Ann Herbert. *On Mother's Lap.*

Sendak, Maurice. *Chicken Soup With Rice.*

Sendak, Maurice. *Where the Wild Things Are.*

Seuss, Dr. (Theodore Geisel). *Horton Hatches the Who.*

Sharmat, Marjorie Weinman. *A Big Fat Enormous Lie.*

Sharmat, Marjorie Weinman. *I Want Mama.*

Sharmat, Marjorie Weinman. *I'm Terrific.*

Sharmat, Marjorie Weinman. *Scarlet Monster Lives Here.*

Simon, Norma. *How Do I Feel?*

Simon, Norma. *I'm Busy, Too.*

Sinberg, Janet. *Divorce Is a Grown Up Problem.*

Smith, Wendy. *The Lonely, Only Mouse.*

Spier, Peter. *Fast-Slow, High-Low: A Book of Opposites by Peter Spier.*

Spier, Peter. *The Fox Went Out on a Chilly Night.*

Spier, Peter. *London Bridge Is Falling Down!*

Spier, Peter. *Rain.*

Stein, Sara Bonnett. *Making Babies.*

Steptoe, John. *My Special Best Words.*

Steptoe, John. *Daddy Is a Monster . . . Sometimes.*

Stevens, Janet. *Goldilocks and the Three Bears.*

Stevenson, James. *Higher on the Door.*

Stiles, Norman. *I'll Miss You, Mr. Hooper.*

Supraner, Robyn. *It's Not Fair.*

Surowiecki, Sandra Lucas. *Joshua's Day*.

Tannenbaum, D. Leb. *Getting Ready for Baby*.

Terris, Susan. *Amanda the Panda and the Redhead*.

Thomas, Marlo (conceived by). *Free to Be . . . You and Me*.

Titherington, Jeanne. *A Place for Ben*.

Tompert, Ann. *Little Fox Goes to the End of the World*.

Tuffy Preschool Books. *Simple Objects See and Say*.

Turkle, Brinton. *Deep in the Forest*.

Waber, Bernard. *Bernard*.

Waber, Bernard. *Ira Sleeps Over*.

Warburg, Sandol Stoddard. *Bedtime for Bear*.

Wells, Rosemary. *Noisy Nora*.

Wilhelm, Hans. *I'll Always Love You*.

Worthington, Phoebe and Joan. *Teddy Bear Gardener*.

Yashima, Taro. *Umbrella*.

Yolen, Jane. *An Invitation to the Butterfly Ball*.

Ziefert, Harriet. *Bear Goes Shopping: A Guessing Game Story*.

Ziefert, Harriet. *Birthday Card, Where Are You?*

Ziefert, Harriet. *Dress Little Bunny: A Sticker Story*.

Ziefert, Harriet. *Harry Takes a Bath*.

Ziefert, Harriet. *Sarah's Questions*.

Zion, Gene. *Harry, the Dirty Dog*.

Zolotow, Charlotte. *Big Brother*.

Zolotow, Charlotte. *Mr. Rabbit and the Lovely Present*.

Zolotow, Charlotte. *The Park Book*.

Zolotow, Charlotte. *William's Doll*.

Four Years

Ackerman, Karen. *Flannery Row, An Alphabet Rhyme*.

Adams, Florence. *Mushy Eggs*.

Ahlberg, Allan. *Each Peach Pear Plum*.

Alexander, Martha. *I'll Be the Horse If You'll Play with Me*.

Alexander, Martha. *I'll Protect You from the Jungle Beasts*.

Alexander, Sue. *Small Plays for You and a Friend*.

Amoss, Berthie. *Tom in the Middle*.

Anderson, C.W. *Billy and Blaze*.

Anno, Mitsumasa. *Anno's Alphabet*.

Asch, Frank. *Just Like Daddy*.

Azarian, Mary. *A Farmer's Alphabet*.

Banish, Roslyn. *I Want to Tell You About My Baby*.

Banner, Angela. *Ant and Bee Time*.

Barlowe, Dot and Sy. *Dinosaurs*.

Baskin, Hosea, Tobias, and Lisa. *Hosie's Alphabet*.

Bass, Ellen. *I Like You to Make Jokes With Me, But I Don't Want You to Touch Me*.

Bauer, Caroline Feller. *My Mother Travels A Lot*.

Behrens, Judy. *Soo-Ling Finds a Way*.

Berenstain, Stan and Jan. *The Berenstain Bears Learn About Strangers*.

Berenstain, Stanley and Janice. *The Berenstain's B Book*.

Bodecker, N.M. *Miss Jaster's Garden*.

Bottner, Barbara. *Jungle Day or How I Learned to Love My Nosey Little Brother*.

Brett, Molly. *An Alphabet by Molly Brett*.

Briggs, Raymond. *The Snowman*.

Bromhall, Winifred. *Middle Mathilda*.

Brown, Judith Gwyn. *Alphabet Dreams*.

Brown, Marcia. *Stone Soup*.

Brown, Margaret Wise. *The Dead Bird*.

Burningham, John. *Granpa*.

Burningham, John. *The Shopping Basket*.

Burningham, John. *Viking Number Play Series*.

Burton, Albert, Jr. *Mine, Yours, Ours*.

Carle, Eric. *1,2,3 to the Zoo*.

Carle, Eric. *The Secret Birthday Message*.

Chalmers, Maru. *Six Dogs, Twenty-Six Cats, Forty-Five Mice and One Hundred Sixteen Spiders*.

Charren, Peggy, and Hulsizer, Carol. *The TV-Smart Book for Kids*.

Chittum, Ida. *The Cat's Pajamas*.

Clifton, Lucille. *Some of the Days of Everett Anderson*.

Clifton, Lucille. *Everett Anderson's Year*.

Clifton, Lucille. *Everett Anderson's Goodbye*.

Cohen, Miriam. *See You Tomorrow, Charles*.

Cole, Joanna. *How You Were Born*.

Cole, Joanna. *My Puppy Is Born*.

Cole, Joanna. *The New Baby at Your House*.

Crary, Elizabeth. *I Want It: A Children's Problem Solving Book*.

Dennis, Wesley. *Flip*.

DePaola, Tomie. *Giorgio's Village*.

Dragonwagon, Crescent. *I Hate My Brother Harry*.

Dragonwagon, Crescent. *Will It Be Okay?*

Drescher, Joan. *Your Family, My Family*.

Eastman, P.D. *Big Dog, Little Dog*.

Ehrlich, Amy. *The Random House Book of Fairy Tales*.

Elliott, Dan. *Grover Goes to School*.

Ellison, Virginia H. *Pooh Bear's Cook Book*.

Eriksson, Eva. *Jealousy*.

Eugene, Toni. *Hide and Seek*.

Farber, Norma. *As I Was Crossing Boston Common*.

Fassler, Joan. *My Grandpa Died Today*.

Feelings, Muriel. *Moja Means One: A Swahili Counting Book*.

Feelings, Muriel. *Zamani Goes to Market*.

Fisher, Aileen. *I Stood upon a Mountain*.

Fisher, Leonard Everett. *Boxes, Boxes*.

Flack, Marjorie and Wiese, Kurt. *The Story About Ping*.

Fleisher, Robbin. *Quilts in the Attic*.

Fletcher, Helen. *Picture Book ABC*.

Florian, Douglas. *People Working*.

Ga'g, Wanda. *The ABC Bunny*.

Galdone, Paul. *The Gingerbread Boy.*

Gerson, Mary-Joan. *Ometiji's Baby Brother.*

Gibbons, Gail. *Toolbox.*

Gibbons, Gail. *Trains.*

Gibbons, Gail. *Up Goes the Skyscraper.*

Glazier, Nancy Hannah. *My Very Own Telephone Book.*

Goodall, John S. *Creepy Castle.*

Goodyear, Carmen. *The Sheep Book.*

Gramatky, Hardie. *Little Toot.*

Greenaway, Kate. *A Apple Pie.*

Greenfield, Eloise. *Honey, I Love, and Other Love Poems.*

Griffith, Helen. *Georgia Music.*

Hague, Kathleen. *Alphabears.*

Hague, Kathleen. *Numbears.*

Hall, Donald. *Ox-Cart Man.*

Harris, Robie H. *I Hate Kisses.*

Hautzig, Deborah. *It's Not Fair.*

Hautzig, Deborah. *A Visit to Sesame Street Library.*

Hayward, Linda. *The Sesame Street Dictionary.*

Hendrickson, Karen. *Baby and I Can Play.*

Hendrickson, Karen. *Fun with Toddlers.*

Hewett, Joan. *Rosalie.*

Hill, Elizabeth Starr. *Evan's Corner.*

Hill, Susan. *Go Away Bad Dreams.*

Himler, Ronald. *Wake Up Jeremiah.*

Hoban, Russell. *Charlie the Tramp.*

Hoban, Tana. *A,B,See!*

Hoban, Tana. *Is It Larger? Is It Smaller?*

Hoban, Tana. *Take Another Look.*

Högner, Franz. *From Blueprint to House.*

Hogrogian, Nonny. *One Fine Day.*

Hoopes, Lyn Littlefield. *Nana.*

Howe, James. *When You Go to Kindergarten.*

Hughes, Shirley. *George the Babysitter.*

Isadora, Rachel. *Jesse and Abe.*

Isadora, Rachel. *Max.*

Isenberg, Barbara, and Jaffee, Marjorie. *Albert the Running Bear's Exercise Book.*

Johnson, Crockett. *Harold and the Purple Crayon.*

Jonas, Ann. *When You Were a Baby.*

Jones, Maurice. *I'm Going on a Dragon Hunt.*

Kalas, Sybille. *The Goose Family Book.*

Kantrowitz, Mildred. *Willie Bear.*

Keats, Ezra Jack. *John Henry.*

Keats, Ezra Jack. *Peter's Chair.*

Keller, Holly. *Goodbye, Max.*

Kellogg, Steven. *Pecos Bill.*

Kightley, Rosalinda. *ABC.*

Kismaric, Susan. *American Children.*

Kitchen, Bert. *Animal Alphabet.*

Krahn, Fernando. *April Fools.*

Kraus, Robert. *Leo, the Late Bloomer.*

Kraus, Robert. *Whose Mouse Are You?*

Krementz, Jill. *Holly's Farm Animals.*

Lalli, Judy. *Feelings Alphabet.*

Lasky, Kathryn and Maxwell. *A Baby for Max.*

Lenett, Robin and Barthelme, Dana. *My Body Is My Own!*

Lionni, Leo. *Alexander and the Wind-Up Mouse.*

Lionni, Leo. *Frederick.*

Lionni, Leo. *Inch by Inch.*

Little, Lessie Jones and Greenfield, Eloise. *I Can Do It Myself.*

Lobel, Anita, with Words by Lobel, Arnold. *On Market Street.*

Lobel, Arnold. *Frog and Toad All Year.*

Lobel, Arnold. *Frog and Toad Are Friends.*

Louie, Ai-Ling. *Yeh-Shen.*

MacDonald, Suse. *Alphabatics.*

Manushkin, Fran. *Little Rabbit's Baby Brother*.

Mari, Iela. *Eat and Be Eaten*.

Marshall, James. *George and Martha*.

Marshall, James. *George and Martha Encore*.

Marshall, James. *George and Martha One Fine Day*.

Marshall, James. *George and Martha Tons of Fun*.

Martin, Elizabeth. *Making Pretzels*.

Martin, Rafe. *Foolish Rabbit's Big Mistake*.

Mattmuller, Felix. *We Want a Little Sister*.

Maury, Inez. *My Mother the Mail Carrier*.

Mayer, Mercer. *There's a Nightmare in my Closet*.

McCloskey, Robert. *Lentil*.

McCloskey, Robert. *Time of Wonder*.

Milne, A.A. *Winnie-the-Pooh*.

Milne, A.A. *The House at Pooh Corner*.

Minarik, Else Holmelund. *Little Bear*.

Mitchell, Joyce Slayton. *My Mommy Makes Money*.

Mitgutsch, Ali. *From Rubber Tree to Tire*.

Mitgutsch, Ali. *From Wood to Paper*.

Moncure, Jane Belk. *My Baby Brother Needs a Friend*.

Musgrove, Margaret. *Ashanti to Zulu*.

Neumeier, Marty and Glaser, Byron. *Action Alphabet*.

Noble, June. *Two Homes for Lynn*.

Omerod, Jan. *101 Things To Do With a Baby*.

Pearson, Susan. *Everybody Knows That!*

Peebles, Lynne. *Cooking With Mother*.

Perrine, Mary. *Salt Boy*.

Peterson, Joan Whitehouse. *I Have a Sister—My Sister Is Deaf*.

Prokofiev, Sergei. *Peter and the Wolf*.

Rabe, Berniece. *The Balancing Girl*.

Rice, James. *Cajun Alphabet*.

Rice, Eve. *New Blue Shoes*.

Robart, Rose. *The Cake That Mack Ate*.

Robbins, Ken. *City/Country*.

Roche, P.K. *I Can Be.* . . .

Rockwell, Anne and Harlow. *My Baby-Sitter*.

Rockwell, Anne. *The Three Sillies and 10 Other Stories To Read Aloud*.

Rosario, Idalia. *Idalia's Project ABC*.

Roser, Wiltrud. *Lena and Leopold*.

Russ, Lavinia. *Alec's Sand Castle*.

Rylant, Cynthia. *The Relatives Came*.

Sasaki, Isao. *Snow*.

Scarry, Richard. *Short and Tall*.

Schlein, Miriam. *The Way Mothers Are*.

Scott, Ann Herbert. *Sam*.

Seeger, Pete. *Abiyoyo*.

Seuss, Dr. (Theodore Geisel). *The 500 Hats of Bartholomew Cubbins*.

Sharmat, Marjorie. *Goodnight Andrew, Goodnight Craig*.

Sharmat, Marjorie Weinman. *I Don't Care*.

Sharmat, Marjorie. *Sometimes Mama and Papa Fight*.

Shiefman, Vicky. *M Is for Move*.

Shyer, Marlene Fanta. *Here I Am, an Only Child*.

Simon, Norma. *I Was So Mad*.

Smith, Jennifer. *Grover and the New Kid*.

Smith, Dian G. *My New Baby and Me*.

Spier, Peter. *Noah's Ark*.

Spier, Peter. *People*.

Stanek, Muriel. *Starting School*.

Stanek, Muriel. *Who's Afraid of the Dark?*

Stecher, Miriam B., and Kandall, Alice S. *Daddy and Ben Together*.

Steichen, Edward. *The Family of Man*.

Steig, William. *Sylvester and the Magic Pebble*.

Stein, Sara Bonnett. *That New Baby*.

Stevens, Janet. *The House that Jack Built*.

Tarrant, Graham. *Frogs.*

Tester, Sylvia. *Sometimes I'm Afraid.*

Tester, Sylvia Root. *We Laughed A Lot, My First Day of School.*

Thomas, Ianthe. *Lordy, Aunt Hattie.*

Udry, Janice May. *Let's Be Enemies.*

Underhill, Liz. *Jack of All Trades.*

Vigna, Judith. *She's Not My Real Mother.*

Viorst, Judith. *The Tenth Good Thing About Barney.*

Viorst, Judith. *Alexander and the Terrible, Horrible, No Good, Very Bad Day.*

Wahl, Jan. *Humphrey's Bear.*

Ward, Lynd. *The Biggest Bear.*

Watson, Jane Werner, Switzer, Robert, and Hirschberg, J.C. *Sometimes I'm Jealous.*

Waxman, Stephanie. *What Is a Girl? What Is a Boy?*

Weiss, Nicki. *A Family Story.*

White, E.B. *Stuart Little.*

Williams, Barbara. *Jeremy Isn't Hungry.*

Williams, Vera B. *A Chair for My Mother.*

Williams, Vera B. *Something Special for Me.*

Willoughby, Elaine Macmann. *Boris and the Monsters.*

Winthrop, Elizabeth. *That's Mine.*

Witcomb, Gerald. *ABC.*

Wittman, Sally. *The Wonderful Mrs. Trumbly.*

Wolf, Janet. *The Best Present Is Me.*

Yolen, Jane. *All in the Woodland Early.*

Yolen, Jane. *Ring of Earth.*

Young, Ed. *The Other Bone.*

Young, Ed. *Up a Tree.*

Ziefert, Harriet. *A New Coat for Anna.*

Zolotow, Charlotte. *Big Sister, Little Sister.*

Zolotow, Charlotte. *Do You Know What I'll Do?*

Zolotow, Charlotte. *The Hating Book.*

Zolotow, Charlotte. *My Grandson Lew.*

Zolotow, Charlotte. *Say It!*

Zolotow, Charlotte. *Timothy Too.*

Five Years

Adler, David A. *The House on the Roof.*

Ahlberg, Janet and Allan. *The Jolly Postman.*

Aliki. *How a Book Is Made.*

Ancona, George. *Helping Out.*

Andersen, Hans Christian. *The Ugly Duckling.*

Anno, Mitsumasa. *All in a Day.*

Anno, Mitsumasa. *Anno's Journey.*

Arkhurst, Joyce Cooper. *The Adventures of Spider.*

Arnstein, Helene. *Billy and Our New Baby.*

Aruego, Jose and Dewey, Ariane. *We Hide, You Seek.*

Bach, Alice. *The Smartest Bear and His Brother Oliver.*

Bahr, Amy C. *It's OK To Say No: A Book for Parents and Children to Read Together.*

Baker, Olaf. *Where the Buffaloes Begin.*

Barklem, Jill. *Winter Story.*

Barrie, J.M. (Retold by Harrison, David L.). *Peter Pan.*

Baylor, Byrd. *Guess Who My Favorite Person Is.*

Baylor, Byrd. *The Way to Start a Day.*

Bierhorst, John (Adaptor). *Songs of the Chippewa.*

Black, Claudia. *My Dad Loves Me, My Dad Has a Disease.*

Blaine, Marge. *The Terrible Thing That Happened at Our House.*

Boegehold, Betty. *Daddy Doesn't Live Here Anymore.*

Braithwaite, Althea. *Special Care Babies.*

Brandenberg, Franz. *Aunt Nina and Her Nephews and Nieces.*

Branley, Franklyn M. *Air Is All Around You.*

Branley, Franklyn M. *What Makes Day and Night.*

Brightman, Alan. *Like Me.*

Brown, Myra Berry. *Amy and the New Baby.*

Bryan, Ashley. *The Cat's Purr.*

Bunting, Eve. *The Happy Funeral*.

Carrick, Carol. *The Accident*.

Chapman, Carol. *The Tale of Meshka the Kvetch*.

Charlip, Remy and Moore, Lillian. *Hooray for Me!*

Clardy, Andrea Fleck. *Dusty Was My Friend: Coming to Terms With Loss*.

Clark, Ann Nolan. *In My Mother's House*.

Clifton, Lucille. *My Brother Fine With Me*.

Clymer, Eleanor. *The Tiny Little House*.

Cohen, Miriam. *Jim's Dog Muffins*.

Conford, Ellen. *Just the Thing for Geraldine*.

Cooney, Barbara. *Miss Rumphius*.

Coutant, Helen. *First Snow*.

Crowley, Arthur. *Bonzo Beaver*.

Dang, Manh Kha. *In the Land of Small Dragon*.

De Poix, Carol. *Jo, Flo, and Yolanda*.

Delton, Julie. *My Uncle Nikos*.

DePaola, Tomie. *The Legend of Bluebonnet*.

DePaola, Tomie. *Now One Foot, Now the Other*.

DePaola, Tomie. *Oliver Button Is a Sissy*.

DePaola, Tomie. *Sing, Pierrot, Sing*.

Dickinson, Mary. *Alex and the Baby*.

Dragonwagon, Crescent. *Always, Always*.

Eber, Christine E. *Just Momma and Me*.

Eisenberg, Phyllis Rose. *A Mitzvah Is Something Special*.

Epstein, Beryl, and Davis, Dorritt. *Two Sisters and Some Hornets*.

Everton, Macduff. *El Circo Magico Modelo/Finding The Magic Circus*.

Fassler, Joan. *Howie Helps Himself*.

Feelings, Muriel. *Jambo Means Hello*.

Florian, Douglas. *Discovering Butterflies*.

Florian, Douglas. *Discovering Trees*.

Fritz, Jean. *The Good Giants and the Bad Pukwudgies*.

Galdone, Paul. *Rumpelstiltskin.*

Galdone, Paul. *The Three Billy Goats Gruff.*

Geisert, Arthur. *Pigs from A to Z.*

Gibbons, Gail. *Department Store.*

Gibbons, Gail. *The Post Office Book: Mail and How It Moves.*

Goffstein, M.B. *School of Names.*

Graham, Ada. Oxford Scientific Films. *Grey Squirrel.*

Greenfield, Eloise. *Me and Nessie.*

Greenfield, Eloise. *She Come Bringing Me That Little Baby Girl.*

Griffith, Helen V. *Georgia Music.*

Haley, Gail E. *A Story, A Story.*

Hawkins, Colin. *Take Away Monsters.*

Hazen, Barbara Shook. *If It Weren't for Benjamin.*

Hazen, Barbara Shook. *Why Couldn't I Be an Only Child Like You, Wigger.*

Hertz, Ole. *Tobias Catches Trout.*

Hertz, Ole. *Tobias Goes Seal Hunting.*

Hest, Amy. *The Purple Coat.*

Hickman, Martha W. *Last Week My Brother Anthony Died.*

Hoban, Russell. *A Baby Sister for Frances.*

Hoban, Russell. *A Birthday for Frances.*

Hoffman, Phyllis. *The Robot Book.*

Hogan, Paula Z. *Sometimes I Get So Mad.*

Holmes, Efner Tudor. *Amy's Goose.*

Homan, Dianne. *In Christina's Toolbox.*

Horwitz, Joshua. *Night Markets: Bringing Food to the City.*

Jarrell, Mary. *The Knee Baby.*

Jewell, Nancy. *Time for Uncle Joe.*

Jones, Hettie, ed. *The Trees Stand Shining: Poetry of the Native American Indian.*

Joslin, Sesyle. *What Do You Say, Dear?*

Kantrowitz, Mildred. *When Violet Died.*

Kay, Helen. *Apron On, Apron Off.*

Klein, Norma. *Girls Can Be Anything.*

Kouzel, Daisy. *The Cuckoo's Reward/El Premio Del Cuco*.

Langner, Nola. *Rafiki*.

Lasker, Joe. *He's My Brother*.

Leaf, Margaret. *Eyes of the Dragon*.

Leiner, Katherine. *Ask Me What My Mother Does*.

Leokum, Arkady. *Tell Me Why #1*.

Lesser, Rika. *Hansel and Gretel*.

Lester, Julius. *The Tales of Uncle Remus and the Adventures of Brer Rabbit*.

Levinson, Irene. *Peter Learns to Crochet*.

Levy, Elizabeth. *Nice Little Girls*.

Lionni, Leo. *The Biggest House in the World*.

Lobel, Arnold. *Fables*.

Locker, Thomas. *The Mare on the Hill*.

Logue, Christopher. *Puss in Boots*.

Longfellow, Henry Wadsworth. *Hiawatha*.

MacDonald, Golden. *The Little Island*.

MacLachlan, Patricia. *Through Grandpa's Eyes*.

Malecki, Maryann. *Mom and Dad and I Are Having a Baby*.

Mannheim, Grete. *The Two Friends*.

Martel, Cruz. *Yagua Days*.

Matsuno, Masako. *Pair of Red Clogs*.

McLerran, Alice. *The Mountain That Loved the Bird*.

Mellonie, Bryan, and Ingpen, Robert. *Lifetimes: The Beautiful Way to Explain Death*.

Mendoza, George. *And I Must Hurry for the Sea Is Coming In*.

Mendoza, George. *Need a House? Call Ms. Mouse!*

Munsch, Robert N. *The Paper Bag Princess*.

Naylor, Phyllis Reynolds. *All Because I'm Older*.

Ness, Evaline. *Do You Have the Time, Lydia?*

Nixon, Joan Lowery. *The Gift*.

Noble, June. *Where Do I Fit In?*

Parents Magazine. *Mike the Mailman*.

Paris, Susan. *Mommy and Daddy Are Fighting*.

Peterson, Jeanne Whithouse. *That Is That.*

Polland, Barbara Kay. *Feelings Inside You & Outloud Too.*

Pollock, Penny. *Water Is Wet.*

Polushkin, Maria. *Baby Brother Blues.*

Pomerantz, Barbara. *Bubby, Me, and Memories.*

Prokofiev, Sergei. *Peter and the Wolf* (A Mechanical Book).

Provensen, Alice. *A Peaceable Kingdom.*

Provensen, Alice and Martin. *The Glorious Flight Across the Channel with Louis Bleriot, July 25, 1909.*

Pryor, Bonnie. *The House on Maple Street.*

Raynor, Dorka. *My Friends Live in Many Places.*

Reit, Seymour. *Child of the Navajos.*

Robbins, Ruth. *Baboushka and the Three Kings.*

Rockwell, Anne. *When We Grow Up.*

Rockwell, Anne and Harlow. *The Emergency Room.*

Root, Phyllis. *Hidden Places.*

Russell, Helen and Ross. *Foraging for Dinner.*

Rylant, Cynthia. *When I Was Young in the Mountains.*

Saul, Wendy. *Butcher, Baker, Cabinetmaker.*

Schick, Eleanor. *City in Winter.*

Schuchman, Joan. *Two Places to Sleep.*

Schwartz, David M. *How Much Is a Million?*

Sendak, Maurice. *Pierre: A Cautionary Tale.*

Sendak, Maurice. *In the Night Kitchen.*

Shulevitz, Uri. *Dawn.*

Simon, Norma. *All Kinds of Families.*

Simon, Norma. *Nobody's Perfect, Not Even My Mother.*

Simon, Norma. *The Saddest Time.*

Simon, Norma. *Why Am I Different?*

Skolsky, Mindy Warshaw. *The Whistling Teakettle.*

Steig, William. *The Amazing Bone.*

Steig, William. *Amos & Boris.*

Stein, Sara Bonnett. *About Handicaps.*

Stenson, Janet Sinberg. *Now I Have a Stepparent and It's Kind of Confusing.*

Steptoe, John. *Birthday.*

Steptoe, John. *Stevie.*

Stull, Edith. *My Turtle Died Today.*

Taylor, Sydney. *All-of-a Kind Family.*

Thomas, Ianthe. *My Street's a Cool Morning Street.*

Thomas, Ianthe. *Walk Home Tired, Billy Jenkins.*

Thomas, Ianthe. *Willie Blows a Mean Horn.*

Turner, Ann. *Dakota Dugout.*

Van Leeuwen, Jean. *Amanda Pig and Her Big Brother Oliver.*

Vigna, Judith. *Daddy's New Baby.*

Viorst, Judith. *I'll Fix Anthony.*

Viorst, Judith. *Sunday Morning.*

Waber, Bernard. *Lorenzo.*

Walker, Jill. *A Caribbean Alphabet.*

Warburg, Sandol Stoddard. *Growing Time.*

Watson, Clyde. *Tom Fox and the Apple Pie.*

Weiss, Nicki. *Chuckie.*

White, E.B. *Charlotte's Web.*

Wildsmith, Brian. *Birds.*

Wolf, Bernard. *Don't Feel Sorry for Paul.*

Wolkstein, Diane. *The Banza: A Haitian Story.*

Wolkstein, Diane. *The Red Lion: A Tale of Ancient Persia.*

Wolkstein, Diane. *Squirrel's Song: A Hopi Tale.*

Wright, Betty Ren. *My New Mom and Me.*

Yarbrough, Camille. *Cornrows.*

Yashima, Taro. *Crow Boy.*

Yolen, Jane. *The Seeing Stick.*

Zelinsky, Paul O. *Rumpelstiltskin.*

Zolotow, Charlotte. *If It Weren't For You.*

Appendix E

List of Wordless Books

Many books exist without any words at all. They are often much more complicated than they first appear. They invite the building of so many talking, reading, and thinking skills that we decided to provide you with a separate list of them. The list is not inclusive, but it does provide a starting point for you and your child to read the pictures, discuss the action, and compose narratives together.

Ahlberg, Allan. *Each Peach Pear Plum*.

Alexander, Martha. *Out! Out! Out!*

Anno, Mitsumasa. *Anno's Alphabet*.

Anno, Mitsumasa. *Anno's Counting Book*.

Anno, Mitsumasa. *Anno's Journey*.

Briggs, Raymond. *The Snowman*.

Bruna, Dick. *Playing in Winter*.

Carle, Eric. *Do You Want to Be My Friend?*

Crews, Donald. *Truck*.

DePaola, Tomie. *Pancakes for Breakfast*.

DePaola, Tomie. *Sing, Pierrot, Sing*.

Goodall, John S. *Creepy Castle*.

Goodall, John S. *The Midnight Adventures of Kelly, Dot, and Esmeralda*.

Goodall, John S. *The Surprise Picnic*.

Hoban, Tana. *Big Ones, Little Ones*.

Hoban, Tana. *Is It Larger? Is It Smaller?*

Hoban, Tana. *Is It Red? Is It Yellow? Is It Blue? An Adventure in Color.*

Hoban, Tana. *Round & Round & Round.*

Hoban, Tana. *Take Another Look.*

Hutchins, Pat. *Changes, Changes.*

Krahn, Fernando. *Who's Seen the Scissors?*

Krahn, Fernando. *April Fools.*

Mari, Iela. *Eat and Be Eaten.*

Mayer, Mercer. *Ah-Choo.*

Mayer, Mercer. *A Boy, a Dog, and a Frog.*

Mayer, Mercer. *Hiccup.*

Mendoza, George. *And I Must Hurry for the Sea Is Coming In.*

Ormerod, Jan. *Moonlight.*

Ormerod, Jan. *Sunshine.*

Oxenbury, Helen. *Beach Days.*

Piers, Helen. *Peekaboo Kitten.*

Piers, Helen. *Peekaboo Mouse.*

Piers, Helen. *Peekaboo Rabbit.*

Sasaki, Isao. *Snow.*

Spier, Peter. *Noah's Ark.*

Spier, Peter. *Rain.*

Turkle, Brinton. *Deep in the Forest.*

Young, Ed. *The Other Bone.*

Young, Ed. *Up a Tree.*

The Bookshelf

The following list of books was selected from many lists of award-winning books, publishers' catalogues, the American Library Association Notable Books, lists of books recommended by experts, librarians, parents, and teachers, and our own preferences.

The books are organized in alphabetical order by author. We have also provided supplementary lists by age. For each of the listings we have included the number of the chapter in which we discuss the book. Although every book on the list is meant to be read aloud, some are so dramatic or flavorful that we mention them specifically in chapter 2, "The Magic of Story." We will therefore indicate "Chap. 2" after the book's age level. We make reference to chapter 3, "The Reading Infant," if a book is especially appropriate for infants from birth to eighteen months. Chapter 4, "Stocking the Storehouse," is indicated for any book that is useful for reinforcing cognitive concepts. If chapter 5, "Whistle While You Work," is mentioned, the book contains material related to work in some way. Reference to chapter 6 signifies a book discussed in "The Beginning Bookbag" or a title that addresses the emotions of children under age five. Mention of chapter 7, "Mirrors and Windows," indicates that the book contains some reference to a child's self-image or an enlarged image of the many cultures in the world. It also reflects books that deal with an issue such as death, divorce, or special needs. A book that looks at sibling relationships will refer to chapter 8, "The Enduring

Bond." Reference to chapter 9 indicates that the book is mentioned in the chapter entitled "Taming the One-Eyed Monster: TV."

Each of the books has a suggested beginning age level attached to it. At best, this is only a suggestion. But keep in mind that children often are interested in books that are supposedly far above or below their intended age level. The ages we have affixed to the books are *starting* levels; we have placed no upper limits on the age that a child might continue to be enthralled by a book. The books that have *birth* as the age level are those we think you will enjoy reading to a newborn or infant under six months.

Some of the books listed may be out of print, but may be available in a local library. Many books are also issued in paperback. It's always a good idea to check with your library or local bookstore.

We have included in this list only those books that we have been able to find and read. There are many more excellent books available. You and your child will grow to prefer certain authors and illustrators over others. Ask for more titles by those authors when you go to bookstores and libraries and, at as young an age as possible, permit your child to accompany you to the library to select books. Together you can form an excellent selection team. Meanwhile, start with the following suggested list. And, above all, enjoy, enjoy, for love of reading.

Aardema, Verna. *Bringing the Rain to Kapiti Plain*. Illustrated by Beatriz Vidal. New York: Dial, 1981. Age: 2. Chaps. 2 and 3.
> A cumulative rhyme relating how Ki-Pat brought rain to the drought-stricken Kapiti Plain. It is in the same style as "The House That Jack Built."

Ackerman, Karen. *Flannery Row, An Alphabet Rhyme*. Illustrated by Karen Ann Weinhaus. Boston: Atlantic Monthly Press, 1986. Age: 4. Chaps. 1 and 4.
> A sea captain's children have names starting with each letter of the alphabet.

Adams, Florence. *Mushy Eggs*. Illustrated by Marilyn Hirsch. New York: Putnam, 1973. Age: 4. Chap. 7.
> Although this single-parent family is coping well, they must cross yet another hurdle when their beloved housekeeper

leaves. The competent mother sensitively acknowledges her children's feelings.

Adler, David A. *The House on the Roof.* Illustrated by Kar-Ben. New York: Bonim, 1976. Age: 5. Chap. 7.
     The children's grandfather secretly brings in materials to their apartment house so that he can surprise them by building a sukkah (little house) for Sukkoth (the harvest festival).

Adoff, Arnold. *Black Is Brown Is Tan.* Illustrated by Emily McCully. New York: Harper & Row, 1973. Age: 3. Chap. 7.
     A story-poem celebrating the color differences in a family where the parents are members of different races.

Ahlberg, Allan. *Each Peach Pear Plum.* Illustrated by Janet Ahlberg. Harmondsworth, England: Viking Kestrel, 1978. Age: 4. Chaps. 1 and 2.
     Familiar nursery characters hide in the colorful pictures of this "I Spy" game book.

Ahlberg, Allan and Janet. *The Baby's Catalogue.* Illustrated by the authors. New York: Viking, 1982. Age: 2. Chaps. 4 and 8.
     Each page of this book labels one event, person, or thing in a baby's life and illustrates it with a number of well-drawn examples. Examples are multicultural, nonsexist, and often amusing. Useful for inviting older siblings to acknowledge a baby's life and routine.

Ahlberg, Janet and Allan. *The Jolly Postman.* Illustrated by the authors. Boston: Little, Brown, 1986. Age: 5. Chap. 5.
     A book with real letters and real envelopes written from one fairy-tale character to another. Children and adults will probably go on to invent their own letters to storybook characters. Hint: Since the letters will be handled frequently, cover them with clear contact paper.

Ahlberg, Janet and Allan. *Peek-A-Boo.* Illustrated by the authors. Harmondsworth, England: Penguin, 1981. Age: 1. Chaps. 2 and 3.
     Children can peek through the openings in the middle of the page to see the small vivid details of a busy family's life as they

might be seen by a small baby living in a comfortably cluttered British home during World War II.

Ahlberg, Janet and Allan. *Playmates*. Illustrated by the authors. New York: Viking Kestrel, 1985. Age: 3. Chap. 4.
    On the left-hand side of double-page spread labeled "swap babies" sits a kangaroo with a baby in its pouch. On the right-hand page is a mother with her baby in a stroller. Both babies can be removed from their slots and placed in any other slot in the book. The game of "Who goes where" is enjoyable, as is the fun of mismatching the babies and their proper places. The publishers have included an extra page of spare playmates. You might still want to laminate each of them so that frequent handling won't tatter them.

Alexander, Martha. *Blackboard Bear.* Illustrated by the author. New York: Dial, 1969. Age: 3. Chaps. 6 and 8.
    When a younger brother is repeatedly told that he is too little to join his older brother and friends, he draws a large bear on the blackboard. When it "comes to life" he won't let the big boys play with the bear when they want to. A story of sibling rivalry and imaginary playmates.

Alexander, Martha. *I'll Be the Horse If You'll Play With Me*. Illustrated by the author. New York: Dial, 1975. Age: 4. Chap. 8.
    Expressive pictures and simple text depict the difficulties of being a middle child. Parents and children can collaborate to find better solutions than the one the child in the story selected.

Alexander, Martha. *Out! Out! Out!* Illustrated by the author. New York: Dial, 1968. Age: 3. Chap. 4.
    When a pigeon flies in the window no one seems to know what to do. No grown-up, that is. A small boy solves the problem. A wordless book that young children will enjoy "reading" to you.

Alexander, Martha. *When the New Baby Comes I'm Moving Out*. Illustrated by the author. New York: Dial, 1979. Age: 3. Chap. 8.
    Oliver decides he is leaving home. He has already lost his high chair, crib, and mother's lap and fears more losses when

the new baby comes. Mother reassures him by telling him he will have an important role as big brother.

Alexander, Sue. *Small Plays for You and a Friend*. Illustrated by the author. New York: Houghton Mifflin, 1973. Age: 4. Chaps. 2 and 6.
Too few books of plays exist for this age group. This book is a good starter.

Aliki. *Go Tell Aunt Rhody*. Illustrated by the author. New York: Macmillan, 1974. Age: Birth. Chaps. 3, 4, and 6.
"Go Tell Aunt Rhody" is a favorite folk song that children love despite its message that "the old gray goose is dead." Aliki's illustrations set the scene, adding warmth and brightness to the end of the tale. The music and words are included at the end of the book.

Aliki. *How A Book Is Made*. Illustrated by the author. New York: Crowell, 1986. Age: 5. Chap. 4.
Describes the stages in making a book, starting with the writing of the manuscript and the drawing of the pictures, and explaining all the technical processes leading to printed and bound copies.

Allen, Robert. *A First Counting Book*. Illustrated by Mottke Weissman. New York: Platt & Munk, 1968. Age: 3. Chap. 4.
A book about numbers. First the numbers one through ten are presented using photographs of familiar items which invite counting. These pictures are labeled: 1 kitten, 2 eggs, 3 dolls, and so forth. The following pages present unlabeled pictures for counting, pictures demonstrating that changes in size and position of items do not change the number of items. The book ends with a pictorial demonstration of addition. Good for many sessions of exploration.

Amoss, Berthie. *Tom in the Middle*. Illustrated by the author. New York: Harper & Row, 1968. Age: 4. Chap. 8.
Tom escapes through fantasy from the realistically portrayed frustrations of being a middle child. He imagines that he and his brothers are playing together.

Ancona, George. *Helping Out*. Illustrated by the author. New York: Clarion, 1985. Age: 5. Chaps. 5 and 8.

Multicultural, nonsexist black-and-white photographs accompanied by simple text enumerate many ways children can feel useful and competent while helping adults.

Andersen, Hans Christian. *The Ugly Duckling*. Illustrated by Robert Van Nutt. New York: Knopf, 1986. Age: 5. Chap. 1.

An ugly duckling spends an unhappy year ostracized by the other animals before he grows into a beautiful swan. Don't miss the opportunity to question the importance of beauty, and to discuss what it means to belong.

Anderson, C.W. *Billy and Blaze*. Illustrated by the author. New York: Collier, 1936. Age: 4. Chap. 1.

The classic story about the friendship of a boy and a horse.

Andry, Andrew C. and Kratka, Suzanne C. *Hi, New Baby*. Illustrated by Thomas Di Grazia. New York: Simon & Schuster, 1970. Age: 2. Chap. 8.

This book is realistic about new babies. It discusses the situations that may cause difficulty for the older sibling and presents realistic suggestions to help cope.

Andry, Andrew C. and Schepp, Steven. *How Babies Are Made*. Illustrated by Blake Hampton. New York: Time-Life Books, 1968. Age: 3. Chap. 4.

Prepared in consultation with the Sex Information and Education Council of the United States (SIECUS) this book gives a clear, straightforward explanation of fertilization in flowers and of conception and birth in chickens, dogs, and humans. Highly recommended.

Anno, Mitsumasa. *All in a Day*. Illustrated by Chengliang, Dillon, Briggs, Brooks, Carle, Calvi, Popov, and Hayashi. New York: Philomel, 1986. Age: 5. Chap. 7.

Eight world-famous illustrators have pictured activities of children in a twenty-four-hour period starting with the evening of December 31. Pictures reveal the uniqueness of each of eight cultures while also showing similarities between them.

Anno, Mitsumasa. *Anno's Alphabet*. Illustrated by the author. New York: Crowell, 1975. Age: 4. Chaps. 1 and 4.

Each letter of the alphabet accompanies a full-page picture of an object beginning with that letter: anvil, bicycle, etc. Each illustration has ingenious surprises, including some that fool the eye. Anno's work attracts readers from the very young through adulthood.

Anno, Mitsumasa. *Anno's Counting Book*. Illustrated by the author. New York: Crowell, 1975. Age: 3. Chaps. 1 and 4.

On each page of this book the same scene gets more complex as the items accumulate, page by page. Each detail bears scrutiny.

Anno, Mitsumasa. *Anno's Journey*. Illustrated by the author. New York: Philomel, 1982. Age: 5. Chap. 1.

Records in drawings the author's journey through northern Europe and his impressions of the land, the people at work and play, and their art, architecture, folklore, and fairy tales.

Arkhurst, Joyce Cooper. *The Adventures of Spider*. Illustrated by Jerry Pinkney. New York: Scholastic, 1964. Age: 5. Chap. 1.

West African folktales explaining natural phenomena. Spider is an example of the trickster character found in the folktales of many cultures. His adventures are a mixture of playfulness and supernatural intervention.

Arnstein, Helene. *Billy and Our New Baby*. Illustrated by M. Jayne Smyth. New York: Behavioral, 1973. Age: 5. Chap. 8.

Billy is impatient, jealous, angry, and regressing after his younger sibling is born. Parents are depicted as good models, showing understanding and providing limits. A guide in the back of the book is directed at adults and gives sound advice.

Aruego, Jose and Dewey, Ariane. *We Hide, You Seek*. Illustrated by the authors. New York: Greenwillow, 1979. Age: 5. Chap. 4.

A multitude of small, humorously drawn animals of the African bush hide from a little red rhino. For example, giraffes become part of the tree trunk and a swarm of didric cuckoos becomes leaves of the tree. This book is highly recommended for children who enjoy the game of hide-and-seek and who are working on visual discrimination skills.

Atkinson, Allen. *Simple Simon and Other Favorites*. Illustrated by the author. New York: Bantam, 1986. Age: Birth. Chaps. 1, 2, and 3.
More familiar nursery rhymes illustrated in a classic fashion.

Asbjornsen, Peter Christen. *The Three Billy Goats Gruff*. Illustrated by Marcia Brown. New York: Harcourt, 1957. Age: 3. Chaps. 1 and 2.
A traditional recounting of the old Norwegian tale. This edition contains no surprises, but provides the familiar story for children to enjoy listening to.

Azarian, Mary. *A Farmer's Alphabet*. Illustrated by the author. Boston: Godine, 1981. Age: 4. Chap. 4.
Framable woodcuts illustrate each letter.

Bach, Alice. *The Smartest Bear and His Brother Oliver*. Illustrated by Steven Kellogg. New York: Harper & Row, 1975. Age: 5. Chap. 8.
Parents acknowledge the differences between their twin boys by giving one a typewriter and the other a bakery truck. Good model for children and parents.

Bahr, Amy C. *It's OK to Say No: A Book for Parents and Children to Read Together*. Illustrated by Frederick Bennett Green. New York: Grosset & Dunlap, 1986. Age: 5. Chap. 6.
A useful basis for discussion of the serious problem of child abuse. Children's intuition is respected and practical advice is given on how to handle uncomfortable situations.

Baker, Olaf. *Where the Buffaloes Begin*. Illustrated by Stephen Gammel. New York: Murray, 1981. Age: 5. Chap. 7.
Vivid recreation of the buffalo and affirmation of the respect that Native Americans have for this beast.

Bang, Molly. *Ten, Nine, Eight*. Illustrated by the author. New York: Greenwillow, 1983. Age: 2. Chaps. 4 and 7.

This Caldecott Honor book is a countdown of familiar items in the room of a little girl at bedtime: ten warm, washed toes; nine soft, stuffed animals; eight windowpanes with falling snow; and so forth. A fine addition to bedtime books as well as counting books.

Banish, Roslyn. *I Want to Tell You About My Baby.* Illustrated with photos from many sources. Berkeley, CA: Wingbow, 1982. Age: 4. Chap. 8.
This story is narrated by a child, telling about the mother's pregnancy, the new baby's birth, and the joys and frustrations of life with the baby. It is a good model of understanding, accepting parents and grandparents. Black-and-white photographs.

Banner, Angela. *Ant and Bee Time.* Illustrated by Bryan Ward. London: Kaye & Ward, 1969. Age: 4. Chap. 4.
The famous English characters Ant and Bee receive a letter inviting them to "the zoo games." The rest of the story is about what they did before getting to the games, with whom, and at what time. All the times before the game are on-the-hour. At the games there are many activities, timed by the minute.

Barklem, Jill. *Winter Story.* Illustrated by the author. New York: Philomel, 1980. Age: 5. Chaps. 4 and 5.
Accurate depiction of hedgerow life and Cornish culture form the basis of these stories for young children about the mice of Brambly Hedge.

Barlowe, Dot and Sy. *Dinosaurs.* Illustrated by the authors. New York: Random House, 1977. Age: 4. Chap. 4.
For children who are fascinated with dinosaurs, this pop-up book is a must. Dinosaurs emerge from eggs, slink through the bushes, and walk off the page.

Barrie, J.M. (Retold by Harrison, David L.). *Peter Pan.* Illustrated by Bob Brackman. Kansas City, MO: Hallmark Books, 1962. Age: 5. Chaps. 1 and 2.
A retold version using pop-up illustrations. The pop-ups are well executed, especially the one of the flying child. The

story is a classic, but take care to address any stereotypes that may be conveyed by the book.

Baskin, Hosea, Tobias, and Lisa. *Hosie's Alphabet*. Illustrated by Leonard Baskin. New York: Viking, 1972. Age: 4. Chap. 4.
Words and pictures that appeal as much to adults as to children. A book to treasure, but not for initial introduction to the alphabet.

Bass, Ellen. *I Like You to Make Jokes with Me, But I Don't Want You to Touch Me*. Illustrated by Marti Betz. Chapel Hill, NC: Lollipop Power, 1981. Age: 4. Chap. 6.
Told from the child's point of view, this is a story of a little girl who enjoys making jokes with Jack, an older man in a supermarket, but does not like it when Jack gets too close to her or tickles her. Her mother helps her practice telling Jack how she feels by talking to the refrigerator. The next time she sees Jack, she is able to tell him what she likes and what she doesn't like.

Bauer, Caroline Feller. *My Mother Travels A Lot*. Illustrated by Nancy Winslow Parker. New York: Viking Penguin, 1981. Age: 4. Chap. 4.
A child describes, on alternating pages, the pluses and minuses of having a mother who must travel a great deal for her work. The father is shown as frequently present.

Baum, Louis. *One More Time*. Illustrated by Paddy Bouma. New York: Morrow, 1986. Age: 3. Chap. 7.
Simon and his daddy spend a lovely Sunday afternoon. When they arrive home, the father leaves Simon with his mother. The reader now realizes that Simon's mother and father are divorced.

Bayley, Nicola. *As I Was Going Up—and Down—*. Illustrated by the author. New York: Macmillan, 1985. Age: Birth. Chaps. 3, 4, and 6.
An upside-down piano player and a cow who comes to dinner are among the cast of characters in these traditional nonsense rhymes that have been delighting children for centuries.

They can be recited to children long before they can hold the book by themselves. A good introduction to the fun books can be.

Bayley, Nicola. *Hush-A-Bye and Other Bedtime Rhymes.* Illustrated by the author. New York: Macmillan, 1985. Age: Birth. Chaps. 2 and 3.
A bedtime book written to soothe young children.

Baylor, Byrd. *Guess Who My Favorite Person Is.* Illustrated by Robert Andrew Parker. New York: Atheneum, 1977. Age: 5. Chaps. 6 and 7.
A little girl and a sensitive young man meet and play a game of deciding what is each of their favorite things: activities, colors, odors, shapes, weather, time of day, dream, food, and many more categories. Their descriptions invite readers to play the game on their own.

Baylor, Byrd. *The Way to Start a Day.* Illustrated by Peter Parnall. New York: Scribners, 1978. Age: 5. Chap. 7.
Text and illustrations describe how people all over the world celebrate the sunrise. Perhaps too sophisticated for a child to handle alone, but the text combines with the illustrations to nurture a sense of beauty and respect for people's diverse feelings.

Behrens, Judy. *Soo-Ling Finds a Way.* Illustrated by Taro Yashima. Golden Gate, 1985. Age: 4. Chap. 5.
A Chinese-American child rescues her grandfather's laundry business when it is threatened by a laudromat across the street.

Behrens, June. *Can You Walk the Plank?* Illustrated by Tom and Michele Grimm. Chicago: Children's Press, 1976. Age: 3. Chap. 6.
Color photographs depict children from a variety of ethnic backgrounds demonstrating their physical capabilities and combining movement with fantasy.

Bemelmans, Ludwig. *Madeline.* Illustrated by the author. New York: Viking, 1939. Age: 3. Chaps. 1 and 2.

Madeline, smallest and naughtiest of the twelve little charges of Miss Clavel, wakes up one night with an attack of appendicitis. The other books in this classic series include *Madeline's Rescue, Madeline and the Bad Hat, Madeline and the Gypsies,* and *Madeline in London.*

Bemelmans, Ludwig. *Parsley.* Illustrated by the author. New York: Harper & Row, 1953. Age: 3. Chap. 6.
A pine tree and a stag grow old together and outwit the hunters. Unusually large pictures illustrate this fantasy.

Berenstain, Stan and Jan. *The Berenstain Bears Learn About Strangers.* Illustrated by the authors. New York: Random House, 1985. Age: 4. Chap. 6.
The Berenstain bear cubs learn not to be overly friendly with strangers and give rules for dealing with them.

Berenstain, Stanley and Janice. *The Berenstains' B Book.* Illustrated by the authors. New York: Random House, 1971. Age: 4. Chap. 4.
Big Brown Bear, Blue Bull, and Beautiful Baboon only encounter objects or meet people whose names begin with the letter *B*. One of the few alphabet books devoted entirely to a single letter.

Berger, Barbara. *Grandfather Twilight.* Illustrated by the author. New York: Philomel, 1984. Age: 3. Chaps. 6 and 8.
A reassuring, poetic bedtime book showing Grandfather Twilight performing his very special evening task. Good for special sharing between parent and child after a long day.

Bierhorst, John (Adaptor). *Songs of the Chippewa.* Illustrated by Joe Servello. New York: Farrar, Straus, Giroux, 1974. Age: 5. Chap. 7.
Bierhorst respects and understands Native American culture. This volume presents the songs carefully and authentically.

Black, Claudia. *My Dad Loves Me, My Dad Has a Disease.* Illustrated by children. Denver: MAC, 1979. Age: 5. Chaps. 4 and 6.

This is a workbook for adults to use with children growing up in alcoholic families. The goal of this book is to give children an opportunity to share their thoughts and feelings and to better understand the disease of alcoholism. This book is a real breakthrough for confused and silent children of alcoholics.

Blaine, Marge. *The Terrible Thing That Happened at Our House.* Illustrated by John C. Wallner. New York: Parents Magazine Press, 1975. Age: 5. Chaps. 1 and 7.
A child feels as if her whole world has fallen apart when her mother resumes her career. The new arrangements that the family has to make are completely unacceptable to her. She wants her old, comfortable life back again. A solution comes about after a major confrontation, when the family decides on a course of action satisfactory to all.

Blance, Ellen and Cook, Ann. *Monster Looks for a Friend.* Illustrated by Quentin Blake. Glendale, CA: Bowmar, 1973. Age: 2. Chap. 6.
A very appealing tall, large-handed, small-headed, purple monster is lonely and finds a friend. A good discussion starter.

Blegvad, Lenore. *This Is Me.* Illustrated by Erik Blegvad. New York: Random House, 1986. Age: 6 mos. Chap. 2.
In this tiny chunky board book a little boy points out parts of his body, some pieces of his clothing, toys, and other familiar objects. Children will enjoy joining him at his labeling task.

Bodecker, N.M. *Miss Jaster's Garden.* Illustrated by the author. New York: Golden Press, Western Pub., 1972. Age: 4. Chap. 6.
The unlikely friendship between a hedgehog and an old woman is tenderly recounted. The illustrations complement the gentle story.

Boegehold, Betty. *Daddy Doesn't Live Here Anymore.* Illustrated by Deborah Borgo. New York: Golden Books, 1985. Age: 5. Chap. 7.
Casey is a young girl whose parents fight with each other, all the while pretending that everything is normal. Her father

eventually moves out of the house and Casey is furious, then feels guilty, thinking she has been at fault. She pretends to be ill, "runs away" (to the backyard), and is frightened that her parents will stop loving her. Her mother finally persuades her that all will be well, that she is loved, and that they are both still her parents. A useful book for young children.

Boegehold, Betty. *Hurray for Pippa!* Illustrated by Cyndy Szekeres. New York: Dell, 1980. Age: 2. Chap. 6.
The first in a series of woodland adventures of characters that toddlers love: Pippa Mouse, Weber Duck, Ripple Squirrel, Cricket and Gray Bird. Full of fun and feeling children readily identify with and enjoy sharing. Short chapters. Other books in this series include: *Here's Pippa Again!, Hurray for Pippa!*, and *Pippa Pops Out!*

Bonne, Rose. *I Know an Old Lady.* Illustrated by Abner Graboff. New York: Scholastic, 1961. Age: 3. Chap. 2.
Cumulative story about an old lady who swallows a variety of animals, initially a fly. Told in verse and set to music.

Bonsall, Crosby. *The Day I Had to Play with My Sister.* Illustrated by the author. New York: Harper & Row, 1972. Age: 3. Chap. 8.
This book invites sympathy for an older brother whose younger sister violates the rules of hide-and-seek.

Bornstein, Ruth. *Little Gorilla.* Illustrated by the author. New York: Clarion, 1976. Age: 2. Chap. 6.
As a baby and a toddler, little gorilla is adored by all the animals in the forest. Then he starts to grow and grow and grow, and to doubt whether he is still lovable in his large form. His birthday party confirms that he is. A good book to build a positive sense of self.

Bottner, Barbara. *Jungle Day or How I Learned to Love My Nosey Little Brother.* Illustrated by the author. New York: Delacorte, 1978. Age: 4. Chap. 8.
Older child who is struggling with a project finally realizes she can't complete it without her younger sibling's help. Simple text, enhanced by cartoonlike illustrations, provides

opportunities for discussion of building respect and cooperation between siblings.

Bracken, Carolyn. *Kitten's Animal Friends*. Illustrated by the author. New York: Random House, 1985. Age: 6 mos. Chap. 3.
A ten-inch stuffed cloth kitten holds a tiny cloth book showing her animal friends. An innovative addition to the cloth book library.

Bradbury, Lynne. *My Day*. Illustrated by Martin Aitchison. Loughborough, England: Ladybird, 1983. Age: 2. Chap. 4.
On each page a number of children are shown at the same time of day and engaged in the same activity: rising, dressing, shopping, eating, playing, going to the park, and so on. Part of the extensive Ladybird series, this one is aimed at helping children understand the sequence of a routine day. It is also designed to promote discussion between the adult reader and the child.

Bradbury, Lynne. *On the Move*. Illustrated by Ken McKie. Loughborough, England: Ladybird, 1983. Age: 1. Chap. 4.
A brightly illustrated book with bold, realistic drawings of different vehicles. Many are large. Each page has a sentence or two naming the vehicle and describing its use.

Braithwaite, Althea. *Special Care Babies*. Illustrated by Nicola Spoor. London, England: Dinosaur Pub., 1986. Age: 5. Chap. 8.
A British book about premature babies and their care told by the brother of one such baby. Clear text.

Brandenberg, Franz. *Aunt Nina and Her Nephews and Nieces*. Illustrated by Aliki. New York: Greenwillow, 1983. Age: 5. Chap. 6.
Aunt Nina lives alone. To celebrate her cat's birthday, she invites her six nephews and nieces to her junk-filled house. They all spend an adventurous day together. Through the illustrations, the reader is exposed to a house rich in love and treasures.

Brandenberg, Franz. *I Wish I Was Sick Too*. Illustrated by the author. New York: Greenwillow, 1976. Age: 3. Chap. 8.

When Edward, a small cat, is sick, his mother and his grandmother take loving care of him. Elizabeth, his sister, is
jealous and wishes she were sick too. Her wish comes true.

Branley, Franklyn M. *Air Is All Around You*. Illustrated by Holly
Keller. New York: Harper & Row, 1986. Age: 5. Chap. 4.
Describes the various properties of air and shows how to
prove that air takes up space and that there is air all around
us.

Branley, Franklyn M. *What Makes Day and Night*. Illustrated by
Arthur Dorros. New York: Harper & Row, 1986. Age: 5. Chap. 4.
A simple explanation of how the rotation of the earth causes
night and day. A good resource for children who are curious
about the world around them and ready for simple scientific
information.

Brett, Molly. *An Alphabet by Molly Brett*. Illustrated by the
author. London: Medici Society, 1980. Age: 4. Chap. 4.
A cornucopia of woodland flora and fauna illustrate this pretty
alphabet book.

Bridwell, Norman. *Clifford, the Big Red Dog*. Illustrated by the
author. New York: Scholastic, 1985. Age: 3. Chap. 7.
One of a number of popular stories that this publisher has
printed for the Spanish-reading population. This book introduces Clifford, a gigantic fantasy dog, who functions as a
benign superhero.

Briggs, Raymond. *The Snowman*. Illustrated by the author. New
York: Random House, 1978. Age: 4. Chap. 1.
When his snowman comes to life, a little boy invites him
home and in return is taken on a flight above beautiful cities
and strange lands.

Brightman, Alan. *Like Me*. Illustrated by the author. Boston:
Little, Brown, 1976. Age: 5. Chap. 7.
Narrated by a child who has Down's syndrome, this photo
story invites sympathetic understanding on the part of non-
disabled children.

Bromhall, Winifred. *Middle Mathilda*. Illustrated by the author. New York: Knopf. Age: 4. Chap. 6.

A good story to read to a middle child who sometimes feels that nothing special happens to her.

Brown, Judith Gwyn. *Alphabet Dreams*. Illustrated by the author. Englewood Cliffs, NJ: Prentice-Hall, 1976. Age: 4. Chap. 4.

An introduction to the alphabet using the ball-bounce and jump-rope rhyme, "A my name is Anna."

Brown, Marcia. *Stone Soup*. Illustrated by the author. New York: Scribners, 1947. Age: 4. Chaps. 1 and 2.

The classic edition of this old folktale of a soldier who tricks people of a village into feeding him by promising them that he will teach them to make soup from stones.

Brown, Margaret Wise. *A Child's Good Night Book*. Illustrated by Jean Charlot. New York: Harper & Row, 1986. Age: 1. Chap. 6.

Baby animals go to sleep, each in its own way, in its own place. The child, too, goes to sleep. The book closes with a prayer.

Brown, Margaret Wise. *The Country Noisy Book*. Illustrated by Leonard Weisgard. New York: Harper & Row, 1940. Age: 1. Chaps. 1 and 4.

The second in this series of classic stories about Muffin, the black puppy. This time he is confined to a box while traveling to the country and hears many new sounds while in his box and while exploring the farm.

Brown, Margaret Wise. *The Dead Bird*. Illustrated by Remy Charlip. New York: Dell, 1958. Age: 4. Chaps. 2, 4, and 7.

The first book to discuss the topic of death with very young children, this is the story of children's reactions to finding a dead bird in the woods.

Brown, Margaret Wise. *The Golden Egg Book*. Illustrated by Leonard Weisgard. New York: Golden Press Western Pub., 1947. Age: 2. Chaps. 1 and 6.

An unusually large book about the friendship between two animals, a bunny and a duckling.

Brown, Margaret Wise. *Goodnight Moon*. Illustrated by Clement Hurd. New York: Harper & Row, 1947. Age: 1. Chaps. 1, 2, and 6.
  A classic good-night story blending fantasy and reality. The book has been a favorite for many years partly because of its deep understanding of children's need for a soothing goodnight ritual. A classic.

Brown, Margaret Wise. *The Important Book*. Illustrated by Leonard Weisgard. New York: Harper & Row, 1949. Age: 3. Chap. 6.
  The importance of different objects is described from a child's perspective and illustrated with paintings. Although you may sometimes disagree with the text, you and your child can add your own ideas about a thing's importance and go on to select other items and their special qualities.

Brown, Margaret Wise. *The Indoor Noisy Book*. Illustrated by Leonard Weisgard. New York: Harper & Row, 1942. Age: 1. Chaps. 3 and 4.
  Muffin, the little puppy, is confined to the house because he has a cold. From his room he listens carefully and hears many different household sounds.

Brown, Margaret Wise. *The Noisy Book*. Illustrated by Leonard Weisgard. New York: Harper & Row, 1939. Age: 1. Chaps. 1 and 3.
  When a little black dog named Muffin gets a cinder in his eye, the veterinarian bandages his eyes. With his eyes covered, Muffin hears all sorts of interesting noises.

Brown, Margaret Wise. *The Runaway Bunny*. Illustrated by Clement Hurd. New York: Harper & Row, 1972. Age: 18 mos. Chaps. 1, 2, and 6.
  The author provides a model for a satisfactory solution to the problem of a child's dual needs for security and independence.

Brown, Myra Berry. *Amy and the New Baby*. Illustrated by the author. New York: Watts, 1965. Age: 5. Chap. 8.
  The new baby cries a lot, requires a lot of mother's attention, and stays longer than Amy thought she would. Parents dem-

onstrate affection and understanding and help reshape the family to include all members.

Bruna, Dick. *The Apple*. Illustrated by the author. New York: Methuen, 1975. Age: 3. Chap. 4.
Bruna's familiar style presents the alphabet with a clear relation between letter and picture.

Bruna, Dick. *The King*. Illustrated by the author. New York: Two Continents, 1964. Age: 3. Chap. 6.
Illustrating with brightly colored, simple forms outlined in black, Dick Bruna tells of a little boy-king who gets tired of playing alone. When his caretakers tell him that he should not play with Rose, a little girl friend, because she has no crown, he is very sad. He ingeniously solves the problem by removing his crown.

Bruna, Dick. *Playing in Winter*. Illustrated by the author. Great Britain: Methuen, 1984. Age: 6 mos. Chap. 3.
This is a very simple wordless story that opens out and becomes a two-sided mural. On the first side a child dresses in warm clothes to go out to play on a snowy day. On the opposite side of the same six panels or pages, the appropriately dressed child skis, skates, sleds, and builds a snowman. Dick Bruna's distinctive drawings of simple shapes outlined in black, filled with a few strong colors, appeal to young and old alike.

Bryan, Ashley. *The Cat's Purr*. Illustrated by the author. New York: Atheneum, 1985. Age: 5. Chaps. 2 and 7.
This old Indian folktale is designed to be read aloud. Complete with sound effects, it tells the story of why rat and cat are enemies, and how the cat got its purr.

Bryan, Ashley. *Walk Together Children*. Illustrated by the author. New York: Atheneum, 1974. Age: Birth. Chap. 1.
A collection of black American spirituals illustrated with woodcuts that evoke the spirit and culture of the songs.

Bunting, Eve. *The Happy Funeral*. Illustrated by Vo-Dinh Mai. New York: Harper & Row, 1982. Age: 5. Chap. 7.

Chinese funeral rituals are respectfully described and illustrated. Laura, a young child, is included in all of the family
ceremonies celebrating the grandfather's life and marking his
death.

Burningham, John. *Cluck, Baa.* Illustrated by the author. New
York: Viking, 1984. Age: 1. Chap. 4.
An early labeling book, executed in the author/illustrator's
inimitable style. This book depicts animals and presents their
sounds.

Burningham, John. *Granpa.* Illustrated by the author. New York:
Crown, 1984. Age: 4. Chaps. 6 and 7.
A touching story of the close relationship between a young
girl and her grandfather. In sparse prose the quality of the
love shines through. The last few pictures show the young girl
alone. It is clear that the grandfather has died.

Burningham, John. *John Burningham's Colors.* Illustrated by the
author. New York: Crown, 1985. Age: 2. Chap. 4.
On the left-hand page of each spread John Burningham
presents a color with a simple lowercase word and a bowler
hat of that color. On the right is one of his witty children,
dressed all in that color and interacting with things of that
color. In fact, the picture is solely in tones of the color being
taught, except for skin tones. The child wears the bowler hat,
which is the main color.

Burningham, John. *John Burningham's 1 2 3.* Illustrated by the
author. New York: Crown, 1985. Age: 3. Chap. 4.
Page by page, an enormous, delicately drawn tree occupying
each double-page spread is filled with ten children. One
child is added per page and each child is full of facial expression, movement, and enjoyment. A surprising ending adds to
the fun of this counting book.

Burningham, John. *Mr. Gumpy's Motor Car.* Illustrated by the
author. New York: Crowell, 1973. Age: 3. Chap. 4.
When Mr. Gumpy goes for a ride in his car, the animals ask if
they may come along. The jaunt in the countryside is lovely

until it rains and the car becomes stuck in the mud. All ends well in this cheerful fantasy.

Burningham, John. *The Shopping Basket*. Illustrated by the author. New York: Crowell, 1980. Age: 4. Chap. 5.
A little boy encounters greedy animals on his way home from a shopping trip. This fantasy flight is also a counting book.

Burningham, John. *Viking Number Play Series*. Illustrated by the author. New York: Viking, 1983. Age: 4. Chap. 4.
Although these six books require adult participation, they introduce children to mathematical principles through their enjoyable pictures and playful format. Concepts introduced are: in *Pigs Plus*, addition; in *Ride Off*, subtraction; in *Read One*, numbers as words; in *Five Down*, numbers as signs; in *Count Up*, sets; and in *Just Cats,* groups. Helps people appreciate the many mathematical ideas we take for granted.

Burningham, John. *Wobble Pop*. Illustrated by the author. New York: Viking, 1984. Age: 2. Chap. 5.
One-word verbs accompany pictures of a small child's adventures with his teddy bear.

Burton, Albert, Jr. *Mine, Yours, Ours*. Illustrated by Lois Axeman. Chicago: Whitman, 1977. Age: 4. Chap. 4.
In this self-starter book, illustrations and a very simple text use words and phrases such as mine, yours, ours, my friend, and your friend to provide a format for understanding the concepts of belonging and sharing. Parts of the body, clothing, playthings, grandfather, houses, and friends are topics presented for labeling ownership and for discussion. The book provides an abundance of cultural diversity. The somewhat awkward text needs supplementing by an adult reader.

Burton, Virginia Lee. *Katy and the Big Snow*. Illustrated by the author. New York: Scholastic, 1971. Age: 3. Chaps. 1, 4, and 6.
Katy is a big red crawler tractor who pushes dirt around in the summer and plows the snow in the winter. After one great winter storm, Katy plows out the whole city of Geopolis.

Burton, Virginia Lee. *The Little House*. Illustrated by the author. Boston: Houghton Mifflin, 1942. Age: 3. Chaps. 1 and 2.

The curious little country house learns what it is like to live in the city when the city expands around her. Happily, she is moved out into the countryside again.

Burton, Virginia Lee. *Mike Mulligan and His Steam Shovel.* Illustrated by the author. New York: Scholastic, 1967. Age: 3. Chaps. 1, 2, and 6.
Mike Mulligan is proud of Mary Anne, his steam shovel. The two of them work well together and face the challenge of being able to dig a foundation in a very short period of time.

Burton, Terry. *Let's Go Shopping.* Illustrated by the author. Loughborough, England: Ladybird, 1985. Age: 2. Chap. 5.
A father and his child shop at the supermarket. Children will enjoy "reading" this book to you. Excellent starter for a discussion of shopping.

Byers, Betsy. *Go and Hush the Baby.* Illustrated by Emily A. McCully. New York: Viking, 1971. Age: 3. Chap. 8.
Older brother, with baseball glove in hand, is asked to quiet the baby. He does so with great creativity, energy, and good will.

Caldecott, Randolph. *A First Caldecott Collection.* Illustrated by the author. Harmondsworth, England: Frederick Warne, 1986. Age: Birth. Chaps. 1, 2, and 3.
Includes "The House That Jack Built" and "A Frog He Would A-Wooing Go." The illustrations are the attraction.

Caldecott, Randolph. *A Second Caldecott Collection.* Illustrated by the author. Harmondsworth, England: Frederick Warne, 1986. Age: Birth. Chaps. 1, 2, and 3.
Includes "Sing a Song for Sixpence" and "The Three Jovial Huntsmen." You will enjoy the illustrations as you sing these songs to your child.

Caldecott, Randolph. *A Third Caldecott Collection.* Illustrated by the author. Harmondsworth, England: Frederick Warne, 1986. Age: Birth. Chaps. 1, 2, and 3.
Includes the "Queen of Hearts" and "The Farmer's Boy." A reproduction of one of the early Mother Goose collections.

Campbell, Rod. *Dear Zoo*. Illustrated by the author. New York: Four Winds, 1982. Age: 18 mos. Chap. 4.

Each page of this book has a flap concealing an animal from the zoo that is sent to the young writer on request. The elephant is too big, the giraffe is too tall, the lion is too fierce, the camel is too grumpy, and so forth. Finally the child receives a perfect gift from his friends at the zoo.

Campbell, Rod. *Pet Shop*. Illustrated by the author. New York: Scholastic, 1984. Age: 3. Chap. 5.

A board book that permits children to feed six animals using cardboard inserts.

Caple, Kathy. *The Purse*. Illustrated by the author. Boston: Houghton Mifflin, 1986. Age: 3. Chaps. 4, 5, and 6.

After being convinced that she should keep her money in a purse rather than an old Band-Aid box, Katie purchases a yellow purse. She does odd jobs so she will have some money to put into it. When she misses the clinking sound the money made in the Band-Aid box, her father helps her work out a solution. A good book to start discussions about decision making.

Carle, Eric. *Catch the Ball!* Illustrated by the author. New York: Putnam, 1982. Age: 6 mos. Chaps. 3 and 4.

This well-designed board book allows children to pass the red ball that is attached to a string back and forth between the animal characters. This book is good for learning animal names and for just having fun.

Carle, Eric. *Do You Want to Be My Friend?* Illustrated by the author. New York: Harper & Row, 1971. Age: 1. Chap. 6.

A tiny mouse is looking for a friend. All the large animals, the crocodile, lion, hippo, walrus, monkey, peacock, fox, kangaroo, and giraffe (all brightly rendered by the artist) show no interest. In the end a suitable companion is found. Each animal's tail precedes it by one page, allowing children to predict what animal will follow.

Carle, Eric. *Let's Paint a Rainbow*. Illustrated by the author. New York: Philomel, 1982. Age: 2. Chap. 4.

A large sturdy board book about two painters who paint a rainbow. They add two colors per page until they have eight. Children will enjoy naming the colors and copying their design.

Carle, Eric. *My Very First Book of Numbers.* Illustrated by the author. New York: Crowell, 1984. Age: 3. Chap. 4.
This book is probably not ideal for introducing counting, but it is excellent for children who recognize the numbers one through ten. The format of the book is fun: the pages are horizontally split in two. The top segments show a numeral and a corresponding number of black squares. Bottom pages, not in numerical order, have pictures of brightly colored fruits. The goal is to flip the pages and make the number of fruits correspond with the number of black squares.

Carle, Eric. *My Very First Book of Touch.* Illustrated by the author. New York: Crowell, 1986. Age: 1. Chap. 4.
This spiral-bound board book invites participation but has no certain right answers. The pages are cut in half. The top half has a word describing texture: soft, rough, fluffy, furry, hard, wet, smooth, etc. The bottom halves have pictures of animals: bear, fish, turtle, chicks, etc. Pictures and words are to be paired. Good to read aloud with a very young child or for a beginning reader to work with alone.

Carle, Eric. *1,2,3 to the Zoo.* Illustrated by the author. New York: Philomel, 1968. Age: 4. Chap. 4.
Huge, colorful, textured circus animals ride through this book on the flatbed cars of a train. On each page there is a different species and a different number of animals waiting to be counted.

Carle, Eric. *The Secret Birthday Message.* Illustrated by the author. New York: Harper & Row, 1986. Age: 4. Chap. 4.
On his birthday, Tim finds a message with shapes standing for clues of where he must hunt for his present. Children get thoroughly involved as they join Tim on his search, through full-color pages, designed with cut-out shapes. An original and exciting book.

Carle, Eric. *The Very Busy Spider*. Illustrated by the author. New York: Philomel, 1984. Age: 18 mos. Chaps. 1 and 2.

> The farm animals try to divert a busy little spider from spinning her web, but she persists and produces a thing of beauty and usefulness. The web is textured and raised, so that the book is fun to touch as well as see.

Carle, Eric. *The Very Hungry Caterpillar*. Illustrated by the author. New York: Scholastic. Age: 18 mos. Chaps. 1 and 2.

> A hungry caterpillar literally eats its way through this book. Children may count the numbers of holes as well as the prodigious amount of food the caterpillar eats on its way to becoming a beautiful butterfly.

Carle, Eric. *What's for Lunch?* Illustrated by the author. New York: Putnam, 1982. Age: 18 mos. Chaps. 4 and 5.

> On each page of this well-illustrated board book, there is a different fruit growing on a vine or tree. A monkey hanging on a string can be slipped through a slot on each page. He refuses each fruit until the bananas at the book's end.

Carlson, Nancy White. *Jesse Bear, What Will You Wear?* Illustrated by Bruce Degen. New York: Macmillan, 1987. Age: 2. Chap. 4.

> When Jesse Bear is asked what he will wear, he answers in verse. The poetry of this book bounces along and so does Jesse in the lively illustrations.

Carrick, Carol. *The Accident*. Illustrated by Donald Carrick. New York: Clarion, 1976. Age: 5. Chaps. 4 and 7.

> After his dog is hit by a truck and killed, Christopher and his family deal with their feelings of guilt, anger, and depression.

Cartlidge, Michelle. *Teddy's House*. Illustrated by the author. New York: Simon & Schuster, 1985. Age: 6 mos. Chap. 3.

> A cheery teddy bear is shown interacting with a different object on each page. All are familiar household items that children can label and identify in their own homes.

Chalmers, Maru. *Six Dogs, Twenty-three Cats, Forty-five Mice, and One Hundred Sixteen Spiders*. Illustrated by the author. New York: Harper & Row, 1986. Age: 4. Chap. 4.

For children who love animals, counting, and fantasy this book is ideal. This story is of conflicting friendships: the protagonist loves her animal friends but she also loves her aunt who isn't used to so many animals. A resolution is reached.

Chapman, Carol. *The Tale of Meshka the Kvetch*. Illustrated by Arnold Lobel. New York: Dutton, 1980. Age: 5. Chap. 7.
This amusing story, written in folktale style, is greatly enhanced by its illustrations. An old woman learns an important lesson about being positive rather than always complaining.

Charlip, Remy and Moore, Lillian. *Hooray for Me!* Illustrated by Vera Williams. New York: Parents Magazine Press, 1975. Age: 5. Chap. 7.
Many kinds of families are illustrated here, including blended and extended families.

Charren, Peggy and Hulsizer, Carol. *The TV-Smart Book for Kids*. Illustrated by Marilyn Hafner. New York: Dutton, 1986. Age: 4. Chap. 9.
Produced by Action for Children's Television (ACT), this calendar-book contains puzzles, games, and activities to help children and their parents guide the children's television viewing.

Chevalier, Christa. *Spence Isn't Spence Any More*. Illustrated by the author. Niles, IL: Whitman, 1985. Age: 3. Chap. 4.
Spence and his mother play a game where they both pretend to be someone else. They return to their real selves when they realize that they prefer it that way.

Chevalier, Christa. *Spence Makes Circles*. Illustrated by the author. Niles, IL: Whitman, 1982. Age: 3. Chap. 6.
Spence is having a good time on his own with his pencil, scissors, and glue. When he gets glue in his hair, he remedies the problem by cutting it out. When he creates a moustache by scratching his nose with fingers full of hair and glue, his mother laughs good-naturedly—joined by Spence, who is also relieved that his mother is not angry at his mess.

Child, Lydia Maria. *Over the River and Through the Wood.*
Illustrated by Brinton Turkle. New York: Scholastic, 1974. Age: 18
mos. Chaps. 1 and 2.
  Brinton Turkle uses juxtaposed color and black-and-white
  drawings to illustrate this traditional song for Thanksgiving.
  Music and lyrics are included at the end of the book.

Chittum, Ida. *The Cat's Pajamas.* Illustrated by Art Cumings.
New York: Parents Magazine Press, 1980. Age: 4. Chap. 5.
  Fred makes his cat a pair of pajamas, but the cat won't wear
  them. Fred sews, washes clothes, and is a very active boy.

Clardy, Andrea Fleck. *Dusty Was My Friend: Coming to Terms
with Loss.* Illustrated by Eleanor Alexander. New York: Human
Sciences Press, 1984. Age: 5. Chap. 7.
  Describes the difficult situation of the death of a young child
  as told from the perspective of his friend.

Clark, Ann Nolan. *In My Mother's House.* Illustrated by Velino
Herrara. New York: Viking, 1941. Age: 5. Chap. 7.
  We see the importance of the Tewa Indian houses through the
  eyes of five Tesqueque children. A strong message of family
  and community and the importance of nature and land to the
  way of life.

Clifton, Lucille. *Don't You Remember.* Illustrated by Evaline
Ness. New York: Dutton, 1973. Age: 3. Chaps. 7 and 8.
  Lively, four-year-old Desire Mary Tate is taken care of by
  one of her older brothers while both her parents work outside
  the home. Good model of family dealing with the universal
  tasks of cooperating and sharing chores in a nonsexist
  manner.

Clifton, Lucille. *Everett Anderson's Goodbye.* Illustrated by Ann
Grifalconi. New York: Holt, 1983. Age: 4. Chaps. 1 and 7.
  Everett Anderson has a difficult time coming to terms with
  his grief after his father dies. His mother's understanding that
  his reaction is normal and to be respected provides a strong
  model.

Clifton, Lucille. *Everett Anderson's Year.* Illustrated by Ann
Grifalconi. New York: Holt, 1974. Age: 4. Chaps. 7 and 8.

Everett still misses and loves his father, though he has left Everett and his mother. Mother manages well and so does Everett, an only child, in the loving environment they have created. Part of a fine series of books with Everett Anderson as the protagonist.

Clifton, Lucille. *Good, Says Jerome*. Illustrated by Stephanie Douglas. New York: Dutton, 1973. Age: 3. Chaps. 7 and 8.
When Jerome tells his worries and anxieties to his older sister, Janice Marie, she helps him resolve them. The relationship between them is a model of warmth and good communication between siblings of different age and sex.

Clifton, Lucille. *My Brother . . . Fine with Me*. Illustrated by Moneta Barnett. New York: Holt, 1975. Age: 5. Chaps. 7 and 8.
A child overcomes her jealousy of her younger brother. Clifton's ear for the authentic language of children is notable.

Clifton, Lucille. *Some of the Days of Everett Anderson*. Illustrated by Evaline Ness. New York: Holt, 1970. Age: 4. Chaps. 6 and 7.
Poems expressing the feelings a young child experiences, including fears and joys. This six-year-old boy goes through the days of the week in verse that provides the reader with an intimate acquaintance of Everett Anderson's feelings about such topics as missing his father, sharing activities with his mother, and refusing to carry an umbrella.

Clymer, Eleanor. *The Tiny Little House*. Illustrated by Ingrid Fetz. New York: Scholastic, 1964. Age: 5. Chap. 6.
Children befriend an elderly woman by helping her to set up a cookie shop in the tiny little house.

Cohen, Miriam. *Will I Have a Friend?* Illustrated by Lillian Hoban. New York: Macmillan, 1967. Age: 3. Chap. 6.
Before he goes to school, Jim wonders whether he will have a friend. At first he feels lonely and excluded, but by the end of the day he has made contact with another child and feels certain that he too has a friend.

Cohen, Marsha. *Baby's Favorite Things*. Illustrated by the author. New York: Random House, 1986. Age: 6 mos. Chap. 3.

Simple pictures of familiar items in a baby's world are drawn on the cloth pages of this child-size book.

Cohen, Miriam. *Best Friends*. Illustrated by Lillian Hoban. New York: Macmillan, 1971. Age: 3. Chap. 6.
A story of friendship, found, lost, and regained. The protagonists' feelings ring true.

Cohen, Miriam. *Jim's Dog Muffins*. Illustrated by Lillian Hoban. New York: Greenwillow, 1984. Age: 5. Chap. 7.
Even though Jim's friends try to help and comfort him, he is distraught over the death of his dog. A surface look at the issue of death, but a good discussion starter for young children.

Cohen, Miriam. *See You Tomorrow, Charles*. Illustrated by Lillian Hoban. New York: Greenwillow, 1983. Age: 4. Chap. 7.
Charles, who is blind, joins a group of children who can see. They learn from one another and enjoy one another's company.

Cole, Joanna. *How You Were Born*. Illustrated by Hella Hammid, et al. New York: Morrow, 1984. Age: 4. Chaps. 4 and 8.
Straightforward text, clear photographs, and sketches inform children about conception, fetal growth, labor, birth, and early infancy. Opens with a useful four-page parent guide.

Cole, Joanna. *My Puppy Is Born*. Illustrated by Jerome Wexler. New York: Scholastic, 1973. Age: 4. Chap. 4.
The story of Sausage, the puppy, from the moment she is born until the moment she is ready to leave her mother and become the storyteller's very own. Photographs of the newborn puppy as it matures.

Cole, Joanna. *The New Baby at Your House*. Illustrated by Hella Hamid. New York: Morrow, 1985. Age: 4. Chap. 8.
An informative book aimed at older siblings who are dealing with the many issues surrounding the birth of a baby.

Conford, Ellen. *Just the Thing for Geraldine*. Illustrated by John Larrecq. Boston: Little, Brown, 1974. Age: 5. Chap. 8.

Geraldine, a young possum, recognizes her own talents with the help of her brother. Her parents try to impose all sorts of lessons on Geraldine, but she refuses. She is a talented juggler, and she proves her ability to everyone's satisfaction, including her own.

Cooney, Barbara. *Miss Rumphius.* Illustrated by the author. New York: Viking, 1982. Age: 5. Chap. 1.

Great-aunt Alice Rumphius was once a little girl who loved the sea, longed to visit faraway places, and wished to do something to make the world more beautiful. She succeeds in doing all three.

Corey, Dorothy. *You Go Away.* Illustrated by Lois Axeman. Niles, IL: Whitman, 1976. Age: 2. Chap. 6.

A perfect story for children who are dealing with separation anxiety. Pictures show babies playing peek-a-boo, toddlers darting away from their parents and returning, parents leaving their children and coming back. In some later scenes, the children move away and return. As it progresses, the book describes ten different situations involving children at various ages.

Corey, Dorothy. *New Shoes!* Illustrated by Dora Leder. Niles, IL: Whitman, 1985. Age: 18 mos. Chap. 5.

Every other family member seems to be getting shoes. The little girl in the story finds it hard to wait for her turn. When it comes, she gets to select a new pair from the ten pairs she is shown. She is so pleased with her new shoes that she sleeps with them.

Coutant, Helen. *First Snow.* Illustrated by Vo-Dinh Mai. New York: Knopf, 1974. Age: 5. Chap. 7.

Lien is experiencing her first snow after moving from Vietnam to New England. Her grandmother is dying and Lien is confused and disturbed until her grandmother directs her to experience the snow. She becomes more content after recognizing the cyclical nature of life.

Crary, Elizabeth. *I Want It: A Children's Problem Solving Book.* Illustrated by Marina Megale Horosko. Seattle, WA: Parenting Press, 1982. Age: 4. Chap. 8.

A book that can be read traditionally, from cover to cover, or as an activity book where children choose among alternatives and then see the outcomes of their choices. Describes two children having trouble sharing and offers seven different solutions, including the consequences of each.

Crews, Donald. *Carousel*. Illustrated by the author. New York: Greenwillow, 1982. Age: 3. Chap. 4.
Donald Crews's pictures in this book familiarize the reader with a carousel and convey the feeling of riding on it.

Crews, Donald. *Flying*. Illustrated by the author. New York: Greenwillow, 1986. Age: 3. Chap. 4.
One of the latest of award-winning artist/author Donald Crews's books about large vehicles. In this book the reader looks down on different city and country scenes.

Crews, Donald. *Harbor*. Illustrated by the author. New York: Greenwillow, 1982. Age: 3. Chap. 4.
Boats move in and out of the harbor, an environment not familiar to most small children, in this book by award-winning author/artist Donald Crews. Different boats are named.

Crews, Donald. *School Bus*. Illustrated by the author. New York: Greenwillow, 1984. Age: 3.Chap. 6.
Another book showing, from close-up, a large vehicle from a child's familiar world.

Crews, Donald. *Truck*. Illustrated by the author. New York: Greenwillow, 1980. Age: 3. Chaps. 1 and 4.
This Caldecott Honor Book shows a large red truck from many different angles and in many different settings and weather conditions. Excellent for children who are interested in large vehicles and who are ready to learn how perspective changes the appearance of an object.

Crowley, Arthur. *Bonzo Beaver*. Illustrated by Annie Gusman. Boston: Houghton Mifflin, 1980. Age: 5. Chap 8.
Shows the younger of two beaver brothers, who is too small to do many of the things his older sibling can, using his mind rather than strength to overcome this problem.

Crowther, Robert. *The Most Amazing Hide-and-Seek Opposites Book*. Illustrated by the author. New York: Viking Kestrel. Age: 3. Chap. 4

Expressive animals, outlined in black and colored brightly, hide under flaps, requiring pulling tabs to emerge or jump out at you to illustrate sixteen opposites. An unforgettable experience.

Daly, Niki. *Look at Me*. Illustrated by the author. New York: Viking Kestrel, 1986. Age: 3. Chap. 8.

When Andy comes over to play with Suzie, her little brother, Josh, tries acting like a robot, becoming a Karate King, and balancing on one foot on top of a table to get their attention. His final antic is so inviting that the big kids want to join him and he wins a hug from his sister.

Dang, Manh Kha. *In the Land of Small Dragon*. Illustrated by Tony Chen. New York: Viking, 1979. Age: 5. Chap. 7.

A Vietnamese Cinderella story. The details are similar to the Chinese version of this tale. A good story to have on hand for widening children's horizons.

De Angeli, Marguerite. *Book of Nursery and Mother Goose Rhymes*. Illustrated by the author. Garden City, NY: Doubleday, 1953. Age: Birth. Chap. 1.

An old-fashioned rendering of the major Mother Goose rhymes.

De Poix, Carol. *Jo, Flo, and Yolanda*. Illustrated by Stephanie Sove Ney. Chapel Hill, NC: Lollipop Power, 1973. Age: 5. Chap. 8.

A rare book showing the individuality of three siblings, even though they are triplets.

De Regniers, Beatrice Schenk. *May I Bring a Friend?* Illustrated by Beni Montresor. Bloomfield, CT: Atheneum, 1964. Age: 2. Chap. 1.

A royal romp of a book in which a young boy tests the king and queen's acceptance of him by bringing a wild assortment of "friends" to dinner. The king and queen are models of adults who grant unconditional love and acceptance to their children. The illustrations are striking for their unusual colors and their amusing depictions of the various animal friends.

De Regniers, Beatrice Schenk. *Waiting for Mama*. Illustrated by Victoria de Larrea. Boston: Houghton Mifflin, 1984. Age: 3. Chap. 6.
   An amusing story about a little girl who is told to wait on a bench while her mother makes a quick trip into the grocery store. As she waits and waits, she feels enough time is passing that she is getting old enough to marry, have children, and have her hair turn gray, all of which is humorously illustrated.

Delton, Julie. *My Uncle Nikos*. Illustrated by Marc Simont. New York: Crowell, 1983. Age: 5. Chap. 7.
   Helena's annual summer visit to her Uncle Nikos in Greece helps her and the reader appreciate the richness of contemporary life in a small Greek village.

Dennis, Wesley. *Flip*. Illustrated by the author. Harmondsworth, England: Puffin, 1941. Age: 4. Chap. 6.
   A little colt manages to rejoin his mother who is across the brook after he is inspired by a dream of growing wings. This is a story about emerging competence.

DePaola, Tomie. *Giorgio's Village*. Illustrated by the author. New York: Putnam, 1982. Age: 4. Chap. 4.
   A pop-up book with six colorful stagelike settings that take the reader into the world of an Italian Renaissance village.

DePaola, Tomie. *The Legend of Bluebonnet*. Illustrated by the author. New York: Putnam, 1983. Age: 5. Chap. 7.
   This is the story of an orphaned Comanche Indian girl who sacrifices what she loves best to save her tribe. It is based on Comanche lore, and the illustrations are authentically Comanche.

DePaola, Tomie. *Nana Upstairs and Nana Downstairs*. Illustrated by the author. New York: Putnam, 1973. Age: 3. Chap. 7.

A young boy's great grandmother dies after having been inca-
pacitated. The child and the old woman share mutual affection. Children are given a sense of the progression from very
old age to death, in a gentle and endearing story form.

DePaola, Tomie. *Now One Foot, Now the Other.* Illustrated by the
author. New York: Putnam, 1981. Age: 5. Chaps. 4 and 7.
Bobby's grandfather helped him learn to walk. When grandfather suffers a stroke it is Bobby's turn to help him.

DePaola, Tomie. *Oliver Button Is a Sissy.* Illustrated by the
author. New York: Harcourt, 1979. Age: 5. Chap. 6.
Oliver Button doesn't like to do the things boys usually do. He
prefers drawing pictures and dancing. The boys tease him,
the girls defend him; Oliver goes on tap dancing. When
Oliver enters a talent show, even though he doesn't win, his
classmates (boys and girls) construct a sign saying OLIVER
BUTTON IS A STAR. Oliver is accepted at last. Children can
discuss the importance of acceptance, and what Oliver would
have done even if he had not been accepted by the boys in his
class.

DePaola, Tomie. *Pancakes for Breakfast.* Illustrated by the author. New York: Harcourt, 1978. Age: 3. Chaps. 2 and 4.
This wordless book tells the story of a woman who decides to
have pancakes for breakfast, gets the needed eggs from
chickens, milk from her cow, and maple syrup from her
neighbor. When her pets make a mess of her plan, she finds a
lucky solution.

DePaola, Tomie. *Sing, Pierrot, Sing.* Illustrated by the author.
San Diego: Harcourt, 1983. Age: 5. Chap. 2.
Simple Pierrot dreams of his saucy sweetheart, Columbine,
in this mime story. Although there are no words in this book,
the story's sophistication requires skill in sequence and comprehension.

DePaola, Tomie. *Strega Nona.* Illustrated by the author. Englewood Cliffs, NJ: Prentice-Hall, 1975. Age: 3. Chaps. 1, 2,
and 6.

The classic folk theme of the overflowing pot is enlivened by the Italian setting and characters brought to life by DePaola's illustrations and text. Strega Nona is a benevolent witch. Together with her well-intentioned but bumbling assistant, Big Anthony, they cook up an unforgettable pot of pasta. Children will also enjoy the sequel, *Strega Nona's Magic Lessons*.

Dragonwagon, Crescent. *Always, Always*. Illustrated by Arieh Zeldich. New York: Macmillan, 1984. Age: 5. Chap. 7.
A little girl discovers that although her parents are divorced, it in no way changes their love for her. The book also presents two different life-styles and makes no negative judgments.

Dragonwagon, Crescent. *I Hate My Brother Harry*. Illustrated by Dick Gackenback. New York: Harper & Row, 1983. Age: 4. Chap. 8.
Harry's sister has many reasons to feel her brother's teasing indicates that he hates her. Mother reminds her of her brother's kindness to her when she was very little and says the teasing is "something brothers and sisters go through," not hatred. This leads to a gesture toward friendship on the child's part.

Dragonwagon, Crescent. *Will It Be Okay?* Illustrated by Ben Schecter. New York: Harper & Row, 1977. Age: 4. Chap. 7.
A child's fears of death and abandonment are acknowledged and dealt with in a poetic, gentle, and developmentally appropriate manner.

Dragonwagon, Crescent. *Wind Rose*. Illustrated by Ronald Himler. New York: Harper & Row, 1976. Age: 3. Chap. 6.
In poetic language, a mother tells her daughter just what she and daddy felt, dreamed, and planned while waiting for her to be born.

Drescher, Joan. *Your Family, My Family*. Illustrated by the author. New York: Walker, 1980. Age: 4. Chap. 7.
This book describes all sorts of families and shows respect for each kind.

Dubov, Christine Salac. *Aleksandra, Where Are Your Toes?* Illustrated by Josef Schneider. New York: St. Martin's, 1986. Age: 6 mos. Chaps. 2 and 3.

A baby points out various parts of her body in answer to simple questions.

Dubov, Christine Salac. *Aleksandra, Where Is Your Nose?* Illustrated by Josef Schneider. New York: St. Martin's, 1986. Age: 6 mos. Chaps. 2 and 3.

A baby points out different parts of her face and head in response to questions. The color photographs of this small board book add to the appeal of this always popular naming game.

Duke, Kate. *Clean-Up Day*. Illustrated by the author. New York: Dutton, 1986. Age: 1. Chap. 5.

A "guinea pig board book" about cleaning up the house. This small book is a model of fun and cooperation.

Dunn, Phoebe. *Farm Animals*. Illustrated by the author. New York: Random House, 1984. Age: 6 mos. Chap. 3.

Tiny twenty-four-page board book with color photographs of animals found on a farm. Many double-page spreads.

Dunn, Phoebe. *I'm A Baby*. Illustrated by the author. New York: Random House, 1987. Age: 6 mos. Chap. 3.

Excellent clear photographs show babies from infancy through age one engaged in typical activities of increasing difficulty.

Durrell, Julie. *The Pudgy Book of Toys*. Illustrated by the author. New York: Grosset & Dunlap, 1983. Age: 6 mos. Chap. 3.

Five-by-five-inch, sixteen-page board book with one drawing per page of a familiar toy. Addition of animal on each page may be distracting or may add interest for young readers.

Dyer, Jane. *Moo, Moo, Peekaboo!* Illustrated by the author. New York: Random House, 1986. Age: 1. Chaps. 4 and 6.

A board book with different-size holes or slots on each page, which give the reader a glimpse of an animal that will be shown in its entirety on the following page.

Eastman, P.D. *Are You My Mother?* Illustrated by the author.
New York: Random House Books, 1960. Age: 2. Chaps. 6 and 7.
The story of a newborn bird who goes searching for his
mother, who was off finding food when he hatched. The little
bird asks many animals if they are his mother, including an
old airplane and a small boat, and is disappointed each time
he is mistaken. Just as he feels overwhelmingly alone, he is
reunited with Mother by a steam shovel.

Eastman, P.D. *Big Dog, Little Dog.* Illustrated by the author.
New York: Random House, 1973. Age: 4. Chap. 4.
This book of opposites is much more of a story than most
others. Two dogs are friends and enjoy many activities together, although their tastes are frequently opposites.

Eber, Christine E. *Just Momma and Me.* Illustrated by the author.
Chapel Hill, NC: Lollipop Power, 1975. Age: 5. Chap. 7.
Regina must adjust when Karl comes to live with her and her
Momma, and then again when her Momma has a baby. The
mother is warm and loving. She is a student with a range of
interests and abilities including sports. Karl is patient and
loving. He gardens, helps keep the home clean, and cares for
Regina and the rest of the family. All of the characters are
respected by the author. The message comes through that
this is a strong and loving family.

Edelman, Elaine. *I Love My Baby Sister (Most of the Time).*
Illustrated by Wendy Watson. New York: Puffin/Viking Penguin,
1984. Age: 3. Chap. 8.
An amusing and balanced picture of a small child's adjustment to life with a new sibling. Even though the baby
screams, tugs hair, and demands lots of attention, she is also
cuddly and cheerful at times. The older sibling anticipates a
future of friendship between the two.

Edwards, Ron. *The Postal Service.* Illustrated by Tim Clark.
Loughborough, England: Ladybird Books, 1983. Age: 3. Chap. 5.
Color photographs and a well-written text explain how the
British postal system works. Fascinating inside look at the
many people and machines needed to process the mail.

Ehrlich, Amy. *The Random House Book of Fairy Tales*. Illustrated by Diane Goode. New York: Random House, 1985. Age: 4. Chap. 1.

> Nineteen of the best-known fairy tales, including "Rapunzel," "Beauty and the Beast," "Thumbelina," and "Hansel and Gretel."

Eichler, Margrit. *Martin's Father*. Illustrated by Bev Magennis. Chapel Hill, NC: Lollipop Power, 1971. Age: 3. Chap. 6.

> The story describes the everyday activities that Martin and his father engage in. It is clear that his father is a single parent whose relationship with his son is a nurturing one.

Eisenberg, Phyllis Rose. *A Mitzvah Is Something Special*. Illustrated by Susan Jeschke. New York: Harper & Row, 1978. Age: 5. Chap. 7.

> In their behavior, Lisa's two grandmothers are very different. Both love Lisa and both enjoy it enormously when Lisa does a mitzvah (good deed) and invites them both over for an evening.

Elliott, Dan. *Grover Goes to School*. Illustrated by Normand Chartier. New York: Random House/Children's Television Network, 1982. Age: 4. Chaps. 6 and 9.

> Grover's first day at school makes him very unhappy because he is so eager to make friends that he neglects his own true feelings. A new friend helps him to see that he has the right to his own preferences.

Ellison, Virginia H. *Pooh Bear's Cook Book*. Illustrated by Ernest Shepard. New York: Dell, 1969. Age: 4. Chap. 5.

> Recipes of all sorts, particularly those such as Pooh's "smackerels."

Emberley, Barbara (adaptor). *One Wide River to Cross*. Illustrated by Ed Emberley. New York: Scholastic, 1966. Age: 6 mos. Chaps. 3, 4, and 6.

> Ed Emberley's woodcuts are set against brightly colored backgrounds to accompany the words of this traditional song. Older toddlers will love naming the animals and counting them.

Emberley, Ed. *Animals*. Illustrated by the author. Boston: Little, Brown, 1987. Age: 6 mos. Chap. 3.

Eleven animals are pictured and labeled in this clear, simple board book for very young children.

Emberley, Ed. *Cars, Boats, and Planes*. Illustrated by the author. Boston: Little, Brown, 1987. Age: 1. Chap. 4.

Seven types of vehicles are illustrated and labeled in this very simple and clear board book.

Emberley, Ed. *First Words: Sounds*. Illustrated by the author. Boston: Little, Brown, 1987. Age: 6 mos. Chaps. 3 and 4.

This small board book has very clear illustrations of animals, vehicles, and one friendly little ghost. Each is labeled with the sound it makes.

Emberley, Ed. *Home*. Illustrated by the author. Boston: Little, Brown, 1987. Age: 6 mos. Chap. 3.

A small, clearly illustrated board book of twelve familiar things found in many homes. Particularly amusing are the pictures of a mother and father from below the knees—a child's-eye view.

Epstein, Beryl and Davis, Dorritt. *Two Sisters and Some Hornets*. Illustrated by Rosemary Wells. New York: Holiday House, 1972. Age: 5. Chap. 8.

Two aged sisters reminisce together about an incident from their childhood. Their spats now are very similar to the ones they had then. The younger remains petulant into old age, the other is superior and smug.

Erikson, Karen. *I Can Share*. Illustrated by Maureen Roffey. New York: Scholastic, 1985. Age: 2. Chaps. 4 and 6.

This small book uses bold, colorful, and clear illustrations to present some of the problems youngsters have in sharing.

Erikson, Karen. *No One Is Perfect*. Illustrated by Maureen Roffey. New York: Viking Kestrel, 1987. Age: 3. Chap. 6.

A little girl learns that making mistakes needn't make her feel sad, cry, or hide. Everyone makes mistakes, even grown-ups in this humorous, but useful, book.

Eriksson, Eva. *Jealousy*. Illustrated by the author. Minneapolis: Carolrhoda, 1985. Age: 4. Chap. 6.

Victor and Rosalie are very best friends. They play together everyday. Then Rosalie gets the mumps and Victor starts playing with Sophie. Rosalie gets jealous, but a solution is found. Excellent for discussion of the powerful feelings evoked by jealousy and the ways it can be handled.

Ets, Marie Hall. *In the Forest*. Illustrated by the author. New York: Viking, 1944. Age: 3. Chap. 6.

A very popular, gentle fantasy tale about a little boy who imagines going for a walk alone in a forest and meeting a number of friendly animals who join him on a parade.

Ets, Marie Hall. *Just Me*. Illustrated by the author. New York: Viking, 1965. Age: 3. Chap. 6.

A little boy imitates the movements of many animals. When his father calls him, he delightedly runs to him in his own special gait.

Ets, Marie Hall. *Play with Me*. Illustrated by the author. New York: Penguin, 1955. Age: 2. Chap. 6.

A little girl eagerly invites the animals of the meadow to play with her, but they all run away. Finally she sits down by the pond and is very still. Then the animals slowly approach her. A book about friendship and accommodation.

Ets, Marie Hall. *Talking Without Words*. Illustrated by the author. New York: Viking, 1968. Age: 2. Chap. 4.

The nonverbal communication of animals is described by the author whose expressive black-and-white illustrations have been enjoyed for twenty years. Examples of human gestures, from sticking out one's tongue to giving someone a hug, are provided.

Eugene, Toni. *Hide and Seek*. Illustrated by Barbara Gibson. Washington, DC: National Geographics, 1985. Age: 4. Chap. 4.

A pop-up creation using multilevel pop-out environments to camouflage animals. Five natural settings are presented. Many animals are made to move or appear by the reader pulling tabs. Well-illustrated with much detail.

Everton, MacDuff. *El Circo Magico Modelo/Finding the Magic Circus*. Illustrated by the author. Minneapolis: Carolrhoda, 1982. Age: 5. Chap. 7.

> Done in the style of Huichol Indian yarn paintings, this story is based on a real-life trip that the author and his son took to Mexico to visit friends and to revisit the Yucatan circus where the author was once a performer. There are Spanish translations and a pronunciation guide at the end of the book.

Fadiman, Clifton. *The World Treasury of Children's Literature (Vols. I, II, III)*. Illustrated by Leslie Morrill. Boston: Little, Brown, 1984. Age: 1. Chap. 2.

> A three-volume anthology of classical and contemporary children's stories, poems, myths, and legends from many countries.

Farber, Norma. *As I Was Crossing Boston Common*. Illustrated by Arnold Lobel. Berkeley, CA: Creative Arts, 1982. Age: 4. Chap. 4.

> A rhymed account of all the unusual animals seen when crossing Boston Common.

Fassler, Joan. *Howie Helps Himself*. Illustrated by Joe Lasker. Chicago: Whitman, 1975. Age: 5. Chap. 7.

> Howie learns to wheel his own wheelchair without requiring other people to help him. This is a triumph for him.

Fassler, Joan. *My Grandpa Died Today*. Illustrated by Stewart Kranz. New York: Behavioral, 1971. Age: 4. Chap. 7.

> When a young boy's grandfather dies, he mourns for him in his own way, and is permitted by his parents to resume his ordinary activities. He knows that he will always lovingly remember his grandfather.

Feelings, Muriel. *Jambo Means Hello*. Illustrated by Tom Feelings. New York: Dial, 1974. Age: 5. Chaps. 4 and 7.

> The twenty-four letters of the Swahili alphabet are illustrated with words and pictures. Each page provides information about Swahili culture.

Feelings, Muriel. *Moja Means One: A Swahili Counting Book*. Illustrated by Tom Feelings. New York: Dial, 1971. Age: 4. Chaps. 4 and 7.

Illustrations and text combine to celebrate the richness of Swahili culture, while at the same time helping young children to reinforce their counting skills.

Feelings, Muriel. *Zamani Goes to Market*. Illustrated by Tom Feelings. New York: Seabury, 1970. Age: 4. Chap. 6.
When Zamani is at last old enough to accompany his father and brothers to market, he is shown further evidence of his growing maturity by spending his money on a gift for his mother.

Felt, Sue. *Rosa Too Little*. Illustrated by the author. Garden City, NY: Doubleday, 1950. Age: 3. Chap. 8.
Rosa is too young to take books from the library, to jump rope with her sister, or to go on the roof with her brother. Finally, Rosa is old enough to go to school with her siblings and get a library card of her own.

Fisher, Aileen. *I Stood upon a Mountain*. Illustrated by Blair Lent. New York: Crowell, 1979. Age: 4. Chap. 6.
A child asks four people how the world began. She receives four different answers — an egg, a word, a world of fire, and an explosion. No answer is affirmed, only the wonder that led to the question.

Fisher, Leonard Everett. *Boxes, Boxes*. Illustrated by the author. New York: Viking, 1984. Age: 4. Chap. 4.
Eighty boxes, boldly colored, interestingly detailed, many-shaped and multipurpose.

Flack, Marjorie. *Ask Mr. Bear*. Illustrated by the author. New York: Macmillan, 1932. Age: 18 mos. Chaps. 4 and 6.
Danny is looking for a perfect birthday gift for his mother. Each animal he asks offers a gift that Danny's mother already has and then suggests he ask another animal. Each animal joins the search. Finally Danny asks Mr. Bear and finds the perfect gift he has been seeking. This classic has endured for more than fifty years.

Flack, Marjorie and Wiese, Kurt. *The Story About Ping*. Illustrated by Kurt Wiese. New York: Scholastic, 1933. Age: 4. Chaps. 1 and 6.

Ping is a duckling who lives on a boat on the Yangtse River. He learns that it is better to endure a small reprimand than to lose the security of one's own home and family.

Fleisher, Robbin. *Quilts in the Attic*. Illustrated by Ati Forberg. New York: Macmillan, 1978. Age: 4. Chap. 8.
Two young sisters are playing with quilts up in their attic, thinking up all sorts of imaginative games. At one point, they get into a fight but find a way to resolve the quarrel.

Fletcher, Helen. *Picture Book ABC*. Illustrated by Jennie Williams. New York: Platt & Munk, 1978. Age: 4. Chap. 4.
A very first alphabet book using brightly colored pictures.

Florian, Douglas. *Discovering Butterflies*. Illustrated by the author. New York: Scribners, 1986. Age: 5. Chap. 4.
Describes the structure, life cycle, and behavior of butterflies and depicts different species found in North America, Africa, and South America. A good book to use as a first reference.

Florian, Douglas. *Discovering Trees*. Illustrated by the author. New York: Scribners, 1986. Age: 5. Chap. 4.
An introduction to trees, their growth, reproduction, usefulness, and varieties.

Florian, Douglas. *People Working*. Illustrated by the author. New York: Crowell, 1983. Age: 4. Chap. 4.
This book briefly describes in words and pictures how and where people work.

Ford, George. *Baby's First Picture Book*. Illustrated by the author. New York: Random House, 1979. Age: 6 mos. Chap. 3.
A cloth book with one-word, one-picture format.

Fowke, Edith (lyrics). *Roll Over! A Counting Song*. Illustrated by Merle Peek. New York: Clarion, 1981. Age: 2. Chap. 4.
Before falling asleep a little boy keeps rolling over, and the animals (imaginary and stuffed) that are in bed with him fall out one by one. Good for counting backward or learning to subtract one.

Frank, Josette. *Poems to Read to the Very Young*. Illustrated by Eloise Wilkin. New York: Random House, 1982. Age: Birth. Chap. 1.

A collection of short poems on various subjects, by Robert Louis Stevenson, A. A. Milne, Christina Rossetti, and others. Begin reading these to your infant and then see how he or she remembers them fondly at age 3, 4, and up.

Fritz, Jean. *The Good Giants and the Bad Pukwudgies*. Illustrated by Tomie DePaola. New York: Putnam, 1982. Age: 5. Chap. 7.

This story is a somewhat modernized amalgam of several tales telling of the creation of the islands off Cape Cod according to the legends of the Wampanoag Indians of New England. This book encourages young readers to read more tales of Native Americans.

Frost, Robert. *Stopping by Woods on a Snowy Evening*. Illustrated by Susan Jeffers. New York: Dutton, 1978. Age: Birth. Chap. 1.

Illustrations of wintry scenes accompany each line of the well-known poem. An edition for parents to enjoy when the children are babies, and for the children to appreciate as they grow up.

Fujikawa, Gyo. *Let's Eat*. Illustrated by the author. New York: Grosset & Dunlap, 1975. Age: 18 mos. Chaps. 4 and 5.

A board book about many different foods. Children will enjoy naming foods they know, learning about new things to eat, and discussing their preferences.

Ga'g, Wanda. *The ABC Bunny*. Illustrated by the author. New York: Coward McCann, 1933. Age: 4. Chap. 4.

An old-fashioned alphabet book that children may enjoy because it is so different from slick, modern versions. The rhyming story about a bunny adds to the fun.

Ga'g, Wanda. *Millions of Cats*. Illustrated by the author. New York: Scholastic, 1928. Age: 3. Chap. 1.

An old man and woman are lonely, so the old man searches for a cat. He brings home millions of cats who finally destroy each other in a quarrel over who is the prettiest. The thinnest, most scraggly kitten survives. The old couple lovingly nurture it. The refrain is one that children enjoy chanting.

Galdone, Paul. *The Gingerbread Boy*. Illustrated by the author. New York: Clarion, 1975. Age: 4. Chaps. 1, 2, and 4.
The Gingerbread Boy eludes the hungry grasp of everyone he meets until he happens upon a fox more clever than he. The cumulative nature of the story is one of its major attractions.

Galdone, Paul. *Henny Penny*. Illustrated by the author. New York: Clarion, 1968. Age: 3. Chap. 1.
A bold and brightly illustrated version of this well-known cumulative story.

Galdone, Paul. *Little Bo-Peep*. Illustrated by the author. New York: Clarion, 1986. Age: Birth. Chaps. 1 and 2.
An illustrated rendition of the traditional nursery rhyme about the little girl who lost her sheep.

Galdone, Paul. *The Little Red Hen*. Illustrated by the author. New York: Scholastic, 1973. Age: 3. Chap. 1.
A well-illustrated and witty version of the traditional story about the value of working together.

Galdone, Paul. *Rumpelstiltskin*. Illustrated by the author. New York: Clarion, 1985. Age: 5. Chap. 1.
Galdone boldly illustrates this faithful rendition of the classic fairy tale that retains its popularity despite the negative implications of much of its plot.

Galdone, Paul. *The Teeny-Tiny Woman: A Ghost Story*. Illustrated by the author. New York: Houghton Mifflin, 1984. Age: 3. Chap. 2.
A retelling of the story of the teeny woman who finds a tiny bone in a churchyard and regrets putting it into her cupboard.

Galdone, Paul. *The Three Bears*. Illustrated by the author. New York: Clarion, 1972. Age: 3. Chaps. 1 and 2.

The illustrations are lively and realistic, but the ending is very hard on Goldilocks. Think about whether you want to use it.

Galdone, Paul. *The Three Billy Goats Gruff.* Illustrated by the author. New York: Seabury, 1973. Age: 5. Chaps. 1 and 2.
Galdone's renditions of the classic tales never spare the villains. His illustrations are popular with many children.

Galdone, Paul. *Three Little Kittens.* Illustrated by the author. New York: Clarion, 1986. Age: Birth. Chaps. 1 and 2.
Three little kittens lose, find, soil, and wash their mittens. Another classic rhyme song to sing to your infant and enjoy later as well.

Geisert, Arthur. *Pigs from A to Z.* Illustrated by the author. Boston: Houghton Mifflin, 1986. Age: 5. Chap. 4.
An intricate alphabet book detailing the construction of a house by pigs. The illustrations are quirky line drawings.

Geringer, Laura. *Molly's New Washing Machine.* Illustrated by Petra Mathers. New York: Harper & Row, 1986. Age: 3. Chap. 5.
A new washing machine is delivered by two rabbits to Molly's house. Molly, a human being, and many of her zany animal friends run a test load and dance to the "music" of the machine's different cycles. Lots of fun for a washday at home.

Gerson, Mary-Joan. *Ometiji's Baby Brother.* Illustrated by Eliza Moon. New York: Henry Z. Walk, 1974. Age: 4. Chap. 8.
Ometiji, a young Nigerian boy, feels pushed aside when the baby is born. Nobody seems to want or need him. When he overcomes his feelings and creates a very special gift for his new sibling's naming party, he sees how proud his parents and guests are and reaches out for his new sibling for the first time.

Gibbons, Gail. *Boats.* Illustrated by the author. New York: Holiday House, 1983. Age: 3. Chap. 4.
This book introduces the young reader to a large variety of floating vessels: kayaks, rowboats, canoes, shells, sailboats,

speed boats, and many larger vehicles such as cruise ships and submarines.

Gibbons, Gail. *Department Store*. Illustrated by the author. New York: Harper & Row, 1984. Age: 5. Chap. 4.
A behind-the-scenes view of a department store, its various areas, personnel, and inner workings.

Gibbons, Gail. *The Post Office Book: Mail and How It Moves*. Illustrated by the author. New York: Harper & Row, 1982. Age: 5. Chaps. 4 and 5.
A step-by-step description of what happens to mail from the time it is deposited in the mailbox to its arrival at its destination. Also contains brief historical facts about mail service in the United States.

Gibbons, Gail. *Toolbox*. Illustrated by the author. New York: Holiday House, 1982. Age: 4. Chaps. 4 and 5.
Brightly colored, clearly drawn tools labeled to teach their names and functions.

Gibbons, Gail. *Trains*. Illustrated by the author. New York: Holiday House, 1987. Age: 4. Chap. 4.
Gail Gibbons's recent book gives young readers lots of verbal and pictorial information about many kinds of trains, some of which we rarely see anymore.

Gibbons, Gail. *Tunnels*. Illustrated by the author. New York: Holiday House, 1984. Age: 3. Chap. 4.
A bright introduction to the dark world of tunnels, their builders (ants, moles, chipmunks, prairie dogs, and people), and the various shapes and sizes in which they can be built.

Gibbons, Gail. *Up Goes the Skyscraper*. Illustrated by the author. New York: Macmillan, 1986. Age: 4. Chap. 4.
A must for every urban child who has walked past empty lots walled in with boards providing only adult-height peepholes. A fine description, using colorful linear pictures and simple text, of the building of a skyscraper from permit and excavation to interior decoration. Adults will love this one too.

Gillham, Bill. *Can You See It?* Illustrated by Fiona Horne. New York: Putnam, 1986. Age: 3. Chap. 4.
> Each left-hand page has a close-up picture of an object. In the picture to the right, the object is to be found but is often quite well hidden. A real visual discrimination challenge.

Gillham, Bill. *The First Words Picture Book.* Illustrated by Sam Grainger. New York: Coward McCann, 1982. Age: 1. Chap. 3.
> The aim of this book is to stimulate children's language development. The author provides a close-up photograph of an object such as a ball on the left-hand page and shows the same object being used by children on the right-hand page.

Gillham, Bill. *What Can You Do?* Illustrated by Fiona Horne. New York: Putnam, 1986. Age: 3. Chap. 4.
> This book combines colorful photographs and simple text to suggest how familiar objects can be used creatively in play.

Gillham, Bill. *What's the Difference?* Illustrated by Fiona Horne. New York: Putnam, 1986. Age: 3. Chap. 4.
> This book contains paired photographs designed to provide opportunities for comparison and discussions of similarity and difference. The children in the photographs are from a variety of cultural backgrounds and care is taken to avoid gender stereotypes. A book that stimulates thought and visual discrimination.

Gillham, Bill and Hulme, Susan. *Let's Look for Opposites.* Illustrated by Jan Siegieda. New York: Coward McCann, 1984. Age: 3. Chap. 4.
> Paired pictures of children at everyday activities are photographed to illustrate eleven opposite concepts.

Gillham, Bill and Hulme, Susan. *Let's Look for Shapes.* Photos by Jan Siegieda. New York: Coward McCann, 1984. Age: 3. Chap. 4.
> One of a series of four books designed to encourage children to look for shapes in the everyday world. Photographs on the left side of each double page are of an object of the shape being presented. The photograph on the right side is of a child interacting with another object of the same shape.

Other books in this series include *Let's Look for Colors, Let's Look for Numbers,* and *Let's Look for Opposites.*

Ginsburg, Mirra. *The Sun's Asleep Behind the Hill.* Illustrated by Paul O. Zelinsky. New York: Greenwillow, 1982. Age: 1. Chap. 6.
The sun, the leaves, the breeze, the squirrel, and a child each has had a busy day and knows that evening is the time to rest. The text is adapted from an Armenian song.

Girard, Laura Walvood. *You Were Born on Your Very First Birthday.* Illustrated by Christa Kieffer. Niles, IL: Albert Whitman, 1983. Age: 3. Chap. 8.
This book, told by a mother speaking to her child, describes what life was like for the child in utero. The tone is loving and soft, the information clear.

Glazier, Nancy Hannah. *My Very Own Telephone Book.* Illustrated by Ginna Hirtenstein. New York: Grosset & Dunlap, 1986. Age: 4. Chap. 4.
With large spaces to write in important phone numbers and a space to put photographs of the person being called, this telephone-shaped board book can help your child feel that friends, relatives, parents, and emergency workers can be reached when needed. Useful summary pages for your child's personal health information and with information for a babysitter.

Goennel, Heidi. *Seasons.* Illustrated by the author. Boston: Little, Brown, 1986. Age: 1. Chap. 4.
Slabs of unusual colors, strikingly juxtaposed, illustrate this picture book about the special sights and activities children can enjoy in each of the four seasons. The pictures are evocative and invite discussion.

Goff, Beth. *Where Is Daddy? The Story of a Divorce.* Illustrated by Susan Perle. Boston: Beacon, 1969. Age: 3. Chap. 7.
Janeydear experiences fears and self-doubt after her parents' divorce. Gradually the adults help her to understand that she is not to blame, and that her parents will continue to care for her. This is one of the few books on this issue written for children so young.

Goffstein, M.B. *School of Names*. Illustrated by the author. New York: Harper & Row, 1986. Age: 5. Chap. 4.

What it means to live on the Earth and to share a connection with the ocean, the continents, the clouds, the animals, and all the elements of the Earth. Naming is an important part of the understanding process.

Goffstein, M.B. *Sleepy People*. Illustrated by the author. New York: Farrar, Straus, Giroux, 1966. Age: 1. Chap. 6.

Four tiny people in nightshirts and caps yawn, smile, stretch, eat cookies, drink cocoa, and are always very sleepy in this unusual bedtime book.

Goodall, John S. *Creepy Castle*. Illustrated by the author. New York: Atheneum, 1975. Age: 4. Chaps. 2 and 4.

This wordless story told by rich, detailed paintings is of two heroic mice who are locked into a castle by a villainous character (also a mouse). Complete with fair maiden and moat, children will love "reading" and telling this story.

Goodall, John S. *The Midnight Adventures of Kelly, Dot, and Esmeralda*. Illustrated by the author. New York: Atheneum, 1972. Age: 4. Chap. 2.

Three toys go on a magic midnight journey and finally return to their playroom.

Goodall, John S. *The Surprise Picnic*. Illustrated by the author. New York: Atheneum, 1977. Age: 3. Chaps. 2 and 4.

This is the wordless story of a mother cat and her two kittens who take a picnic to an island. Their adventures begin when the "rock" on which they have laid out their lovely lunch disappears. This is just the beginning of their many adventures. Full-page paintings alternate with half-page sections. When the smaller pages are turned and rest against the former full page, the scene changes dramatically. This book is highly recommended for storytelling by adults and children.

Goodyear, Carmen. *The Sheep Book*. Illustrated by the author. Chapel Hill, NC: Lollipop Power, 1972. Age: 4. Chap. 4.

The story of Ba-Ha-He, a real sheep who lives in California, who is born, named, sung about, and shorn. Ba-Ha-He's wool is carded, spun, balled, and knitted into a sweater for the woman who is a farmer and her owner. The book ends with Ba-Ha-He giving birth to her own lamb. Simple and well illustrated in black against strong yellow background.

Gorbaty, Norman. *Baby Animals Say Hello*. Illustrated by the author. New York: Random House, 1986. Age: 6 mos. Chap. 3.
This small cloth book with padded pages introduces babies to ten baby animals and the sounds they make. Color drawings with black outlines and very simple backgrounds make pictures easy to identify.

Gorbaty, Norman. *Baby Ben's Book of Colors*. Illustrated by the author. New York: Random House, 1985. Age: 1. Chap. 4.
A "baby fingers board book," this book is tabbed on the side to help a young child turn the pages and identify objects and colors.

Graboff, Abner. *Old MacDonald Had a Farm*. Illustrated by the author. New York: Scholastic, 1969. Age: 18 mos. Chaps. 1, 2, and 4.
Old MacDonald is a perennial favorite with children learning animal names and sounds and with older children who enjoy the challenge of remember the sequence of animals.

Graham, John. *I Love You, Mouse*. Illustrated by Tomie DePaola. New York: Harcourt, 1976. Age: 2. Chap. 6.
A caring, protective little boy tells each of thirteen animals that he loves it and will provide it with a particularly appropriate home. He will join it in an activity that is special to its kind. As evening approaches, the boy's father joins him. In parallel language, the father tells the boy that he is loved, that he has a home with a bed and warm quilts. A story about learning how to provide security and love.

Gramatky, Hardie. *Little Toot*. Illustrated by the author. New York: Putnam, 1939. Age: 4. Chap. 1.
Little Toot becomes a hero after rescuing an ocean liner from the rocks.

Gray, Genevieve. *Send Wendell*. Illustrated by Symeon Shimin. New York: McGraw-Hill, 1974. Age: 3. Chap. 4.

Wendell is one of seven children. Because all of them are busy and he isn't, Wendell is the one who always has to run errands. After Uncle Robert comes to visit, Wendell is busy, too, writing letters to his uncle.

Greeley, Valerie. *Pets*. Illustrated by the author. New York: Harper & Row, 1981. Age: 6 mos. Chap. 4.
A small board book with very delicate and detailed paintings of seven pets, not all familiar, against lovely backgrounds.

Greenaway, Kate. *A Apple Pie*. Illustrated by the author. London: Frederick Warne, 1886. Age: 4. Chaps. 1 and 4.
A classic alphabet book illustrated with charming children in Victorian dress. Each letter advances the story of what happens to a mammoth apple pie.

Greenfield, Eloise. *Honey, I Love, and Other Poems*. Illustrated by Diane and Leo Dillon. New York: Crowell, 1978. Age: 4. Chap. 7.
A collection of poems. All are personal, evocative, and well-crafted. The illustrations celebrate Afro-American beauty.

Greenfield, Eloise. *Me and Nessie*. Illustrated by Moneta Barnett. New York: Crowell, 1975. Age: 5. Chap. 8.
A young girl has a make-believe friend on whom she blames her own faults and negative behavior. When she is ready for school, she is ready to leave her imaginary friend behind.

Greenfield, Eloise. *She Come Bringing Me That Little Baby Girl*. Illustrated by John Steptoe. Philadelphia: Lippincott, 1974. Age: 5. Chap. 8.
Young Kevin wants a sibling, but when his baby sister finally arrives, he is jealous. When his mother gives him the baby to hold and when his friends admire her, a positive sense of connection begins. He is even able to imagine happy times they will share in the future.

Gregor, Arthur. *Animal Babies*. Illustrated by Ylla. New York: Harper & Row, 1959. Age: 1. Chaps. 3, 4, and 6.
One of the world's foremost animal photographers has put together a collection of large black-and-white photographs of animals and their babies.

Gretz, Susanna. *Hide-and-Seek*. Illustrated by the author. New York: Four Winds/Macmillan, 1985. Age: 18 mos. Chap. 6.

> Four teddy bears play hide-and-seek. One bear is shown trying out a number of hiding places and finally chooses to hide in bed. He is found fast asleep.

Gretz, Susanna. *I'm Not Sleepy*. Illustrated by the author. New York: Four Winds, 1986. Age: 18 mos. Chap. 4.

> While all the other teddy bears are going off to bed John feels wide awake and wants to play. On heavy board pages.

Gretz, Susanna. *Ready for Bed*. Illustrated by the author. New York: Four Winds, 1986. Age: 18 mos. Chap. 4.

> Teddy Bear Andrew has trouble getting ready for bed. On heavy board pages.

Gretz, Susanna. *teddy bears 1 to 10*. Illustrated by the author. New York: Four Winds, 1986. Age: 18 mos. Chap. 5.

> Ten teddy bears emerge from the dry cleaner in a much-improved state.

Gretz, Susanna. *Too Dark!* Illustrated by the author. New York: Four Winds, 1986. Age: 18 mos. Chap. 4.

> Even familiar objects can look scary for a teddy bear trying to fall asleep in a dark room. A charming board book that may help small children to talk about their own fears.

Griego, Margot, and Bucks, Betsy. *Tortillitas Para Mamá*. Illustrated by Barbara Cooney. New York: Holt, 1981. Age: 18 mos. Chap. 2.

> A collection of nursery rhymes, each in both English and Spanish, collected from the Spanish community in the Americas, many with instructions for accompanying finger plays or other activities.

Griffith, Helen V. *Georgia Music*. Illustrated by James Stevenson. New York: Greenwillow, 1986. Age: 4. Chap. 6.

> A young girl takes advantage of the opportunity to reciprocate her grandfather's special gift to her. In his old age, when he is depressed, she sings to him the Georgia songs that he sang to her.

Griffith, Helen V. *Mine Will, Said John.* Illustrated by Muriel Batherman. New York: Greenwillow, 1980. Age: 3. Chap. 5.
John's parents try to interest him in a gerbil or chameleon for a pet, but John will be content only with a puppy.

Gundersheimer, Karen. *Colors to Know.* Illustrated by the author. New York: Harper & Row, 1986. Age: 2. Chap. 4.
Each left-hand page has a thick border, a square, and a color word in large uppercase letters. All are in the color being presented. On the right-hand page is an object of that color and a tiny little person interacting with the object. A small, clear, uncluttered beginning book about color.

Gundersheimer, Karen. *Shapes to Show.* Illustrated by the author. New York: Harper & Row, 1986. Age: 3. Chap. 4.
On each left-hand page of this small book, a shape is drawn and labeled with its name. In each right-hand picture, two clothed mice are interacting with an object of the same shape. Each picture invites storytelling as well as shape naming.

Hader, Berta and Elmer. *The Big Snow.* Illustrated by the authors. New York: Collier, 1948. Age: 3. Chap. 4.
A lovely old book about forest animals' watching for signs of winter and making their yearly preparations. When the big snow comes, they are helped by an old couple. Winner of a Caldecott Medal.

Hadithi, Mwenye. *Greedy Zebra.* Illustrated by Adrienne Kennaway. Boston: Little, Brown, 1984. Age: 3. Chap. 4.
An illustrated story of how the animals of the jungle acquired their glorious coats and horns, and why the zebra has its black and white stripes.

Hague, Kathleen. *Alphabears.* Illustrated by Michael Hague. New York: Holt, 1984. Age: 4. Chap. 4.
On each page of this illustrated book, a bear is introduced and its special qualities are described in rhyme. Each bear's name begins with a different letter of the alphabet. Because no one bear is like another, this book can be used to support respect for individual differences.

Hague, Kathleen. *Numbears*. Illustrated by Michael Hague. New York: Holt, 1986. Age: 4. Chap. 4.

A four-line rhyme describes each of the twelve bears introduced on a page of this book. The poem contains a number in its story. Each poem's story comes to life in the full-page painting on the facing page. For some of the paintings, good visual discrimination skills are required because of the soft, muted tones and detail.

Hale, Sara Josepha. *Mary Had a Little Lamb*. Illustrated by Tomie DePaola. New York: Holiday House, 1984. Age: Birth. Chap. 1.

The famous nineteenth-century nursery rhyme about the schoolgoing lamb is accompanied by the music later written for it.

Haley, Gail E. *A Story, A Story*. Illustrated by the author. New York: Atheneum, 1970. Age: 5. Chaps. 1, 2, and 7.

Anansi tales, well researched, told, and illustrated.

Hall, Donald. *Ox-Cart Man*. Illustrated by Barbara Cooney. New York: Viking, 1979. Age: 4. Chaps. 1 and 2.

Describes the day-to-day life throughout the changing seasons of an early-nineteenth-century New England family. The illustrations, combined with the simple text, are so outstanding that this award-winning book has appeal for adults and children of all ages.

Harmer, Juliet. *The Little Go-to-Sleep Book*. Illustrated by the author. New York: Atheneum, 1986. Age: 6 mos. Chaps. 3 and 6.

To help her baby go to sleep, the mother in this small, illustrated bedtime story tells her child about where each of the animals goes to sleep in the night. A quieting good-night book.

Harper, Anita. *It's Not Fair*. Illustrated by Susan Hellard. New York: Putman, 1986. Age: 3. Chap. 8.

On the cover of this book, a medium-size kangaroo is pictured, midjump, about to squash a baby bottle. The first half of his story depicts his anger at all the things his new sibling is given or permitted to do which he is denied. The second half of the book describes the many things that he is permitted that the baby is not.

Harris, Robie H. *I Hate Kisses.* Illustrated by Diane Paterson. New York: Knopf, 1981. Age: 4. Chap. 6.
A small boy decides he is too big for his stuffed animal and his parents' kisses. He briefly changes his mind when he hurts himself at the end of the day.

Hart, Jane. *Singing Bee!* Illustrated by Anita Lobel. New York: Lothrop, Lee, Shepard, 1982. Age: Birth. Chap. 2.
A collection of over one hundred songs, including lullabies, holiday and traditional songs, singing games, and finger plays.

Haus, Felice. *Beep! Beep! I'm A Jeep!* Illustrated by Norman Gorbaty. New York: Random House, 1986. Age: 2. Chap. 6.
This "Great Big Board Book" is designed especially for graduates of baby-oriented board books—toddlers, who are ready to climb into cardboard boxes, as the protagonist does, and pretend they are in a jeep, a train, a tugboat, a fire truck, or an airplane.

Hautzig, Deborah. *It's Not Fair.* Illustrated by Leigh Tom. New York: Random House/Children's Television Network, 1986. Age: 4. Chaps. 6 and 9.
Bert and Ernie are partners in a lemonade stand, but Bert does all the work and Ernie gets all the credit. In the end all of Ernie's friends make it up to him.

Hautzig, Deborah. *A Visit to Sesame Street Library.* Illustrated by Joe Mathieu. New York: Random House, 1986. Age: 4. Chaps. 4, 5, and 9.
When Big Bird goes to the library with Grover, he is surprised by the many services the library provides. Published in cooperation with the Children's Television Workshop.

Hautzig, Deborah. *Why Are You So Mean to Me?* Illustrated by Tom Cooke. New York: Random House/Children's Television Network, 1986. Age: 3. Chaps. 6 and 9.

When Grover's friends are mean to him because he can't play baseball, he, in turn, is mean to Big Bird. The friends settle their differences, and Grover's mother assures him that he is valued for who and what he is.

Hawkins, Colin and Jaqui. *My First Book*. Illustrated by the authors. New York: Viking Kestrel, 1985. Age: 1. Chaps. 3 and 6.
The top of a frilly bassinet flap opens revealing a smiling infant and, on the back of the flap, a place for mother and/or child to fill in "I came home on . . . with . . . by. . . ." The page labeled MY FIRST SMILE shows a baby under a blanket. When the blanket is flapped open we see a smiling child and a space to fill in "I first smiled on . . . at. . . ." Each page has drawings and a space to record a "first." Children will love reading this with a parent or writing in it when they are older.

Hawkins, Colin. *Take Away Monsters*. Illustrated by the author. New York: Putnam, 1984. Age: 5. Chap. 4.
Pull the tab on each page and some of the colorful, smiling monsters disappear, behind a door, into a cupboard, even into a piano, to act out a subtraction problem for the reader. An amusing book for youngsters who have mastered subtraction.

Hayes, Geoffrey. *Bear by Himself*. Illustrated by the author. New York: Harper & Row, 1976. Age: 2. Chaps. 6 and 8.
A story about a little bear who knows how to enjoy his time alone. Good for only children and for siblings who need to learn the pleasure of solitude and independence.

Hayward, Linda. *The Sesame Street Dictionary*. Illustrated by Joe Mathieu. New York: Random House/Children's Television Network, 1980. Age: 4. Chaps. 4, 6, and 9.
A dictionary of vocabulary very young children can use. Each word is defined, used in a sentence, and illustrated with actions by the Sesame Street characters.

Hazen, Barbara Shook. *Gorilla Wants to Be the Baby*. Illustrated by Jaqueline Bardner Smith. New York: Atheneum, 1978. Age: 3. Chap. 8.

An amusing book that describes a toddler's friendship with a green gorilla who tells all about some of the difficulties of adjusting to life with a new baby.

Hazen, Barbara Shook. *If It Weren't for Benjamin*. Illustrated by Laura Hartman. New York: Human Sciences Press, 1979. Age: 5. Chap. 8.

In this book, a supportive family helps an older brother deal with his feelings of sibling rivalry.

Hazen, Barbara Shook. *Why Couldn't I Be an Only Child Like You, Wigger?* Illustrated by Leigh Grant. New York: Atheneum, 1975. Age: 5. Chap. 8.

Exchanging places appeals to two boys, one an only child, the other from a large family. When they carry out their plan, each comes to appreciate his own situation.

Hazen, Nancy. *Grownups Cry Too/Los Adultos Tambien Lloran*. Illustrated by the author. Chapel Hill, NC: Lollipop Power, 1973. Age: 3. Chap. 6.

This book shows a wide variety of situations that might be the occasion for tears. Grownups are shown crying too.

Hedderwick, Mairi. *Katie Morag and the Tiresome Ted*. Illustrated by the author. Boston: Little, Brown, 1986. Age: 3. Chap. 8.

Katie has been in a bad mood ever since the new baby arrived. She does numerous naughty things and is sent to Grannie's Island where there is a big storm. After the storm she feels much better and decides to end her bad mood. She accepts the new baby and makes a loving gesture to its presence.

Hellard, Susan. *Billy Goats Gruff*. Illustrated by the author. New York: Putnam, 1986. Age: 3. Chaps. 1 and 2.

A lift-the-flap book containing humorous illustrations of the classic Norwegian folktale. The ending provides us with a reformed troll who permits free traffic across the bridge.

Helmering, David Wild, and Williams, John. *We're Going to Have a Baby*. Illustrated by Robert Cassell. Nashville: Abingdon, 1978. Age: 3. Chap. 8.

Describes the apprehensions, fears, and sadness felt by a four-year-old when he learns he will have a new sibling. A six-year-old friend shares his skepticism, but a neighbor reassures Jimmy of his parents' continuing love.

Hendrickson, Karen. *Baby and I Can Play*. Illustrated by Marina Megale. Seattle: Parenting Press, 1985. Age: 4. Chap. 8.
An unusual book that teaches older siblings specific things they can do to interact positively with their new baby. Also advises older siblings that they may have negative feelings which they should bring to their parents.

Hendrickson, Karen. *Fun with Toddlers*. Illustrated by Marina Megale. Seattle: Parenting Press, 1985. Age: 4. Chap. 8.
This book, like the one above, teaches older children how to play constructively and instructively with a sibling, this time a toddler. It also talks about negative feelings and how to handle them. A useful book because of specific suggestions.

Hertz, Ole. Translated from the Danish by Tobi Tobias. *Tobias Catches Trout*. Illustrated by the author. Minneapolis: Carolrhoda, 1981. Age: 5. Chap. 4.
Tobias, a young Greenlander, goes on a trout-fishing expedition with his family in their motor boat.

Hertz, Ole. Translated from the Danish by Tobi Tobias. *Tobias Goes Seal Hunting*. Illustrated by the author. Minneapolis: Carolrhoda, 1981. Age: 5. Chap. 4.
In Greenland, a boy and his father hunt seals in their kayaks.

Hest, Amy. *The Purple Coat*. Illustrated by Amy Schwartz. New York: Four Winds, 1986. Age: 5. Chap. 5.
Despite her mother's reminder that "navy blue is what you always get," Gabby begs her grandfather, who is a tailor, to make her a purple fall coat.

Hewett, Joan. *Rosalie*. Illustrated by Donald Carrick. New York: Lothrop, Lee, Shepard, 1987. Age: 4. Chaps. 5 and 6.
Cindy loves her old dog, Rosalie. She manages to find ways to play with the old dog, and the family clearly takes good care of the animal.

Hickman, Martha W. *Last Week My Brother Anthony Died.* Illustrated by Julien Randie. Nashville: Abingdon, 1984. Age: 5. Chap. 7.

> Julie's four-week-old brother has died. The story is told from her perspective as she describes her feelings. The minister gives spiritual comfort to her parents, and helps her to accept her own responses.

Highwater, Jamake. *Moonsong Lullaby.* Illustrated by Marcia Keegan. New York: Lothrop, Lee, Shepard, 1981. Age: Birth. Chaps. 2 and 7.

> Portrays the activities of a Cherokee camp with photographs. The lullaby affirms the positive quality of life. Sing this book to infants and keep it for older children to enjoy.

Hill, Elizabeth Starr. *Evan's Corner.* Illustrated by Nancy Grossman. New York: Holt, 1967. Age: 4. Chap. 8.

> Evan lives in a very small apartment with his parents, three older sisters, and his younger brother, Adam. A warm, sharing relationship emerges when Evan constructs a place of his own but remains unsatisfied until he also recognizes Adam's needs.

Hill, Eric. *Spot Goes Splash!* Illustrated by the author. New York: Putnam, 1984. Age: 6 mos. Chap. 3.

> Eric Hill's yellow puppy with brown spots is shown splashing in the garden, at the beach, when it rains, and in the bath on the pages of this appealing, brightly colored, waterproof small book.

Hill, Eric. *Where's Spot?* Illustrated by the author. New York: Putnam, 1980. Age: 18 mos. Chaps. 1 and 4.

> Children enjoy searching under the flaps of the pages to see if they can locate the missing puppy, Spot.

Himler, Ronald. *Wake Up Jeremiah.* Illustrated by the author. New York: Harper & Row, 1979. Age: 4. Chap. 6.

> A young boy shares the ecstasy and beauty of the new day with his parents. The author shows us that it is human to be sensitive to beauty, and that this sensitivity is not gender-linked.

Hines, Anna Grossnickle. *All By Myself.* Illustrated by the author. New York: Clarion, 1985. Age: 3. Chap. 6.

> After reviewing with her mother all the things she has learned to do since she was a baby, Josie tells her mother she is ready to go through the night without diapers. Subsequently, she succeeds for many nights. Josie does experience an accident one night and on another she must overcome her fear of the dark to reach the bathroom. She is very proud of this next step toward independence.

Hoban, Russell. *A Baby Sister for Frances.* Illustrated by Lillian Hoban. New York: Harper & Row, 1964. Age: 5. Chap. 8.

> Frances runs away (to a spot under the kitchen table) because her baby sister, Gloria, eclipses some of the attention Frances is used to. Her very loving parents exclaim loudly how much she is missed both by them and Gloria. Frances emerges feeling much better.

Hoban, Russell. *Bedtime for Frances.* Illustrated by Garth Williams. New York: Harper & Row, 1960. Age: 3. Chaps. 1 and 6.

> Another in the series of sensitive books about a little badger whose nighttime fears keep her and her family awake. Their responses are both appropriate and amusing, reflecting a deep understanding of Frances's concerns and needs. Other books in this series include *A Baby Sister for Frances, Bread and Jam for Frances, A Best Friend for Frances,* and *A Birthday for Frances.*

Hoban, Russell. *A Birthday for Frances.* Illustrated by Lillian Hoban. New York: Scholastic, 1968. Age: 5. Chap. 8.

> Frances has ambivalent feelings about her little sister Gloria's birthday which are not resolved until the very end of this warm, understanding book.

Hoban, Russell. *Bread and Jam for Frances.* Illustrated by Lillian Hoban. New York: Harper & Row, 1964. Age: 3. Chap. 1.

> Frances has some real concerns about her food. She prefers bread and jam over the regular family fare. When bread and jam appear for her at every meal she realizes that variety has its advantages.

Hoban, Russell. *Charlie the Tramp.* Illustrated by Lillian Hoban. New York: Scholastic, 1966. Age: 4. Chap. 6.

> A little beaver decides he wants to be a tramp and have a good time rather than be a beaver and work hard. He leaves home, but during his time as a tramp he builds a pond and returns to do odd jobs to earn his lunch and dinner. His parents conclude that he will make a fine beaver some day.

Hoban, Tana. *A, B, See!* Illustrated by the author. New York: Greenwillow, 1982. Age: 4. Chap. 4.

> A collection of photograms of objects that begin with a particular letter of the alphabet.

Hoban, Tana. *Big Ones, Little Ones.* Illustrated by the author. New York: Greenwillow, 1976. Age: 2. Chaps. 4 and 6.

> Black-and-white photographs of great interest illustrate the relative size and relationships of fourteen animals and their young.

Hoban, Tana. *Count and See.* Illustrated by the author. New York: Macmillan, 1972. Age: 2. Chap. 4.

> Another concept book by photographer/author Tana Hoban.

Hoban, Tana. *I Read Signs.* Illustrated by the author. New York: Mulberry/Morrow, 1983. Age: 4. Chap. 5.

> A book of eye-catching photographs of signs that children are likely to see in their daily walks and rides. The author/illustrator has carefully arranged the pages so that children will look for differences and similarities. The signs progress from COME IN WE'RE OPEN to SORRY WE'RE CLOSED.

Hoban, Tana. *Is It Larger? Is It Smaller?* Illustrated by the author. New York: Greenwillow, 1985. Age: 4. Chap. 4.

> Another book by Tana Hoban challenging children to look carefully at her color photographs and compare objects. Sometimes there are only two elements to consider for relative size, sometimes there are three or more.

Hoban, Tana. *Is It Red? Is It Yellow? Is It Blue? An Adventure in Color.* Illustrated by the author. New York: Greenwillow, 1978. Age: 3. Chap. 4.

At the bottom of each photograph are colored dots. They correspond with colors to be found in the picture. Some colors are easy to find, some much more difficult. There are no labels or words. Some ambiguity adds to the interest of a number of pages.

Hoban, Tana. *Over, Under & Through*. Illustrated by the author. New York: Macmillan, 1973. Age: 3. Chap. 4.
Using interesting black-and-white photographs of urban scenes, Tana Hoban illustrates some more sophisticated spatial concepts: over, under, and through; on and in; around, across, and between; beside and below, and against and behind.

Hoban, Tana. *Panda, Panda*. Illustrated by the author. New York: Greenwillow, 1986. Age: 6 mos. Chap. 3.
On each page of this 6-by-6-inch board book there is a color photograph of a panda bear performing a basic act: eating, sitting, rolling, standing, drinking, climbing yawning, sleeping, walking, and standing.

Hoban, Tana. *Push/Pull Empty/Full*. Illustrated by the author. New York: Macmillan, 1972. Age: 2. Chap. 4.
Large black-and-white photographs illustrate fifteen pairs of opposites. Pictures invite careful scrutiny and discussion.

Hoban, Tana. *Round & Round & Round*. Illustrated by the author. New York: Greenwillow, 1983. Age: 3. Chap. 4.
In twenty-eight museum quality photographs, Tana Hoban presents a myriad of round shapes found in the real world. Large and small, rough and smooth, natural and man-made, round shapes are everywhere. Children love finding each example of roundness, obvious and hidden, in these pages. Some pages contain just a few examples; some contain an almost countless number.

Hoban, Tana. *Take Another Look*. Illustrated by the author. New York: Greenwillow, 1981. Age: 4. Chap. 1.
Each interesting black-and-white photograph in this book is preceded with a piece of white paper with a hole two inches

in diameter cut from the center to let a small part of the photograph behind it be seen. Without a single word, the book invites the reader to guess the whole object that is hidden from the small part that can be seen. On the back of each photograph is another picture of the same item seen from a distance.

Hoffman, Phyllis. *Baby's Kitchen*. Illustrated by Carol Hudson. New York: Scholastic, 1985. Age: 3. Chap. 5.
A colorforms book with fifteen reusable vinyl stick-ons including play figures, pots, pans, bowls, apron, cakes, and more. Caution: this book should not be used with or near children who still put small objects in their mouths.

Hoffman, Phyllis. *The Robot Book*. Illustrated by Carol Hudson. New York: Scholastic, 1986. Age: 5. Chap. 4.
This book challenges children to take the vinyl stickers of different shapes, which are provided at the front of the book, and use them to copy an increasingly complex design of a robot who is made solely of geometrical shapes. Stickers are reusable and can be made into an infinite number of designs.

Hogan, Paula Z. *Sometimes I Get So Mad*. Illustrated by Dora Leder. Milwaukee: Raintree, 1980. Age: 5. Chap. 8.
Explores anger in a relationship and shows how it can be expressed. Explains that anger can strengthen the relationship rather than ruin it.

Högner, Franz. *From Blueprint to House*. Illustrated by the author. Minneapolis: Carolrhoda, 1973. Age: 4. Chap. 4.
From the drawing of the blueprint to the family moving in, this book follows the steps necessary in building a house.

Hogrogian, Nonny. *One Fine Day*. Illustrated by the author. New York: Macmillan, 1971. Age: 4. Chaps. 1 and 2.
The story of a greedy fox's adventure adapted from an Armenian folktale.

Holden, Edith. *The Hedgehog Feast*. Illustrated by the author. New York: Windmill/Dutton, 1978. Age: 3. Chap. 5.

A hedgehog family prepares for winter with a sumptuous feast.

Holmes, Efner Tudor. *Amy's Goose*. Illustrated by Tasha Tudor. New York: Harper & Row, 1977. Age: 5. Chap. 6.
Amy, who loves to see the geese return in the fall, nurses one wounded animal and befriends it. When it is healthy again, she succeeds in her struggles to love it enough to let it be free again.

Homan, Dianne. *In Christina's Toolbox*. Illustrated by Mary Heine. Chapel Hill, NC: Lollipop Power, 1981. Age: 5. Chap. 5.
A girl builds a bird-feeder, stilts, and a tree house.

Hoopes, Lyn Littlefield. *Nana*. Illustrated by Arieh Zeldich. New York: Harper & Row, 1981. Age: 4. Chap. 7.
After a little girl's grandmother dies, the child recalls her grandmother's lessons about how to be a part of nature. Thus the child finds a way of always keeping her beloved grandmother with her.

Horwitz, Joshua. *Night Markets: Bringing Food to the City*. Illustrated by the author. New York: Harper & Row, 1984. Age: 5. Chap. 4.
The text and photographs of this book tell the story of how food arrives by land, air, and sea and is transported to a variety of wholesale food markets that supply fish, vegetables, fruits, meat, dairy, and freshly baked goods to New York City retail outlets.

Cheng, Hou-tien. *Six Chinese Brothers*. Illustrated by the author. New York: Holt, 1979. Age: 3. Chap. 8.
A classic tale of brotherly love and mutual help.

Howe, James. *When You Go to Kindergarten*. Illustrated by Betsy Imershein. New York: Knopf, 1986. Age: 4. Chap. 6.
A well-written and well-photographed explanation about what it may be like for a child who first goes to kindergarten. The book acknowledges that it may be hard to say good-bye to parents. It shows long corridors, an empty classroom, bath-

rooms with small toilets and sinks, and children at different activities. The book also explains some common expectations like listening, learning shapes and colors, cleaning up, and practicing a fire drill.

Hughes, Shirley. *Alfie Gives a Hand*. Illustrated by the author. New York: Mulberry, 1985. Age: 2. Chap. 6.
When Alfie learns that he cannot take his mother with him to his first birthday party, he brings his security blanket instead. In the course of the party he has to choose between his blanket and a child who needs a friend.

Hughes, Shirley. *All Shapes and Sizes*. Illustrated by the author. New York: Lothrop, Lee, Shepard, 1986. Age: 3. Chap. 4.
Using amusingly drawn children, Shirley Hughes illustrates a number of concepts having to do with shape and size.

Hughes, Shirley. *Bathwater's Hot*. Illustrated by the author. New York: Lothrop, Lee, Shepard, 1985. Age: 3. Chap. 4.
Famous for her expressive characters, Shirley Hughes has drawn busy pictures illustrating the opposites: hot and cold, young and old, throw away and keep, wide awake and fast asleep, hard and soft, and many more. She has chosen some interesting and unusual ones as well as some standards.

Hughes, Shirley. *George the Babysitter*. Illustrated by the author. Englewood Cliffs, NJ: Prentice-Hall, 1977. Age: 4. Chap. 4.
Three children spend the day with George, their baby-sitter. Together they do chores, play, eat, shop, garden, and enjoy the ups and downs of real people. Not without humor as well as insight, children who spend the day with a caretaker will enjoy this book.

Hughes, Shirley. *Lucy and Tom's Day*. Illustrated by the author. Harmondsworth, England: Puffin, 1960. Age: 3. Chaps. 4 and 5.
Two English children proceed through an ordinary day that includes many activities familiar to American children. They also demonstrate some differences such as drinking tea and eating biscuits and sleeping in cots.

Hutchins, Pat. *Changes, Changes*. Illustrated by the author. New York: Macmillan, 1971. Age: 3. Chap. 4.

Two wooden figures arrange and rearrange their block structure, serving as models for young block builders. The blend of fantasy and reality is appropriate for this age level.

Hyman, Robin and Inge. *Casper and the Rainbow Bird*. Illustrated by Yutaka Sugita. Woodbury, NY: Barron, 1978. Age: 3. Chap. 5.
The story of a young crow who goes to the city for the first time and meets a beautiful caged rainbow bird whom he struggles to free.

Ichikawa, Satomi. *Let's Play*. Illustrated by the author. New York: Philomel, 1981. Age: 2. Chap. 8.
A book showing a group of different-age children playing happily together. Older children are shown including younger ones in their games.

Isadora, Rachel. *I See*. Illustrated by the author. New York: Greenwillow, 1985. Age: 1. Chap. 4.
In soft paintings a toddler in diapers is shown looking at or enjoying some familiar things: her bear, her spoon, her belly button, her stroller, a slide, cat, ball, bird, blocks, bath, book, bottle, and crib.

Isadora, Rachel. *Jesse and Abe*. Illustrated by the author. New York: Greenwillow, 1981. Age: 4. Chap. 7.
Jesse's grandfather, Abe, works backstage in a Broadway theater. He realizes how much his grandfather is valued when he is late for work one night. He also realizes how much he loves his grandfather.

Isadora, Rachel. *Max*. Illustrated by the author. New York: Macmillan, 1976. Age: 4. Chaps. 4 and 6.
Max, a terrific baseball player, takes his sister to ballet class and is invited to join in. He has a wonderful time doing ballet and leaps his way to the baseball field. Ballet becomes Max's weekly baseball warm-up. Humorous pictures augment this story of a boy with enough self-assurance to allow himself to enjoy what is more commonly a girl's activity.

Isenberg, Barbara and Jaffe, Marjorie. *Albert the Running Bear's Exercise Book*. Illustrated by Diane de Groat. New York: Clarion, 1984. Age: 4. Chaps. 4 and 5.

Violet Bear convinces her friend Albert that he should exercise. Albert is shown doing many exercises of increasing difficulty. Children can follow Albert's lead. The book is a nice combination of story and exercises for the child to do.

Jarrell, Mary. *The Knee Baby*. Illustrated by Symeon Shimin. New York: Farrar, Straus, Giroux, 1973. Age: 5. Chap. 8.
After a long wait while his mother is occupied with the new baby, the little boy in this story gets to sit on his mother's lap.

Jeffers, Susan. *All the Pretty Horses*. Illustrated by the author. New York: Macmillan, 1974. Age: Birth. Chap. 2.
An attractive rendering of the well-known lullaby.

Jewell, Nancy. *The Snuggle Bunny*. Illustrated by Mary Chalmers. New York: Harper & Row, 1972. Age: 3. Chap. 6.
A small, lonely bunny searches for company and finds an old man who needs snuggling as much as he does.

Jewell, Nancy. *Time for Uncle Joe*. Illustrated by Joan Sandin. New York: Harper & Row, 1981. Age: 5. Chap. 7.
The changing seasons trigger a little girl's loving memories of her late uncle.

Johnson, B.J., and Aiello, Susan. *A Hat Like That*. Illustrated by the authors. New York: St. Martin's, 1986. Age: 1. Chap. 3.
On each page of this 6-by-6 inch stiff-paged book, a small child dons a different hat and imagines himself in the role of space traveler, underwater diver, baker, artist, and so forth. Each page has a texture to feel or a tab to lift, pull, or turn. Colorful, appealing pictures of close-up heads and hats.

Johnson, B.J., and Aiello, Susan. *My Blanket Burt*. Illustrated by the authors. New York: St. Martin's, 1986. Age: 1. Chaps. 3 and 5.
Each page of this 6-by-6 inch stiff-paged book provides the child with something to lift, feel, or move as the reader helps the protagonist search for his yellow security blanket, Burt. A welcome addition to the library of books with moveable parts.

Johnson, Crockett. *The Blue Ribbon Puppies*. Illustrated by the author. New York: Harper & Row, 1958. Age: 18 mos. Chap. 4.

Instead of choosing among the seven puppies to find the best puppy and award a blue ribbon, each puppy wins a blue ribbon for being the best in its class.

Johnson, Crockett. *Harold and the Purple Crayon.* Illustrated by the author. New York: Harper & Row, 1955. Age: 4. Chap. 6.
A classic, modern fantasy about a little boy who decides to go for a walk in the moonlight. He draws everything he needs with his purple crayon: the moon, the path, the trees, tasty apples, a scary dragon to guard the trees, and many other things which delight, frighten, and rescue him and the reader.

Johnson, Ilse and Hazelton, Nika Standen. *Cookies and Breads: The Baker's Art.* Illustrated by Ferdinand Boesch. New York: Chapman-Reinhold, 1967. Age: 3. Chap. 5.
Based on an exhibition assembled by the Museum of Contemporary Crafts in New York, this book has large photographs of both traditional and creative contemporary breads from around the world. It opens up a whole new world of baking possibilities.

Johnson, John E. *The Me Book.* Illustrated by the author. New York: Random House, 1979. Age: 6 mos. Chap. 3.
A brightly colored cloth book with pictures of a small boy labeling some parts of his body and showing some of the things he can do.

Jonas, Ann. *When You Were a Baby.* Illustrated by the author. New York: Viking Penguin, 1982. Age: 4. Chap. 8.
"When you were a baby you couldn't . . . pile your blocks so high, take your kitty for a ride, or splash in puddles with your new boots . . ." The list goes on, accompanied by large and colorful two-page pictures of boots, blocks, etc. An effective way to help a small child recognize growth and accomplishments.

Jones, Hettie, ed. *The Trees Stand Shining: Poetry of the Native American Indian.* Illustrated by Robert Andrew Parker. New York: Dial, 1971. Age: 5. Chap. 7.

This illustrated book includes chants, songs, and poems of Native Americans across the country.

Jones, Maurice. *I'm Going on a Dragon Hunt*. Illustrated by Charlotte Firmin. New York: Four Winds, 1987. Age: 4. Chap. 2.
    A child's wanderings take him through tall grass, across a wide ravine, over a mud field, and eventually to a cave where it seems a dragon dwells. This is a participation game that builds memory skills.

Joslin, Sesyle. *What Do You Say, Dear?* Illustrated by Maurice Sendak. New York: Scholastic, 1958. Age: 5. Chap. 1.
    A funny book about manners that are to be used in the most outlandish situations. Children will enjoy guessing what to say.

Kahl, Virginia. *The Dutchess Bakes a Cake*. Illustrated by the author. New York: Scribners, 1955. Age: 3. Chap. 5.
    An amusing story about a dutchess and her over-yeasted cake. A good book to stimulate interest in cooking.

Kahn, Peggy. *The Care Bears' Book of Feelings*. Illustrated by Carolyn Bracken. New York: Random House, 1984. Age: 6 mos. Chap. 4.
    The popular care bears are depicted in situations that evoke their feelings. This book provides a nonthreatening way to open conversations with children about their feelings.

Kalan, Robert. *Jump, Frog, Jump!* Illustrated by Byron Barton. New York: Scholastic, 1981. Age: 2. Chap. 4.
    Bright, bold colors, and simple story with easy repetitive words.

Kalas, Sybille. *The Goose Family Book*. Illustrated by the author. London: Neugebauer, 1986. Age: 4. Chap. 4.
    Text and photographs describe the physical characteristics and behavior of a family of goslings from the moment they hatch until they grow to adulthood.

Kantrowitz, Mildred. *When Violet Died*. Illustrated by Emily A. McCully. New York: Parents Magazine, 1973. Age: 5. Chap. 7.
Young children conduct a funeral for their dead bird.

Kantrowitz, Mildred. *Willie Bear*. Illustrated by Nancy Winslow Parker. New York: Four Winds, 1976. Age: 4. Chap. 6.
A little boy deals with his concerns about going to school by pretending that his teddy bear is the one who is going. By the morning of the first day of school, he is well prepared to go off by himself, leaving his bear behind.

Karn, George. *Circus Big and Small*. Illustrated by the author. Boston: Little, Brown, 1986. Age: 3. Chap. 4.
This small board book contains bright, happy drawings of circus animals and entertainers illustrating the opposite concepts of big and small, happy and sad, tall and short, plain and fancy, up and down, in and out, and alone and together. Part of a series including *Circus Colors*, *Circus Train*, *Animal Walk*, *Circus ABC*, *Circus 1,2,3*, *Circus People*, and *Circus Animals*.

Kay, Helen. *Apron On, Apron Off*. Illustrated by Yaroslava. New York: Scholastic, 1968. Age: 5. Chap. 5.
The idea of this book is to demonstrate that wearing an apron is not solely a female act. Joan, the protagonist, meets a number of males who wear aprons: a carpenter, newspaper seller, shoemaker, baker, and Joan's father, a printer. But Joan's mother's apron, in contrast to the males', is decorative rather than utilitarian. At the end of the story, Joan constructs a functional apron for herself.

Keats, Ezra Jack. *John Henry*. Illustrated by the author. New York: Scholastic, 1965. Age: 4. Chaps. 1 and 7.
Bold illustrations accompany this retelling of the story of the steel-driving man.

Keats, Ezra Jack. *A Letter to Amy*. Illustrated by the author. New York: Harper & Row, 1968. Age: 3. Chaps. 5, 6, and 7.
Peter wants to invite Amy to his birthday party in a special way, by writing her a letter. His trip to the mailbox is eventful and nearly spoils the invitation.

Keats, Ezra Jack. *Peter's Chair*. Illustrated by the author. New York: Harper & Row, 1967. Age: 4. Chaps. 7 and 8.

Peter runs away (to the front steps) after his parents paint most of his old furniture pink for the new baby. He salvages his old chair, but discovers that he has outgrown it. The support of his parents, the smell of supper, and his own good judgment allow him to return home and accept his new sister.

Keats, Ezra Jack. *The Snowy Day*. Illustrated by the author. New York: Scholastic, 1962. Age: 2. Chaps. 1 and 7.

Appealing shapes and warm colors are used in this simple story of a young black child's fun in the snow.

Keats, Ezra Jack. *Whistle for Willie*. Illustrated by the author. New York: Viking, 1964. Age: 3. Chaps. 6 and 7.

Peter works very hard at learning to whistle for his dog, Willie. When he finally succeeds, there are more rewards than one.

Keller, Holly. *Geraldine's Blanket*. Illustrated by the author. New York: Greenwillow, 1984. Age: 2. Chap. 6.

When Geraldine Pig's parents insist that she get rid of her blanket, Geraldine finds an original way to keep it with her: she makes it into a dress for her doll, Rosa.

Keller, Holly. *Goodbye, Max*. Illustrated by the author. New York: Greenwillow, 1987. Age: 4. Chap. 7.

Ben grieves over the death of his dog, Max. He demonstrates the normal stages of mourning, especially anger.

Kellogg, Steven. *Chicken Little*. Illustrated by the author. New York: Morrow, 1985. Age: 3. Chap. 1.

Chicken Little and his feathered friends, alarmed that the sky seems to be falling, are easy prey to hungry Foxy Loxy when he poses as a police officer in hopes of tricking them into his truck. You may want to select a version of this story that has a less tragic ending for the fowls.

Kellogg, Steven. *Pecos Bill*. Illustrated by the author. New York: Morrow, 1986. Age: 4. Chap. 1.

Incidents from the life of Pecos Bill, from his childhood among the coyotes to his unusual wedding day. The illustrations convey the sense of fun for this tall tale.

Kightley, Rosalinda. *ABC*. Illustrated by the author. Boston: Little, Brown, 1986. Age: 4. Chap. 6.

Large, colorful, simple shapes depict objects a young child can easily recognize. The "X" problem is resolved by showing a picture of a box with the caption "as in box." The entire alphabet is recapitulated at the end of the book, with miniature replicas of each page.

Kightley, Rosalinda. *Opposites*. Illustrated by the author. Boston: Little, Brown, 1986. Age: 3. Chap. 4.

Simple, large pictures of familiar people, animals, and objects are placed against intensely colored backgrounds to create a book illustrating some basic concepts: a frog leaps up out of the water and down into the water; a juggling clown is happy when successful then sad when he drops his balls, and so forth. The book ends with a lottolike matching game.

Kightley, Rosalinda. *Shapes*. Illustrated by the author. Boston: Little, Brown, 1986. Age: 3. Chap. 4.

Another book which necessitates active involvement on the part of the reader. On the left-hand side of the double-page spread, a very large, brightly colored shape is presented. On the right, an object has been made up of a number of different-sized examples of that shape, and the child is asked to say how many circles, for example, have been incorporated in the object. Some pictures are quite a challenge because they use numerous examples of different shapes to make up the object.

Kilroy, Sally. *Babies' Outings*. Illustrated by the author. New York: Scholastic, 1984. Age: 6 mos. Chap. 3.

Simple, brightly colored drawings with clear black outlines show babies in different out-of-the-home settings: garden, pond, park, backyard, store, restaurant, and beach. One of a series of eight books about baby's world.

Kilroy, Sally. *Grandpa's Garden*. Illustrated by the author. Harmondsworth, England: Viking Kestrel, 1986. Age: 2. Chap. 5.
Two children enjoy gardening with their grandparents.

Kindred, Wendy. *Lucky Wilma*. Illustrated by the author. New
York: Dial, 1973. Age: 5. Chap. 7.
Wilma spends her Saturdays with her father (her parents are
divorced). Most Saturdays are planned around visiting zoos
and museums but one special Saturday forces them to spend
the day with no special plan. This turns out to be the most fun
of all for Wilma.

Kismaric, Susan. *American Children*. New York: Museum of
Modern Art, 1980. Age: 4. Chap. 7.
Series of photographs depicting children of all ages from
many geographic areas. This book begins with more recent
photos (1976) and goes backward in time to the 1890s.

Kitchen, Bert. *Animal Alphabet*. Illustrated by the author. New
York: Dial, 1984. Age: 4. Chap. 4.
Each huge clear letter of the alphabet is accompanied by the
animal it represents. The ostrich peers through the *O* and the
dodo hangs upside down from the *D*.

Klein, Norma. *Girls Can Be Anything*. Illustrated by Roy Doty.
New York: Dutton, 1973. Age: 5. Chaps. 6 and 7.
Adam and Marina are best friends in kindergarten. One day
they have a disagreement because Adam tells Marina she
can't be a doctor: "Girls are always nurses." As the days go by,
Adam displays other sexist ideas. With her parents' help,
Marina points out to Adam several women who are living
examples of the "forbidden" roles. In the end the two children play equitably together.

Kouzel, Daisy. *The Cuckoo's Reward/El Premio Del Cuco*. Illus-
trated by Earl Thollander. New York: Doubleday, 1977. Age: 5.
Chap. 7.
This story is an adaptation of a Mayan legend explaining why
the cuckoo lays her eggs in other birds' nests. It is told in both
Spanish and English.

Krahn, Fernando. *April Fools*. Illustrated by the author. New York: Dutton, 1974. Age: 4. Chap. 2.

Two little boys construct a monster to play a series of April Fools jokes on the townspeople. They succeed admirably.

Krahn, Fernando. *Who's Seen the Scissors?* Illustrated by the author. New York: Dutton, 1975. Age: 3. Chap. 2.

The adventures of a wayward pair of red scissors. The scissors cut clotheslines, dog leashes, flowers, a lion's mane, and more, before returning home to the tailor's shop. A wordless book that invites telling a story.

Krasilovsky, Phyllis. *The Very Little Boy*. Illustrated by Ninon. Garden City, NY: Doubleday, 1962. Age: 3. Chap. 8.

The little boy in this story is smaller than a cornstalk, a baseball bat, even a sled. He is too little to join the parade, feed the elephant, or touch the pedals on a bicycle—he is a toddler. As time passes, the situation changes and we share with him the signs of growing bigger.

Kraus, Robert. *Leo, the Late Bloomer*. Illustrated by Jose Aruego. New York: Simon & Schuster, 1971. Age: 4. Chap. 6.

A story about a little tiger whose father worries because he cannot read, write, talk, draw, or eat neatly. His mother steadfastly believes that nothing is wrong with him and that he will "bloom" in his own good time. When he does, both Leo and his father are reassured and delighted.

Kraus, Robert. *Whose Mouse Are You?* Illustrated by José Aruego. New York: Macmillan, 1970. Age: 4. Chap. 6.

Each time this question is asked, a tail of an animal appears on a page. As the page is turned the rest of the animal appears.

Krauss, Ruth. *A Hole Is to Dig*. Illustrated by Maurice Sendak. New York: Harper & Row, 1952. Age: 2. Chap. 1.

A book of first definitions, reflecting a child's perspective.

Krauze, Andrzej. *Christopher Crocodile Cooks a Meal*. Illustrated by the author. New York: Macmillan, 1985. Age: 2. Chap. 5.

An expressive crocodile prepares an elaborate and humorous meal for his cousins. They enjoy it thoroughly and help with the dishes before they play a board game together.

Krementz, Jill. *Holly's Farm Animals*. Illustrated by the author. New York: Random House, 1986. Age: 4. Chap. 4.
A little girl lives on a farm with her family where they raise animals as a hobby. Holly is shown with a large variety of animals.

Krementz, Jill. *Katherine Goes to Nursery School*. Illustrated by the author. New York: Random House, 1986. Age: 2. Chap. 6.
A large board book with photographs and very clear text about a little girl's day at a nursery that she loves. Shows numerous activities both indoors and out, as well as snack time, group time, rest time, arrival, and going home.

Krementz, Jill. *Lily Goes to the Playground*. Illustrated by the author. New York: Random House, 1986. Age: 1. Chap. 4.
An unusually large board book, especially designed for toddlers, this book has photographs and a simple clear text to describe the activities available at the playground.

Kunhardt, Dorothy. *Mrs. Sheep's Little Lamb*. Illustrated by Garth Williams. New York: Golden Press, 1949. Age: 3. Chap. 6.
In this book a little lamb gets separated from her mother while doing an errand in the grocery store. A friendly manager finds her in tears but, with his help, she is soon reunited with her mother. A fine choice for children working on early issues of separation.

Kunhardt, Dorothy. *Pat the Bunny*. Illustrated by the author. Racine, WI: Western, 1962. Age: 1. Chaps. 1 and 3.
For almost forty-five years this book has been delighting children. A classic, it invites involvement of the very young child. Some pages have a texture to be felt: the bunny's fur, Daddy's scratchy face. Some pages have an activity to explore: a cloth to lift for hide-and-seek, a hole of a ring to poke a finger through, and a small mirror to look into.

Lacome, Julie. *My First Book of Words*. Illustrated by the author. New York: Platt & Munk, 1986. Age: 2. Chap. 4.

Each double-page spread has a brightly colored illustration presenting one category of things: body parts, clothing, foods, actions, toys, household objects, animals, things found on the street, on the beach, and at work, animals and colors. All items are labeled.

Ladybird. *Let's Go Shopping*. Illustrated by Terry Burton. Lewiston, ME: Ladybird, 1985. Age: 2. Chap. 5.
A board book combining simple sentences with colorful pictures about things that toddlers see and do.

Lakin, Patricia. *Don't Touch My Room*. Illustrated by Patience Brewster. Boston: Little, Brown, 1985. Age: 3. Chap. 8.
Both the preparations for the new baby and the reality of the baby are difficult for Aaron, but, with his parents' help, he finds a place of his own and protective feelings for his baby brother.

Lalli, Judy. *Feelings Alphabet*. Illustrated by the author. Rolling Hills Estates, CA: B.L. Winch, 1984. Age: 4. Chaps. 4 and 7.
An album of emotions from *A* to *Z*. Using black-and-white photographs, each emotion is illustrated, for example, *A* is afraid, *C* is curious, and so on.

Langner, Nola. *Rafiki*. Illustrated by the author. New York: Viking, 1977. Age: 5. Chaps. 5, 6, and 7.
Rafiki goes into the jungle to build a house. When she is confronted by the jungle animals who tell her it is not her role to build a house, Rafiki helps them to change their ideas of gender roles, and the lion king admits that he was in error.

Lasker, Joe. *He's My Brother*. Illustrated by the author. Chicago: Whitman, 1974. Age: 5. Chaps. 7 and 8.
Jamie is a slow learner. He has an older sister who is kind to him, and an older brother who sometimes teases him and is impatient with him. The older brother learns to play with Jamie and to understand him better. The book focuses on Jamie's abilities rather than his deficiencies.

Lasker, Joe. *Mothers Can Do Anything*. Illustrated by the author. Chicago: Whitman, 1972. Age: 3. Chaps. 4 and 5.

This book demonstrates the variety of jobs that mothers can hold: lion tamer, scientist, artist, and more.

Lasky, Kathryn and Maxwell. *A Baby for Max*. Illustrated by Christopher Knight. New York: Macmillan, 1984. Age: 4. Chap. 6.
An honest, developmentally appropriate account from the perspective of a five-year-old child awaiting, and then adjusting to, the birth of his baby sister.

Leaf, Margaret. *Eyes of the Dragon*. Illustrated by Ed Young. New York: Lothrop, Lee, Shepard, 1987. Age: 5. Chap. 2.
An artist agrees to paint a dragon on the wall of a Chinese village, but the magistrate's insistence that he paint eyes on the dragon has amazing results.

Lear, Edward. *The Owl and the Pussy-Cat*. Illustrated by Claire Littlejohn. New York: Harper & Row, 1987. Age: 3. Chaps. 4 and 6.
Introducing children to poetry is a joy with this pop-up book. When the owl and the pussy are in the rowboat, the oars of the boat can be made to move as the owl sways to the guitar. There are seven double-page spreads and four designs that pop up.

Leiner, Katherine. *Ask Me What My Mother Does*. Illustrated by Michael H. Arthur. New York: Watts, 1978. Age: 5. Chap. 4.
Photographs portray real women at their actual place of work, doing all sorts of jobs such as "steeplejill," carpenter, photographer, dancer, musician, bus driver, pediatrician, secretary, and others.

Lenett, Robin, and Barthelme, Dana. *My Body Is My Own!* Illustrated by Frank C. Smith. New York: Playmore and Waldman, 1985. Age: 4. Chap. 6.
A coloring book that presents the basic skills of "body safety" for young children. It deals with not only highly charged situations that may involve abuse, but also with everyday encounters.

Lenski, Lois. *Lois Lenski's Big Big Book of Mr. Small*. Illustrated by the author. New York: Derrydale, 1985. Age: 3. Chap. 4.

Lois Lenski's most famous books from the thirties and forties are reprinted here: *Policeman Small, Cowboy Small, The Little Farm, The Little Auto, The Little Sailboat,* and *The Little Airplane*. Full of information as well as fun, the simple stories and charming pictures will be enjoyed today as they have been, in some cases, for more than fifty years.

Lenski, Lois. *Sing a Song of People*. Illustrated by Giles Laroche. Boston: Little, Brown, 1987. Age: 2. Chap. 7.
With colorful cut paper illustrations and poetic text, this book shows people of all sorts enjoying the life of the city.

Leokum, Arkady. *Tell Me Why #1*. Illustrated by Howard Bender. New York: Grossett & Dunlap, 1986. Age: 5. Chap. 5.
A good reference book for parents when children ask questions about our world, how things began, the human body, other creatures, and how things are made.

LeSieg, Theodor. *In a People House*. Illustrated by Roy McKie. New York: Random House, 1972. Age: 2. Chaps. 3 and 4.
A story about cartoon characters, Mr. Bird and Mouse, who enter a house, bounce on chairs, ride on roller skates, and discover and play with a myriad of familiar objects.

Lesser, Rika. *Hansel and Gretel*. Illustrated by Paul O. Zelinsky. New York: Dodd, Mead, 1984. Age: 5. Chap. 1.
A tale from the Brothers Grimm: A poor woodcutter's children, lost in the forest, come upon a house made of bread, cakes, and candy, occupied by a wicked witch who likes to have children for dinner.

Lester, Julius. *The Tales of Uncle Remus and The Adventures of Brer Rabbit*. Illustrated by Jerry Pinkney. New York: Dial, 1987. Age: 5. Chaps. 1 and 7.
A new version of Joel Chandler Harris's *The Adventures of Brer Rabbit*. Lester has made use of Harris's scholarship and has transformed the dialect into a modified contemporary southern Black English. Although Lester inserts some contemporary references into the stories, he is respectful of the authenticity of their source.

Levinson, Irene. *Peter Learns to Crochet*. Illustrated by Ketra Sutherland. Stanford, CA: New Seed, 1976. Age: 5. Chap. 5.
> Peter wants to learn to crochet so that he can make all sorts of useful items. When neither his mother nor father can help him, his teacher shows him how.

Levy, Elizabeth. *Nice Little Girls*. Illustrated by Mordecai Gerstein. New York: Delacorte, 1974. Age: 5. Chap. 6.
> Jackie, the new girl in class, has short hair and wears jeans. Because of this, the teacher and the other children think she's a boy. When Jackie is restricted from doing the activities she likes, her parents intervene and she is able to make some impact on the sexist expectations of her class.

Lewin, Hugh. *Jafta*. Illustrated by Lisa Kopper. Minneapolis: Carolrhoda, 1983. Age: 3. Chap. 4.
> Jafta, a small black boy, compares some of his everyday feelings and actions to those of African animals. The illustrations add to the clarity, warmth, and originality of the text.

Lionni, Leo. *Alexander and the Wind-up Mouse*. Illustrated by the author. New York: Knopf, 1969. Age: 4. Chap. 6.
> Alexander, a real mouse, and Willy, a toy wind-up mouse, are friends. Alexander envies Willy because people love him. One day he discovers that Willy is to be discarded with other toys, and he finds a way to transform Willy into a real mouse. Some philosophical questions are raised here about the advantages of security over temporary pleasure.

Lionni, Leo. *The Biggest House in the World*. Illustrated by the author. New York: Knopf, 1968. Age: 5. Chap. 4.
> In a fable within a fable, a wise snail convinces his son that a small, easy-to-carry shell might be better than the biggest house in the world.

Lionni, Leo. *Fish Is Fish*. Illustrated by the author. New York: Pantheon, 1970. Age: 3. Chaps. 4 and 6.
> A little minnow loses his friend, the tadpole, when the tadpole becomes a frog. When the frog returns, he tells the fish about the extraordinary things he has seen on land. The

large, pastel-colored drawings show a cow and humans as the fish imagines them. When the fish tries to leave the pond and see the frog's world, he is saved and comes to appreciate the beauty of being a fish in a fish's world.

Lionni, Leo. *Frederick*. Illustrated by the author. New York: Pantheon, 1967. Age: 4. Chaps. 1 and 6.
While other mice are gathering food for the winter, Frederick is "gathering words" and seems useless. However, in the deep of winter, the others learn the value of Frederick's special talent for observation and poetry.

Lionni, Leo. *Inch by Inch*. Illustrated by the author. New York: Astor-Honor, 1960. Age: 4. Chaps. 1 and 4.
A large, dramatically illustrated book about an inchworm who proves his worth by measuring the tail of a robin, the long pink patterned neck of the flamingo, the large, rounded beak of the toucan, the whole hummingbird, and so on. A classic.

Little, Lessie Jones and Greenfield, Eloise. *I Can Do It Myself*. Illustrated by Carole Byard. New York: Crowell, 1978. Age: 4. Chap. 7.
Donny is determined to buy his mother's birthday present all by himself, but he meets a scary challenge on the way home.

Lobel, Anita, with words by Lobel, Arnold. *On Market Street*. Illustrated by the author. New York: Scholastic, 1981. Age: 4. Chaps. 1 and 4.
On each page of this book a shopkeeper stands, displaying his or her wares. What is unusual is that the form of the shopkeeper is totally made up of the wares that he or she sells. The pages are arranged in alphabetical order from apples through gloves and lollipops, to zippers. The product appears in profusion, and forms the head, arms, body, legs, and feet of the shopkeepers. Thus the shopkeepers not only display their goods, but also are fancifully constructed of these wares.

Lobel, Arnold. *Fables*. Illustrated by the author. New York: Harper & Row, 1980. Age: 5. Chap. 6.

Arnold Lobel has written twenty short fables, complete with morals, that are as colorful and original as the drawings that accompany them.

Lobel, Arnold. *Frog and Toad All Year.* Illustrated by the author. New York: Harper & Row, 1976. Age: 4. Chaps. 1 and 6.
Five more stories about the lovable pair of amphibians who are fun to read about and who have much to teach children about true friendship and feelings. All of the books in the series (*Frog and Toad Together, Days with Frog and Toad, Frog and Toad Are Friends*) are classics.

Lobel, Arnold. *Frog and Toad Are Friends.* Illustrated by the author. New York: Scholastic, 1970. Age: 4. Chaps. 1, 6, and 8.
Two animals who are models of friendship and goodwill toward each other. Each episode provides an opportunity for children to solve a problem of human interaction. Look for all of the titles in the series.

Lobel, Arnold. *The Random House Book of Mother Goose.* Illustrated by the author. New York: Random House, 1986. Age: Birth. Chaps. 1 and 2.
An illustrated collection of Mother Goose nursery rhymes, including well-known ones such as "Baa, Baa, Black Sheep" and "Little Boy Blue," and less familiar ones such as "Doctor Foster went to Gloucester" and "When Clouds Appear Like Rocks and Towers."

Lobel, Arnold. *The Rose in My Garden.* Illustrated by Anita Lobel. New York: Greenwillow, 1984. Age: 2. Chaps. 4 and 5.
A well-designed and well-illustrated cumulative story about the flowers and animals in a garden.

Locker, Thomas. *The Mare on the Hill.* Illustrated by the author. New York: Dial, 1985. Age: 5. Chap. 2.
Grandfather brings home a fearful mare to breed, hoping that his grandsons can teach her to trust people again. The illustrations are remarkable.

Logue, Christopher. *Puss in Boots.* Illustrated by Nicola Bayley. New York: Greenwillow, 1976. Age: 5. Chap. 1.

A classic story of the clever cat who enables his pleasant, but simple, master to win a fortune.

Longfellow, Henry Wadsworth. *Hiawatha*. Illustrated by Susan Jeffers. New York: Dial, 1983. Age: 5. Chap. 1.
Verses from Longfellow's epic poem depict the boyhood of Hiawatha. The quality and details of the illustrations are noteworthy.

Louie, Ai-Ling. *Yeh-Shen*. Illustrated by Ed Young. New York: Philomel, 1982. Age: 4. Chap. 1.
A young Chinese girl overcomes the wickedness of her stepsister and stepmother to become the bride of a prince. The oldest known version of the Cinderella tale. The details are different: a magic fish figures importantly in this and other Cinderellas.

Lynn, Sara. *Colors*. Illustrated by the author. Boston: Little, Brown, 1986. Age: 2. Chap. 4.
This large book about colors will be a favorite with children who love clowns and their antics. Each left-hand page has an enormous square of the new color being introduced. On the right-hand page a clown is shown painting a large familiar object using the new color. The clown's costume uses the new color and all the colors previously presented. Part of a series that includes: *ABC, 123, Shapes*, and *Opposites*.

Lynn, Sara. *1 2 3*. Illustrated by the author. Boston: Little, Brown, 1986. Age: 3. Chap. 4.
A well-designed simple counting book with bright colors, clear numbers, and amusing animal illustrations, this book invites young fingers to reach out and touch so that counting is a concrete behavior.

MacDonald, Golden. *The Little Island*. Illustrated by Leonard Weisgard. New York: Doubleday, 1946. Age: 5. Chap. 6.
This winner of the 1947 Caldecott Medal invites children to look at some philosophical concepts: how everyone is a part of the world and a world in and of oneself. The little island and a kitten discover this secret together.

MacDonald, Suse. *Alphabatics*. Illustrated by the author. New York: Bradbury, 1986. Age: 4. Chap. 4.

The letters of the alphabet are transformed and incorporated into twenty-six illustrations: an *s* becomes a swan; an *e* becomes the toenails on an elephant's feet.

MacLachlan, Patricia. *Through Grandpa's Eyes*. Illustrated by Deborah Kogan Ray. New York: Harper & Row, 1980. Age: 5. Chap. 1.

A young boy learns a different way of seeing the world from his blind grandfather.

McCloskey, Robert. *Blueberries for Sal*. Illustrated by the author. New York: Viking, 1948. Age: 3. Chaps. 1 and 6.

On one side of Blueberry Hill, Sal and her mother are picking blueberries. Sal loves picking and eating. While she is resting (and eating) she gets separated from her mother. On the other side of the mountain, Mother Bear and Little Bear also become separated while picking berries. A mix-up of mothers ensues but all ends well in this nearly forty-year-old favorite that combines the sensory and somewhat scary into a perfect story for three- and four-year-olds. Take care that children know how dangerous it really is to follow a bear, or have anything to do with a live one.

McCloskey, Robert. *Lentil*. Illustrated by the author. New York: Scholastic, 1940. Age: 4. Chap. 6.

A young boy wants to make music, and despite his seeming lack of talent, manages to succeed in performing on a harmonica, thus pleasing himself and the townspeople.

McCloskey, Robert. *Make Way for Ducklings*. Illustrated by the author. New York: Penguin, 1941. Age: 2. Chaps. 1 and 6.

The mallard parents' quest for the safest place to raise their family takes them into and around the Boston of the 1940s.

McCloskey, Robert. *Time of Wonder*. Illustrated by the author. New York: Viking, 1957. Age: 4. Chaps. 1 and 6.

This Caldecott winner tells of children who enjoy their stay on an island off the coast of Maine, observing the natural wonders of the area. When a storm rises, the whole family gathers inside their house to sing and face their fears together.

McGovern, Ann. *Too Much Noise*. Illustrated by Simms Taback. New York: Scholastic, 1967. Age: 18 mos. Chap. 4.
When the sounds of his house seem unbearable, a wise man suggests that Peter add one animal and then another and another. After they are accumulated, they are eliminated, and the house noises don't seem so bad after all. Based on an old folktale.

McLerran, Alice. *The Mountain That Loved the Bird*. Illustrated by Eric Carle. Natick, MA: Picture Book Studio, 1985. Age: 5. Chap. 6.
A profound book about an unusual friendship between a mountain and a bird whose mutual caring changes each of them, especially the lifeless, stony mountain.

McMillan, Bruce. *Becca Forward, Becca Backward: A Book of Concept Pairs*. Illustrated by the author. New York: Lothrop, Lee, Shepard, 1986. Age: 3. Chap. 4.
Becca is photographed illustrating a number of concept pairs. The photographs are large and colorful.

Mannheim, Grete. *The Two Friends*. Illustrated by the author. New York: Knopf, 1968. Age: 5. Chap. 6.
On Jenny's first day at school, she feels scared and lonely as she looks around the classroom. Nancy invites her to "come and make music," Mark invites her to play with the turtle, and the day goes very well. Excellent photographs accompany this story about a well-integrated kindergarten.

Manushkin, Fran. *Bubblebath*. Illustrated by Ronald Himler. New York: Harper & Row, 1974. Age: 3. Chap. 8.
Two sisters thoroughly enjoy each other's company while getting dirty, clean, then dirty again.

Manushkin, Fran. *Little Rabbit's Baby Brother*. Illustrated by Diane De Groat. New York: Crown, 1986. Age: 4. Chap. 8.

Little Rabbit finds her own way of coming to terms with her new baby brother.

Mari, Iela. *Eat and Be Eaten*. Illustrated by the author. Hauppauge, NY: Barrons, 1980. Age: 4. Chap. 4.
A provocative wordless book about the predatory nature of many animals. A good thought-and-discussion starter.

Marie, Susan. *I Will Not Wear That Sweater*. Illustrated by the author. Los Angeles: Wonder, 1986. Age: 2. Chap. 6.
A little girl is perfectly willing to wear most of the clothes she has, but she refuses to wear one particular piece of clothing.

Marshall, James. *George and Martha*. Illustrated by the author. Boston: Houghton Mifflin, 1972. Age: 4. Chaps. 2 and 6.
Stories about the deep and joyful friendship between two hippopotamuses who know that honesty can be painful but worth the effort. Children will enjoy these sensitive, caring friends.

Marshall, James. *George and Martha Encore*. Illustrated by the author. Boston: Houghton Mifflin, 1973. Age: 4. Chaps. 2 and 6.
Another in the series of George and Martha books. Four stories about two characters who learn from each other, share their feelings, and care about each other's feelings.

Marshall, James. *George and Martha One Fine Day*. Illustrated by the author. Boston: Houghton Mifflin, 1978. Age: 4. Chaps. 2 and 6.
More stories about these direct, honest friends who provide excellent models for human beings.

Marshall, James. *George and Martha Tons of Fun*. Illustrated by the author. Boston: Houghton Mifflin, 1980. Age: 4. Chaps. 2 and 6.
Five brief episodes reveal the ups and downs of a great friendship.

Martel, Cruz. *Yagua Days*. Illustrated by Jerry Pinkney. New York: Dial, 1976. Age: 5. Chap. 7.

On a visit to Puerto Rico to visit relatives, Adam has a wonderful time with his extended family and appreciates the beauty of the land and the diversity and caring of the people.

Martin, Bill, Jr. *Brown Bear, Brown Bear, What Do You See?* Illustrated by Eric Carle. New York: Holt, 1983. Age: 6 mos. Chaps. 3 and 4.
Each large double-page spread holds one of Eric Carle's full-page, strongly colored, cut paper collages of an animal. The animal and its color are labeled. Then the animal is asked what it sees, and the animal on the next page is named. Children can develop their prediction skills by picturing the colored animal that will follow. Yet turning the page to see Carle's collage is always a surprise.

Martin, Bill, Jr., and Archambault, John. *Here Are My Hands*. Illustrated by Ted Rand. New York: Holt, 1985. Age: 1. Chaps. 2 and 4.
A book presenting the parts of the body through rhythmic, rhyming text, and large, colorful pictures of active children. Good for reading aloud.

Martin, Elizabeth. *Making Pretzels*. Illustrated by the author. New York: Viking Kestrel, 1986. Age: 4. Chap. 5.
A laminated, spiral-bound book containing the recipe for making pretzels. Diagrams and instructions are clear enough for young children to follow, although cooking always requires adult supervision.

Martin, Rafe. *Foolish Rabbit's Big Mistake*. Illustrated by Ed Young. New York: Putnam, 1985. Age: 4. Chaps. 1 and 2.
As all the animals panic and flee at Little Rabbit's announcement that the Earth is breaking up, a brave lion steps in and brings sense to the situation. Similar to *Chicken Little* and *Henny Penny*.

Matsuno, Masako. *Pair of Red Clogs*. Illustrated by Kazue Mizumura. Cleveland: World, 1960. Age: 5. Chap. 7.
A taste of Japanese culture. When a Japanese grandmother buys her granddaughter a pair of red lacquer clogs, she

remembers a time long ago when she received just such a pair, cracked them, and desperately wanted them to be brand-new again. A story that portrays universal feelings.

Maury, Inez. Translated by Norah E. Aemany. *My Mother the Mail Carrier*. Illustrated by Lady McCrady. New York: Feminist Press, 1976. Age: 4. Chaps. 5 and 7.
 Spanish title: *Mi Mamá la Cartera*. Written in Spanish and English, the story centers on how a single parent can be an effective mother, mail carrier, and individual, all at the same time. The little boy loves his mother and is very proud of her.

Mayer, Mercer. *Ah-Choo*. Illustrated by the author. New York: Dial, 1976. Age: 3. Chaps. 2 and 4.
 An elephant with an allergy causes a lot of problems because of his large sneezes. He finally meets his match. Children love "reading" this wordless story and telling it to others.

Mayer, Mercer. *A Boy, A Dog and A Frog*. Illustrated by the author. New York: Dial, 1967. Age: 3. Chap. 1.
 A humorous story, without words, about a boy and his dog who try to catch a frog. Although the frog escapes, he decides to join the boy and his dog after all.

Mayer, Mercer. *Hiccup*. Illustrated by the author. New York: Dial, 1976. Age: 3. Chap. 2.
 The amusing and somewhat slapstick story of two hippos who suffer from the hiccups and who try some unpleasant cures on each other.

Mayer, Mercer. *There's a Nightmare in My Closet*. Illustrated by the author. New York: Dial, 1968. Age: 4. Chap. 6.
 A little boy overcomes his nightmare by bullying it and then by protecting it.

Mellonie, Bryan and Ingpen, Robert. *Lifetimes: The Beautiful Way to Explain Death*. Illustrated by the authors. New York: Bantam, 1983. Age: 5. Chap. 7.
 Death is a natural part of life, but the life cycle varies depending on the sort of creature. All, however, share in the

passage of time. Death is not something to be feared. All of these messages are presented with simplicity and directness.

Mendoza, George. *And I Must Hurry for the Sea Is Coming In.* Illustrated by the author. Englewood Cliffs, NJ: Prentice-Hall, 1971. Age: 5. Chaps. 2 and 7.
   A city child dreams of the ocean and lets his imagination transform the city setting.

Mendoza, George. *Need a House? Call Ms. Mouse!* Illustrated by Doris Smith. New York: Grosset & Dunlap, 1981. Age: 5. Chaps. 5 and 6.
   Henrietta, a mouse, is a famous decorator whose work is in great demand. She is not only creative and hardworking, she is also a chief executive. A role model, but be certain to discuss different definitions of success and different styles of achieving it.

Merriam, Eve. *Mommies at Work.* Illustrated by Beni Montresor. New York: Knopf, 1961. Age: 3. Chaps. 4 and 5.
   Mommies of all sorts are shown at work to help dispel gender-role stereotypes.

Merrill, Susan. *Washday.* Illustrated by Harriet Sherman. New York: Clarion, 1978. Age: 2. Chaps. 5 and 6.
   In this picture book, a family shares the work, pleasures, and small adventures of washday.

Miller, J.P. *Big and Little.* Illustrated by the author. New York: Random House, 1976. Age: 3. Chap. 4.
   In this fair-sized board book, simply drawn animals are used to illustrate concepts such as tall and short, fat and thin, few and many, over and under, up and down, and in and out. Bright background colors add interest.

Miller, J.P. *Little Rabbit's Garden.* Illustrated by the author. New York: Random House, 1985. Age: 6 mos. Chap. 3.
   A tiny cloth book about a rabbit and his garden. The book is attached to a cloth rabbit.

Miller, J.P. *Little Rabbit Goes to the Doctor.* Illustrated by the author. New York: Random House, 1987. Age: 3. Chap. 4.

Little Rabbit does not want to go to the doctor when he is sick, but his mother says he must. He has a good experience and is soon better.

Miller, J.P. *Little Rabbit Takes a Walk*. Illustrated by the author. New York: Random House, 1987. Age: 6 mos. Chap. 3.
This five-inch book about Little Rabbit on Easter morning is accompanied by a same-size stuffed cloth version of the character, just the right size for an infant to hold.

Miller, J.P. *Yoo-hoo, Little Rabbit: A Peek-a-Board Book*. Illustrated by the author. New York: Random House, 1986. Age: 2. Chap. 4.
When Little Rabbit finishes his chores he goes looking for his friends. Each animal he invites to play appears first through a hole in the previous page. Disappointed that no one will play, Rabbit is about to return home when all his friends appear.

Milne, A.A. *The House at Pooh Corner*. Illustrated by Ernest H. Shepard. New York: Dutton, 1986. Age: 4. Chaps. 1 and 2.
A continuation of the tales of Pooh, Tigger, Eeyore, Piglet, Kanga, and Roo, under the watchful eyes of Christopher Robin.

Milne, A.A. *Pooh's Counting Book*. Illustrated by Ernest H. Shepard. New York: Dutton, 1982. Age: 3. Chaps. 2 and 4.
Poems and prose from the four classic Pooh books are used in this small story because they contain the numbers one through ten. Large numerals stand out for children to "read" while an adult reads the story.

Milne, A.A. *When We Were Very Young*. Illustrated by Ernest H. Shepard. New York: Dutton, 1924. Age: 6 mos. Chaps. 1, 2, and 3.
Some of the best-known and best-loved verses of modern times by the author of the *Winnie-the-Pooh* stories. Also look for the second volume of poems, *Now We Are Six*.

Milne, A.A. *Winnie-the-Pooh*. Illustrated by Ernest H. Shepard. New York: Dell, 1926. Age: 4. Chaps. 1 and 2.
Christopher Robin and company have small, gentle adventures. The language and accompanying pictures, together with memorable characters, make this one a classic.

Minarik, Else Holmelund. *Little Bear*. Illustrated by Maurice Sendak. New York: Harper & Row, 1957. Age: 4. Chaps. 1, 2, and 6.

Four short stories in which Little Bear explores his world with his imagination, safely nurtured and reassured by his loving mother. Other titles in the series are *A Kiss for Little Bear, Father Bear Comes Back, Little Bear's Friend,* and *Little Bear's Visit.*

Mitchell, Joyce Slayton. *My Mommy Makes Money*. Illustrated by True Kelley. Boston: Little, Brown, 1984. Age: 4. Chap. 5.

Mothers are described as pursuing all sorts of careers, from fixing washing machines to performing marriage ceremonies. Different ages, heritages, and physical appearances are included. Mothers and children are seen cooperatively and happily living productive lives.

Mitgutsch, Ali. *From Lemon to Lemonade*. Illustrated by the author. Minneapolis: Carolrhoda, 1986. Age: 3. Chap. 4.

Perhaps the least complicated of this "from start to finish" series, this small book follows the steps used in manufacturing commercial lemonade.

Mitgutsch, Ali. *From Rubber Tree to Tire*. Illustrated by the author. Minneapolis: Carolrhoda, 1980. Age: 4. Chap. 4.

This book, originally written in German, traces the latex taken from the rubber tree through many stages until it is made into rubber that is used in many diverse ways.

Mitgutsch, Ali. *From Wood to Paper*. Illustrated by the author. Minneapolis: Carolrhoda, 1982. Age: 4. Chap. 4.

This small book describes the steps it takes to make paper from wood. Large interesting machines are described.

Moncure, Jane Belk. *My Baby Brother Needs a Friend*. Illustrated by Frances Hook. Chicago: Children's Press, 1979. Age: 4. Chap. 8.

Illustrated with colorful and realistic drawings, this book shows specific ways siblings can interact with a new baby. It also anticipates activities they will share when the baby is older.

Moorat, Joseph. *Thirty Old-Time Nursery Songs*. Illustrated by Paul Woodroffe. New York: Metropolitan Museum of Art, 1980. Age: Birth. Chap. 1.

> An illustrated collection of thirty familiar nursery songs including "Three Blind Mice," "Yankee Doodle," and "Ding Dong Bell."

Moss, Elaine. *In the Garden*. Illustrated by Celia Berridge. London: Deutsch, 1984. Age: 3. Chap. 5.

> A handy model for young children who want to garden.

Murray, W. *Talkabout Home*. Illustrated by Eric Winter and Harry Wingfield. Loughborough, England: Ladybird, 1973. Age: 2. Chap. 4.

> Using familiar objects that are very clearly depicted, children are asked which ones they have seen, touched, heard, tasted, and smelled. Other easy activities using familiar household objects can be enjoyed and talked about.

Musgrove, Margaret. *Ashanti to Zulu*. Illustrated by Leo and Diane Dillon. New York: Dial, 1976. Age: 4. Chaps. 4 and 7.

> Cultural information about twenty-six African peoples from the Ashanti through Masai and Ndaka to the Yoruba and Zulu. An interesting fact, story, or custom accompanies each letter, along with illustrations that earned the book the Caldecott Award.

Naylor, Phyllis Reynolds. *All Because I'm Older*. Illustrated by Leslie Morrill. New York: Atheneum, 1981. Age: 5. Chap. 8.

> Eldest children will appreciate John's dilemma and his solution when he is asked to keep his younger siblings out of trouble in a supermarket.

Ness, Evaline. *Do You Have the Time, Lydia?* Illustrated by the author. New York: Dutton, 1971. Age: 5. Chap. 8.

> Lydia, her brother, and their father live together on an island. Lydia is so busy that she often disappoints her younger brother. At last she becomes sympathetic to her brother's feelings and decides to change.

Neumeier, Marty and Glaser, Byron. *Action Alphabet*. Illustrated by the authors. New York: Greenwillow, 1984. Age: 4. Chap. 4.

The letters of the alphabet appear as parts of pictures representing sample words, such as a drip formed by a *D* coming out of a faucet and a vampire with *V*s for fangs.

Nixon, Joan Lowery. *The Gift*. Illustrated by the author. New York: Macmillan, 1983. Age: 5. Chap. 7.

A boy visits his relatives on their farm in Ireland. The story revolves around great-grandfather's tales of Irish folklore, especially of leprechauns. He becomes enchanted with these tales and sets out to prove to his aunt that they are true. The story conveys the love between generations as well as the beauty of the Irish countryside. The folklore of Ireland is vividly portrayed.

Noble, June. *Two Homes for Lynn*. Illustrated by Yuri Salzman. New York: Holt, 1979. Age: 4. Chap. 7.

A child has an imaginary friend who helps her to adjust to her parents' divorce and to the two homes she now can call home.

Noble, June. *Where Do I Fit In?* Illustrated by Yuri Salzman. New York: Holt, 1981. Age: 5. Chap. 7.

John's mother and stepfather are expecting a new child, and John is anxious. His grandparents help him to realize he is an important family member.

O'Brien, Anne Sibley. *Come Play with Us*. Illustrated by the author. New York: Holt, 1985. Age: 1. Chap. 6.

A board book about a little girl who is unhappy when her father leaves her at her day care center. She is helped to make the transition, enjoys her day, and is also very pleased when her father returns to pick her up. Useful for children seeking reassurance about separations from their parents.

O'Brien, Anne Sibley. *Don't Say No!* Illustrated by the author. New York: Holt, 1986. Age: 1. Chaps. 3 and 6.

Close to mealtime a toddler is told *no* once too often. Her mother's understanding helps her identify and cope with her frustration. Many children will identify readily with the text and watercolor illustrations of this board book.

O'Brien, Anne Sibley. *I Don't Want to Go*. Illustrated by the author. New York: Holt, 1986. Age: 1. Chaps. 3 and 6.

Another in Anne Sibley O'Brien's series of board books mirroring one of the typical frustrations faced by a small child. This time, a little boy does not want to go home for lunch while he is having a good time at the playground.

O'Brien, Anne Sibley. *I'm Not Tired.* Illustrated by the author. New York: Holt, 1986. Age: 18 mos. Chaps. 4 and 6.
Taking a nap is not always what a child wants to do, but as this book demonstrates, it is a necessity.

O'Brien, Anne Sibley. *It Hurts!* Illustrated by the author. New York: Holt, 1986. Age: 18 mos. Chaps. 4 and 6.
A child's feelings are respected and dealt with by a loving mother who gently cleanses the child's scraped knee.

O'Brien, Anne Sibley. *It's Hard to Wait.* Illustrated by the author. New York: Holt, 1986. Age: 1. Chap. 6.
Realistic illustrations and situations depict a little boy whose time with his father is postponed by chores and a telephone call. The difficulty of waiting is acknowledged; the child's patience is rewarded.

O'Brien, Anne Sibley. *I Want That!* Illustrated by the author. New York: Holt, 1985. Age: 1. Chaps. 3 and 6.
In this fourteen-page board book an older child takes a desired toy from a younger child and makes him cry, then feels bad and resolves the problem by sharing. Realistic text, illustrations, and solution.

O'Brien, Anne Sibley. *Where's My Truck?* Illustrated by the author. New York: Holt, 1985. Age: 18 mos. Chaps. 4 and 6.
Jason's mother helps him to see the importance of putting things away in their proper place.

O'Donnell, Elizabeth Lee. *Maggie Doesn't Want to Move.* Illustrated by Amy Schwartz. New York: Four Winds, 1987. Age: 2. Chaps. 4 and 6.
An older brother attributes his many fears and doubts about moving to his little sister. Finally, when he meets his new teacher his feelings begin to change. A fine addition to the small group of books about the experience of moving.

Ogle, Lucille and Thoburn, Tina. *I Spy*. Illustrated by Joe Kaufman. New York: New Heritage, 1970. Age: 1. Chap. 4.

On each page of this book two objects are carefully drawn and labeled. There are more than 300 objects in the book, and they are arranged by category. The familiar game "I Spy" can be played at many levels of sophistication. Games and goals are explained at the beginning and end of the book.

Omerod, Jan. *101 Things to Do with a Baby*. Illustrated by the author. Harmondsworth, England: Puffin, 1984. Age: 4. Chap. 8.

An older sister is shown doing 101 different things with her baby sibling, all of them parts of simple daily routines. Some are simple chores and kindnesses, others are marvelously creative games. She is also shown enjoying her parents' company and attention when the baby is asleep.

Ong, Cristina. *Gymboree Back and Forth!* Illustrated by the author. New York: Random House, 1986. Age: 3. Chap. 4.

In this small board book, children are shown playing and illustrating the concepts of up and down, big and little, over and under, in and out, noisy and quiet.

Ong, Cristina. *Gymboree Jump Like Me!* Illustrated by the author. New York: Random House, 1986. Age: 1. Chaps. 3 and 4.

Each left-hand page of this small board book depicts an animal in motion. Each right-hand page shows a small child imitating the behavior. Children may also enjoy trying to imitate the animals and children in the pictures.

Ong, Cristina. *Gymboree Wee Workout*. Illustrated by the author. New York: Random House, 1986. Age: 6 mos. Chap. 3.

This small board book has brightly colored, delicate drawings of young children wiggling, reaching, twisting, jumping, bouncing, and performing a variety of exercises that children may enjoy trying at home.

Ong, Cristina. *We Sing Out*. Illustrated by the author. New York: Random House, 1986. Age: 6 mos. Chap. 3.

This small board book has poems full of action and movement directions so the child can act out the poem. The aim of the book is to give children "the joy of exercise and noncompetitive group play." Parental involvement is necessary for very young children.

Opie, Iona and Peter. *The Oxford Nursery Rhyme Book*. Illustrated by Joan Hassall. Oxford, England: Oxford, 1980. Age: Birth. Chaps. 2 and 3.
    A comprehensive and scholarly collection of 800 rhymes and songs illustrated with black-and-white woodcuts.

Ormerod, Jan. *Moonlight*. Illustrated by the author. New York: Lothrop, Lee, Shepard, 1982. Age: 3. Chap. 2.
    A good-night book showing parents' interactions with their children in the hours before bedtime.

Ormerod, Jan. *Sunshine*. Illustrated by the author. New York: Lothrop, Lee, Shepard, 1982. Age: 3. Chap. 2.
    A wordless book that reflects a child's activities. This one focuses on a child's experiences in the early morning hours.

Ormondroyd, Edward. *Theodore*. Illustrated by John Larrecq. Berkeley, CA: Parnassus, 1966. Age: 3. Chap. 5.
    When a toy bear accidentally gets washed and cleaned, the little girl who owns him does not recognize him until he becomes his dirty old self once more.

Orska, Krystyna. *A Special Collection—Illustrated Poems for Children*. Illustrated by the author. Northbrook, IL: Hubbard, 1973. Age: Birth. Chaps. 2 and 3.
    A classic volume of carefully selected poems suitable for young children.

Oxenbury, Helen. *Animals*. Illustrated by the author. London: Walker, 1982. Age: 18 mos. Chaps. 1, 2, and 4.
    A toddler imitates a succession of animals. Oxenbury's illustrations are always a treat.

Oxenbury, Helen. *Beach Days*. Illustrated by the author. New York: Dial, 1982. Age: 2. Chap. 2.
    A wordless creation in the same style of this popular author-illustrator. Children will find it easy to invent their own narrative to this book.

Oxenbury, Helen. *Dressing*. Illustrated by the author. New York: Simon & Schuster, 1981. Age: 6 mos. Chaps. 2 and 4.
> On each left-hand page there is a large, clearly drawn piece of clothing. On the right-hand page a toddler is shown wearing that piece of clothing and all others from previous pages.

Oxenbury, Helen. *I Can*. Illustrated by the author. New York: Random House, 1986. Age: 6 mos. Chaps. 3, 4, and 6.
> An appealing and expressive toddler is depicted sitting, crawling, jumping, stomping, dancing, falling, running, sliding, stretching, kicking, bending, and waving on the pages of this board book.

Oxenbury, Helen. *I Hear*. Illustrated by the author. New York: Random House, 1986. Age: 6 mos. Chaps. 2, 3, and 4.
> On each left-hand page of this small board book the source of a sound is drawn: a bird, the rain, a dog, a watch, a telephone, and a baby. On the right-hand side of each page a young child is shown listening to the animal or object's sound. The noises are not described, yet they can almost be heard.

Oxenbury, Helen. *I See*. Illustrated by the author. New York: Random House, 1986. Age: 6 mos. Chaps. 2 and 3.
> This small board book shows an animal, object, person, or vehicle on each left-hand page. On each right-hand page a small child is shown interacting with the object. The object is labeled.

Oxenbury, Helen. *I Touch*. Illustrated by the author. New York: Random House, 1986. Age: 6 mos. Chaps. 2, 3, and 4.
> On the left-hand side of each page an object is drawn. On the right-hand page a young child is shown touching the object. The drawings are so expressive that the reader can almost feel the items.

Oxenbury, Helen. *Playschool*. Illustrated by the author. London: Walker, 1983. Age: 3. Chap. 6.
> On her first day at playschool, a little girl is reluctant to let go of her mother. Then she meets a friend, Nana, and together they enjoy the teacher's games and eat their snacks. Oxen-

bury's pictures and text have a message that is warm and reassuring.

Oxford Scientific Films. *Grey Squirrel*. Illustrated by George Bernard and John Paling. New York: Putnam, 1982. Age: 5. Chap. 4.
Describes the habits and characteristics of the grey squirrel, a North American native that has also has become established in Great Britain.

Paris, Susan. *Mommy and Daddy Are Fighting*. Illustrated by Gail Labinski. Seattle, WA: New Leaf/Seal, 1986. Age: 5. Chap. 6.
A little girl knows that cats, siblings, and even parents fight, but she finds her parents' arguing frightening. She and her sister have questions about the future of their family which they ask Mother when she comes to comfort them after an argument and Daddy is "taking a walk to cool off." It is clear that the fight is part of a disturbing pattern. A good book for children in similar circumstances if read with a close, understanding adult. A discussion guide for parents is included.

Pearson, Susan. *Everybody Knows That!* Illustrated by Diane Paterson. New York: Dial, 1978. Age: 4. Chap. 4.
A little boy stops playing with his best friend, a girl, after they start kindergarten. She wants to be a pilot, not a stewardess. To get even, when she bakes cookies, she tells him he can't help. In the end they both finish the cookies and play together and it is her turn to be the pilot.

Peebles, Lynne. *Cooking with Mother*. Photographs by John Moyes. Illustrated by John Hall. Loughborough, England: Ladybird, 1977. Age: 4. Chap. 5.
Another in this English series that encourages parent-child interaction and learning through doing.

Peek, Merle. *Roll Over*. Illustrated by the author. New York: Clarion, 1981. Age: 3. Chap. 4.
A version of the traditional counting song in which one character is eliminated from the ten in the bed until only one is left.

Peppe, Rodney. *Circus Numbers*. Illustrated by the author. New York: Delacorte, 1969. Age: 2. Chap. 4.

Colorful illustrations of the circus enliven the process of practicing counting.

Perrine, Mary. *Salt Boy*. Illustrated by Leonard Weisgard. Boston: Houghton Mifflin, 1968. Age: 4. Chap. 7.

A young Navajo boy wants his father to teach him how to rope. His father promises to teach him when he learns to be more responsible in caring for his mother's sheep. After the boy rescues a lamb, he earns his reward and learns to rope.

Petersham, Maud and Miska. *The Box with Red Wheels*. Illustrated by the author. New York: Macmillan, 1949. Age: 2. Chaps. 1 and 2.

An affectionate story of a baby and inquisitive but friendly animals. Each of the animals is attracted to the baby, and the baby is entranced by the animals. The box with red wheels is the baby's carriage.

Peterson, Jeanne Whitehouse. *I Have a Sister—My Sister Is Deaf*. Illustrated by Deborah Kogan Ray. New York: Harper & Row, 1977. Age: 4. Chap. 8.

A young girl describes how her deaf sister experiences everyday life, how others react to her, and how she feels about her sister's condition.

Peterson, Jeanne Whitehouse. *That Is That*. Illustrated by Deborah Ray. New York: Harper & Row, 1979. Age: 5. Chaps. 7 and 8.

When her father leaves home, Emma Rose helps her brother Meko to cope with the loss, and then to accept the fact that the father will not return. Emotions are respected here: both parents cry, the mother is short-tempered afterward, the children are unhappy for a long while. Eventually everyone has at least accepted the situation.

Petty, Kate and Kopper, Lisa. *What's That Taste?* Illustrated by the authors. New York: Watts, 1986. Age: 18 mos. Chap. 4.

Children are shown tasting different foods and the text describes each taste with one or two adjectives.

Phillips, Joan. *Peek-a-Boo! I See You!* Illustrated by Kathy Wilburn. New York: Grosset & Dunlap, 1983. Age: 2. Chaps. 4 and 6.

> In this large board book children, a baby bear, a bunny, a duckling, a puppy, and a lamb each play peek-a-boo. Each hides in a different place and is found by an adult seeker.

Piers, Helen. *Peekaboo Kitten.* Illustrated by the author. New York: Harcourt, 1986. Age: 6 mos. Chap. 4.

> A fluffy gray kitten is pictured with twelve familiar items in this colorful board book that opens to become a two-sided mural.

Piers, Helen. *Peekaboo Mouse.* Illustrated by the author. San Diego: Harcourt, 1986. Age: 6 mos. Chaps. 2 and 3.

> A wordless fold-out board book with color photos of a mouse peeking out of various objects.

Piers, Helen. *Peekaboo Rabbit.* Illustrated by the author. Great Britain: Methuen, 1986. Age: 6 mos. Chap. 3.

> Colorful photographs show a fuzzy tan bunny with twelve familiar objects. This board book is wordless and opens up to become an attractive two-sided mural.

Piper, Watty. *The Little Engine That Could.* Illustrated by Richard Walz. New York: Platt & Munk, 1984. Age: 3. Chap. 1.

> The story of the little blue engine who thought she could, and she did. This edition contains pop-up pages and an abbreviated text.

Piper, Watty. *The Little Engine That Could.* Illustrated by George and Doris Hauman. New York: Platt & Munk, 1986. Age: 3. Chap. 1.

> The newest reprint of the story of the determined little blue engine whose effort and faith in herself pays off.

Platt and Munk. *Baby's First Counting Book.* New York: Platt & Munk, 1985. Age: 1. Chap. 4.

> A board book matching numbers with baby animals.

Platt and Munk. *Baby's First Toys.* New York: Platt & Munk, 1986. Age: 6 mos. Chap. 3.

Color photographs of ten familiar toys that are labeled.

Platt and Munk. *Baby's Things*. New York: Platt & Munk, 1985. Age: 6 mos. Chaps. 1 and 3.
  Board book with photographs of familiar items, one to a page. Each object labeled.

Platt and Munk. *My First Book of Animal Babies*. Illustrated by Karen Lee Schmidt. New York: Platt & Munk, 1986. Age: 6 mos. Chap. 3.
  A board book that shows baby animals along with their mothers. It is clear that these mothers are taking loving care of their babies.

Polland, Barbara Kay. *Feelings Inside You & Outloud Too*. Illustrated by Craig DeRoy. Berkeley, CA: Celestial Arts, 1975. Age: 5. Chaps. 4 and 6.
  Explores various feelings and emotions and discusses how to express and deal with them.

Pollock, Penny. *Water Is Wet*. Illustrated by Barbara Beirne. New York: Putnam, 1985. Age: 5. Chap. 4.
  Brief text and photographs introduce the characteristics and uses of water.

Polushkin, Maria. *Baby Brother Blues*. Illustrated by Ellen Weiss. New York: Bradbury, 1987. Age: 5. Chap. 8.
  As she describes a day in the life of her baby brother and the family's reaction to everything he does, a six-year-old girl decides that maybe she likes him after all.

Pomerantz, Barbara. *Bubby, Me, and Memories*. Illustrated by Leon Urie. New York: Union of Hebrew Congregations, 1983. Age: 5. Chap. 7.
  The child's sadness at her grandmother's death is assuaged by the positive and palpable memories she has of the special times she shared with her grandmother. Black-and-white photographs accompany the sensitive text in this beneficial and loving book.

Pomerantz, Charlotte. *The Half-Birthday Party*. Illustrated by Anne Di Salvo-Ryan. New York: Clarion, 1984. Age: 3. Chap. 8.

Daniel celebrates his baby sister's attainment of the grand age of six months by holding a "half-birthday" party.

Potter, Beatrix. *Cecily Parsley's Nursery Rhymes.* Illustrated by the author. London: Frederick Warne. Age: 2. Chaps. 1, 2, and 4.
Eight short nursery rhymes are accompanied by Beatrix Potter's famous illustrations in this small treasure. The rhymes can be recited to children long before they are ready to handle the book. These are real classics.

Potter, Beatrix. *Meet Peter Rabbit.* Illustrated by the author. Harmondsworth, England: Frederick Warne, 1986. Age: 2. Chap. 2.
A very first board book to introduce babies to the "Tale of Peter Rabbit." With original illustrations by Beatrix Potter.

Potter, Beatrix. *The Tale of Peter Rabbit.* Illustrated by the author. New York: Scholastic, 1903. Age: 3. Chaps. 1 and 2.
The beloved story of the naughty bunny and his adventures in Mr. MacGregor's garden. Other stories in this series are *The Tale of Mrs. Tiggy-Winkle, The Tale of Benjamin Bunny,* and *The Tale of Squirrel Nutkin.*

Prelutsky, Jack. *Read-Aloud Rhymes for the Very Young.* Illustrated by Marc Brown. New York: Knopf, 1986. Age: Birth. Chap. 1.
A collection of over 200 short poems by both known and anonymous American and English authors.

Prestine, Joan Singleton. *Sometimes I'm Afraid.* Illustrated by Meredith Johnson. Los Angeles: Price, Stern, Sloan, 1987. Age: 3. Chap. 6.
Tim articulates his fears very well, and even acknowledges that some of them are somewhat unreasonable. (He sometimes is afraid when his mother and father go out, even though he knows they will return; and he's sometimes afraid of the doctor, even though he knows that the doctor will make him feel better.) After he acknowledges his fears, Tim's mother confesses some of her fears, and they both say how much it helps when they talk to someone special, like each other.

Preston, Edna Mitchell. *The Temper Tantrum Book*. Illustrated by Rainey Bennett. New York: Scholastic, 1969. Age: 2. Chap. 6.
> Numerous animals describe their hates and what causes them to have a temper tantrum. Many young children will readily identify with the situations described. A good opening for dialogue.

Price, Mathew. *My Daddy*. Illustrated by Jean Claverie. New York: Knopf, 1986. Age: 2. Chap. 4.
> A lift-up board book for toddlers and fathers. The toddler in the book has a delightful time playing with his doting father, who serves as his horse, bicycle, swing, ski-lift, and airplane.

Prokofiev, Sergei. Translated by Maria Carlson. *Peter and the Wolf*. Illustrated by Charles Mikolaycak. New York: Viking, 1982. Age: 4. Chap. 1.
> Retells the classic tale of the boy who captures a vicious wolf despite his grandfather's dire warnings. This version makes no reference to orchestral work, but depicts the story in bright, realistic paintings.

Prokofiev, Sergei. *Peter and the Wolf* (A Mechanical Book). Illustrated by Barbara Cooney. Paper Engineering by John Strejan and David A. Carter. New York: Viking, 1985. Age: 5. Chaps. 1 and 2.
> The design and format will astound adults and children. The classic story is sketchily told, but well-illustrated by Barbara Cooney, a Caldecott Medal winner.

Prokofiev, Sergei. *Peter and the Wolf*. Illustrated by Erna Voigt. Boston: Godine, 1980. Age: 5. Chaps. 1, 2, and 4.
> Each page introducing a character contains a picture of that character and the instrument of the orchestra that signals its arrival. A line of music is also included that contains the theme for the character.

Provensen, Alice. *A Peaceable Kingdom*. Illustrated by Alice and Martin Provensen. New York: Viking, 1985. Age: 5. Chaps. 1 and 4.
> A classic, but complex, alphabet book using unusual animals and Shaker designs.

Provensen, Alice and Martin. *The Glorious Flight Across the Channel with Louis Bleriot, July 25, 1909.* Illustrated by the authors. New York: Viking, 1983. Age: 5. Chap. 6.

This Caldecott Medal winner takes us from the beginning of Louis Bleriot's obsession with flying, through many mishaps and approximations, to his flight across the channel in his eleventh plane. The story allows children to identify with the growing boy, and later, the man, whose perseverance enables him to prove that an airplane can make this daring trip. A good book for children who are struggling with challenges of their own.

Pryor, Bonnie. *Grandpa Bear.* Illustrated by Bruce Degen. New York: Morrow, 1985. Age: 3. Chap. 6.

Four episodes demonstrate the affection between Samantha and her grandfather. The two of them play many imaginative games together.

Pryor, Bonnie. *The House on Maple Street.* Illustrated by Beth Peck. New York: Morrow, 1987. Age: 5. Chap. 4.

When the children living at 107 Maple Street find a treasure in the backyard, they wonder about who lost it. Flashing back over a hundred-year period, the author tells the story of the people who roamed and settled the site before the children— Indians, settlers, townspeople—each of whom changed the setting.

Rabe, Berniece. *The Balancing Girl.* Illustrated by Lillian Hoban. New York: Dutton, 1981. Age: 4. Chaps. 6 and 7.

Margaret is very good at balancing. She can balance cylinder blocks and magic markers, balance on her crutches, and balance a book on her head while rolling along in her wheel-chair. One of her classmates is not impressed until she designs the best fund-raising event at the school carnival. The author describes this as an "ordinary book which just happens to have a handicapped child as the main character." It conveys a "can-do" attitude.

Raynor, Dorka. *My Friends Live in Many Places.* Illustrated by the author. Chicago: Whitman, 1980. Age: 5. Chap. 7.

Photographs record the activities of children in many different countries. The book clearly celebrates diversity as well as conveying the universalities of childhood.

Reit, Seymour. *Child of the Navajos*. Illustrated by Paul Conklin. New York: Dutton, 1981. Age: 5. Chap. 7.
A Navajo boy lives at a government school during the week and on the reservation on the weekends. A good introduction to the issues attendant upon Native American life in our country.

Rey, H.A. *Curious George*. Illustrated by the author. New York: Scholastic, 1941. Age: 3. Chap. 1.
The little monkey gets into trouble because of his overwhelming curiosity, but he manages to come out safe and happy in the end.

Rey, H.A. *See the Circus*. Illustrated by the author. New York: Houghton Mifflin, 1956. Age: 2. Chaps. 1 and 4.
This small book has delighted children for years. On each page a two-stanza rhyme invites children to guess with what animal the pictured circus performer will be acting. The picture flaps open to reveal the circus animal. Some are quite a surprise.

Rey, H.A. *Where's My Baby?* Illustrated by the author. Brookings, OR: Sandpiper, 1943. Age: 2. Chap. 6.
Each folded page gives the toddler an opportunity to find the baby that belongs to the mother animal.

Rice, James. *Cajun Alphabet*. Illustrated by the author. Gretna, LA: Pelican, 1985. Age: 4. Chap. 4.
Short alphabetical rhymes introduce Cajun vocabulary and culture. Several items are given for each letter of the alphabet. Many of the words are French, and readers may need the accompanying glossary because not all of them are illustrated. For example, "A is arpent, le measure du terre, to own more than forty c'est extraordinaire." Inference skills may be practiced here to good effect.

Rice, Eve. *Goodnight, Goodnight*. Illustrated by the author. New York: Greenwillow, 1980. Age: 1. Chap. 6.

A friendly nighttime neighborhood is created in this endearing good-night book. When one little kitten wants to keep on playing instead of coming in for the night, his mother finds him and takes him home.

Rice, Eve. *New Blue Shoes*. Illustrated by the author. Middlesex, England: Puffin, 1975. Age: 4. Chaps. 5 and 6.
A little girl asserts her independence by insisting on getting blue shoes instead of the brown ones her mother prefers. On the way home from shopping, the child has second thoughts about her choice. In a special way, her mother helps her regain confidence in her choice.

Ringi, Kjell. *The Winner*. Illustrated by the author. New York: Harper & Row, 1969. Age: 3. Chap. 4.
This wordless book is a powerful story of two competitors, the escalation of this conflict, and their mutual destruction. Not without humor, the illustrations that tell the story are colorful and amusing. A fine book to stimulate thought and discussion.

Robart, Rose. *The Cake That Mack Ate*. Illustrated by Maryann Kovalski. Boston: Atlantic Monthly Press, 1986. Age: 4. Chap. 5.
A cumulative story similar in form to "The House That Jack Built."

Robbins, Ruth. *Baboushka and the Three Kings*. Illustrated by Nicolas Sidjakov. Boston: Houghton Mifflin, 1960. Age: 5. Chap. 4.
An old Russian folktale about the old woman who, declining to accompany the three kings as they followed the star in search of the baby Jesus, fails to find him on her own. Each year she renews her endless search.

Robbins, Ken. *City/Country*. Illustrated by the author. New York: Viking Kestrel, 1985. Age: 4. Chap. 4.
Large, somewhat muted color photographs document a car trip from urban high rises and crowds into small towns and farm land.

Roberts, Sarah. *I Want to Go Home!* Illustrated by Joe Mathieu. New York: Random House/Children's Television Network, 1985. Age: 3. Chaps. 6 and 9.

Big Bird's summer visit to his grandmother's house is in danger of becoming an unhappy experience because of Big Bird's homesickness. His grandmother's understanding and his acquisition of a new friend help Big Bird adjust.

Roche, P.K. *I Can Be . . .* Illustrated by the author. Englewood Cliffs, NJ: Prentice-Hall, 1967. Age: 4. Chap. 6.
A little boy can be "quiet as snowflakes falling to the ground," as shy as a lamb, as lively as a big, brass band, and much more. This simple book invites children to appreciate and explore their many moods by comparing them to things in the world around us.

Roche, P.K. *Webster and Arnold and the Giant Box.* Illustrated by the author. New York: Dial, 1980. Age: 3. Chap. 8.
Two animal brothers play together happily, confront each other angrily, and then return to mutual enjoyment.

Rockwell, Anne. *In Our House.* Illustrated by the author. New York: Crowell, 1985. Age: 1. Chap. 4.
Each room of a bear family's house is presented and the bears are performing the many activities appropriate in that room. Good for learning verbs and the different functions of different rooms.

Rockwell, Anne. *The Three Sillies and 10 Other Stories to Read Aloud.* Illustrated by the author. New York: Harper & Row, 1979. Age: 4. Chap. 2.
Contains "The Old Woman and Her Pig," "The Three Sillies," "The Travels of a Fox," "The Milkmaid and the Bucket of Milk," "Lambikin," "The Tortoise and the Hare," "The Bremen Town Musicians," "The Fox and the Crow," and more.

Rockwell, Anne. *When We Grow Up.* Illustrated by the author. New York: Dutton, 1981. Age: 5. Chaps. 4 and 5.
A wide variety of career choices is available to both males and females, as evidenced by the fact that Amy wants to be a writer, Edmund wants to be a veterinarian, Nancy wants to be a plumber, and Emily wants to walk on the moon. Chil-

dren's career aspirations can provide adults with interesting information about the children's self-concept and their notions of gender expectations.

Rockwell, Anne and Harlow. *The Emergency Room*. Illustrated by the authors. New York: Macmillan, 1985. Age: 5. Chap. 4.
Explores the equipment and procedures of a hospital room by describing what one patient sees while being treated for a sprained ankle.

Rockwell, Anne and Harlow. *My Baby-Sitter*. Illustrated by the authors. New York: Macmillan, 1985. Age: 4. Chap. 4.
A little boy describes what he does with his fifteen-year-old baby-sitter when his parents go out for the evening. Realistic and amusing, their activities include doing the dishes after eating cheeseburgers, dancing to the music the sitter brings with her, watching TV, regular bedtime preparations, the sitter's homework, phone calls to friends, and a snack when the little boy is in bed.

Rockwell, Harlow. *My Dentist*. Illustrated by the author. New York: Greenwillow, 1975. Age: 3. Chap. 6.
With characteristic clarity, the author details for children the experience of going to the dentist.

Rockwell, Harlow. *My Kitchen*. Illustrated by the author. New York: Greenwillow, 1980. Age: 1. Chaps. 3 and 4.
This book's simple drawings and text depict the many familiar items to be found in the kitchen at lunchtime or anytime.

Rockwell, Harlow. *My Nursery School*. Illustrated by the author. New York: Greenwillow, 1976. Age: 3. Chap. 6.
By describing in very simple language and pictures what one child and her friends are choosing to do in their nursery school during one day, the author gives children a good sense of the range of activities, the pattern of the day, and the atmosphere of a typical nursery school.

Rogers, Fred. *Going to Day Care*. Illustrated by Jim Judkis. New York: Putnam, 1985. Age: 2. Chaps. 4 and 6.

Part of Fred Rogers's *First Experiences* series, this book is designed to help children cope with starting day care. This book shows routines and equipment in both school and home day care settings, shows both men and women as day care providers, and children at play. The text is factual, realistic, and refers frequently to feelings.

Rogers, Fred. *Going to the Doctor*. Illustrated by Jim Judkis. New York: Putnam, 1986. Age: 2. Chap. 6.
Another *First Experiences* book. The photographs show fathers as well as mothers accompanying their children to the doctor's office. Many parts of the examination procedure are shown and de-mystified.

Rogers, Fred. *Going to the Potty*. Illustrated by Jim Judkis. New York: Putnam, 1986. Age: 18 mos. Chaps. 4 and 6.
With excellent photographs and sensitive text, Fred Rogers of "Mr. Rogers Neighborhood" introduces children to the new experience of using the potty or toilet.

Rogers, Fred. *The New Baby*. Illustrated by Jim Judkis. New York: Putnam, 1985. Age: 3. Chap. 8.
Part of the new *First Experiences* series and designed to help lessen children's fears about facing something new and difficult. Through large photographs and clear text, this book tells an older child what the new baby will be like, and the good and bad feelings he may have in reaction. Especially useful is the acknowledgment of anger and the statement "you can do things when you're mad that don't hurt you or anybody else," accompanied by a photograph of a child knocking down a block building.

Rojankovsky, Feodor. *Feodor Rojankovsky's Great Big Animal Book*. Illustrated by the author. Racine, WI: Western, 1950. Age: 1 up. Chaps. 1, 3, and 4.
For more than thirty-five years Rojankovsky's paintings of farm animals have been delighting young children. They still do. This book is excellent for learning the names of animals and forming clear mental pictures of them.

Root, Phyllis. *Hidden Places*. Illustrated by Daniel San Sousi. Milwaukee: Raintree, 1983. Age: 5. Chap. 7.

Evan stays at his Uncle Joe's farm while his parents try to resolve their marital problems. Uncle Joe helps Evan to face his own feelings and come to terms with them.

Rosario, Idalia. *Idalia's Project ABC*. Illustrated by the author. New York: Holt, 1981. Age: 4. Chap. 4.
Introduces the alphabet by means of brief bilingual descriptions of city life. In Spanish and English.

Rosenberg, Amye. *1,2, Buckle My Shoe*. Illustrated by the author. New York: Simon & Schuster, 1981. Age: 6 mos. Chaps. 3 and 4.
A cloth book that infants will enjoy looking at and toddlers will enjoy manipulating. A modern version of the old rhyme.

Rosenberg, Amye. *The Pudgy Peek-a-Boo Book*. Illustrated by the author. New York: Grosset & Dunlap, 1983. Age: 1 up. Chaps. 3, 4, and 6.
Mice, rabbits, kittens, piglets, baby bears, and a dog play peek-a-boo in this colorful small board book.

Roser, Wiltrud. *Lena and Leopold*. Illustrated by the author. New York: McElderry, 1985. Age: 4. Chap. 4.
Lena finally finds out why her cat, Leopold, won't play with the new toy mouse.

Roth, Harold. *A Goodnight Hug*. Illustrated by the author. New York: Grosset & Dunlap, 1986. Age: 6 mos. Chap. 3.
This board book describes a toddler's nighttime routine. The father in this family is particularly active in the rearing and nurturing of the child. The mother and father are parenting partners. Color photographs add to the appeal of the familiar tasks and rituals.

Roth, Harold. *Nursery School*. Illustrated by the author. New York: Grosset & Dunlap, 1986. Age: 2. Chaps. 4 and 7.
Photographs of children of different races are combined with a simple text to tell children what happens during the course of a day at nursery school.

Roth, Harold. *The Playground*. Illustrated by the author. New York: Grosset & Dunlap, 1986. Age: 18 mos. Chaps. 4 and 7.

The color photographs of this board book for toddlers shows a multiracial group of children thoroughly enjoying many playground activities. Readers are invited to answer questions about whether they like some of the pictured equipment.

Roth, Harold. *Spring Days*. Illustrated by the author. New York: Grosset & Dunlap, 1986. Age: 1 up. Chap. 4.
Young children are shown enjoying spring's special pleasures: picking dandelions, sniffing daffodils, playing in the rain, and so on.

Roth, Harold. *Summer Days*. Illustrated by the author. New York: Grosset & Dunlap, 1986. Age: 1. Chap. 4.
Brightly colored photographs show young children enjoying typical summertime activities such as going to the beach and eating watermelon.

Russ, Lavinia. *Alec's Sand Castle*. Illustrated by James Stevenson. New York: Harper & Row, 1972. Age: 4. Chap. 6.
A little boy is crowded by interfering relatives when he is building a sand castle. He separates himself from them and their "help." In the private spaces of his mind, he builds wonderful castles and fantasies that neither his relatives nor the rain can spoil.

Russell, Helen and Ross. *Foraging for Dinner*. Illustrated by the author. Nashville: T. Nelson, 1975. Age: 5. Chap. 5.
A good resource for an enthusiastic gardener or cook, this book tells about edible foods found in the wild.

Rylant, Cynthia. *Night in the Country*. Illustrated by Mary Szilagyi. New York: Bradbury, 1986. Age: 1. Chaps. 3, 4, and 6.
This book helps the reader see and hear nighttime in the country. The pace of this book is very slow so that young readers can savor each of the images and sounds as they turn the pages. The images are commonplace but the treatment is extraordinary.

Rylant, Cynthia. *The Relatives Came*. Illustrated by Stephen Gammell. New York: Bradbury, 1985. Age: 4. Chaps. 2 and 6.

A Caldecott Medal winner about a family reunion. Full of
warmth and humor, it is a celebration of family togetherness.

Rylant, Cynthia. *When I Was Young in the Mountains*. Illustrated
by Diane Goode. New York: Dutton, 1982. Age: 5. Chap. 6.
Grandmother tells an unseen grandchild about the small
daily pleasures of her early life in the mountains. Her happi-
ness and deep commitment to the ways of her childhood
permeate the sharing. Another Caldecott honor book.

Samton, Sheila White. *The World from My Window*. Illustrated
by the author. New York: Crown, 1985. Age: 3. Chap. 4.
Color blocks and cut-out shapes illustrate a simple counting
rhyme. The author/illustrator is known for her murals, wall
hangings, and pictures.

Sasaki, Isao. *Snow*. Illustrated by the author. New York: Viking,
1980. Age: 4. Chap. 4.
A wordless story about a tiny train station from early morning
to late night when the day's snowfall finally stops. Good for
children learning to read detail and to follow sequence.

Saul, Wendy. *Butcher, Baker, Cabinetmaker*. Illustrated by
Abigail Heyman. New York: Crowell, 1978. Age: 5. Chaps. 4
and 5.
Photographs illustrate the many occupations women can hold
and can be competent in.

Savage, Dorothy. *The Yellow Peephole Book*. Illustrated by Gillian
Chapman. New York: Dutton, 1986. Age: 2. Chap. 4.
Through a hole in each page children see the color yellow.
The yellow circle on each page becomes part of the picture,
for example, a sun, an egg yolk, or a balloon. Labels identify
objects only. Readers should supply the adjective *yellow* each
time to fulfill the purpose of the book. Part of a series, which
includes a separate book on the colors red, black, and green.

Scarry, Richard. *Early Words*. Illustrated by the author. New
York: Random House, 1976. Age: 1. Chap. 3.
On each page of this 6-by-8 inch board book, Scarry's famous
rabbit-child engages in a simple activity. Unlike most of the

other Scarry books, these pages are uncluttered. The pictures are simply and colorfully drawn.

Scarry, Richard. *Richard Scarry's Best First Book Ever!* Illustrated by the author. New York: Random House, 1979. Age: 2. Chap. 4.
Each page of this very large book has detailed, labeled pictures of items relating to one topic. Clothing, colors, manners, the alphabet, a visit to the doctor, shapes, school, the playground, and counting are among the many topics.

Scarry, Richard. *Richard Scarry's What Animals Do.* Illustrated by the author. Racine, WI: Western, 1963. Age: 1. Chaps. 3 and 4.
Each double-page spread of this large board book presents a handsome close-up picture of an animal and labels the animal and its typical movement. For example: the rooster struts, the duck waddles, the bear snuffles, the worm wiggles, and so forth.

Scarry, Richard. *Short and Tall.* Illustrated by the author. Racine, WI: Western, 1976. Age: 4. Chap. 4.
For children who enjoy Richard Scarry's tiny animal characters and silly situations this book will appeal greatly. Each page tells a story or two illustrating a concept of opposites in a humorous manner.

Scheffler, Ursel. *A Walk in the Rain.* Illustrated by Ulises Wensell. New York: Putnam, 1984. Age: 3. Chap. 6.
Josh goes for a walk in the rain with his grandmother and wears his new rainwear. The grandmother enjoys the rain as much as the child.

Schick, Eleanor. *City in Winter.* Illustrated by the author. New York: Macmillan, 1970. Age: 5. Chap. 6.
Jimmy stays home from school because of a blizzard and spends the day with his grandmother. Several of Jimmy's activities are described. His mother returns home from work at the end of the day, demonstrating one arrangement for single-parent families.

Schlein, Miriam. *The Way Mothers Are.* Illustrated by Joe Lasker. New York: Whitman, 1963. Age: 4. Chaps. 6 and 7.

A story about a little kitten who wonders why he is loved when he is naughty as well as good. Through this well-crafted story, one mother explains a parent's unconditional love.

Schlesinger, Alice. *Baby's Mother Goose*. Illustrated by the author. New York: Grosset & Dunlap, 1986. Age: 6 mos. Chap. 3.
   This board book permits a child to hold the book and turn the pages while you read the rhymes aloud.

Schmidt, Karen Lee. *My First Book of Baby Animals*. Illustrated by the author. New York: Grosset & Dunlap, 1986. Age: 1. Chap. 4.
   Nicely drawn, benign-looking wild animals are shown with their young.

Schuchman, Joan. *Two Places to Sleep*. Illustrated by Jim LaMarche. Minneapolis: Carolrhoda, 1979. Age: 5. Chap. 7.
   David describes living with his father and visiting his mother on weekends after his parents' divorce.

Schwartz, David M. *How Much is a Million?* Illustrated by Steven Kellogg. New York: Scholastic, 1985. Age: 5. Chap. 4.
   Marvelosissimo the Magician illustrates a million in many many ways to help children grasp its size and meaning.

Scott, Ann Herbert. *On Mother's Lap*. Illustrated by Glo Coalson. New York: McGraw-Hill, 1972. Age: 3. Chaps. 7 and 8.
   A young child learns that there is ample room on his mother's lap for both her children. The Alaskan setting is a bonus.

Scott, Ann Herbert. *Sam*. Illustrated by Symeon Shimin. New York: McGraw-Hill, 1967. Age: 4. Chaps. 6, 7, and 8.
   Sam needs to feel useful. His siblings and parents are too busy to pay attention to him until his mother invites him to join her in making raspberry tarts.

Seeger, Pete. *Abiyoyo*. Illustrated by Michael Hays. New York: Macmillan, 1986. Age: 4. Chap. 2.
   Banished from the town for making mischief, a little boy and his father are welcomed back when they find a way to make the dreaded giant Abiyoyo disappear.

Seidenn, Art. *Counting Rhymes*. Illustrated by the author. New York: Grosset & Dunlap, 1985. Age: 2. Chap. 4.
This large board book contains many traditional rhymes. The unifying theme is time and numbers.

Sendak, Maurice. *Chicken Soup with Rice*. Illustrated by the author. New York: Harper & Row, 1962. Age: 3. Chap. 4.
Whether to help learn the months of the year or just to have fun, children will love the monthly poems about eating chicken soup and rice at all seasons and months of the year.

Sendak, Maurice. *In the Night Kitchen*. Illustrated by the author. New York: Harper & Row, 1970. Age: 5. Chap. 2.
A young boy dreams of being baked in a batter. He turns out fine.

Sendak, Maurice. *Pierre: A Cautionary Tale*. Illustrated by the author. New York: Harper & Row, 1962. Age: 5. Chap. 6.
A little boy lives to regret his temper tantrums in this tongue-in-cheek tale.

Sendak, Maurice. *Where the Wild Things Are*. Illustrated by the author. New York: Harper & Row, 1963. Age: 3. Chaps. 1, 2, and 6.
After Max has been sent to his room without supper, he sails off in his imagination to the land of the wild things. He tames the wild things and returns to his own room, where he finds his supper waiting. This modern classic reflects children's need to tame the wild things within themselves.

Seuss, Dr. (Theodore Geisel). *The 500 Hats of Bartholomew Cubbins*. Illustrated by the author. New York: Scholastic, 1938. Age: 4. Chap. 1.
Bartholomew tries to take off his hat to show respect for the king, but each time he does, a new, more elaborate one, appears.

Seuss, Dr. (Theodore Geisel). *Horton Hatches the Who*. Illustrated by the author. New York: Random House, 1940. Age: 3. Chap. 6.

A much-loved fantasy about Horton the Elephant who is recruited by Lazy Mayzie, the bird, to sit on her nest. He endures rain, ice, teasing, and capture, but faithfully sits on the egg. When it hatches, Horton and everyone else are in for a surprise.

Sharmat, Marjorie Weinman. *A Big Fat Enormous Lie*. Illustrated by David McPhail. New York: Dutton, 1978. Age: 3. Chap. 4.

When asked by his father, a small boy lies and says he did not eat the jar of cookies. He feels stuck with his lie and it becomes like a monster that grows until he tells his parents about it. This is a good opener for discussions about honesty and the feelings a person might have that could lead him or her to lie in the first place.

Sharmat, Marjorie. *Goodnight Andrew, Goodnight Craig*. Illustrated by Mary Chalmers. New York: Harper & Row, 1969. Age: 4. Chap. 8.

After two brothers are put to bed by their father, they take a long time falling asleep. They sleep only after the older boy has promised the younger that he will play with him. A generally realistic and positive picture of brothers.

Sharmat, Marjorie Weinman. *I Don't Care*. Illustrated by Lillian Hoban. New York: Macmillan, 1977. Age: 4. Chaps. 6 and 7.

The story reflects the stages of mourning over a loss. This book deals with the loss of a balloon, but the stages are the same, no matter what the loss.

Sharmat, Marjorie Weinman. *I'm Terrific*. Illustrated by Kay Chorao. New York: Holiday House, 1977. Age: 3. Chaps. 1 and 6.

A bear cub named Jason thinks he's terrific and awards himself gold stars. He also boasts to his friends who do not enjoy this trait. Jason realizes he has to change if he wants to have friends, so he tries being unpleasant. Finally he decides just to be himself, gives away his gold stars, and gains friends. Through all this self-discovery Jason's mother is supportive, encouraging, and nondirective. The pictures are charming.

Sharmat, Marjorie. *I Want Mama*. Illustrated by Emily Arnold McCully. New York: Harper & Row, 1974. Age: 3. Chap. 6.

A little girl experiences and expresses many feelings while her mother is in the hospital. This book would be helpful to children separated from a loved one because of illness. A good place to begin a dialogue between reader and child.

Sharmat, Marjorie Weinman. *Scarlet Monster Lives Here*. Illustrated by Dennis Kendrick. New York: Harper & Row, 1979. Age: 3. Chap. 6.

Scarlet Monster moves to a new neighborhood, prepares for new friends, and looks forward to meeting them. When no one visits, she thinks something is wrong with her. She is surprised to learn that they have not visited because they thought she would not like them.

Sharmat, Marjorie. *Sometimes Mama and Papa Fight*. Illustrated by Kay Chorao. New York: Harper & Row, 1980. Age: 4. Chap. 6.

A brother and sister are scared and worried when their parents argue, even though it is explained that arguments "sometimes happen and we get over them." Children will identify with many of the feelings of the children in the story and may feel reassured if this book is read to them by a parent who believes in its happy conclusion. Could also be useful in different circumstances with a changed ending.

Shiefman, Vicky. *M Is For Move*. Illustrated by Bill Miller. New York: Dutton, 1981. Age: 4. Chap. 4.

Presents an illustrative action word for each consonant in the alphabet.

Shulevitz, Uri. *Dawn*. Illustrated by the author. New York: Farrar, Straus, Giroux, 1974. Age: 5. Chap. 1.

This book was inspired by an ancient Chinese poem. Simple text and luminous pictures describe the transition from night to day in the process of the camping trip of a grandson and grandfather.

Shulevitz, Uri. *One Monday Morning*. Illustrated by the author. New York: Macmillan, 1967. Age: 2. Chap. 6.

This fantasy is adapted from an ancient folk song but seems very modern. Set in a tenement, each day a king, queen, and growing entourage come to visit a little boy who isn't home. The last page reveals the source of the child's fantasy, a deck of cards.

Shyer, Marlene Fanta. *Here I Am, an Only Child*. Illustrated by Donald Carrick. New York: Scribners, 1985. Age: 4. Chap. 8.
An only child lists many things he has against his status as an only child. He also realizes many advantages come from his position. This is a good conversation opener.

Silverstein, Shel. *Where the Sidewalk Ends: The Poems and Drawings of Shel Silverstein*. Illustrated by the author. New York: Harper & Row, 1974. Age: 2. Chap. 2.
Quirky and funny poems, some of them with a bite. Toddlers may not understand all of the poems, but they will enjoy hearing them. Also try *A Light in the Attic* by the same author-illustrator, published by Harper in 1981.

Simon, Norma. *All Kinds of Families*. Illustrated by Joe Lasker. Niles, IL: Whitman, 1976. Age: 5. Chaps. 7 and 8.
Through words and pictures, this book explores and acknowledges families of all sorts, including those that are not traditional or conforming to the conventional definition.

Simon, Norma. *How Do I Feel?* Illustrated by Joe Lasker. Niles, IL: Whitman, 1970. Age: 3. Chaps. 4 and 6.
This book is designed to help children understand their feelings and express them in words. The book tells about different situations in the lives of two children and their varied reactions.

Simon, Norma. *I'm Busy, Too*. Illustrated by Dora Leder. Niles, IL: Whitman, 1980. Age: 3. Chap. 5.
This book shows that it is not just grown-ups who have very busy days. The three children in this book are from families that are different in many ways, but the caring and routines that each family engages in show definite similarities as well as a respect for the child's activities.

Simon, Norma. *I Was So Mad*. Illustrated by Dora Leder. Chicago: Whitman, 1974. Age: 4. Chaps. 4 and 8.

This book depicts many varied situations that can evoke angry feelings in children. It is a good tool for helping children understand that their feelings are normal and acceptable, although their behavior may not be.

Simon, Norma. *Nobody's Perfect, Not Even My Mother.* Illustrated by Dora Leder. Chicago: Whitman, 1981. Age: 5. Chap. 6.
Simon reminds children that it's good to try hard, but that they can't expect perfection from anyone. Sample situations are presented showing parents, teachers, and other grownups having difficulties doing their jobs, dealing with people, and trying to give up smoking.

Simon, Norma. *The Saddest Time.* Illustrated by Jacqueline Rogers. Niles, IL: Whitman, 1986. Age: 5. Chap. 7.
Explains death as the inevitable end of life and provides three situations in which children experience powerful emotions when someone close has died.

Simon, Norma. *Why Am I Different?* Illustrated by Dora Leder. Niles, IL: Whitman, 1976. Age: 5. Chap. 7.
Numerous children detail their differences and demonstrate a respect for everyone.

Sinberg, Janet. *Divorce Is A Grown-Up Problem.* Illustrated by Nancy Gray. New York: Avon, 1978. Age: 3. Chap. 7.
Acknowledges children's feelings and helps them to deal with the negative feelings after a divorce. A bibliography of references is included.

Skolsky, Mindy Warshaw. *The Whistling Teakettle.* Illustrated by Karen Ann Weinhaus. New York: Harper & Row, 1977. Age: 5. Chap. 7.
The first in a series of four stories about Hannah. The other titles are *Carnival and Kopek, Hannah Is a Palindrome,* and *Hannah and the Best Father on Route 9W.* These are continuing stories about Hannah, a young Jewish girl growing up in the 1930s in rural New York.

Slier, Debby. *What Do Babies Do?* Illustrated by photographs selected by the author. New York: Random House, 1985. Age: 6 mos. Chaps. 3 and 7.

The color photographs of this small board book present babies in various typical activities: sleeping, drinking, reading, looking in a mirror, laughing, crying, crawling, playing in the bath, clapping hands, standing, and going for a walk. Babies seem to love seeing pictures of other babies.

Slier, Debby. *What Do Toddlers Do?* Illustrated by photographs selected by the author. New York: Random House, 1985. Age: 1. Chaps. 3 and 7.

In color photographs multiracial toddlers are shown enjoying typical activities, which are simply labeled.

Slier, Debby. *Whose Baby Are You?* Illustrated by photographs selected by author. Philip Lief, 1987. Age: 1. Chaps. 3, 6, and 7.

This large board book is also a game. The pages are split horizontally: the top halves have pictures of adult animals and the bottom halves have pictures of baby animals to match with their parents. Color photographs are clear and very appealing.

Slobodkina, Esphyr. *Caps for Sale.* Illustrated by the author. New York: Scholastic, 1968. Age: 2. Chap. 6.

A classic that has delighted children for more than forty years, this tale is about monkeys who steal a cap seller's wares and how he manages to outsmart the clever animals to regain possession of his colorful caps.

Smith, Dian G. *My New Baby and Me.* Illustrated by Douglas Sardo. New York: Scribners, 1986. Age: 4. Chap. 8.

A workbook for older siblings that invites them to describe themselves and their new sibling in creative ways. Some well-structured, positive comparison is encouraged and an appreciation of self and baby is built.

Smith, Jennifer. *Grover and the New Kid.* Illustrated by Tom Cooke. New York: Random House/Children's Television Network, 1987. Age: 4. Chaps. 6 and 9.

Although Grover tries to be kind to the new boy in school, the boy is selfish and rude to him and everyone else in the class. In the end the new boy mends his ways, and everyone understands that he misbehaved because of his own fears.

Smith, Wendy. *The Lonely, Only Mouse*. Illustrated by the author. New York: Viking Kestrel, 1986. Age: 3. Chap. 8.

> Thelonius, an only mouse, wishes he had a sibling. He is delighted when his cousin Charlie comes to visit, but in the process learns that there are some advantages to being "an only."

Spier, Peter. *Fast-Slow, High-Low: A Book of Opposites by Peter Spier*. Illustrated by the author. Garden City, NY: Doubleday, 1972. Age: 3. Chap. 4.

> On each double-page spread Peter Spier gives many examples of the concept he is presenting using the amusing, detailed drawings for which he has become acclaimed.

Spier, Peter. *The Fox Went Out on a Chilly Night*. Illustrated by the author. Garden City, NY: Doubleday, 1961. Age: Birth. Chap. 1.

> Intricate and detailed illustrations of a traditional folk song. Parents will enjoy the pictures as they sing the song to their babies.

Spier, Peter. *Gobble, Growl, Grunt*. Illustrated by the author. Garden City, NY: Doubleday, 1971. Age: 1. Chaps. 3 and 4.

> This illustrator has crowded his pages with expressive animals of every variety. The sound of each and every animal labels its picture. A delight for people of all ages.

Spier, Peter. *London Bridge Is Falling Down!* Illustrated by the author. Garden City, NY: Doubleday, 1967. Age: 3. Chaps. 2 and 4.

> Mr. Spier's detailed illustrations bring each stage of the famous London Bridge's history to light. The reader sees each time it is built and each time it collapses. The music for the song and a history of the bridge follow at the end of the story.

Spier, Peter. *Noah's Ark*. Illustrated by the author. Garden City, NY: Doubleday, 1977. Age: 4. Chap. 1.

> A humorously detailed illustrated version of the Noah story, taken from the sixteenth-century Dutch poem, "The Flood" by Jacobus Rivius.

Spier, Peter. *People*. Illustrated by the author. Garden City, NY: Doubleday, 1980. Age: 4. Chaps. 1 and 4.

An enormous book in both size and concept, this book fills us, through pictures, with example after example of our human differences, but also with our common humanity. For example, half of one page is filled with fifty-four profiles, illustrating that "noses come in every shape imaginable." Just a few of the other illustrated categories are people's sizes, shapes, eyes, ears, hairstyles, clothing, wisdom, foolishness, games, houses, tastes, holidays, pets, and many more.

Spier, Peter. *Rain*. Illustrated by the author. Garden City, NY: Doubleday, 1982. Age: 3. Chap. 4.

Rain, wind, and children combine to make a detailed story when depicted in the many many lively, humorous drawings of Peter Spier. Mr. Spier communicates a sense of wonder, beauty, and enjoyment in the natural world.

Stanek, Muriel. *Starting School*. Illustrated by Betty and Tony Deluna. Chicago: Whitman, 1981. Age: 4. Chap. 6.

A small book with simple drawings that introduce children to school. Tells about looking forward to school over the summer, having a physical examination, a trip to the dentist, and a trip to the shoe store during the summer to get ready.

Stanek, Muriel. *Who's Afraid of the Dark?* Illustrated by Helen Cogancherry. Chicago: Whitman, 1980. Age: 4. Chap. 6.

Kenny is afraid of the dark and his sister and father each think of ways to help him overcome his special fear. Kenny's grandfather is also helpful, as is a new child in Kenny's class who shares the same fear. No simple solutions are offered in this story, but the validity and commonality of fears are acknowledged.

Stecher, Miriam B. and Kandell, Alice S. *Daddy and Ben Together*. Illustrated by Alice S. Kandell. New York: Lothrop, Lee, Shepard, 1981. Age: 4. Chap. 6.

Dad and Ben have a good relationship, but when Mommy has to go away on a business trip for a few days, they have a hard time. Ben decides he needs to change his mood and he succeeds; from then on, all goes well.

Steichen, Edward. *The Family of Man*. Photographs selected by the author. New York: Maco Magazine, 1955. Age: 4. Chaps. 1 and 7.

A collection of photographs from all over the world, celebrating humanity, its differences, and similarities.

Steig, William. *The Amazing Bone*. Illustrated by the author. New York: Penguin, 1976. Age: 5. Chap. 4.

A fantasy about a little pig who finds an amazing bone that saves her from a hungry fox. The story, language, and pictures represent the style for which Mr. Steig is famous.

Steig, William. *Amos & Boris*. Illustrated by the author. New York: Farrar, Straus, Giroux, 1971. Age: 5. Chap. 6.

A moving story about an exemplary friendship between a mouse and a whale, each of whom saves the other.

Steig, William. *Sylvester and the Magic Pebble*. Illustrated by the author. New York: Scholastic, 1969. Age: 4. Chaps. 2 and 6.

Through an accidental misuse of a magic pebble, Sylvester becomes a rock. His parents never give up their search for him and finally, magically, find him.

Stein, Sara Bonnett. *About Handicaps*. Illustrated by Dick Frank. New York: Walker, 1974. Age: 5. Chaps. 4 and 7.

An open family book for parents and children, using two texts, one for adults to read to children, and one providing information for parents and caretakers. The photographs permit children to stare without interruption at a prosthetic hand and arm.

Stein, Sara Bonnett. *Making Babies*. Illustrated by Doris Pinney. New York: Walker, 1974. Age: 3. Chap. 8.

An *Open Families* series book that discusses the importance of an open atmosphere for understanding sex, love, birth, and families. A somewhat value-laden presentation of topics.

Stein, Sara Bonnett. *That New Baby*. Photographs by Dick Frank. New York: Danbury, 1974. Age: 4. Chap. 8.

Another in the *Open Family* series. Text for children depicts older children feeling jealousy and sense of loss when a new sibling is expected. Text for adults alongside children's text.

Stenson, Janet Sinberg. *Now I Have a Stepparent and It's Kind of Confusing*. Illustrated by Nancy Gray. New York: Avon, 1979. Age: 5. Chap. 7.

Although the young boy in the story accepts his parents' divorce as well as he can, he becomes confused and upset when his mother plans to remarry. All of the adults behave reasonably and lovingly, and the boy comes to accept the new marriage. A preface giving advice and guidance to parents and stepparents is a beneficial aspect of this book.

Steptoe, John. *Birthday*. Illustrated by the author. New York: Holt, 1972. Age: 5. Chaps. 7 and 8.

Everyone in this black community is represented as part of a loving extended family in which Javaka celebrates his birthday.

Steptoe, John. *Daddy Is a Monster . . . Sometimes*. Illustrated by the author. New York: Lippincott, 1980. Age: 3. Chaps. 6 and 7.

The children in this story feel their Daddy is like some kind of monster when he gets angry. They are astounded when he tells them that they are sometimes monsters, too.

Steptoe, John. *My Special Best Words*. Illustrated by the author. New York: Viking, 1974. Age: 3. Chaps. 6, 7, and 8.

A three-year-old helps her one-year-old brother with toilet training, nose blowing, and speaking. They also quarrel, share special words, and present a happy picture of sibling togetherness.

Steptoe, John. *Stevie*. Illustrated by the author. New York: Harper & Row, 1969. Age: 5. Chaps. 7 and 8.

When Robert's mother takes in another child to care for, her son experiences feelings very similar to sibling rivalry. But, when Stevie leaves, Robert misses him.

Stevens, Janet. *Goldilocks and the Three Bears*. Illustrated by the author. New York: Holiday House, 1986. Age: 3. Chap. 1.

A little girl wanders by the home of three bears and seeing no one at home goes inside, helps herself to food, and falls asleep. In the end, she sees the error of her ways, and vows to bother the bears no more.

Stevens, Janet. *The House That Jack Built*. Illustrated by the author. New York: Holiday House, 1965. Age: 4. Chaps. 1 and 2.
Amusingly irreverent illustrations of the classic cumulative rhyme.

Stevenson, James. *Higher on the Door*. Illustrated by the author. New York: Greenwillow, 1987. Age: 3. Chap. 6.
A man who is a grandfather recalls many of the small, every-day delights, fears, disappointments, and special times he had as a child. He remembers feeling eager to get older, "higher on the door."

Stevenson, Robert Louis. *A Child's Garden of Verses*. Illustrated by Michael Foreman. New York: Delacorte, 1985. Age: Birth. Chaps. 1 and 2.
The familiar poems are notably wrought by the illustrator.

Stevenson, Robert Louis. *A Child's Garden of Verses*. Illustrated by Tasha Tudor. New York: Rand McNally, 1981. Age: Birth. Chap. 1.
Victorian settings appropriately illustrate the poetry.

Stevenson, Robert Louis. *The Moon*. Illustrated by Denise Saldutti. New York: Harper & Row, 1984. Age: 2. Chap. 2.
Illustrations portray a father and daughter going fishing against a background of Stevenson's poem about nightly happenings in the light of the moon.

Stiles, Norman. *I'll Miss You, Mr. Hooper*. Illustrated by Joe Mathieu. New York: Random House, 1984. Age: 3. Chaps. 7 and 9.
Based on the script for "Sesame Street" after the death of Will Lee who created the role of Mr. Hooper. The book is sensitive and honest. Big Bird takes on the role of a preschooler and the adults answer his questions. The book stresses the important things people should do for one another. The book is a supportive one, especially since young viewers probably remember Mr. Hooper fondly.

Stull, Edith. *My Turtle Died Today*. Illustrated by Mamoru Funai. New York: Holt, 1964. Age: 5. Chap. 7.

A boy grieves over the death of his turtle. A good model for coping with the death of a pet.

Super, Terri. *The Pudgy Pat-A-Cake Book*. Illustrated by the author. New York: Grosset & Dunlap, 1983. Age: 6 mos. Chap. 4.
Familiar nursery and action rhymes presented one to a page by friendly and cheerful pastel-colored animals.

Supraner, Robyn. *It's Not Fair*. Illustrated by Randall Enos. New York: Warne, 1976. Age: 3. Chap. 8.
An older sibling is offended because the baby always seems to get what she wants. The tables are turned when the firstborn has a day out alone with the parents.

Surowiecki, Sandra Lucas. *Joshua's Day*. Illustrated by Patricia Riley Lenthall. Durham, NC: Lollipop Power, 1972. Age: 3. Chap. 4.
Page by large page, the reader sees Joshua's day unfold. He wakes with his mother and has breakfast with her. She leaves him at day care and goes to her job as a photographer. Joshua's time at day care is chronicled. At five his mother comes, picks him up, and the evening is spent together.

Tallarico, Tony. *Shapes: See and Say*. Illustrated by the author. Harrison, NY: Tuffy Books, 1986. Age: 2. Chap. 4.
Part of the Tuffy Books preschool series, each brightly colored, laminated page presents a large picture of a shape and a smaller picture of a familiar object illustrative of that shape. Both pictures are labeled. A very simple, clear book for children beginning to learn their shapes. A companion book to *Simple Objects See and Say*.

Tannenbaum, D. Leb. *Getting Ready for Baby*. Illustrated by Anthony Rao. New York: Simon & Schuster, 1982. Age: 3. Chap. 8.
A book that describes one child, Heather, learning about pregnancy, fetal growth, prenatal care, family trees, the hospital, equipment for babies, the nature of infants, and birth. At each stage there are games and activities for the reader to reinforce and personalize the information.

Tarrant, Graham. *Frogs*. Illustrated by Tony King. Los Angeles: Intervisual Communications, 1983. Age: 4. Chap. 4.

In this pop-up book a large green frog opens and closes his large mouth, rolls his round eye, and fathers a tiny tadpole who slowly develops into another green frog.

Tax, Meredith. *Families*. Illustrated by Marilyn Hafner. Boston: Little, Brown, 1981. Age: 2. Chap. 7.

With sometimes humorous text and drawings, this book depicts many different sorts of families in an accepting and informative way. The book stresses the message that what is important is not a family's size or location. What is important is their love for one another.

Taylor, Sydney. *All-Of-A Kind Family*. Illustrated by Helen John. New York: Dell, 1951. Age: 5. Chaps. 5. and 7.

All of the books in this series describe a Jewish family living in the Lower East Side of Manhattan in the early part of this century. This first book of the series introduces readers to the family of five girls and their parents. It also conveys the values of love of learning and books as well as responsibility for one's actions, all portrayed in a light and loving manner.

Terris, Susan. *Amanda the Panda and the Redhead*. Illustrated by Emily McCully. Garden City, NY: Doubleday, 1975. Age: 3. Chap. 8.

When Amanda doesn't get attention because her parents are busy with her baby brother and breakfast, she first becomes enraged and then chooses to be silent. After trying to work out her feelings through her toy panda, she goes to bed. When her parents seek her out and tell her she is special, amicable relations seem to be restored.

Tester, Sylvia Root. *We Laughed A Lot, My First Day of School*. Illustrated by Frances Hook. New York: Children's Press, 1979. Age: 4. Chap. 7.

A small child's parents invest much hope in him; they did not have the opportunity to go to school. The child's fears are not really acknowledged, but his first day is a huge success. The Mexican-American ethnicity of the family is a plus.

Thomas, Ianthe. *Lordy, Aunt Hattie*. Illustrated by Thomas Di-Grazia. New York: Harper & Row, 1978. Age: 4. Chap. 7.

Jeppa Lee and her Aunt Hattie have a loving visit with each other, demonstrating their affection in a conversation that is depicted in a tone poem by the author.

Thomas, Ianthe. *My Street's A Cool Morning Street*. Illustrated by Emily A. McCully. New York: Harper & Row, 1976. Age: 5. Chap. 7.

Illustrations of a busy and friendly, though realistic, city as a young boy walks to school.

Thomas, Ianthe. *Walk Home Tired, Billy Jenkins*. Illustrated by Thomas DiGrazia. New York: Harper & Row, 1974. Age: 5. Chap. 8.

Billy Jenkins is very tired when he leaves the playground with his older sister, Nina. She lovingly helps him imagine that the walk home is a magic ride. Gentle illustrations of people and city add to this sensitive story about a nurturing older sister.

Thomas, Ianthe. *Willie Blows A Mean Horn*. Illustrated by Ann Toulmin-Rothe. New York: Harper & Row, 1981. Age: 5. Chaps. 4 and 7.

A young boy adores his father, who is a jazz musician. The boy wants to be a performer too. The child's love and admiration for his father are returned with warmth in his father and mother's affection for him.

Thomas, Marlo (conceived by). *Free to Be . . . You and Me*. Illustrated by Samuel N. Antupit. New York: McGraw-Hill, 1974. Age: 3. Chaps. 1 and 7.

A compilation of societally conscious stories, songs, and poems that are fun as well as thought provoking.

Titherington, Jeanne. *A Place for Ben*. Illustrated by the author. New York: Greenwillow, 1970. Age: 3. Chap. 8.

When baby Ezra's crib is moved into Ben's room, Ben seeks out a place where he can be alone. Ben realizes privacy sometimes means loneliness and soon appreciates a visit from his crawling brother.

Tobias, Tobi. *Moving Day*. Illustrated by William Pene du Bois. New York: Knopf, 1976. Age: 2. Chaps. 4 and 6.

An amusing, yet realistic, picture of moving told from a child's perspective. A good book to use to reflect the sometimes difficult process of letting go of one home and moving into a new one.

Tompert, Ann. *Little Fox Goes to the End of the World*. Illustrated by John Wallner. New York: Crown, 1976. Age: 3. Chap. 2.

Little Fox tells her mother all the frightening things she'll see and do when she travels to the end of the world.

Turkle, Brinton. *Deep in the Forest*. Illustrated by the author. New York: Dutton, 1976. Age: 3. Chap. 2.

A reversal of the Goldilocks story. A little bear visits Goldilocks's house, with the same consequences that Goldilocks suffered in the more familiar version of the tale.

Turner, Ann. *Dakota Dugout*. Illustrated by Ronald Himler. New York: Macmillan, 1985. Age: 5. Chap. 4.

Poetic description of experiences in a sod house long ago on the Dakota prairie.

Udry, Janice May. *Let's Be Enemies*. Illustrated by Maurice Sendak. New York: Harper & Row, 1961. Age: 4. Chaps. 6 and 7.

Two friends have an argument and make up without either one's conceding that he was wrong.

Underhill, Liz. *Jack of All Trades*. Illustrated by the author. Boston: Godine, 1985. Age: 4. Chap. 5.

A nonsensical tour of different professions, culminating in the young protagonist's decision to remain what he is, a puppy.

Van Leeuwen, Jean. *Amanda Pig and Her Big Brother Oliver*. Illustrated by Ann Schweninger. New York: Dial, 1982. Age: 5. Chap. 8.

Older brother Oliver is wonderfully understanding when his little sister, Amanda, wants to do everything he does. Their mother finally gets her involved in a separate activity, playing with blocks.

Venables, Bob. *Jungle*. Illustrated by the author. London, England: Blackie, 1983. Age: 2. Chap. 4.

A short six-line poem introduces the camouflaged animals to be found on this green and brown, two-sided mural. Animals, once found, lift out and can be used as puzzle pieces. Animals are labeled.

Vigna, Judith. *Daddy's New Baby*. Illustrated by the author. Chicago: Whitman, 1982. Age: 5. Chap. 8.

A good book for children coping with the birth of a stepbrother or sister. Acknowledges the situation and the jealous feelings a child may have. Ends with a positive connection between the protagonist and her baby stepsister.

Vigna, Judith. *She's Not My Real Mother*. Illustrated by the author. Chicago: Whitman, 1980. Age: 4. Chaps. 4 and 7.

When Miles gets lost, his stepmother comes to his rescue. He now begins to view her with affection, and to reconcile his anxiety about his sense of loyalty to his birthmother.

Viorst, Judith. *Alexander and the Terrible, Horrible, No Good, Very Bad Day*. Illustrated by Ray Cruz. New York: Atheneum, 1972. Age: 4. Chaps. 1, 6, and 8.

Everything goes wrong for Anthony, one of three brothers. Some of the mishaps can be blamed on his brothers but some are simply "life." The book helps children see that other people have bad days too.

Viorst, Judith. *I'll Fix Anthony*. Illustrated by Arnold Lobel. New York: Harper & Row, 1969. Age: 5. Chap. 8.

A younger brother dreams of being old enough to take revenge on his mean older brother. Accurately depicts younger child's feelings.

Viorst, Judith. *Sunday Morning*. Illustrated by Hillary Knight. New York: Atheneum, 1968. Age: 5. Chap. 8.

Two brothers have fun together on a Sunday morning when they awaken hours before their parents.

Viorst, Judith. *The Tenth Good Thing About Barney*. Illustrated by Erik Blegvad. New York: Atheneum, 1973. Age: 4. Chaps. 1 and 7.

When the little boy's pet cat, Barney, dies, he grieves. His family helps him to plan a funeral, and the child is charged with thinking of ten good things about his pet. The tenth good thing is that Barney is now part of the cycle of life, helping the flowers grow.

Voce, Louise. *My First Book of Animals*. Illustrated by the author. New York: Platt & Munk, 1986. Age: 1. Chap. 4.

A comprehensive introduction through labeled pictures of the animal world. Each very large double-page spread contains many examples of one category of animals: jungle animals, animals in cold places, animals found on safari, sea animals, farm animals, pets, baby animals, and silly animals. Also a section on what animals eat, their homes, sounds, and babies.

Waber, Bernard. *Ira Sleeps Over*. Illustrated by the author. Boston: Houghton Mifflin, 1972. Age: 3. Chaps. 1 and 7.

Ira learns that he is not alone in his need for security. He and his friend both need their stuffed animals to have a comfortable night's sleep.

Waber, Bernard. *Lorenzo*. Illustrated by the author. New York: Houghton Mifflin, 1981. Age: 5. Chap. 6.

Lorenzo is a fish who learns his survival skills so well that he can take care of himself when he gets separated from his family. He misses his family and shows his vulnerability without losing his sense of self.

Wadsworth, Olive A. *Over in the Meadow*. Illustrated by Ezra Jack Keats. New York: Scholastic, 1971. Age: 6 mos. Chaps. 3, 4, and 6.

Babies will enjoy hearing this traditional song while older children will appreciate Ezra Jack Keats's soft drawings of animals that accompany the lyrics.

Wahl, Jan. *Humphrey's Bear*. Illustrated by William Joyce. New York: Holt, 1987. Age: 4. Chaps. 2 and 6.

Humphrey has wonderful adventures with his toy bear after they go to bed at night, just as his father did before him.

Walker, Jill. *A Caribbean Alphabet*. Illustrated by the author. Barbados: Best of Barbados Ltd., 1979. Age: 5. Chaps. 4 and 7.
An alphabet book designed especially so that children from the Caribbean can have familiar objects with which to identify, and so that non-Caribbean children can acquire some information about a different culture. The illustrations of houses, foods, animals, and people working are remarkably true to their real-life counterparts.

Warburg, Sandol Stoddard. *Bedtime for Bear*. Illustrated by Lynn Munsinger. New York: Houghton Mifflin, 1985. Age: 3. Chap. 6.
Children can compare their nighttime rituals with those of this little bear.

Warburg, Sandol Stoddard. *Growing Time*. Illustrated by Leonard Weisgard. Boston: Houghton Mifflin, 1969. Age: 5. Chap. 7.
After a little boy's pet dies, the adults in his family help him to understand about death. He wisely understands that there can never be a replacement for his beloved pet.

Ward, Lynd. *The Biggest Bear*. Illustrated by the author. Boston: Houghton Mifflin, 1952. Age: 4. Chaps. 1, 4, and 6.
When a small boy's "pet" bear becomes a "trial and tribulation to the whole valley" and the boy cannot make his beloved animal-friend stay in the woods, the boy is told to do "the only thing to do." Just as he is about to shoot the bear, a whole new sequence of events begins. This is a fine story that invites discussion of important themes such as responsibility, loyalty, love, and priorities. Famous for illustrations.

Watanabe, Shigeo. *Daddy, Play with Me*. Illustrated by Yasuo Ohtomo. New York: Philomel, 1984. Age: 2. Chap. 4.
A little bear cub involves his father in all sorts of play until his father falls asleep reading a story before naptime.

Watanabe, Shigeo. *I Can Build a House*. Illustrated by Yasuo Ohtomo. New York: Philomel, 1982. Age: 2. Chap. 6.
Seventh in a series of *I Can Do It All by Myself* books, this is the story of a small bear who experiments with blocks, cush-

ions, and cartons until he succeeds in building himself a house. Toddlers will identify with his failures, his persistence, and pleasure at success. Other books in this series are *How Do I Put It On?*, *Get Set! Go!*, *What a Good Lunch!*, *I'm the King of the Castle!*, *I Can Ride It!*, *Where's My Daddy?*, and *I Can Take a Walk!*

Watanabe, Shigeo. *I Can Ride It!* Illustrated by Yasuo Ohtomo. New York: Philomel, 1981. Age: 2. Chaps. 4 and 6.
  Bear can ride his tricycle and a bike (with training wheels). With characteristic pluck and persistence he tries roller skates and a skate board despite numerous falls. He imagines himself being able to drive a car, bus, and plane. Another book in the *I Can Do It All By Myself* series.

Watson, Clyde. *Tom Fox and the Apple Pie*. Illustrated by Wendy Watson. New York: Crowell, 1972. Age: 5. Chap. 8.
  The youngest sibling in this large family is the "pet" although he is greedy, lazy, and somewhat selfish. He indulges himself by eating a whole apple pie without sharing. The ending is satisfying because the naughty boy gets his comeuppance in the end.

Watson, Jane Werner, Switzer, Robert, and Hirschberg, J.C. *Sometimes I'm Jealous*. Illustrated by Irene Trivas. New York: Orown, 1986. Age: 4. Chap. 8.
  A very clear and well-written story about a child's feelings of loss and jealousy as well as gains when a new baby causes him to lose his status as "baby of the family." Unusually specific and complex. Short text for parents at the beginning.

Waxman, Stephanie. *What Is a Girl? What Is a Boy?* Photographs by Dennis Hicks, Robert Liu, and Stephanie Waxman. Culver City, CA: PEACE, 1976. Age: 4. Chaps. 4 and 7.
  Discusses what makes girls and boys different, pointing out that they can have the same names, enjoy the same activities, and feel the same emotions. The conclusion is that the only differences are physical.

Weiss, Nicki. *Chuckie*. Illustrated by the author. New York: Greenwillow, 1982. Age: 5. Chap. 8.

A story about an older sister who resents her new brother until a very special personal connection is made between them: Chuckie's first word is "Lucy."

Weiss, Nicki. *A Family Story*. Illustrated by the author. New York: Greenwillow, 1987. Age: 4. Chap. 8.
A story about the special relationship between Rachel and her younger sister, Annie, and how this relationship is passed on from one generation to the next.

Welber, Robert. *Goodbye, Hello*. Illustrated by Cyndy Szekeres. New York: Pantheon, 1974. Age: 1. Chaps. 3 and 6.
In this illustrated, very small volume, a kitten leaves its mother and discovers a bug; a puppy leaves its mother and discovers a toad; a mouse finds a tree to climb; a bird finds the sky. Other animals are described, then a child is shown leaving his mother and greeting his teacher.

Wells, Rosemary. *Max's First Word*. Illustrated by the author. New York: Dial, 1979. Age: 1. Chap. 3.
A small board book in the *Very First Book* series. Other titles include *Max's Toys, Max's Ride,* and *Max's New Suit*. In this book Max's older sister tries to coax him to say simple, one-syllable words. Max finally reacts to an apple with his first word: *delicious*.

Wells, Rosemary. *Noisy Nora*. Illustrated by the author. New York: Scholastic, 1973. Age: 3. Chaps. 7 and 8.
Nora, a tiny, yellow-smocked mouse, suffers many frustrations as a middle child. She demonstrates her anger in many ways and finally runs away (to a closet). She is found by concerned parents. Amusing and well illustrated.

Wescott, Nadine. *The Old Lady Who Swallowed a Fly*. Illustrated by the author. New York: Pantheon, 1984. Age: Birth. Chap. 2.
A silly song detailing the animals consumed by a voracious old lady.

Wheeler, Cindy. *Marmalade's Nap*. Illustrated by the author. New York: Knopf, 1983. Age: 1. Chap. 3.

Marmalade, a cat, looks for a quiet place in the barn to sleep, away from all the baby animals. Marmalade is disturbed over and over until he discovers a perfect, quiet spot—the room where the baby is sleeping.

White, E.B. *Charlotte's Web*. Illustrated by Garth Williams. New York: Harper & Row, 1952. Age: 5. Chaps. 1 and 2.
Charlotte, an extraordinary spider, saves the life of her true friend, Wilbur the Pig. The story is concerned with deep friendship and the continuity of life.

White, E.B. *Stuart Little*. Illustrated by Garth Williams. New York: Harper & Row, 1945. Age: 4. Chaps. 1, 2, and 8.
Children enjoy the adventures of this small mouse who was born to a human family. Stuart is brave, kind, and clever. Younger siblings especially appreciate the way Stuart outshines his older brother.

Wik, Lars. *Baby's First Words*. Illustrated by the author. New York: Random House, 1985. Age: 6 mos. Chap. 3.
Colorful photographs of familiar items and activities in a toddler's daily life.

Wilburn, Kathy. *Pudgy Pals*. Illustrated by the author. New York: Grosset & Dunlap, 1983. Age: 6 mos. Chap. 3.
This small board book presents drawings of ten baby animals whose sweetness may appeal to babies. Each animal is labeled with a noun and adjective.

Wilburn, Kathlene. *The Pudgy Rock-A-Bye Book*. Illustrated by the author. New York: Grosset & Dunlap, 1983. Age: Birth. Chaps. 1 and 3.
This small board book contains several traditional nursery rhymes. Babies enjoy holding the book and toddlers enjoy looking at the pictures and turning the pages while the rhymes are read or sung.

Wildsmith, Brian. *Birds*. Illustrated by the author. Oxford, England: Oxford, 1967. Age: 5. Chap. 4.
Textured, intensely colored, accurately rendered drawings of birds are accompanied by the labels for their plurals: a stare of owls, a watch of nightingales, and a party of jays.

Wildsmith, Brian. *The Island*. Illustrated by the author. Oxford, England: Oxford, 1983. Age: 2. Chaps. 2 and 4.

> Told in bright, textured illustrations, for which Brian Wildsmith is famous, and just a few words, this is the story of a leopard, goat, and monkey who ride on a raft until they land on an island full of colorful birds. The island sinks "down, down . . . down," then suddenly rises to reveal itself as a hippopotamus. This is a wonderful story, especially for children learning animal names and the concepts up and down.

Wilhelm, Hans. *I'll Always Love You*. Illustrated by the author. New York: Crown, 1985. Age: 3. Chaps. 6 and 7.

> A little boy and his dog, Elfie, grow up together. The boy takes good, loving care of the dog. He watches his beloved pet grow old and die, and is glad that he always rememberd to tell Elfie of his undying love.

Williams, Barbara. *Jeremy Isn't Hungry*. Illustrated by Martha Alexander. New York: Dutton, 1978. Age: 4. Chap. 8.

> When older brother Davey is asked by his mother to feed his younger brother, he discovers that this can be a difficult task. This is a down-to-earth, amusing model of an older sibling entrusted with some responsibility for his younger brother.

Williams, Vera B. *A Chair for My Mother*. Illustrated by the author. New York: Greenwillow, 1982. Age: 4. Chap. 6.

> This Caldecott Honor Book tells the story of a child, mother, and grandmother who live together and have a special jar for saving coins they get from tips, odd jobs, and finding bargains. They use the money to buy a special and badly needed chair for the hardworking mother, who is a waitress.

Williams, Vera B. *Something Special for Me*. Illustrated by the author. New York: Greenwillow, 1983. Age: 4. Chap. 6.

> Rosa has difficulty choosing a birthday gift to buy with the coins her mother and grandmother have saved until she hears a man playing an accordion. In this sequel to *A Chair for My Mother*, Rosa buys an old accordion, certain that she will continue to get pleasure from her choice.

Willoughby, Elaine Macmann. *Boris and the Monsters*. Illustrated by Lynn Munsinger. Boston: Houghton Mifflin, 1980. Age: 4. Chap. 6.

> A young boy fears the monsters of the night. He finally is able to overcome his fears when he receives a new puppy to love and cuddle. This solution to a child's nighttime fears is respectful of the child's feelings and is, at the same time, a practical solution. The puppy is both a protector and a creature in need of protection.

Wingfield, Ethel and Harry. *A Ladybird First Picture Book*. Illustrated by the authors. Loughborough, England: Ladybird, 1970. Age: 1. Chaps. 3 and 4.

> The first in a series of books designed to be read by parents and children to build vocabulary and encourage comment and conversation. Carefully drawn, large, simple color pictures of familiar items are labeled.

Wingfield, Ethel and Harry. *A Ladybird Fifth Picture Book*. Illustrated by the authors. Loughborough, England: Ladybird, 1973. Age: 1. Chaps. 3 and 4.

> Part of a large series of books from England that are designed for parents to use with children to "stimulate your child's natural development." Nicely drawn familiar objects are presented and labeled. Each page contains a few suggestions to parents who wish to encourage comment or conversation. Although the books in this sound and well-researched series are not slickly packaged, their content generally holds young children's interest.

Winn, Chris. *Playing*. Illustrated by the author. New York: Holt, 1985. Age: 1. Chaps. 3 and 5.

> One of a series of four "busy day board books" with colorful, crayonlike drawings of children engaged in various activities. All activities are labeled with verbs. Other books in the series include: *Helping*, *My Day*, and *Holiday*.

Winn, Marie and Miller, Allan. *Fireside Book of Children's Songs*. Illustrated by John Alcorn. New York: Simon & Schuster, 1966. Age: Birth. Chaps. 1, 2, and 3.

> A collection for refreshing your memory about old favorites.

Winter, Jeanette. *Come Out to Play.* Illustrated by the author. New York: Knopf, 1986. Age: Birth. Chap. 2.
>Presents the Mother Goose rhyme inviting girls and boys to leave supper and sleep and come out to play in the street by the light of the moon.

Winter, Jeanette. *Hush Little Baby.* Illustrated by the author. New York: Pantheon, 1984. Age: Birth. Chaps. 2 and 3.
>A contemporary rendering of the American folk song. In this version, the father tends to the child at nap time.

Winthrop, Elizabeth. *That's Mine.* Illustrated by Emily McCully. New York: Holiday House, 1977. Age: 4. Chap. 8.
>Brother and Sister begin competing over who can build the best castle. They realize they can have more fun if they cooperate and build together. When they complete a building, they have their baby sibling join them.

Withall, Sabrina. *The Baby's Book of Babies.* Illustrated by many credited photographers. New York: Harper & Row, 1977. Age: 6 mos. Chap. 3.
>Twelve close-up black-and-white photographs of children of different races with a variety of facial expressions and moods. Babies love looking at other babies. Space to include your children's pictures.

Witte, Pat and Eve. *The Touch Me Book.* Illustrated by Harlow Rockwell. Racine, WI: Western, 1975. Age: 1. Chap. 3.
>On each page of this small stiff-paged book children are invited to feel a different texture that is described in the text. Pages are sturdy.

Wittman, Sally. *The Wonderful Mrs. Trumbly.* Illustrated by Margot Apple. New York: Harper & Row, 1982. Age: 4. Chap. 6.
>Martin likes his teacher, Mrs. Trumbly, very much. In fact, he could be said to have a crush on her. Mrs. Trumbly is a widow who becomes involved with another teacher, Mr. Klein, all of which makes Martin very jealous. When Mrs. Trumbly announces her engagement to Mr. Klein, Martin feels sick. A compassionate Mrs. Trumbly helps Martin to understand that they can still be special friends.

Wolde, Gunilla. *Betsy and the Doctor*. Illustrated by the author.
New York: Random House, 1978. Age: 2. Chap. 6.
   A small, useful book about a cheery child who falls from a tree
   at school, cuts her forehead, and has to go to the doctor with
   her teacher to get stitches. Betsy is shown having the cut
   cleaned, getting a shot of local anesthesia, getting her
   stitches, and cheerfully recounting her experience to anxious
   classmates and her parents.

Wolde, Gunilla. *Betsy's Baby Brother*. Illustrated by the author.
New York: Random House, 1975. Age: 2. Chap. 8.
   Betsy can enjoy and help with her baby brother. She can also
   be jealous and can find him loud and unaware of her feelings.
   A generally positive picture of life with a new baby.

Wolde, Gunilla. *This Is Betsy*. Illustrated by the author. New York:
Random House, 1975. Age: 2. Chap. 4.
   Betsy smiles and frowns, wears pants on her legs and pants on
   her head, a shirt on her chest and a shirt on her legs, wears
   her hair smooth, and makes her hair purposely messy. Children love the nonsense and pluck of this charming character.

Wolf, Bernard. *Don't Feel Sorry for Paul*. Illustrated by the author. Philadelphia: Lippincott, 1976. Age: 5. Chap. 7.
   Paul has multiple physical disabilities, but the book focuses
   on his strengths. The clear, black-and-white photographs
   show the reader what prosthetic hands and legs look like, and
   how they work.

Wolf, Janet. *The Best Present Is Me*. Illustrated by the author. New
York: Harper & Row, 1984. Age: 4. Chap. 6.
   A young girl and her family go to celebrate grandmother's
   birthday with her. When it comes time to give gifts, the child
   cannot find the special drawing she has made. Her grandmother understands and says, "The best present is you."

Wolkstein, Diane. *The Banza: A Haitian Story*. Illustrated by
Marc Brown. New York: Dial, 1981. Age: 5. Chaps. 2 and 7.
   A well-researched tale of the cleverness of Cabree the little
   goat, who uses a magical instrument called a banza to van-

quish all who threaten her. Her friend Teegra, a tiger, gave her the banza and told her that "the banza belongs to the heart, and there is no stronger protection than the heart."

Wolkstein, Diane. *The Red Lion: A Tale of Ancient Persia.* Illustrated by Ed Young. New York: Crowell, 1977. Age: 5. Chap. 2.
Prince Azid must fight the red lion and prove his courage before he can be crowned king. He is afraid and runs away, but when he conquers his fear and confronts the lion, the lion is tame and the prince realizes that "only fear would make him ferocious." A tale that invites discussion about fear and courage.

Wolkstein, Diane. *Squirrel's Song: A Hopi Tale.* Illustrated by Lillian Hoban. New York: Knopf, 1976. Age: 5. Chaps. 2 and 7.
It is important for children to have access to the traditional stories from a Native American heritage. This tale of the friendship between a squirrel and a chipmunk deals with the power of song while at the same time telling of their adventure in the peach orchard.

Worthington, Phoebe and Joan. *Teddy Bear Gardener.* Illustrated by Joan Worthington. New York: Viking Penguin, 1983. Age: 3. Chap. 5.
A pleasant model for children who want to garden.

Wright, Betty Ren. *My New Mom and Me.* Illustrated by Betsy Day. Milwaukee: Raintree, 1981. Age: 5. Chap. 7.
The story of how a young child and her family can adjust to the death of a parent and come to accept a new mother.

Yarbrough, Camille. *Cornrows.* Illustrated by Carole Byard. New York: Coward, McCann, 1979. Age: 5. Chaps. 2 and 7.
As Mama and Great-grammaw braid the children's hair into cornrows they tell of the meanings of the designs of the cornrows and present some of the traditions of Afro-American history and culture.

Yashima, Taro. *Crow Boy.* Illustrated by the author. New York: Viking, 1955. Age: 5. Chaps. 6 and 7.

A Caldecott Honor book set in rural Japan about Chibi, an unusual, shy child who comes over the mountain to school every day yet is not well known by his classmates. When in the sixth grade a new teacher arrives at school and takes the class to the countryside, Chibi shares his special knowledge and talents with his newly appreciative schoolmates.

Yashima, Taro. *Umbrella*. Illustrated by the author. New York: Viking, 1958. Age: 3. Chaps. 1 and 7.
Momo eagerly waits for a rainy day so she can use the red boots and umbrella she received on her third birthday. When that day finally arrives, Momo is so proud of her new umbrella that she walks alone, without having to hold either her mother or father's hand.

Yolen, Jane. *All in the Woodland Early*. Illustrated by Jane Breskin Zalben. New York: Philomel, 1979. Age: 4. Chap. 4.
Music and lyrics by the author add to the attraction of this ABC book in which a little boy goes hunting for friends and encounters animals from *A* to *Z* "all in the woodland early."

Yolen, Jane. *The Fireside Song Book of Birds and Beasts*. Illustrated by Peter Parnall. New York: Simon & Schuster, 1972. Age: Birth. Chaps. 2 and 3.
A collection of animal songs arranged by Barbara Green.

Yolen, Jane. *An Invitation to the Butterfly Ball*. Illustrated by Jane Breskin Zalben. New York: Putnam, 1983. Age: 3. Chap. 4.
A gentle, rolling counting rhyme in which woodland animals prepare for a ball. The cumulative verse helps reinforce the counting.

Yolen, Jane. *The Lullaby Songbook*. Illustrated by Charles Mikolaycak. San Diego: Harcourt, 1986. Age: Birth. Chaps. 1 and 2.
A collection of fifteen lullabies, each with a historic note and a musical arrangement.

Yolen, Jane. *Ring of Earth*. Illustrated by John Wallner. New York: Harcourt, 1986. Age: 4. Chap. 2.

Four interlocking poems about the seasons, each told by a creature specially linked to that season: the winter weasel, spring peeper, summer's dragonfly, and the goose flying south in the autumn.

Yolen, Jane. *The Seeing Stick*. Illustrated by Remy Charlip and Demetra Marsalis. New York: Crowell, 1977. Age: 5. Chaps. 1, 2, and 7.

With the help of a blind old man, the young daughter of the emperor learns to "see with her fingers." This illustrated story is a treasure.

Yolen, Jane. *The Three Bears Rhyme Book*. Illustrated by Jane Dyer. New York: Harcourt, 1987. Age: 2. Chaps. 2 and 6.

Gentle rhymes for the very young from Baby Bear's point of view about such childhood concerns as nap time, getting angry, night fears, and walking in the rain.

Young, Ed. *The Other Bone*. Illustrated by the author. New York: Harper & Row, 1984. Age: 4. Chap. 2.

In a story similar to the Aesop's fable, a dog dreams of finding a bone, does find one, and then loses it because he sees its reflection in a pool of water and grasps for what he thinks will be a second bone. Although the book is wordless, the pictures require a high level of comprehension.

Young, Ed. *Up a Tree*. Illustrated by the author. New York: Harper & Row, 1983. Age: 4. Chap. 2.

In a series of amusing and graphic pictures we see the adventures of a feisty cat who has managed to be trapped in a tree. Children will find no difficulty in adding their own narrative.

Zelinsky, Paul O. *Rumpelstiltskin*. Illustrated by the author. New York: Dutton, 1986. Age: 5. Chaps. 1 and 2.

A strange little man helps the miller's daughter spin straw into gold for the king on the condition that she give him her firstborn child. The illustrations literally illuminate the book; the straw looks as if it contains gold even before it is spun. The story needs lot of discussion: why were the miller and the king so greedy? Why did the young woman want to marry the greedy king?

Ziefert, Harriet. *Baby Ben's Busy Book*. Illustrated by Norman Gorbaty. New York: Random House, 1984. Age: 1. Chaps. 2 and 3.

A *Baby Ben* book. It presents the world of sights, sounds, colors, and early learning concepts from a baby's point of view.

Ziefert, Harriet. *Bear Goes Shopping: A Guessing Game Story*. Illustrated by Arnold Lobel. New York: Harper & Row, 1986. Age: 3. Chap. 5.

A fold-out, guessing game story with a little bear shopping for different things on each day of the week.

Ziefert, Harriet. *Birthday Card, Where Are You?* Illustrated by Richard Brown. New York: Viking Penguin, 1985. Age: 3. Chap. 5.

A lift-the-flap book showing what happens to a birthday card in the mail.

Ziefert, Harriet. *Clappity Clap*. Illustrated by Rudi Tesa. New York: Viking, 1984. Age: 1. Chaps. 3 and 5.

Fun for introducing verbs and activities children can share, this little colorful board book shows a girl and boy working and playing together.

Ziefert, Harriet. *Dress Little Bunny: A Sticker Story*. Illustrated by Lisa Campbell Ernst. New York: Viking Penguin, 1986. Age: 3. Chap. 6.

A board book with reusable vinyl stickers that can be used to dress the bunny in appropriate clothes for different weather and for nighttime. While the book is NOT for very young children who are still at a stage of putting objects in their mouths, the book is useful for slightly older toddlers who are learning "to do" by themselves.

Ziefert, Harriet. *Harry Takes a Bath*. Illustrated by Mavis Smith. New York: Viking Penguin, 1987. Age: 3. Chap. 5.

One of a series of *Hello Reading* books, this is a very short chapter book for the beginning reader. Harry the Hippo takes a long playful bath and even cleans up afterwards!

Ziefert, Harriet. *Munchety Munch: A Book About Eating*. Illustrated by Rudi Tesa. New York: Viking, 1984. Age: 1. Chaps. 3 and 5.

Brightly colored photographs and clear, simple text describe different actions of eating: biting, licking, tasting, sipping, drinking, and crunching.

Ziefert, Harriet. *A New Coat for Anna*. Illustrated by Anita Lobel. New York: Knopf, 1986. Age: 4. Chap. 4.
Even though there is no money, Anna's mother finds a way to make Anna a badly needed winter coat. The information on how wool is made into cloth is incorporated into the story.

Ziefert, Harriet. *Sarah's Questions*. Illustrated by Susan Bonners. New York: Lothrop, Lee, Shepard, 1986. Age: 4. Chap. 5.
A little girl and her mother take a walk in the countryside. First they play "I Spy." Later the little girl asks questions about nature that the mother responds to with respect and accuracy. The book's tone and illustrations foster an appreciation of and interest in nature.

Zion, Gene. *Harry, the Dirty Dog*. Illustrated by Margaret Bloy Graham. New York: Harper & Row, 1956. Age: 3. Chaps. 4 and 6.
A little dog gets so dirty that his family does not recognize him. Finally, he jumps into the bath. Once he is scrubbed clean, he is recognized. A perennial favorite, perhaps because children are somewhat afraid that they will not be recognized and acknowledged as they change.

Zolotow, Charlotte. *Big Brother*. Illustrated by Mary Chalmers. New York: Harper & Row, 1960. Age: 3. Chap. 8.
Big brother is an effective tease. He finds many ways to make his little sister cry. One day she is too absorbed in her own activity to take notice. Her brother ends up joining her.

Zolotow, Charlotte. *Big Sister, Little Sister*. Illustrated by Martha Alexander. New York: Harper & Row, 1976. Age: 4. Chap. 8.
Big sisters sometimes need help too. This awareness makes a little sister who doesn't like to always be "taken care of" feel better about her relationship with her sister.

Zolotow, Charlotte. *Do You Know What I'll Do?* Illustrated by Garth Williams. New York: Harper & Row, 1950. Age: 4. Chap. 8.

This classic expresses the love of a child for a young baby by describing her willingness to share the experiences she enjoys.

Zolotow, Charlotte. *The Hating Book*. Illustrated by Ben Schecter. New York: Harper & Row, 1969. Age: 4. Chap. 8.
A story of one little girl's anger and puzzlement at some of her friend's hurtful behavior. She initially handles her frustration by pretending not to care but, with her mother's help, learns how to confront her friend and resolve the conflict.

Zolotow, Charlotte. *Hold My Hand*. Illustrated by Thomas Di Grazia. New York: Harper & Row, 1972. Age: 2. Chap. 6.
Two little girls walk together sensing first the coming storm and then enjoying the snowflakes when they come.

Zolotow, Charlotte. *If It Weren't for You*. Illustrated by Ben Schecter. New York: Harper & Row, 1966. Age: 5. Chap. 8.
An older brother resents his baby brother, and recounts all of the things he could do if it weren't for his baby brother.

Zolotow, Charlotte. *I Have a Horse of My Own*. Illustrated by Yoko Mitsuhashi. New York: Abelard-Schuman, 1964. Age: 2. Chaps. 4 and 6.
Illustrated with pink and gray woodcuts, this story of a girl's dream is evocative and lovely. In the morning she eats her breakfast and goes to school to play with her friends, making a clear distinction between night and day, dream and reality.

Zolotow, Charlotte. *Mr. Rabbit and the Lovely Present*. Illustrated by Maurice Sendak. New York: Harper & Row, 1962. Age: 3. Chap. 6.
A child's generous feelings are rewarded when she and an enormous fantasy rabbit determine the perfect gift for the child's mother.

Zolotow, Charlotte. *My Grandson Lew*. Illustrated by William Pene du Bois. New York: Harper & Row, 1974. Age: 4. Chaps. 1, 6, and 7.
A little boy and his mother share loving memories of the boy's dead grandfather. Both of them are helped to cope with their grief through these affirming reflections.

Zolotow, Charlotte. *One Step, Two*. Illustrated by Cindy Wheller. New York: Lothrop, Lee, Shepard, 1955. Age: 2. Chap. 6.

> While out for a walk, a little girl points out a yellow crocus, a fat gray cat, a blue bird, a round white pebble, dancing laundry on the line, and things the mother would otherwise have overlooked. At the end of their walk, the mother thanks the child who is now in her arms and fast asleep.

Zolotow, Charlotte. *The Park Book*. Illustrated by H.A. Rey. New York: Harper & Row, 1972. Age: 3. Chap. 1.

> The comings and goings, the events and activities of a city park as told to a little boy from the country.

Zolotow, Charlotte. *Say It!* Illustrated by James Stevenson. New York: Greenwillow, 1980. Age: 4. Chaps. 4 and 6.

> A little girl and her mother go on a walk. Each time the mother remarks on the beauty of something she sees, the child begs her to "say it." Finally the mother tells her daughter that she loves her and that that is what she's been saying all along.

Zolotow, Charlotte. *Three Funny Friends*. Illustrated by Mary Chalmers. New York: Harper & Row, 1961. Age: 2. Chap. 6.

> When a little girl moves to a new town, she invents three playmates to assuage her loneliness. When she befriends a real little boy, she is happy enough to give up her other "friends."

Zolotow, Charlotte. *Timothy Too*. Illustrated by Ruth Robbins. New York: Harper & Row, 1986. Age: 4. Chap. 8.

> A younger brother wants very much to be included in his brother's play. A book both younger and older siblings can identify with.

Zolotow, Charlotte. *Wake Up and Goodnight*. Illustrated by Leonard Weisgard. New York: Harper & Row, 1971. Age: 2. Chap. 6.

> A book that moves from morning to night and creates a pleasant quiet atmosphere for bedtime.

Zolotow, Charlotte. *William's Doll*. Illustrated by William Pene du Bois. New York: Harper & Row, 1972. Age: 3. Chaps. 1, 6, and 7.

The story of a competent young boy who expresses the wish to have a doll. His father finds his wish unacceptable but his grandmother understands it well and succeeds in persuading the father that little boys can practice their nurturing skills on dolls.

The Bookshelf for Parents

The following books were selected for their usefulness as aids to designing activities for children, as sources of professional information on child development, and as practical resources for dealing with specific issues. Most of the books labeled *resource* contain annotated bibliographies.

Adams, Caren and Fay, Jennifer. *No More Secrets: Protecting Your Children from Sexual Assault*. San Luis Obispo, CA: Impact, 1981.

Aston, Athina. *How to Play with Your Baby*. Charlotte, NC: Fast & Macmillan, 1964. (Activities)
  Ideas for beneficial playing with your infant.

Bank, Stephen P. and Kahn, Michael D. *The Sibling Bond*. New York: Basic Books, 1982. (Child Development)
  The authors, clinical psychologists, offer a theory of the way siblings attach to each other and engage in lifelong relationships.

Bernath, Maja. *Parents' Book for Your Baby's First Year*. New York: Ballantine, 1983. (Child Development)
  Advice of a comprehensive nature focusing on the first year.

Bernstein, Joanne E. *Books to Help Children Cope with Separation and Loss*. New York: Bowker, 1983. (Resource)
> An excellent reference for finding books to help with such issues as death, divorce, serious illness, moving, and any form of loss.

Brazelton, T. Berry, M.D. *Toddlers And Parents: A Declaration of Independence*. New York: Dell, 1974. (Child Development)

Calladine, Carole and Andrew. *Raising Siblings*. New York: Delacorte, 1979. (Child Development)

Caplan, Frank. *The First Twelve Months of Life: Your Baby's Growth Month by Month*. New York: Grosset & Dunlap, 1973. (Child Development)

Caplan, Frank and Theresa. *The Early Childhood Years: The Two- to Six-Year-Old*. New York: Perigee/Putnam, 1983. (Child Development)

Caplan, Frank and Theresa. *The Second Twelve Months of Life: A Kaleidoscope Of Growth*. New York: Putnam, 1977. (Child Development)

De Franco, Ellen B. *TV On/Off: Better Family Use of Television*. Santa Monica: Goodyear, 1980. (Activities)
> Ideas for activities to do with children from four years old and up to help them control and improve their television viewing.

Dreyer, Sharon Spredemann. *The Bookfinder: When Kids Need Books*. Circle Pines, MI: American Guidance Service, 1985. (Resource)
> An extensive annotated bibliography of books to help children solve problems.

Dunn, Judy. *Sisters and Brothers*. Cambridge, MA: Harvard, 1985. (Child Development)

Fisher, John J. *Toys to Grow With Infants and Toddlers*. New York: Putnam, 1986. (Activities)

Lots of good ideas on how to make toys for your child that will be both entertaining and beneficial.

Graves, Ruth. *The RIF Guide to Encouraging Young Readers.* Garden City, NY: Doubleday, 1987. (Activities)
Many activities are suggested for children from age four up.

Grollman, Earl A. *Explaining Death to Children.* Boston: Beacon, 1967. (Child Development)
This book has chapters by experts from different fields discussing various aspects of death.

Grollman, Earl A. *Talking About Death.* Boston: Beacon, 1971. (Child Development)
A short book for parents to help them talk to their children about death.

Ilg, Frances L., M.D., and Ames, Louise Bates, Ph.D. *The Gesell Institute's Child Behavior.* New York: Harper & Row, 1955. (Child Development and Rescource)
Based directly on research work done over many years at Yale University, this book has two parts. The first part presents the ages and stages of typical child development and a discussion of individuality. The second part discusses thirteen specific issues, such as eating, sexuality, and fears. The book closes with a discussion of discipline.

Kaplan, Louise. *Oneness and Separateness: From Infant to Individual.* New York: Simon & Schuster, 1978. (Child Development)

Kaye, Evelyn. *How to Treat TV With TLC: The ACT Guide to Children's Television.* Boston: Beacon, 1979. (Resource)
Information and ideas for helping children get the most out of viewing television, ACT publishes a number of helpful handbooks. Send for their list: Action for Children's Television, 20 University Rd., Cambridge, MA 02138.

Larrick, Nancy. *A Parent's Guide to Children's Reading.* New York: Bantam, 1982. (Resource)
Guidance from a thoughtful expert in children's literature to books for children from age four up.

Leach, Penelope. *Your Baby and Child from Birth to Age Five.* Mount Vernon, NY: Consumers Union, 1987. (Child Development)
A comprehensive look at your child's development.

Lee, Barbara, and Rudman, Masha. *Leading to Reading.* New York: Berkeley, 1984. (Activities)
Resources and activities to do with the child from four years of age up, to motivate reading and writing.

Marzollo, Jean, and Lloyd, Janice. *Learning Through Play.* New York: Harper & Row, 1974. (Activities)
Tons of activities to do with your preschool child to encourage cognitive skills.

Montessori, Maria. *The Discovery of the Child.* New York: Ballantine, 1967. (Child Development)

Oppenheim, Joanne, Brenner, Barbara, and Boegehold, Betty. *Choosing Books for Kids.* New York: Ballantine, 1986. (Resource)
Published by the well-known and respected Bank Street College of Education, this book provides an excellent overview of books for children from babies to age twelve.

Pulaski, Mary Ann Spencer. *Your Baby's Mind and How It Grows: Piaget's Theory for Parents.* New York: Harper & Row, 1978. (Child Development)

Rudman, Masha Kabakow. *Children's Literature: An Issues Approach.* New York: Longman, 1984. (Resource)
Discussion and recommendations for books on death, old age, sibling relationships, war, adoption, foster care, special needs, gender, heritage, and sex education.

Sparling, Joseph, and Lewis, Isabelle. *Learning Games for the First Three Years.* New York: Walker, 1979. (Activities)

Spock, Benjamin, and Rothenberg, Michael. *Baby and Child Care*. New York: Simon and Schuster, 1985. (Child Development)

Trelease, Jim. *The Read-Aloud Handbook*. New York: Penguin, 1985. (Resource)
    An excellent guide to good read-alouds for children up to age 12.

Sources

In researching the text, the authors consulted the following works:

Adams, Virginia. "The Sibling Bond: A Lifelong Love/Hate Relationship." *Psychology Today:* June, 1981.

Adcock, Don and Segal, Marilyn. *Play and Learn: From Two to Three Years*. La Jolla, CA: Oak Tree, 1980.

Anderson, Dan, and Collins, Patricia. *The Impact on Children's Education: TV's Influence on Cognitive Development*. Washington, DC: U.S. Department of Education, 1988.

Bader, Barbara. *American Picturebooks From Noah's Ark to the Beast Within*. New York: Macmillan, 1976.

Baker, Augusta and Greene, Ellin. *Storytelling: Art and Technique*. New York: R.R. Bowker, 1977.

Barbe, Walter B., Ph.D. *Growing Up Learning: The Key to Your Child's Potential*. Washington, DC: Acropolis, 1985.

Beard, Ruth M. *Outline of Piaget's Developmental Psychology for Students and Teachers*. New York: Basic Books, 1969.

Bettelheim, Bruno. *The Uses of Enchantment*. New York: Random House, 1977.

Bettelheim, Bruno and Zelan, Karen. *On Learning to Read*. New York: Knopf, 1982.

Brazelton, T. Berry, Koslowski, B., and Main, Mary. *The Origins of Reciprocity: The Early Mother-Infant Interaction*. New York: Wiley, 1974.

Burke, Eileen M. *Early Childhood Literature: For Love of Child and Book*. Newton, MA: Allyn and Bacon, 1986.

Butler, Dorothy. *Cushla and her Books*. Boston: The Horn Book, 1980.

Chance, Paul. "Your Child's Self-Esteem." *Parents Magazine:* January, 1982.

Cianciolo, Patricia Jean (ed). *Picture Books for Children*. Chicago: American Library Association, 1981.

Coody, Betty. *Using Literature with Young Children*. Dubuque, IA: Wm. C. Brown, 1973.

Covington, Martin V. and Beery, Richard G. *Self-Worth and School Learning*. New York: Holt, 1976.

Despert, Louise J., M.D. *The Inner Voices of Children*. New York: Simon & Schuster, 1975.

Gillespie, John T., and Gilbert, Christine B. *Best Books for Children*. New York: R.R. Bowker, 1985.

Huck, Charlotte. *Children's Literature in the Elementary School*. New York: Holt, 1979.

Mahler, Margaret S., Pine, Fred, and Bergman, Anni. *The Psychological Birth of the Human Infant*. New York: Basic Books, 1975.

Mahoney, Ellen, and Wilcox, Leah. *Ready, Set, Read*. Metuchen, NJ: The Scarecrow Press, 1985.

Markus, Hazel. "Sibling Personalities: The Luck of the Draw." *Psychology Today:* June, 1981.

Norton, Donna E. *Through the Eyes of a Child*. Columbus, Ohio: Merrill, 1987.

Rutter, Michael. "Resilient Children." *Psychology Today:* March, 1984.

Schmidt, Fran, and Friedman, Alice. *Creative Conflict Solving for Kids*. Miami: G.C. Abrams Peace Fund, 1985.

Sroufe, Alan L. "The Coherence of Individual Development." *American Psychologist:* Vol. 34, No. 10, 1979.

Sutherland, Zena, et al. *Children and Books*. Glenview, IL: Scott Foresman, 1981.

Trotter, Robert J. "You've Come a Long Way, Baby." *Psychology Today:* May, 1987.

WGBH Transcripts. *Life's First Feelings*. Boston: WGBH Educational Foundation, 1986.

White, Burton. *The First Three Years of Life*. New York: Avon, 1975.

White, Dorothy. *Books Before Five*. Portsmouth, NH: Heinemann, 1984.